Principles and Practices of CAD/CAM

CAD/CAM systems are perhaps the most crucial advancement in the field of new technology relating to engineering, design and drawing in all technical domains. CAD/CAM stands for computer-aided design and computer-aided manufacturing. These systems are useful in all facets of contemporary design and architecture. The fundamentals of CAD/CAM systems are covered in detail throughout this book.

This book aims to introduce the fundamental aspects, complete with an adequate number of illustrations and examples, without delving too deeply into the specifics of the subject matter. This book is valuable in the classroom for both teachers and students.

Features

- Each chapter begins with the Learning Outcomes (LOs) section, which highlights the critical points of that chapter.
- All LOs, solved examples and questions are mapped to six Bloom Taxonomy levels (BT levels).
- Offers fundamental concepts of CAD/CAM without becoming too complicated.
- Solved examples are presented in each section after the theoretical discussion to clarify the concept of that section.
- Chapter-end summaries reinforce key ideas and help readers recall the concepts discussed.

Students and professionals need to have a working knowledge of CAD/CAM since it has many applications and continues to expand. Students at the undergraduate and graduate levels of engineering courses use this book as their primary textbook. It will also be helpful for managers, consultants and professionals.

Principles and Practices of CAD/CAM

Vikram Sharma, Vikrant Sharma
and Om Ji Shukla

CRC Press
Taylor & Francis Group
Boca Raton London New York

CRC Press is an imprint of the
Taylor & Francis Group, an **informa** business

A CHAPMAN & HALL BOOK

Front cover image: Aleksandr Artt/Shutterstock

First edition published 2024
by CRC Press
2385 NW Executive Center Drive, Suite 320, Boca Raton FL 33431

and by CRC Press
4 Park Square, Milton Park, Abingdon, Oxon, OX14 4RN

CRC Press is an imprint of Taylor & Francis Group, LLC

© 2024 Vikram Sharma, Vikrant Sharma, and Om Ji Shukla

ISBN: 978-1-032-38781-9 (hbk)
ISBN: 978-1-032-39676-7 (pbk)
ISBN: 978-1-003-35084-2 (ebk)
ISBN: 978-1-032-39677-4 (eBook+)

DOI: 10.1201/9781003350842

Typeset in Times New Roman
by Deanta Global Publishing Services, Chennai, India

Contents

Preface

The globalisation of the economy necessitates the development of new products that have improved characteristics at prices that are competitive. Another difficulty arises from the shortening of the product's lifespan. Because of this, the time required for the product development cycle has to be significantly compressed. Engineers today use CAD/CAM systems for every activity because of the tremendous increases in processing power and the broader availability of software tools for design and manufacturing.

The idea behind this book is straightforward, yet it works quite well. In order for the reader to become successful in utilising any CAD/CAM system, they need to obtain information from a source that is both thorough and complete. This expertise covers a comprehension of the design process, the role of computers in design and production, geometric modelling, computer graphics, three-dimensional modelling, the principles of computer-aided manufacturing (CAM) and numerically controlled (NC) part programming. In addition to that, the topics covered in this book include the principles of automation, automated material handling and inspection and industrial robots. In light of these considerations, readers should find this book helpful since it offers a comprehensive solution to all of their CAD/CAM, automation and industrial robot education requirements under one roof.

MAPPING WITH BLOOM'S TAXONOMY

The main feature of this book is the mapping of chapters with the revised Bloom Taxonomy Level (BT level). Bloom's Taxonomy was created to promote a higher level of cognitive thought, such as analysis, evaluation and creation, rather than simply to remember facts. Bloom's Taxonomy has six learning stages from the lower level through to higher-level thinking.

> *BT level 1. Remembering:* Recall information or data.
> *BT level 2. Understanding:* Understand the meaning of written, oral and graphics.
> *BT level 3. Applying:* Applying a concept in a new situation.
> *BT level 4. Analysing:* Breaking down the concepts into the constituent parts and drawing inferences.
> *BT level 5. Evaluating:* Making judgements based on standards and sets of criteria.
> *BT level 6. Creating:* Create a new thing or model based on prior learning.

All chapter learning outcomes, solved examples, questions and practice problems are mapped to a Bloom's Taxonomy level.

PEDAGOGICAL FEATURES

This book includes a variety of valuable pedagogical features to help the readers understand and retain the content.

1. Each chapter begins with the Learning Outcomes (LOs) section, which highlights the critical points of each chapter,
2. LOs are presented in the box within the specific section of each chapter,
3. Solved examples are presented in each section after the theoretical discussion to clarify the concept of that section,
4. At the end of each chapter, a summary reinforces key ideas and helps readers recall the concepts discussed,
5. Questions are provided at the end of each chapter to test the understanding of the concept discussed in the chapter,
6. Competency checks using six levels of Bloom's Taxonomy help readers assess their understanding of the material.

Acknowledgements

We would like to thank our colleagues and our family members for their encouragement and moral support in bringing this book to fruition. We do appreciate CRC Press for their diligent effort in rendering this book elegant, in a prompt manner.

The Authors

About the Authors

Vikram Sharma, PhD, is an Associate Professor in the Mechanical-Mechatronics Engineering Department at the LNM Institute of Information Technology (LNMIIT), Jaipur, India. He has over 20 years of teaching and research experience. He holds a BE degree in Mechanical Engineering, an ME degree in CAD/CAM and a PhD degree in the field of Automobile Supply Chains. His current research interests include lean and green manufacturing. He has published several papers in national and international journals and conferences.

Vikrant Sharma, PhD, is an Assistant Professor in the Department of Mechanical Engineering, Mody University of Science and Technology, Lakshmangarh, India. He graduated in Production Engineering from the University of Pune in 2004. He obtained a Master's degree in Manufacturing System Engineering from Malaviya National Institute of Technology (MNIT), Jaipur, in 2007. He received his doctorate in Production Engineering from Mechanical Engineering Department, Rajasthan Technical University, Kota. He has research and teaching experience of about 15 years and about 30 publications in international journals of repute. He has published five textbooks. He also won the first prize for the book *CNC Machines and Automation* from the All-India Council for Technical Education (AICTE) in the all-India level competition under the scheme named "Takniki Pathyapustak Puraskar Yojana-2014" (Technical Text Book Prize Distribution Scheme of 2014). He is a life member of the Institution of Engineers (India) and the Institution of Engineering and Technology (IET, UK).

His research interests include industrial engineering, optimisation techniques, production and operations management, plant layout, multicriteria decision making and product design.

Om Ji Shukla, PhD, is an Assistant Professor at the Department of Mechanical Engineering, National Institute of Technology (NIT), Patna, India. He received his doctorate from Malaviya National Institute of Technology (MNIT), Jaipur, and an ME from Birla Institute of Technology & Science (BITS), Pilani. During his PhD, he worked on multi-agent-based production systems that involved real-time production scheduling problems. He has published several research papers in international journals and conference proceedings. He has also authored several book chapters in edited books. His research interests are agent-based modelling, AI in manufacturing, operations management, supply chain management, and e-waste management. He is currently heading the Entrepreneurship Cell at NIT Patna as Professor-in-Charge.

1 Introduction to CAD

Learning Outcomes: After studying this chapter, the reader should be able

LO 1: To understand computer-aided engineering (BT level 2).
LO 2: To understand product lifecycle management (BT level 2).
LO 3: To understand the design process and application of computers in design (BT level 2).
LO 4: To understand computer fundamentals: computer input devices, output devices and CPU (BT level 2).

VIDEO 1

1.1 INTRODUCTION TO COMPUTER-AIDED ENGINEERING (CAE)

CAE refers to any use of computers to solve engineering problems. Computer-assisted processes include computer-aided design (CAD), computer-assisted manufacturing (CAM), computer-integrated manufacturing (CIM), computer-assisted analysis (CAA), material requirements planning (MRP) and computer-assisted planning (CAP). CAE is the use of software to forecast or analyse the mechanical, thermal, magnetic or other qualities and states of a system. Software for CAE may simulate the effects of wind, temperature, weight and stress on the design or assembly of a product. Before committing to actual construction, engineers may model the effects of stress on components of an internal combustion engine, such as pistons, or on structures, such as bridges or aircraft wings, using computers.

> *LO 1. To understand Computer-Aided Engineering (CAE)*

CAE is the use of interactive computer graphics to solve engineering issues, made feasible by the rapid growth of computing technology and the improvement of graphics displays, engineering workstations and graphics standards. CAE software may run on mainframes, supercomputers, minicomputers, engineering workstations and even personal computers. The selection of a computer system is influenced by the processing capacity required by the CAE application software or the desired degree and speed of graphical interface. Increasing numbers of firms are using engineering workstations. A typical CAE software package consists of several mathematical models encoded in algorithms developed in a suitable programming language. An engineering model represents the phenomenon being studied. A geometric model may be used to describe the physical arrangement. On a display device such as a cathode ray tube (CRT), liquid crystal display (LCD), or plasma display, the user interface displays the results alongside the geometry. CAE can be coupled with optimisation systems to find iterative solutions to the engineering design problems, thus improving productivity and the quality of design.

Figure 1.1 illustrates a CAE application running on a computer used in engineering. To begin a physical analysis, mathematical equations representing the phenomenon of interest must be written. Equations like Newton's second law may be used in this engineering model to explain the behaviour

DOI: 10.1201/9781003350842-1

1

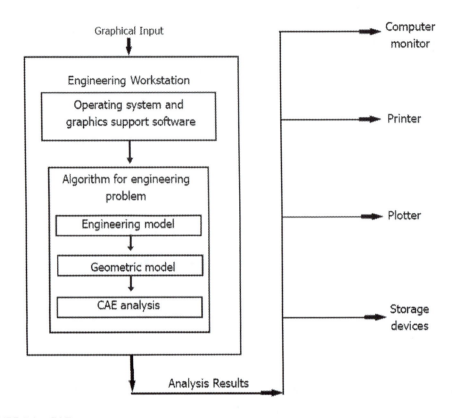

FIGURE 1.1   CAE system

of a spring-mass-damper system, for instance. The next step is to construct an analogue of the actual setup. This geometric model may include lines, surfaces and solids of any number of dimensions. Displaying the outcome of an engineering study on a geometric model by changing the colour and intensity of a scalar parameter is a common practice. The contemporary software makes use of special rendering schemes to improve the display of results.

Each product and service has a finite lifetime. Lifecycle refers to the period between a product's debut on the market and its final retirement. For any company, whether it is an automobile manufacturer or any other engineering goods manufacturer, the lifecycle of a product is something that must be understood and managed properly. So, let us try to understand it briefly.

1.2   PRODUCT LIFECYCLE MANAGEMENT (PLM)

The purpose of PLM is to manage a product from its conception to its ultimate decommissioning. The management structure of PLM is applicable to the software and service sectors in addition to the manufacturing industry. There are typically five distinct stages that make up a product's lifecycle or phases (Figure 1.2):

LO 2. To understand Product life cycle management

1. Product development,
2. Product introduction,
3. Product growth,
4. Product maturity,
5. Product decline.

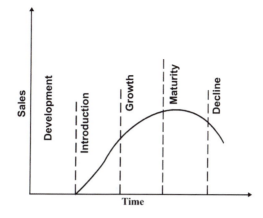

FIGURE 1.2   Product lifecycle curve

Figure 1.2 illustrates these phases. The first phase is the beginning of life, which includes new product development and design processes. When a company develops a new product idea, it enters the product development phase. We translate and integrate new information into an existing product as part of this procedure. In the beginning, while a product is still in the testing phase, there are no sales. Today is a day when money may be spent without the possibility of recovering it. When a product reaches its second phase, known as "introduction," it is made available to the general public. During this period, it is common to invest heavily in marketing and promotion, and it is often necessary to execute new service requirements fast at the price of quality. As product sales surge during the growth period, this is the opportunity to reap the rewards of the investment. Now is the time to make further efforts to increase market share. This level encompasses supply chain coordination, controlled product data and warranty management. The company must exhibit all of its products and make an attempt to distinguish them from the competitors.

When there are several variants of the original product on the market, the product has attained its full potential. During this time period, the product is most profitable. In this last phase, it is typical for product sales to decline with the market. Before the decision to remove a product from the market, there are several questions that must be answered.

It is difficult to decide to remove a product from sale due to problems such as maintaining the device's functionality, assuring a sufficient supply of replacement components and forecasting how rivals would react to the market vacancy. Companies would often maintain a high price plan for diminishing products in order to increase their profit margin and ultimately alienate the few remaining loyal customers from buying the product. This phase can also be referred as the end-of-life phase.

1.3   DEVELOPMENT IN MICROELECTRONICS AND COMPUTER HARDWARE

The 19th century experienced an industrial revolution which considerably enhanced the physical power of human beings. In the 20th century there was another revolution when computers were introduced. These computers offered an enhancement of man's mental capabilities. Computers are now being widely used in all the engineering fields, and computers are essential to each significant engineering endeavour. Recent advancements in computer memory and processing power have made it possible to solve more difficult problems and do more computations in less time. More importantly, this has become possible due to developments in the field of *microelectronics* and integrated chips (IC). We are witnessing the phenomenon of ever-increasing chip density.

Due to very large scale integration (VLSI), the price of computer hardware has dropped dramatically, putting it within the financial grasp of most industrial companies. In addition, VLSI and Ultra

Large Scale Integration (ULSI) have contributed to the miniaturisation of computer components. Because of these advancements in computer science, CAD and CAM are quickly becoming the norm in the engineering industry. They can boost output because of this potential.

Now computers play an essential role in the product design and development processes. Computers have become a powerful tool for rapid and economic production of graphic pictures. CAE design and CAE are the advancement of CAD. These are fast evolving concepts that make use of computers and CAD in other fields of engineering like process planning, production, quality and maintenance, etc.

1.4 COMPUTER-AIDED DESIGN (CAD) DEFINED

A simple definition of CAD is the use of computers in the design process. CAD technologies are now commonly utilised in the design of engineering components, vehicles, aeroplanes, ships, spacecraft, buildings, textiles, machine tools, consumer goods and many other types of items. Tools for design analysis (such as finite element analysis and the finite element method), optimisation, testing, etc. are all a part of this suite. The field of CAD and CAM focuses on the use of computers in all stages of production, from the design office to the machine shops and assembly shops, from the inspection and quality control departments to the final components store. Conceptual design, analysis, rapid prototyping, component design, documentation, process planning and manufacturing are just few of the areas where CAD systems are being utilised extensively. CAD and CAM are two distinct areas that are combined in CAD/CAM. Over the course of the last 40 years, these two fields have grown separately. Nowadays, CAD/CAM systems include both of these methodologies. A CAD/CAM system enables a single system to be used for both the design and control of the production process.

In order to create and modify images on a display device with the assistance of a computer, a sophisticated approach known as interactive computer graphics is used as the foundation for CAD.

CAE is the practice of using computers to help in the engineering of a product in areas such as quality assurance, optimisation, analysis, manufacturability, etc.

VIDEO 2

1.5 DESIGN PROCESS

Let us now study the use of computers in design. Every product to be manufactured goes through two basic processes. These are

LO 3. To understand Design process and application of computers in design

1. Design process,
2. Manufacturing process.

First, the design is prepared by the design department. Then the machining operations, sequence of machining, tooling, etc. is decided by the process planning department. This information is sent to the machine shop to manufacture the components. After manufacturing and quality checks, the final product is marketed by the sales and marketing department.

1.5.1 PRODUCT CONCEPTUALISATION

Initially, the concept of design of the product starts emerging when the need is felt. Design conceptualisation does not have any laid-down procedures. It is the knowledge and experience of the engineers that help them in formulating the concept of a new product and its design.

1.5.2 Design Modelling and Simulation

In order to give final form to the concept of design, rough sketches or layouts of the product are drawn. This helps in giving a form to the concept by the engineers. This process is known as "*Design modelling and simulation*." These days advance CAD software such as IDEAS, Pro/E, Catia and SOLIDWORKS are available for product modelling and simulation.

Both product conceptualisation and design modelling and simulation are also called the "*synthesis process*" of design. Nowadays, due to the non-availability of engineers with vast experience, Artificial Intelligence and Expert systems are being developed which can help in the synthesis process.

1.5.3 Design Analysis

The design, once formulated, needs to be analysed for stress distribution using various theories such as theory of failure, bending stresses and torsion theory, etc. It is important to check that the maximum stress induced should be less than ultimate stress of the material, so that the product does not fail during its intended life. Design analysis can be simplified by using computers.

The Finite Element Method (FEM) is an advanced numerical analysis technique that is becoming popular for various types of analysis like stress analysis, thermal analysis, fluid flow analysis and acoustic analysis, etc. FEM software packages like Pro/MACHINICA, IDEAS, SIMULATION, NISA, ANSYS and NASTRAN are nowadays being used by CAD/CAM engineers for identifying stress distribution in machine components, buildings and bridges.

1.5.4 Design Optimisation

The term "optimised design" refers to a plan that has been finetuned to ensure maximum effectiveness under certain circumstances.

Various parameters are used to optimise the design process. Factors that can be taken into consideration are weight factors, cost factor, minimum deflection and maximum energy absorption, etc. The complexity in design optimisation increases with an increase in the number of constraints.

1.5.5 Design Evaluation

After the design optimisation process, the final design part is still not over, and the design is not communicated to the process planning or manufacturing departments unless it is tested. The design can be tested by two methods: Either by making a prototype of the *product* and then testing the prototype, but this is a time-consuming process; or the other method (which is much faster) makes use of concept called *virtual manufacturing*. In this technique, a solid model of the component is prepared on some software package like IDEAS, Pro/E or Solid Edge and then it is subjected it to various types of testing by making use of the testing module in these packages.

1.5.6 Design Documentation and Communication

After the design evaluation stage, documentation of design is carried out by preparing drawings either manually or using a CAD package. Use of computers for drawings helps in systematic storage of the drawings and making suitable modifications as desired. CAD packages help in making the design process fast, accurate and easy.

1.5.7 Computer-Aided Process Planning

Process planning is a very important task carried out before the actual machining of the designed part. In this task, planning of all the machining operations is carried out. In this process, tooling

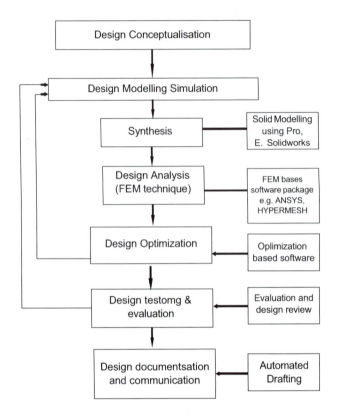

FIGURE 1.3   Computer application in design

and fixture planning of all the machines is decided. Process planning is carried out by highly experienced engineers. Nowadays *computer-aided process planning* (CAPP) is becoming popular due to availability of various CAPP software packages.

   Manufacturing: Conventional machines, numerically controlled (NC) machines or computer numerically controlled (CNC) machines are used for machining when process planning is complete. Using computers has become an integral part of the design process, which is shown in the flowchart in Figure 1.3.

1.6   IMPORTANCE AND NECESSITY OF CAD

The importance and necessity of CAD has been recognised mainly due to following reasons:

1. Data collected throughout the design, process planning, production, analysis, etc. phases may all be stored and managed by a computer system.
2. Second, 3-D models allow for visual inspection and checking of complex geometric designs before real prototypes are made.
3. Use of CAD packages make design modelling and simulation an easy task.
4. Before putting a concept into action, it may be analysed and optimised using CAD/CAM software.
5. Using CAD to streamline the product design and development process shortens production times.
6. Effective use of CAD tools improves the productivity of the design processes. It enhances the capabilities of the design engineer in both quality and quantity. Development of interactive graphics software and versatile graphic facilities make simulation an easy task.

7. Design is an interactive process. The number of iterations to be performed depends on the complexity of the problem. Using CAD, it is simple to evaluate and compare many design options and then execute the one that works best.

8. A CAD system can be integrated with a CAM system. This means that CNC machines can receive CAD data in real time and use them to generate part programs for producing the components.

1.7 APPLICATIONS OF CAD

The applications of CAD in industry are enumerated below:

1. Developing solid models of various components and assemblies using CAD software packages,
2. Changing and enhancing component models,
3. Picking colours for 3-D models,
4. Seeing the object or its parts from various perspectives and cutaways,
5. Studying the product for its manufacturing planning, standardisation and simplification,
6. Performing an interference test on an assembly's mating components,
7. Analysis of mechanical parts, structures and bridges for stress,
8. Studying the product for material requirement, costing and value engineering,
9. Preparing detailed component drawings and assembly drawings,
10. Preparing a database for future reference and record.

Because of such user-friendly applications, CAD has been widely implemented in the automobile, aerospace, shipbuilding, machine tools consumer goods and other engineering industries.

1.8 COMPUTER-AIDED MANUFACTURING (CAM)

With the advancement of computer technology, computers have been implemented in almost every kind of industry including the manufacturing sector. One possible definition of "Computer-Aided Manufacturing" is "any computer-based assistance in the production of a specified product." Computers may play a direct role or indirect role in manufacturing a given product.

The direct role refers to computerised operation and control of a manufacturing process. For example, consider a lathe machine being operated by a computer. The computer can used to control the production equipment while making a component.

Several process variables may be tracked. In order to control the machining process, the computer may take appropriate action based on the machining requirements stored in its memory.

The indirect role of computers in manufacturing refers to:

1. Computer-aided process planning,
2. Computer-aided NC part programming,
3. Computer-aided material requirement planning and manufacturing planning,
4. Computer-aided material handling and storage,
5. Computer-aided inspection and quality control, etc.

1.9 COMPUTER-INTEGRATED MANUFACTURING (CIM)

CIM is an extension of CAD/CAM. It integrates a CAD/CAM system with the business functions of an organisation.

CIM aims at integration of:

1. Manufacturing tools like CAD/CAM, flexible manufacturing systems, robotics, materials requirement planning, group technology, just-in-time concept, production planning, capacity planning, inventory control, etc.,

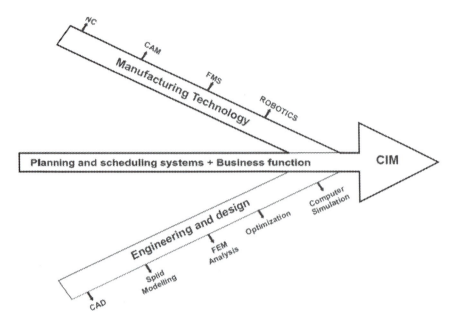

FIGURE 1.4   Integration of technical and business function in CIM

2. Other functional areas of organisation including marketing, purchase order control, vendors and personnel management, etc.,

Hence, all of CAD/technical CAM's features, plus all of the company's administrative tasks, are part of CIM (see Figure 1.4). From the moment an order is received all the way through the manufacturing process, including product design, production, marketing and shipping, computer technology is used as part of a CIM system. CIM is a broader concept than CAD/CAM since it encompasses the commercial operations of a company.

CAD and manufacturing (MM) is the focus of CIM. This field is focused on automating every step of the design and production processes with the help of computers. Distributed data processing, computer networks and database management systems all play significant roles in CIM's technological infrastructure.

1.10   COMPUTER FUNDAMENTALS

Any computer system consists of three main units. These are as follows:

LO 4. To understand computer fundamentals

1. Input devices,
2. Processing unit,
3. Output devices.

To interact with the CAD packages several input devices are used. These facilitate in feeding data or other input to the computer system. A keyboard, mouse, light pen, joystick, touch screen and digitiser are some of the input devices commonly used in CAD systems.

The processing device of a computer is called a central processing unit or CPU. A CPU is also considered to be the brain of the computer because all the processing of data is carried out there. The CPU consists of three components or subunits. These are:

1. Storage,
2. Arithmetic and logic unit,
3. Control unit.

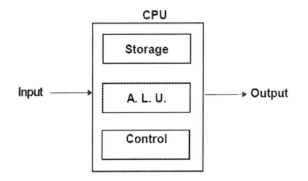

FIGURE 1.5 CPU components

The flow of information in a computer system is as shown in Figure 1.5

The capacity of the storage unit to store data is expressed in terms of bits. A bit is the unit of binary numbers, which are formed by 0 and 1 only, in various combinations. Computers can understand the language of binary numbers only. Hence it converts all the information and data into bits; 0 and 1 represent the status of electronic signals that are passed to and from a computer.

For example, **1101** is a binary number with 4 bits (it should not be confused with decimal number one thousand one hundred and one). A bit is a very small unit for storage, there are larger units for memory as follows:

1 byte = 8 bits,
1 kilobyte = 1024 bytes,
1 megabyte = 1024 kilobytes,
1 gigabyte = 1024 megabytes.

A computer system has two types of memory:

1. Main memory or Random Access Memory (RAM),
2. Secondary memory or Read Only Memory (ROM).

When the computer is switched off, RAM loses the data stored in it. ROM is permanent memory and retains data and information stored in it even after the computer is switched off. This data can be retrieved again and again.

A computer system is a combination of hardware and software. Hardware is defined as the physical unit of a computer that can be seen by the naked eye. Software may be defined as a link between the hardware and the user. Software is used to activate hardware in order to get the desired results.

There are two types of software. These are *application software and system software*. The system software is developed by those with a detailed knowledge of hardware. Examples of such software are operating systems, like DOS, Windows, UNIX, LINUX, etc. The software on which a user works is called applications software. Application software interacts with system software which in turn interacts with the hardware.

The commonly used *output devices* for a CAD system are plotter, printer, copiers and camera systems. Different types of plotters available are flat bed plotter, drum plotter, and pinch roller plotter, etc. These may be either pen plotters or electrostatic plotters.

The different types of printers available are electrostatic printers, inkjet printers, laser printers, impact printer, thermal printers and line printers.

Let us study input and output devices used for computer graphics in more detail.

1.10.1   INPUT DEVICES

Information and commands are fed into the computer through input devices like keyboards and mice. A digital computer's input device takes whatever data or signal it receives as input and transforms it into the binary format the computer understands. Input is handled through a keyboard and a few switches. Physical quantities such as temperature, pressure, speed, location, etc. are measured and controlled using computers as well. For this, we use transducers, which are devices that take in measurements of the physical world and output electric impulses that are proportionate to those measurements.

1.10.1.1   Keyboard

Computer keyboards have descended from typewriters. A keyboard sends information to the CPU each time a key is pressed or released. Keyboards available on the market may have a variety of sizes and shapes but most keyboards have following types of keys in common:

1. Standard typewriter keys that are used to type text and other data,
2. Function keys labelled F1, F2, F3 and so on, also called programmable keys,
3. Special purpose keys such as Ctrl (Control), Del (Delete), Ins (Insert), Alt (Alternate), Caps Lock, Scroll Lock and Num Lock,
4. Cursor movement keys used to move the cursor on the screen. The keys have directional arrows on them,
5. Numeric keys are used to enter numbers for mathematical calculations.

The most common **keyboard design** uses a sheet of elastomeric substance (i.e., an artificial rubber) placed between keys and a printed circuit board. This rubber sheet has a dome shape in it directly beneath each key. When the key is pressed, it pushes down the dome which comes into contact with an electronic circuit board below. There is a conductive spot on the inside of each of the dome which completes the circuit on the printed circuit board, signalling to the CPU that the key has been pressed.

Computers that are intended for use in hazardous environments use keyboards that are often sealed. Such keyboards use a membrane or a simple capacitive switch. These keyboards have sensitive regions called keypads which when pushed generate signals for the CPU. Though these keyboards last longer in hostile environments the disadvantage is that you cannot type as quickly and accurately when compared to a regular one.

For those who are not good at typing, using a **voice recognition** system is an easy way out. This system converts spoken words into electrical signals by comparing the electrical pattern produced by the user's voice with a set of pre-recorded patterns.

1.10.1.2   Mouse

A mouse is a pointing device which when moved on a surface, generates digital signals that are sent to the CPU. These signals are used by the mouse program to control the location of the on-screen cursor. One of the mouse's buttons may be used to choose an item or file from the display.

An **optomechanical mouse** is most popular these days and is a hand-held device with a rubber ball protruding from the underside. Moving the mouse causes the ball to roll. This ball makes continuous contact with the x-roller and y-roller. When the rubber ball moves, it in turn rotates x- and y-rollers and optical encoders close to it generate signals to indicate the amount of motion in each of the two perpendicular directions. The disadvantage of such a mouse is that it tends to pick up dust as the ball rolls on a flat surface. This tends to damage the mechanism that converts that ball's rolling motion into x and y displacement signals. The mouse can be opened at the bottom to clean the dust accumulated inside the mouse. An *optomechanical mouse* is a hand-held device with a rubber ball protruding from the underside.

The problem has been eliminated in the optical mouse which is most popular these days. An LED is located underneath the mouse. It moves the cursor on basis of light reflected from a shiny flat surface beneath the mouse.

1.10.1.3 Graphics Digitiser Tablets

A graphics tablet is a flat, rectangular input device with a stylus shown in Figure 1.6. Each point on the tablet corresponds to a point on a PC's screen. The stylus is like a pen with a pressure switch in the tip. It may be cordless or connected to the tablet with a wire. As you move the stylus with its tip on the tablet, the cursor moves through the corresponding points on the screen. The digitiser tablet uses a technology in which a grid of wires is buried in the surface of the tablet. The tablet's electronic circuitry sends signals through these wires which are received by the stylus placed over tablet. The signal returned by the stylus to the tablet's electronic circuitry determines the point over which the stylus tip was positioned. Other technologies used by digitiser tablets are based on the sonic and magneto-secretive effects. The digitiser tablet is primarily used for tracing over existing drawings. Three dimensional tablets have also been developed to enter 3-D coordinates into a computer system.

1.10.1.4 Scanners

After the keyboard, mouse and digitiser tablet, a scanner is the most common input device.

Basically, they are classified into two types:

1. **Drum scanners (sheet fed scanners):**
   They can scan only flat sheets of paper or film.
2. **Flatbed scanners:**
   They can scan bulkier objects such as pages of a book.

Both charge-coupled device (CCD) and charge-independent pixel (CIS) are popular technologies used for creating scanners (contact image sensor). CCD scanners employ a moving mirror and focusing optics to project an image of whatever is on the scanner's window onto a linear array of light sensors. A bright light inside the scanner illuminates a band on the window that moves along the mirror's motion, thus permitting the scanner to read the contents of the document placed on the top of the window.

A contact image sensor is an array of light sensors that can be moved along with the linear light source on the underside of the scanner window and receive the reflected light from the document directly without using focusing optics. But the disadvantage of such scanners is that they have lower image quality and resolution compared to CCD scanners.

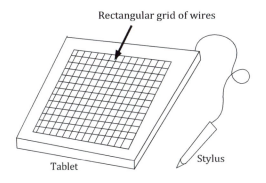

FIGURE 1.6 Tablets

Some other special purpose input devices popular these days are optical character readers, digital cameras and digital video cameras.

1.10.2 OUTPUT DEVICES

Whenever the computer processes data, it will transmit the results to the appropriate output. To regulate or activate machinery, an output device may either store data, print information or display information. Standard output devices include the following: Printers, CRTs, LEDs, digital to analog converters (D/A) converters, controllers, actuators, etc.

The most commonly used output devices in computers are monitor, printer and plotter.

1.10.2.1   Monitor

In almost all computers the information output is obtained primarily by means of video display, also called monitor or screen. The monitor consists of the hardware that actually creates the image you see and some electronic circuitry to activate the display. The monitor may be based on various technologies to display the image, for example, *cathode ray tube* (CRT), *liquid crystal display* (LCD) and *plasma display*. In CRTs a beam of electrons is made to hit a phosphor-coated screen. The spot on the screen at which many electrons hit each microsecond will glow brightly.

1.10.2.2   Printer

After a monitor, a printer is the most common means of getting an output. Some of the printers used these days are enumerated as follows:

1.10.2.2.1   Impact Printers

These were the first to be developed. In these printers, a ribbon soaked with ink is positioned in front of piece of paper, then hit upon with a hammer bearing shape of some character. The impact drives ink out of ribbon onto the page. Character printers and dot matrix printers are the two main categories of impact printers. Dot matrix printers create an image by printing individual dots, whereas character printers utilise curved hammers to create a full sign or letter in a single stroke.

1.10.2.2.2   Inkjet Printers

These printers spray a liquid ink onto the page using multiple jets or nozzles aligned in the print head on a carriage that moves horizontally across the page. Each ink droplet is charged as it passes through a value. Then it passes through horizontal and vertical deflecting plates which direct the ink drops to the desired spot on the paper.

1.10.2.2.3   Laser Printers

These printers have a photosensitive transfer surface built in the form of a rigid cylinder of metal with a thin coating of the photoconductor on its outer surface. The photoconductive material acts as an insulator in the dark but as a good electrical conductor in presence of light. The photoconductive surface which is in a darkened space is charged to a high electrostatic potential. This charge is selectively drained off by shining light on to selected regions of the photoconductive surface.

The surface is flooded with toner particles (mixture of tiny, coloured material and plastic bond material). The toner particles stick only the portions carrying an electrostatic charge.

Paper with an opposite electric charge is pressed against the toner-coated photoconductive charge. Opposite electrostatic charges attract each other. The paper is then separated from the photoconductive surface and most of the toner comes along with the paper by electrostatic attraction. The toner-laden paper is heated to fuse ink particles to the paper.

1.10.2.3   Plotter

A plotter is a computer-driven output device used to make drawings. It has an automatic arm that holds a pen and can press the pen down against the sheet of paper or raise it up at the same time, moving in a prescribed manner. Commonly used plotters are a drum plotter, flat bed plotter and inkjet plotter.

A drum plotter has a long cylinder with a drawing sheet rolled over it, and a pen carriage. Under the computer's control, the drum rotates back and forth while the pen carriage moves horizontally along the cylinder axis to generate the desired drawing. A flat bed plotter uses a horizontal flat surface on which drawing sheet is fixed. The pen carriage and the flat bed under the computer control move along the x- and y-axes to generate the drawing. An inkjet plotter employs inkjets mounted on the carriage and the paper is placed on the drum. Ink of different colours may be used to produce multicoloured drawings. These are more reliable compared to pen plotters.

1.11 SUMMARY

- Rapid development in the field of computers has become possible due to developments in the field of microelectronics and integrated chips.
- CAD can be defined as use of computers to aid the design process.
- CAD and CAM originally developed independently but have now been integrated into CAD/CAM systems.
- CAE can be defined as an engineering philosophy which brings together all the engineering activities such as computer simulation, computer aided analysis and optimisation, CAD, computer-aided drawing, computer-aided process planning, computer-assisted production management, computer-aided manufacturing and numerical control, CAD and computer-aided drafting.
- Design process involves the following steps: Product conceptualisation, design modelling and simulation, design analysis, design optimisation, design evaluation, design documentation and communication.
- The importance of CAD can be realised from the fact that computers can store large amounts of engineering data, create complex geometrical shapes, perform modelling and simulation, etc.
- CIM includes all the engineering functions of CAD/CAM as well as business functions such as order entry, payroll and accounting, customer billing, etc.
- Common input devices used for CAD are keyboard, mouse, light pen, joystick, touch screen and digitisers, etc.
- Common output devices used for CAD are monitor, printer, plotter, etc.
- Auto CAD, Pro/E, CATIA, Solid Edge, SOLIDWORKS and NISA are some of the commonly used CAD packages.

1.12 EXERCISE

1. What do you understand by computer-aided design? Discuss reasons for implement CAD in industry (BT level 2).
2. What are different phases of product development cycle (BT level 1)?
3. Describe various stages in design and development of a piston. How can CAD be used to accelerate the development process (BT level 2)?
4. Give specific advantages of using CAD in product development cycle (BT level 2).
5. Discuss the statement "CAD is only a tool in the design process" (BT level 2).
6. Define the term, "computer-aided engineering" (CAE) (BT level 1).
7. Suppose you are a design engineer in a CNC cylindrical grinding machine manufacturing company. How will you implement CAD in your company? How will you use CAD to improve your design productivity (BT level 4)?
8. What do you mean by computer hardware and software? What are the input and output devices used for CAD? Name some important CAD software popular in design and development industry (BT level 1).

9. Why is the application of computers in the engineering industry becoming so popular? Name a few areas in which CAD is being widely used in industry (BT level 2).
10. What should be the qualities of a CAD engineer? (BT Level 1).
11. Differentiate between classical design and CAD procedures (BT level 4).
12. Explain the functions of basic hardware components of a general-purpose digital computer (BT level 2).
13. Describe design related tasks which are performed by a modern CAD system (BT level 2).
14. What are the benefits of CAD (BT level 1)?
19. Make a table of important design phases. What are the CAD tools to support various design phases (BT level 2)?
20. What do you understand by computer memory? Name two types of computer memory (BT level 2).

1.13 MULTIPLE-CHOICE QUESTIONS

1. What is the primary purpose of CAE software?
   a. To create 3-D models of products.
   b. To simulate and analyse product designs.
   c. To generate engineering drawings and specifications.
   d. To optimise production processes.
2. Which of the following is not a common feature of CAE software?
   a. Pre-processing tools for model setup.
   b. Solver engines for performing calculations.
   c. Post-processing tools for interpreting results.
   d. Design optimisation tools for generating CAD models.
3. Which of the following is a common application of CAE software?
   a. Creating marketing materials for products.
   b. Generating 2-D drawings for product manufacturing.
   c. Simulating the behaviour of structures under load.
   d. Designing user interfaces for software applications.
4. What is the primary goal of Product Lifecycle Management (PLM)?
   a. To manage product costs throughout the product lifecycle.
   b. To optimise product design and development.
   c. To increase product profitability.
   d. To manage product information and data throughout the product lifecycle.
5. Which of the following is not a benefit of implementing a PLM system?
   a. Improved collaboration and communication among team members.
   b. Reduced product development time and costs.
   c. Increased risk of product failure or recall.
   d. Improved quality and reliability of products.
6. What does CAD stand for?
   a. Computer-Aided Drawing.
   b. Computer-Aided Design.
   c. Computer-Assisted Drafting.
   d. Computer-Assisted Design.
7. What is the primary purpose of CAD software?
   a. To create 2-D and 3-D models of products.
   b. To simulate and analyse product designs.
   c. To generate engineering drawings and specifications.
   d. To optimise production processes.

8. Which of the following is not a common feature of CAD software?
   a. Drawing tools for creating 2-D geometry.
   b. Modelling tools for creating 3-D geometry.
   c. Simulation tools for analysing product designs.
   d. Manufacturing tools for producing products.
9. Which of the following is a common application of CAD software?
   a. Creating marketing materials for products.
   b. Generating 2-D drawings for product manufacturing.
   c. Simulating the behaviour of structures under load.
   d. Designing user interfaces for software applications.
10. Which of the following is not a benefit of using CAD software for product design?
    a. Improved accuracy and precision of product designs.
    b. Reduced product development time and costs.
    c. Increased manual labour required in the product design process.
    d. Improved collaboration and communication among team members.
11. What does CAM stand for?
    a. Computer-Aided Management.
    b. Computer-Aided Manufacturing.
    c. Computer-Assisted Machining.
    d. Computer-Assisted Modelling.
12. What is the primary purpose of CAM software?
    a. To create 2-D and 3-D models of products.
    b. To simulate and analyse product designs.
    c. To generate engineering drawings and specifications.
    d. To control manufacturing processes and machinery.
13. What does CIM stand for?
    a. Computer-Integrated Manufacturing.
    b. Computer-Implemented Machining.
    c. Computer-Influenced Modelling.
    d. Computer-Integrated Modelling.
14. Which of the following is not a common feature of CAM software?
    a. Tool path generation for machining operations.
    b. CNC machine simulation for verifying programs.
    c. Design optimisation tools for generating CAD models
    d. Post-processing tools for generating G-code.
15. Which of the following is a common application of CIM?
    a. Controlling manufacturing processes and machinery.
    b. Creating marketing materials for products.
    c. Simulating the behaviour of structures under load.
    d. Designing user interfaces for software applications.

Answers

1. Answer: b. To simulate and analyse product designs.
2. Answer: d. Design optimisation tools for generating CAD models.
3. Answer: c. Simulating the behaviour of structures under load.
4. Answer: d. To manage product information and data throughout the product lifecycle.
5. Answer: c. Increased risk of product failure or recall.
6. Answer: b. Computer-Aided Design
7. Answer: a. To create 2-D and 3-D models of products.

8. Answer: c. Simulation tools for analysing product designs.
9. Answer: b. Generating 2-D drawings for product manufacturing.
10. Answer: c. Increased manual labour required in the product design process.
11. Answer: b. Computer-Aided Manufacturing.
12. Answer: d. To control manufacturing processes and machinery.
13. Answer: a. Computer-Integrated Manufacturing.
14. Answer: c. Design optimisation tools for generating CAD models.
15. Answer: a. Controlling manufacturing processes and machinery.

2 Computer Graphics

Learning Outcomes: After studying this chapter, the reader should be able

LO 1: To know about CAD graphics software and its categorisation (BT level 1).
LO 2: To understand the configuration of CAD software systems (BT level 2).
LO 3: To understand the software standards (BT level 2).
LO 4: To explain the graphics kernel system (BT level 2).
LO 5: To know about display devices (BT level 1).
LO 6: To understand the graphics functions (BT level 2).
LO 7: To explain geometric transformations and 3-D viewing (BT level 2).

2.1 INTRODUCTION

In computer-aided design (CAD) systems, computer graphics is extensively used to display drawings, solid models of the components, wireframe geometry and animation, etc. Computer graphics methods can also be used in painting and art applications and for generation of reports using graphical tools. To understand the technique of generating drawing entities like *lines* and *circles*, *colours*, *shading* and *hidden* lines, it is necessary to understand the intricacies of computer graphics.

LO 1. To know about CAD graphics software and its categorization

The graphics software has been divided into two categories:

(1) **General purpose programming packages** like Graphics Library (GL), which provide a set of graphics functions that can be used in high-level programming languages such as C and C++. These graphics functions are used for making drawing entities like straight line, circle, spline, polygon, ellipse, etc. using the programming languages.
(2) **Special purpose applications packages** include AutoCAD, IDEAS, PRO/ Engineer, Catia, Ansys, SolidWorks, Solid Edge, Unigraphics and Mechanical Desktop, etc. These application packages are used by application engineers and designers rather than software programmers. They can make use of drawing commands and icons without bothering about the software program involved.

2.2 GRAPHICS SOFTWARE

Software for digitally synthesising and manipulating visual material on a computer screen is the focus of computer graphics, a subfield of computer science. It includes software for two-dimensional (2-D) and three-dimensional (3-D) computer graphics and image processing. CAD/CAM software comprises of programs which can generate CAD images on screen and at the same time can establish an interaction between the user and the system. CAD/CAM software may also include programs for design analysis and optimisation (finite element method (FEM) analysis, kinetic simulation), process planning programs (resource planning, route sheets), and subroutines for computer numerical control (CNC) part programming. It is important to understand that computer graphics software is used for a particular CAD application package (such as AutoCAD, Pro/E, SolidWorks). Graphics programs are written giving due consideration to the type of display device and input

DOI: 10.1201/9781003350842-2

device used with the computer. It is recommended that graphics software should be simple, consistent, robust, fast and economically viable.

2.3 SOFTWARE CONFIGURATION OF CAD SOFTWARE SYSTEM

A CAD software system can be basically divided into three subparts. These are:

LO 2. To understand the configuration of CAD software systems

1. Application software (such as AutoCAD, Pro/E, SolidWorks, ANSYS, etc.),
2. Computer graphics software (such as GKS, IGES, etc.),
3. Applications and graphics information database.

The configuration of CAD software can be understood from Figure 2.1. The applications software is used by CAD engineers to generate 3-D solid models of components, assemblies, 2-D drawings, etc. An application program is often tailormade for a particular field of engineering such as mechanical components, civil engineering, architectural, automobile or aerospace engineering. Specialised CAD application software also addresses various other engineering requirements such as simulation, mathematical modelling, FEM-based mesh generation and analysis, bill of material, mass and inertia properties of solid models, etc.

The applications software can be used by the CAD engineer only through computer graphics software. If appropriate graphics software is not loaded in the computer, the CAD application software cannot work. The graphics software works as an interface between user and applications software. The graphics software comprises of input and output routines/functions. The task of input routines is to accept input commands and data entered by a CAD engineer and sends it further to the application program for execution. The output routine controls the display devices such as ***monitor, printer, plotter***, etc. The application program interacts with the database for performing most of its functions.

The database comprises of basic drawing primitives, solid models of standard engineering component, designs, drawings, assemblies, standard formats of desired engineering information such as bill of material, etc.

The database can be organised in various ways. One method of organising a database is shown in Figure 2.2.

One possible data structure for 3-D solid models involves storing the coordinates of vertices. But this method may not completely define the shape, e.g., whether the component is hollow or solid inside. Another method of making a database is the graph-based model as shown in Figure 2.3. Points are connected to form edges; three or more edges combine to form surfaces which in turn combine to form solids. Note that wall surfaces must enclose the solid space from all sides, i.e., the solid should not be open on any side.

Boolean operations such as ADD, SUBTRACT, UNION, INTERSECTION can be used to join the solid entities to form solids of different shapes. For the graphical database, the relational database structure is the most common. In this system, the database exists in the form of tables which are interlinked by pointer relations as shown in Figure 2.4. Files present in the table are linked by pointers.

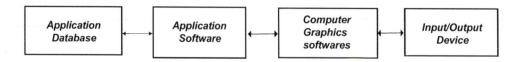

FIGURE 2.1   Software configuration of CAD graphics system

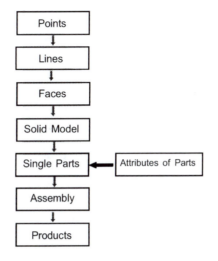

FIGURE 2.2 Organising database

FIGURE 2.3 Graph based model for database

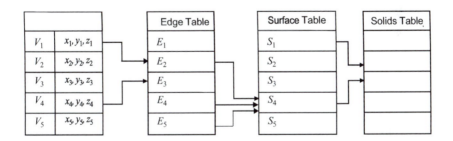

FIGURE 2.4 Relational data structure for 3-D geometric models

2.4 SOFTWARE STANDARDS

When creating graphics software, compatibility is the primary standardising objective. The mobility of CAD software is enhanced by the use of industry-standard graphical elements. Without standards, it is not possible to execute a program designed for one hardware system on another without making the necessary modifications.

LO 3. To understand the software standards

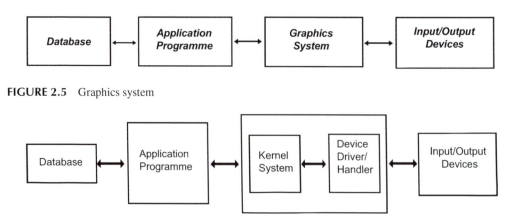

FIGURE 2.5   Graphics system

FIGURE 2.6   Graphics system with Kernel and device driver

Prior to standardisation, the CAD application program with a database is used to interact with graphic systems in order to display output or interact with input. This can be contemplated by the block diagrams given in Figure 2.5.

In such systems, the suitability of an applications program was affected, because if there is any change in the input or output, the graphics system needs to be changed and hence the application program also needs to be changed. Thus, the application program was hardware dependent. Hence, a need for standardisation of graphics software was also felt. Several International Organisations for Standardisation (ISOs) and International Organisations for Planning IOPs) worked together to develop a widely used graphical standard. This standardisation was achieved by dividing the graphics system into two subparts as shown in Figure 2.6.

This led to development of the ***Graphical Kernel System*** (GKS). In this standard, the applications program interacts with the Kernel System which in turn interacts with the device handler and driver. The device driver/handler in turn interacts with input and output devices. So, if there is any change in input and output devices, only the device driver handler needs to be changed. The Kernel and the applications program remain unaffected. Thus, the graphics program becomes hardware independent. There are different types of graphic standard systems like GKS, PHIGS and CORE.

2.5   GRAPHIC KERNEL SYSTEM (GKS)

GKS is a set of subroutines or functions that are used for graphical work in a language-independent manner. These subroutines are used in application programs through a process called language binding. The language independent and device independent functions of GKS make the graphics programs compatible with a diverse selection of computer systems.

LO 4. To explain the graphics kernel system

The graphics input and output devices connected to GKS are called workstations. A device driver/handler assigned to each workstation translates the device-independent representation to a device-dependent or workstation-specific one (i.e., using a technique known as language binding, programmers may use the syntax of their favourite programming language to invoke a range of standardised graphical functions). This can be conceived from Figure 2.7.

For example, in GKS, the subroutine for specifying a sequence of n connected straight line segments is

$$\text{polyline } (n + 1, x, y)$$

In C, the procedure will be invoked with graphics function

$$\text{gpolyline } (n + 1, \text{points})$$

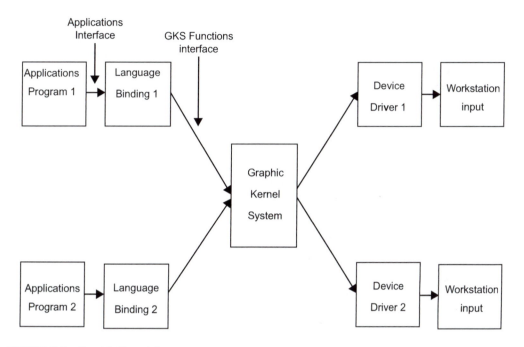

FIGURE 2.7 Graphic Kernal System

where points is the list of end point position coordinates.

A list of output primitives provided in GKS is given below:

(1) **Polyline:** It is a line primitive. For each set of coordinates, a succession of straight lines is generated.
(2) **Polymarker:** It is a point primitive. It generates a set of specified type of symbol at a given position.
(3) **Text:** The text primitive generates a character string at specified position.
(4) **Fill Area:** It is a raster primitive used to fill a polygon with a specified style.
(5) **Cell Array:** It is a raster primitive that generates a grid of rectangular cells, each with a distinct colour.
(6) **Generalised Drawing Primitive (GDP):** It is a general-purpose primitive used for drawing entities like curves, circles, splines, etc.

GKS Inputs: GKS defines a set of logical input devices, which can be mapped on physical input devices like mouse, digitiser, light pen, etc. GKS provides the following logical input device:

(1) **Locator:** Provides position by specifying x–y coordinates,
(2) **Valuators:** Provides real number through keyboard,
(3) **Pick:** Provides segment name and pick identifier,
(4) **Choice:** Provides non-negative integer which represents a selection from a given number of choices,
(5) **String:** Provides a character string,
(6) **Stroke:** Provides a sequence of positions.

Other popular graphics systems are:

1. **Programmer's Hierarchical Interactive Graphics Standard** (PHIGS), which is an extension of GKS and has been approved by standards organisations. It's the international standard for merging application modelling with CGI interactivity. In PHIGS,

structure networks, which are hierarchical data structures, are used to represent applications. Fundamental to PHIGS is the concept of application models which are hierarchical. Hierarchies arise naturally in the modelling process, when the model is constructed from multiple instances of entities which are themselves a collection of instances of simpler components and so on.

2. **SIGGRAPH's** CORE is the first graphics standard to be developed. The CORE graphic system was developed by the graphics standard planning committee of the graphics special interest group on graphics (SIGGRAPH) of the Association for Computing Machinery (ACM). CORE was a hardware- and language-agnostic collection of instructions for manipulating the creation and presentation of graphical content. Therefore, CORE-based code is platform-agnostic. It initially provided for line drawing in 2-D and 3-D graphics and later versions induced faster operations such as Areafill, etc.

2.6 DISPLAY DEVICES

In CAD applications, screens are the primary output medium. They help in making use of interactive graphics for solid modelling and design using CAD systems. Such technologies allow for effective two-way interaction between humans and computers. To increase efficiency and speed up the design process, CAD systems have replaced the traditional drawing board with a digital interface.

LO 5. To know about the display devices

The display devices can be classified into two subgroups:

(1) Display based on the Cathode Ray Tube (CRT) principle,
(2) Solid State Monitors (flat screens).

2.6.1 CRT

Most of the interactive graphics display devices are based on the CRT principle. A CRT is a glass-enclosed tube in which an electron beam is produced by an electron gun and is finally focused and deflected to a specific position on the phosphor-coated screen.

Wherever the electron beam hits the phosphor, the phosphor emits a brilliant light. The screen thus glows to produce a visible trace. The basic arrangement of a CRT is shown in Figure 2.8.

The primary components of a CRT are electron gun, electron beam focusing system, deflection system and phosphor-coated screen.

The electron gun of CRT is shown in Figure 2.9.

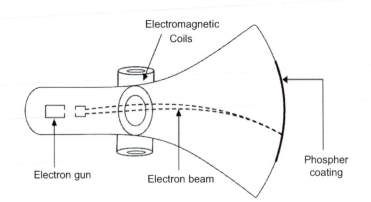

FIGURE 2.8 Basic construction of CRT

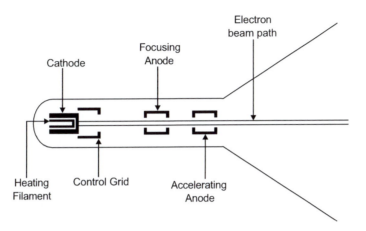

FIGURE 2.9   Basic operation of electron gun

Electron gun: It consists of a metal cathode and a control grid. The cathode is heated by a heating filament when a current is passed through the filament. It thus causes the electrons to reach an excited state and leave the hot cathode surface.

The cathode is covered by the control grid, a metal cylinder. The control grid voltage levels influence the power of the electron beam generated by the cathode. A negative voltage is applied to the gird. Due to this negative voltage, control grid repels the electrons coming from cathode and hence reduces the intensity of electron beam that passes through a small hole in control grid. The intensity of electron beam will vary inversely with the negative voltage over the control gird. This can vary the brightness of the display over the screen.

Focusing system: The need for a focusing system in the CRT arises from the fact that the electrons in the beam, being negatively charged, will repel each other and thus the beam may spread over the screen.

The focusing of an electron beam is accomplished by using a focusing system which comprises of an electric focusing anode. The anode-focusing electrostatic lens is a positively charged metal cylinder. Electrostatic lenses focus electron beams similar to how optical lenses focus light rays.

Focusing an electron beam can also be accomplished by making use of a magnetic field forming a magnetic lens. Magnetic lenses are used in precision equipment because they provide pictures that are crisp and in focus.

Deflection system: As in the case of focussing, deflection of beams can also be regulated either with electric fields or with magnetic fields. However, magnetic field deflection has become more common in the CRT. In this instance, we use a total of four coils, arranged in two sets of two. Each pair of coils is attached to the exterior of the CRT's housing, but on different sides of the neck. Both the left and right sides of the neck include a set of earrings, while the top and bottom of the neck feature their own. Each set of coils creates a magnetic field, and that field causes a transverse deflection force that is perpendicular to the magnetic field and the electron beam's direction of motion.

Screen: The display screen of a visual display unit is coated with phosphor. When the electron beam impinges on the phosphor-coated screen, the kinetic energy of the electrons is absorbed by the phosphor. A part of the kinetic energy is transferred to the phosphor electrons, which as a result get excited and rise to higher energy levels. The remaining kinetic energy is converted by friction into heat. After some time, the excited phosphor electrons lose their extra energy and return to their ground state (stable state) emitting small quantums of light energy.

Different kinds of phosphor having different levels of persistence are available for coating the screen. The duration of persistence is measured in milliseconds, or the time it takes for the screen's light output to fade to 10% of its initial level. Low-persistence phosphors need frequent picture

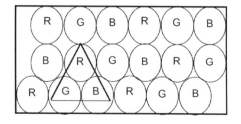

FIGURE 2.10   Arrangement of phosphor dots

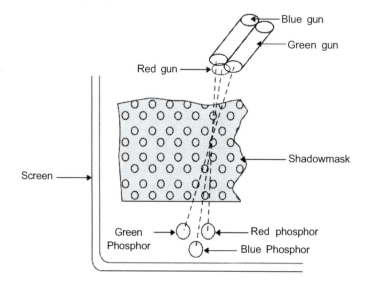

FIGURE 2.11   The shadow mask CRT

updates to prevent flicker. The phosphor on the screen of a raster CRT is composed of a myriad of small spots in a fixed pattern.

In a colour CRT, each of the three primary colours – red, green and blue – is represented by an electron gun. The phosphor dots on the screen create a triangular grid, as shown in Figure 2.10.

The electron guns are arranged in a similar fashion and the individual beams converge or intersect at a shadow mark as shown in Figure 2.11. The shadow mask directs the beam to the red phosphor dot and prevents it from impinging on the green or blue dot. In the simplest case, each pixel has a triad.

Due to the rapid light degradation of phosphor, engineers have invented techniques to prevent the picture on the screen from vanishing.

Scanning the electron beam across the tube several times over various bright spots on the screen at a fast enough rate to create the illusion of a continuous image is one method for keeping the images lighted for longer. It has been observed that if the repetition rate is at least 30 times per second, the human eye will perceive a steady picture, without any flicker. Typically, the scanning rate is kept between 30 and 60 times per second to obtain a flicker-free image. This display is called "*refresh*" CRT since the entire picture is refreshed during each scan.

In refresh type video displays, the electron beam scans the phosphor-coated glass screen by using two techniques: Raster scan and random scan.

2.6.2   RASTER SCAN DISPLAY

In raster scan the electron beam follows a fixed path as shown in Figure 2.12.

The electron beam traverses vertically and horizontally, row by row (scan line). The horizontal trajectory of the beam starts in upper left corner and finishes in the bottom right. During the scan,

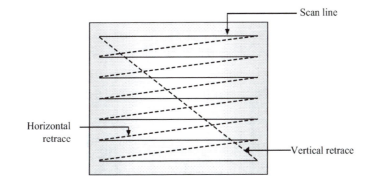

FIGURE 2.12   Raster scan technique

the intensity of the beam is modified to produce the desired picture pattern. When the beam hits the right side of the screen, it is blanked out and transferred to the left, where it starts a one-unit-lower drop. This is illustrated in the figure by a dashed line. Continue scanning until the screen's lower right corner is reached. Upon completion of a scan, the beam is shifted to upper left corner of display to prepare for the subsequent scan.

In raster scan technique the screen is divided into small squares called ***picture elements*** or ***pixels***. An important feature of a pixel is that it is addressable. The image is displayed by illuminating the pixel. The quality of a monitor is referred to in terms of resolution. The more pixels there are on the screen, the higher will be the resolution and clarity of the picture.

The frame buffer or refresh buffer is a piece of memory used by raster scan systems. The array of intensity values for each component of the image is kept in this section of memory. Then, the intensity values are read from the refresh buffer and painted onto the screen one row at a time. At each pixel, the beam's intensity is set to reflect the pixels' intensity. In colour systems, three beams are controlled – one each for the red, green and blue primary colours. The basic architecture of a raster display system is shown in Figure 2.13.

To simplify, think of a frame buffer as a block of RAM. The simplest raster configuration uses one bit per pixel. Bit plane is the term given to this kind of memory storage. Thus, 64K memory bits are needed for a single plane of a 320 200 raster. Each memory bit may take on a value of either 0 or 1. The bit in the frame buffer corresponding to the desired pixel is set to 1 if that pixel is to be addressed. The digital data of the frame buffer must be transformed to an analogue voltage via a digital-to-analogue convertor since the raster CRT is an analogue device (DAC). This is schematically shown in Figure 2.14.

A monochromatic image is created by employing just one bit plane. Additional bit planes enable the generation of a broader spectrum of greyscales and colour palettes. Here, the pixel intensity of

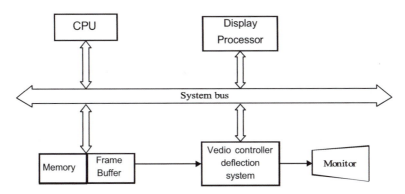

FIGURE 2.13   Raster display system architecture

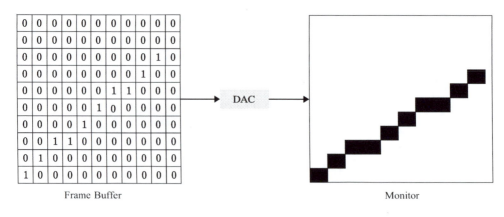

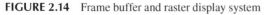
Frame Buffer   Monitor

FIGURE 2.14   Frame buffer and raster display system

the CRT is influenced by a variety of parameters. Consider the number of configurations that may be stored in a frame buffer using just four bits of data: 24 (= 16). This arrangement allows for 16 distinct greyscale or colour tones.

A colour graphics display requires just a simple frame buffer with three-bit planes for each primary colour. Such an arrangement can lead to 2^3 (= 8) colours as given in table below:

	Bit Plane 1	Bit Plane 2	Bit Plane 3
Black	0	0	0
Red	1	0	0
Green	0	1	0
Blue	0	0	1
Yellow	1	1	0
Cyan	0	1	1
Magenta	1	0	1
White	1	1	1

A basic problem with raster images arises due to the discrete array of pixels on the monitor. As a result, although lines that are horizontal and vertical look perfectly straight, those at some other angle have a pronounced jagged appearance as shown in Figure 2.15. This effect is called "*staircasing*." It is present due to the fact that the pixels appear on the screen as small rectangular boxes, with horizontal and vertical sides.

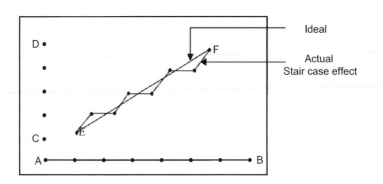

FIGURE 2.15   Display of lines with raster scan technique

It can be observed from Figure 2.15 that while lines AB and CD are straight, the line EF is showing a "*staircase*" effect.

The advantage of implementing a raster scan is that it is possible to show coloured images, shaded and animation images.

2.6.3 RANDOM SCAN

The electron beam in the random scan method travels in a way that may be controlled either by the user or by the computer. In a random scan system, the lines that make up an item are drawn in a completely arbitrary sequence, as seen in Figure 2.16.

After the electron beam generates the complete image, it is repeatedly retracted by the electron beam. Hence, such a display is also called refresh display.

Refresh display terminals have the disadvantage that they cannot display coloured images, shaded and animation images. Also, the display image starts flickering if a substantial amount of data is stored on the screen. Due to these disadvantages, random scan is not recommended for CAD systems.

The main advantage of random scan is that the image is characterised by high brightness and resolution. Also, unlike in the case of raster scan where a jagged line is plotted on pixels, a random scan produces a smooth line drawing since there are no pixels on the screen. Remember that a picture is not defined by its intensity levels, but rather by a set of line drawing instructions.

2.6.3.1 Direct View Storage Tube (DVST)

Another method of maintaining the image on the screen is to store the picture information inside the CRT instead of refreshing the screen.

An improvement on the CRT is the direct view storage tube (DVST). A DVST employs a main gun and a flood gun, both of which are types of electron gun. The image pattern is stored in the primary gun, and the display is continuously updated by the flood gun. A DVST works by encoding an image's details as a distribution of charges on a dielectric-coated wire grid placed directly below the phosphor screen. A constant stream of electrons is released from a separate flood cannon in order to transmit a positive charge pattern from the grid to the phosphor. Thus, the image is traced only once and is stored directly on the screen instead of making use of solid-state memory. Figure 2.17 shows the general arrangement of a DVST.

One of the important merits of a DVST is that the large amounts of graphics data can be shown on the screen without flickering the image. This is because the image is stored on the screen itself rather than being constantly refreshed from the computer memory.

But a DVST has some major disadvantages; because of this, the device is not popular. Since the image is not refreshed, the display has low brightness and contrast: Because of this, it requires dimmed ambient lighting. Also, there is absence of selective erasure. Once the image is displayed

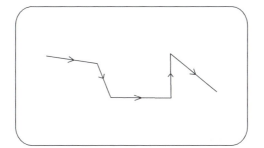

FIGURE 2.16   Random scan

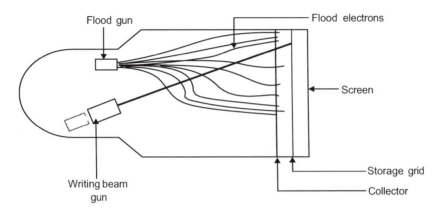

FIGURE 2.17   The direct view storage tube

and stored, it cannot be changed without repainting the entire screen. This reduces the productivity in drafting.

2.6.4   FLAT PANEL DISPLAY

The CRT has some disadvantages. It is very bulky which reduces its portability. Furthermore, a CRT has a high power consumption and high heat dissipation demand. Such drawbacks motivated manufacturers to create a wide variety of flat panels for use as computer output devices. Portable electronic devices including laptops, notebooks and palmtops increasingly often use flat screen displays. The following are examples of flat-screen technology:

(a) **Plasma Screen**

The basic design of a plasma panel display device is shown in Figure 2.18. It consists of two glass plates arranged very close to each other. The region between the glass plates is filled with inert gas, usually argon. On the interior of one glass plate is a set of very tiny vertical conducting wires, while on the other glass plate is a set of horizontal conducting wires. Gas at the intersections of this tiny mesh of horizontal and vertical conductors breaks down into incandescent plasma of electrons and ions when an appropriate voltage is applied. Pixel positions are refreshed at a rate of 60 hertz by

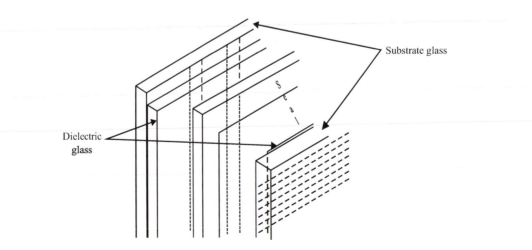

FIGURE 2.18   Plasma display

storing definition-related data in a refresh buffer and periodically applying voltage to the display. As in a storage tube, pixels remain lit until they are erased.

(b) Liquid Crystal Display (LCD)

Liquid crystal display is being widely used in small computers, laptops, calculators and notebooks. It has several advantages like less space requirement and low power consumption. These are non-emissive devices. LCD makes use of liquid crystalline material through which polarised light is passed. The liquid crystal material has special characteristics that, despite its crystalline molecular structure, is fluid.

2.7   COORDINATE REPRESENTATION

Every CAD/CAM system has a coordinate representation system associated with it. Most of the CAD and other general graphics packages make use of a Cartesian coordinate system. Image points defined in a non-Cartesian coordinate system must be translated to Cartesian coordinates before being used in a graphics program.

In a graphics image, the shape of individual objects can be created using separate coordinate reference frames called a local coordinate system. Once all the objects in an image have been defined by their individual local coordinate reference frames, all these objects can be placed in the image with reference to one single reference frame called the world coordinate system. Every user defines his own drawing limits in order to edit the drawing. This coordinate system used by the user is called the world coordinate system.

Now, the image generated has to be displayed on an output device like a monitor, printer, plotter. The coordinate system used by an output device is called a device coordinate system.

Since each of the output devices being used may have a different coordinate system, the problem of compatibility may arise. Hence, it is desirable to convert the world coordinates into another coordinate system to make the system independent of various output devices being used at a particular workstation. Such a coordinate system is called a normalised coordinate system. Hence, the world coordinates are first converted to normalised coordinates which have a range from (0, 0) to (1, 1).

The output device thus interacts with a normalised coordinate system. By doing so it is convenient for the output system to interact with the world coordinate system. The transformation from one coordinate system to another is shown in Figure 2.19.

2.8   GRAPHICS FUNCTIONS

Every CAD graphics program has a number of graphics features to assist the user to make and alter drawings and pictures. You may use these procedures to collect various types of data (output, input, transformations, characteristics, etc.).

LO 6. To understand the graphics functions

Output primitives are the entities that are directly involved in the creation of a painting. These may be either strings of characters or more complex shapes like points, lines, circles, ellipses, polygons, and so on.

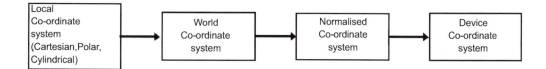

FIGURE 2.19   The transformation sequences from local coordinate system to device co-ordinate system

Output primitives have attributes that describe them. In the case of a line object, the properties include things like line type, colour, thickness, etc.

Positioning, rotation and scaling are all possible with the use of transformation methods.

2.8.1   OUTPUT PRIMITIVES

These are the lines, circles, polygons, ellipses and spheres that make up CAD drawings and models. Output primitives are the graphical components that are generated. It just takes a few simple instructions to draw these output primitives. Creating a line requires the input of two coordinates (start and finish), whereas drawing a circle requires the input of two coordinates (centre and radius).

It is important to understand algorithms to generate these output primitives. Different algorithms are available for generating lines and circles.

2.8.1.1   Line-Generating Algorithms

There are basically three types of algorithms used for generating lines:

1. Algorithm for line drawing using slope method,
2. Digital Differential Analyser (DDA) algorithm,
3. Bresenham's line-drawing algorithm.

What are the characteristics of lines generated by a good line-drawing algorithm? As many mechanical engineers would agree, the answer is to ensure that the lines are straight, that their ends are accurate, that their thickness is constant and that the lines themselves are drawn correctly.

It is known that the screen is divided into pixels that are rectangular in shape. Hence, vertical and horizontal lines can be drawn exactly straight. But the problem arises when you have drawn lines with some other slope. An unpleasant staircase-like quantisation effect is induced in the picture. In order to keep the staircase effect to a minimum, we must choose which pixel should be black and which white. This is determined by the algorithms.

Algorithm for drawing line using the slope method:

Assume that the equation of line is $y = mx + b$

1. Compute $dx : dx = x_2 - x_1$.
2. Compute $dy : dy = y_2 - y_1$.
3. Compute slope $m : m = \dfrac{dy}{dx}$.
4. Compute $b : b = y_1 - mx_1$.
5. Set (x, y) equal to lower left hand end point and set x_{end} equal to largest value of x.

   If $dx < 0$, $x = x_2$, $y = y_2$ and $x\text{end} = x_1$

   If $dx > 0$, $x = x_1$, $y = y_1$ and $x\text{end} = x_2$
6. Test to determine whether the entire line has been drawn. If $x = x_{end}$, stop.
7. Plot the point at the current (x, y) coordinates.
8. Increment $x = x + 1$.
9. Compute the nearest integer value of y, $y = m\,x + b$.
10. Go to step 6.

2.8.1.1.1   DDA Line-Drawing Algorithm

From differential equations, the DDA creates lines. It is a scan conversion line method that calculates either y or x. We sample the line at unit intervals in one coordinate and calculate the line path's equivalent values in other coordinates.

$$\text{Slope,} \quad m = \frac{y_2 - y_1}{x_2 - x_1} = \frac{\Delta y}{\Delta x}$$

$$\text{Hence} \quad \Delta y = mx$$

$$\text{or} \quad \Delta x = \frac{\Delta y}{m}$$

1. If slope (m) is less than one and positive and the start point of the line is at the left, then set the increment in x coordinate to unity (i.e., $\Delta x = 1$).

Hence if (x_i, y_i) is any point on the line then the coordinate of the next point will be

$$x_{i+1} = x_i + 1$$

$$\text{and } y_{i+1} = y_i + m$$

If the start point is to the right, the procedure remains the same, except that now the coordinates will be obtained using relation

$$x_{i+1} = x_i - 1$$

$$\text{and } y_{i+1} = y_i - m$$

2. If the slope is greater than one (i.e., $m > 1$) and start point is at the left, then change in y-coordinate is set to unity and x-coordinate is found out as follows:

Since, $\Delta y = 1$

$$\text{i.e., } y_{i+1} = y_i + 1$$

$$x_{i+1} = x_i - \frac{1}{m}$$

If the start point is to the right, then the above equations are suitably modified to follow the same procedure as given above.

Hence, when the starting point is to the right

$$y_{i+1} = y_i - 1$$

$$\text{and} \quad x_{i+1} = x_i - \frac{1}{m}$$

3. If the slope of the line is negative, then the procedure followed is as given below:

If absolute value of m is less than one, follow the procedure for $m < 1$ as explained in step one, with the modification that one coordinate decreases and the other coordinate increases.

If absolute value of m is greater than one, follow the procedure for $m > 1$ as explained in step two, with the modification that one coordinate decreases and the other coordinate increases.

The DDA is a fast method for generating a line but has some inherent disadvantage. The value of slope m may be a real number. Hence the value of new coordinates calculated using the equations $y_{i+1} = y_i + m$ or $x_{i+1} = x_i + \frac{1}{m}$ may also be real numbers.

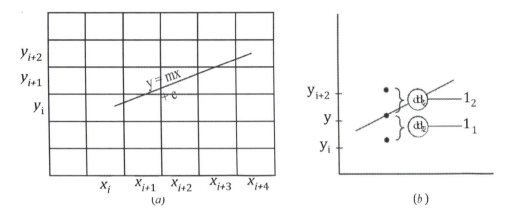

FIGURE 2.20   Bresenham's Algorithm

Hence it becomes necessary to round off the values of y_i+1 and x_i+1 to some integer values because the pixels are arranged on the screen in integer fashion. The rounding-off operation and real arithmetic calculations become imperative which makes line generation using a DDA algorithm a slow process. In low-resolution monitors, the staircase effect is quite prominent. Nowadays DDA is not preferred in CAD systems.

2.8.1.1.2   Bresenham's Algorithm

Bresenham has created a widely used method for drawing lines. Like the DDA, it is built such that one of the coordinate values shifts by 1 at each iteration. Depending on the value of the algorithm's decision variable, the other coordinate may or may not change. The basic problem of DDA, i.e., rounding of operations is eliminated in Bresenham's algorithm.

Consider drawing a line with a positive slope, less than 1. The coordinate position of the pixel to be brightened is determined by increasing the value of x by unity. The corresponding y value is determined by taking the value of y which is closest to the true line path. Figure 2.20(a) and (b) shows the process for ith step.

Let the first pixel to be brightened is (x_i, y_i). The next pixel position can be either

$$(x_{i+1}, y_i) \text{ or } (x_{i+1}, y_{i+1}).$$

Now
$$y = m (x1 + 1) + c$$

$$1_1 = y - y_i$$

$$= \left[m(x_i + 1) + c \right] - y_i$$

$$= m(x_i + 1) + c - y_i$$

$$1_2 = (y_i + 1) - y$$

$$= (y_i + 1) - \left[m(x_i + 1) + c \right]$$

$$= y_i + 1 - m(x_i + 1) - c$$

$$1_1 - 1_2 = m(x_i + 1) + c - y_i - (y_i + 1) + m(x_i + 1) + c$$

$$= 2m(x_i + 1) - 2y_i + 2c - 1$$

where $\qquad\qquad\qquad\qquad\qquad\qquad\qquad m = dy/dx$

Defining

$$P_i = dx\left(l_1 - l_2\right)$$

$$= dx\left[2m\left(x_i + 1\right) - 2y_i + 2c - 1\right]$$

$$= dx\left[2\frac{dy}{dx}\left(x_i + 1\right) - 2y_i + 2c - 1\right]$$

$$= 2dy\left(x_i + 1\right) - 2y_i dx + 2cdx - dx \qquad\qquad (2.1)$$

$$= 2dyx_i + 2dy - 2y_i dx + 2cdx - dx$$

$$= 2dyx_i - 2dxy_i + \left(2cdx + 2dy - dx\right)$$

$$= 2dyx_i - 2dx\, y_i + c_1$$

$$P_{i+1} = 2dyx_{i+1} - 2dxy_{i+1} + c_1$$

Now

$$P_{i+1} - P_i = 2dy\left(x_{i+1} - x_i\right) - 2dx\left(y_{i+1} - y_i\right)$$

$$= 2dy \times 1 - 2dx\left(y_{i+1} - y_i\right) \qquad\qquad (2.2)$$

$$P_{i+1} = P_i + 2dy - 2dx\left(y_{i+1} - y_i\right)$$

If $P_i < 0$, $l1$ is less than l_2 (since dx is positive in Equation (2.1)). So, the pixel corresponding to y_i should be brightened.

So $y_i+1 = y_i$. From Equation (2.2), since $y_i+1 = y_i$ hence $y_i+1 - y_i = 0$.

Therefore, for $P_i < 0$

$$yi+1 = yi$$

$$P_i+1 = P_i + 2dy$$

If $Pi > 0$, $l1$ is greater than l_2 in Equation (2.1). So, the pixel corresponding to y_{i+1} is nearer to the ideal line. Hence, the pixel corresponding to y_{i+1} should be brightened. Now since $y_i+1 = y_i + 1$, so $y_i+1 - y_i = 1$.

Hence, $\qquad\qquad\qquad\qquad\qquad\qquad\qquad P_{i+1} = P_i + 2dy - 2dx$

The first parameter P_o is evaluated for the starting pixel position (x_o, y_o) as:

$$P_o = 2dy - dx$$

2.8.1.2 Algorithms to Generate Circles

Circular and elliptical shapes are often employed in several types of applications, especially those that involve the presentation of mechanical engineering components. Circular- and arc-plotting algorithms have been created. Bresenham's circle algorithm and the midpoint circle algorithm are two popular methods for producing circles.

2.8.1.2.1 Bresenham's Circle Algorithm

If the centre of the circle is (0, 0), then start making the circle from its topmost points i.e., (O, R). To locate the next pixel assuming that (x_i, y_i) is a general point on the circle, then to obtain the next pixel, we increase the value of x by 1 i.e., $x_i + 1 = x_i + 1$, But the corresponding value of y will be either y_i or $y_i - 1$, as shown in Figure 2.21. The actual value of y on the circle can be computed using the equation

$$y_2 = R_2 - (x_i + 1)_2 \tag{2.3}$$

Now let us define
d_1, and d_2 as $d_1 = y_i^2 - y^2$

$$d_2 = y^2 - (y_i - 1)^2$$

Thus $d1$ and $d2$ is the difference of square of y values for two possible points Now substituting the value of $y2$ from
Equation (2.3), we get

$$d_1 = y_i^2 - \left\{ R^2 - \left(x_i + 1 \right)^2 \right\}$$

$$= \quad y_i^2 - R^2 + x_i^2 + 1 + 2x_i$$

$$\text{Also } d_2 = \left\{ R^2 - \left(x_i + 1 \right)^2 \right\} - \left(y_i - 1 \right)^2$$

$$= \quad R^2 - x_i^2 - 1 - 2x_i - y_i^2 - 1 + 2y_i$$

$$= \quad y_i^2 - R^2 + x_i^2 + 1 + 2x_i$$

Let us assume P_i as the decision variable, where

$$P_i = d_1 - d_2$$

$$= y_i^2 - R^2 + x_i^2 + 1 + 2x_i - R^2 + x_i^2 + 1 + 2x_i + y_i^2 + 1 - 2y_i$$

Thus $P_i = \quad 2y_i^2 - 2R^2 - 2y_i + 3 + 2x_i^2 + 4x_i$

According to the algorithm. if $P_i < 0$, Pixel at Position $(x_i + 1, y_i)$ is to be turned On. But if $P_i \geq 0$, pixel $(x_i + 1, y_i - 1)$ has to be turned On.

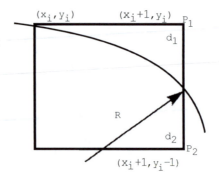

FIGURE 2.21 Bresenham's Circle Algorithm

The initial value of P_i (i.e., $P1$) is obtained for $x1 = 0$ and $y1, = R$ from the equation of P_i as

$$(P1 = 3 - 2R)$$

Subsequent Values of P_i can be obtained as follows: If $P_i < 0$

$$x_i + 1 = x_i + 1, y_i + 1 = y_i$$

As $P_i = 2y\,2 - 2R2 - 2y + 3 + 2\,x2 + 4x_i$

Hence $\quad P_{i+1} \quad = 2y_i^2 - 2R^2 - 2y_i + 3 + 2(x_i + 1)^2 + 4(x_i + 1)$

$$= Pi + 4x_i + 6$$

If $\qquad\qquad\qquad\qquad\qquad\qquad P_i > 0$

$$x_i + 1 = x_i + 1, y_i + 1 = y_i - 1$$

Hence

$$P_{i+1} = 2(y_i - 1)^2 - 2R^2 - 2(y_i - 1) + 2(x_i + 1)^2 + 4(x_i + 1)$$

$$= 2y_i^2 + 2 - 4y_i - 2R^2 - 2y_i + 2 + 2x_i^2 + 2 + 4x_i + 4x_i + 4$$

$$= (2y_i^2 - 2R^2 - 2y_i + 3 + 2x_i^2 + 4x_i) + 4x_i - 4y_i + 10$$

$$= P_i + 4(x_i - y_i) + 10$$

Using this algorithm, one starts plotting at $x = 0$, $y = R$. The algorithm helps selecting the next pixel position until $x_i = y_i$ is reached. The remaining points on the circle can be obtained by taking reflection of these points about $x = y$, $y = 0$ and $x = 0$ lines. The steps in Bresenham's circle algorithm can be enumerated as follows:

1. Set the initial value of the variables:

Let coordinates of circle centre = (h, k). Shift centre to origin. Start by plotting topmost point on circle by setting

$$X = 0$$

$$Y = \text{circle radius } r$$

We keep plotting until we reach 45° in a clockwise direction from vertical initial decision variable, $P = 3 - 2 \times r$

2. Test to determine if the entire circle has been scan converted:

i.e., If $x > y$; stop.

3. Compute location of next pixel. If $P < 0$:

$x_i + 1 = x_i + 1$

$$y_i + 1 = y_i$$

$$\text{and } P_i + 1 = P_i + 4x + 6$$

If $P > 0$:

$$x_i + 1 = x_i + 1$$

$$y_i + 1 = y_i - 1$$

$$\text{and } P_i + 1 = P_i + 4(x - y) + 10$$

4. Plot remaining points by taking mirror image about $x = y$, $y = 0$ and $x = 0$ axis. Shift centre back to its original position by adding h to the x-coordinate and k to the y-coordinate.

$$[x + h, y + k]$$

$$[x + h, -y + k]$$

$$[-x + h, y + k]$$

$$[-x + h, -y + k] \, [y + h, x + k]$$

$$[-y + h, x + k]$$

$$[y + h, -x + k] \text{ and } [-y + h, -x + k]$$

Go to step 2.

2.8.1.2.2   Midpoint Circle Algorithm

This is another popular algorithm used for drawing circles.

1. Set the initial value of variables:

Let coordinates of circle centre $= (h, k)$ $x = 0$
   $Y =$ circle radius r

$$P = 5/4 - r$$

2. Test to determine whether the entire circle has been scan converted:

i.e., if $x > y$; stop.

3. To compute the location of next pixel along the circle centred at $(0, 0)$ if $P < 0$:

$$x_i + 1 = x_i + 1$$

$$y_i + 1 = y_i$$

$$\text{and } P_i + 1 = P_i + 2x_i + 1 + 1$$

If $P > 0$

$$x_i+1 = x_i + 1$$

$$y_i+1 = y_i - 1$$

$$\text{and } P_i+1 = P_i + 2x_i+1 + 1 - 2y_i+1$$

4. Determine symmetry points in the other seven octants.
5. Show each calculated pixel position (x, y) onto the circular path centred on(h, k) and plot the coordinate values:

$$X = x + h \; y = y + k$$

6. Go to step. 2.

Example 2.1: *Utilise the midpoint circle method to convert a circle with a centre at (10, 20) and a radius of 10 units.*
   Solution: Let the centre of the circle be shifted to (0, 0). Then the starting point of the circle is (0, 10). The points on the circle i.e., (x, y) can be calculated using midpoint circle algorithm as shown in table below.

x	y	P	Circle points $(X = x + 10)$	$(Y = y + 20)$
0	10	$P0 = 1 - r = 1 - 10 = -9 \ (P < 0)$	10	30
1	10	$P1 = -9 + 2 \times 1 + 1 = -6 \ (P < 0)$	11	30
2	10	$P2 = -6 + 2 \times 2 + 1 = -1 \ (P < 0)$	12	30
3	10	$P3 = -1 + 2 \times 3 + 1 = 6 \ (P > 0)$	13	30
4	9	$P4 = 6 + 2 \times 4 + 1 - 2 \times 9 = -3 \ (P < 0)$	14	29
5	9	$P5 = -3 + 2 \times 5 + 1 = 8 \ (P > 0)$	15	29
6	8	$P6 = 8 + 2 \times 6 + 1 - 2 \times 8 = 5(P > 0)$	16	28
7	7	$P7 = 5 + 2 \times 7 + 1 - 2 \times 5 = 10(P > 0)$	17	27

As discussed in step 2 of the algorithm, we stop when $x > y$. The remaining points can be determined by taking a mirror image of these points about $x = y$, x-axis and y- axis.

Example 2.2: *Digitise a circle with centre (150, 200) and radius 10. Use midpoint circle algorithm.*
   Solution: Let the centre of the circle be shifted to (0, 0). Then, the starting point of the circle algorithm as in the table below:

x	y	P	$X = x + 150$	$Y = y + 200$
0	10	$P_0 = 1 - x = 1 - 10 = -9$	150	210
1	10	$P_1 = -9 + 2 \times 1 + 1 = -6$	151	210
2	10	$P_2 = -6 + 2 \times 2 + 1 = -1$	152	210
3	10	$P_3 = -1 + 2 \times 3 + 1 = 6$	153	210
4	9	$P_4 = 6 + 2 \times 4 + 1 - 2 \times 9 = -3$	154	209
5	9	$P_5 = -3 + 2 \times 5 + 1 = 8$	155	209
6	8	$P_6 = 8 + 2 \times 6 + 1 - 2 \times 8 = 5$	156	208
7	7	$P7 = 5 + 2 \times 7 + 1 - 2 \times 5 = 10(P > 0)$	157	207

The remaining points can be calculated by taking a mirror image of these points about $x = y$, x-axis and y-axis.

2.9   WINDOWING AND CLIPPING

When only a part of a big drawing is to be modified, a concept of window is used. For example, in AutoCAD, we zoom in on a small area on the entire screen to make changes in the drawing. A *window* is a rectangular area created by the user on the drawing. It can be created by giving the end points of the diagonal of the window. The graphical entities inside the window are thus selected for manipulation. The part of the screen where the window is mapped is called the view port.

The process of displaying an expanded section of an image involves more than just applying the right scaling and translation; we also need to determine which elements of the image are visible and include them in the final product. It's not a picnic to go through this choosing procedure. There may be lines that are partially inside the viewable region and partially beyond it. Only the portion of lines inside the window should be displayed.

Clipping, a procedure that separates each image component into its visible and unseen halves, is the proper method for selecting visible information for display. Points, vectors, curves, straight lines, text characters and polygons are just some of the many different kinds of drawing objects that may be clipped.

2.9.1   POINT CLIPPING

It is possible to determine whether a point (x, y) is inside the window or outside the window.
The point (x, y) lies inside the window if

(i) $x_{\text{left}} \leq x \leq x_{\text{right}}$ and
(ii) $y_{\text{bottom}} \leq y \leq y_{\text{top}}$

where x_{left}, x_{right}, y_{bottom} and y_{top} are position of the edges of the window.

2.9.2   LINE-CLIPPING ALGORITHM

Line-clipping algorithms are designed to determine what proportion of a line should be confined inside a certain window. The Cohen–Sutherland method and the midpoint subdivision algorithm are two of the most used cutting line methods.

2.9.2.1   Cohen–Sutherland Algorithm

This algorithm considers the orientation of a line with respect to a window from three aspects:

(i) If the line is completely outside the window, it is rejected.
(ii) If the line lies entirely inside the window, it is selected for display.
(iii) If the line is intersecting the window boundaries, the point of intersection is calculated and only the portion of the line inside the window is selected and the portion lying outside the window is rejected.

1001	1000	1010
0001	window 0000	0010
0101	0100	0110

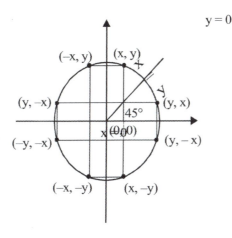

FIGURE 2.22   Plotting point by mirror image

The rejection test is accomplished by expanding the window's boundaries such that they partition the area filled by the unclipped image into nine regions as shown in the matrix above. Each of these regions is accorded a four-bit code and the two end points of the line are assigned codes corresponding to the regions they are in. The four-bit code is assigned as shown in Figure 2.22.

(i)   The window will have the region code 0000.
(ii) The region above the window will have 1 in the first bit position of the region code.
(iii) For the region below the window, 1 appears in the second bit position of the region code.
(iii) For the region to the right of the window, 1 appears in the third bit position of the region code.
(v)   For the region to the left of the window, 1 appears in the fourth bit position of the region code.

Clearly, if the four-bit codes for both endpoints are zero, the line is completely contained inside the window and is chosen or visible.

If the logical intersection of the two codes is not zero, the line must be outside the window totally and is rejected. (i.e., the logical AND operation is not 0000).

2.9.2.2   Midpoint Subdivision Algorithm

The line may be split in half along its equidistant point, enabling us to avoid directly calculating the point where it meets the window frame.

In this algorithm, equation of line is not used. Only the midpoint of the line is calculated. The midpoint divides the line into two equal halves and each half is analysed for the window.

In Figure 2.23 say line AB is to be analysed using midpoint algorithm. M_1 is the midpoint of AB. So, the line is divided into two halves, AM_1 and BM_1. The part BM_1 is completely outside the window hence it is rejected. For the portion AM_1, again the mid- point is calculated. M_2 is the midpoint. The part AM_2 is completely inside the window and it is selected. For the part M_1M_2, again midpoint is found out. M_3 is the midpoint of M_1M_2. Hence the parts M_1M_3 and M_2M_3 are analysed. This procedure is continued until we reach the window boundary. Thus, the part of the line inside the window can be selected by using this procedure.

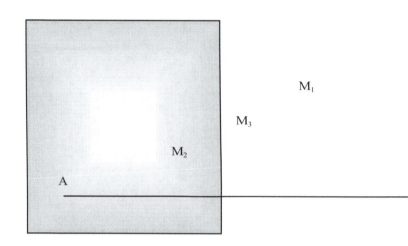

FIGURE 2.23 Midpoint Subdivision Algorithm

2.10 GEOMETRIC TRANSFORMATIONS

Any geometric entity or drawing can be manipulated using transformation routines. If a real drawing has to be produced using a computer, the limitation on the size of display screen poses a problem. There is only a fixed number of pixels on a display surface. The device coordinate system for output devices like plotter, CMM, etc. in pixels is too restrictive for many applications. A solid model needs to be rotated to give a clear picture of its shape. An engineer can make use of transformation techniques to overcome such difficulties. Transformation in a single plane is called 2-D transformation.

LO 7. To explain geometric transformations and 3D viewing

There are basically five types of transformation routines:

1. Translation,
2. Scaling,
3. Rotation,
4. Reflection,
5. Shear.

2.10.1 TRANSLATION

Any graphical entity can be translated or moved in X or Y direction by using this routine.
Basic equations used in this subroutine are

$$X' = Y + Tx$$

$$Y' = Y + Ty$$

(X', Y') are the new coordinates after translation and (X, Y) are the old coordinates before translation. T_x and T_y is the distance to be translated in x and y direction respectively.

The equations can be written in matrix form as

$$\begin{bmatrix} X' & Y' & 1 \end{bmatrix} = \begin{bmatrix} X & Y & 1 \end{bmatrix} \times \begin{bmatrix} 1 & 0 & 0 \\ 0 & 1 & 0 \\ T_x & T_y & 1 \end{bmatrix}$$

$$\text{Here matrix} \begin{bmatrix} 1 & 0 & 0 \\ 0 & 1 & 0 \\ T_x & T_y & 1 \end{bmatrix} \text{ is called the translation matrix.}$$

2.10.1.1 Matrix Representation and Homogeneous Coordinates

The composite transformation (i.e., carrying out two or more transformations at a time) can be carried out conveniently by using matrix representation of transformation routines. A concept of homogeneous coordinates is used. Every point having coordinates (x, y) can be represented in matrix form as $[X, Y, W]$. Here W represents a parameter which defines the class of transformation. The representation of a coordinate in a matrix as shown above is called homogeneous coordinates.

For all 2-D transformations the value of W is 1. Hence the equation of any transformation of a point can be represented in matrix form as

$$[X'\ Y'\ 1] = [X\ Y1]'\ [\text{Transformation Ma t r ix}]_{3\times3}$$

It is obvious that for 2-D problems, the dimensions of a transformation matrix must be 3×3.

2.10.2 SCALING

This routine is used to enlarge the object or make it small.

The basic equations are

$$X' = X.\ S_x$$

$$Y' = Y.\ S_y$$

where S_x and S_y are the scaling factor in x and y direction respectively. To enlarge an image, the value of scaling factor will be greater than one and to reduce an image, the value of scaling factor will be less than one.

$$\text{Scaling matrix will be} \begin{bmatrix} S_x & 0 & 0 \\ 0 & S_y & 0 \\ 0 & 0 & 1 \end{bmatrix}$$

Hence the matrix form of equations for scaling will be

$$\begin{bmatrix} X' & Y' & 1 \end{bmatrix} = \begin{bmatrix} X & Y & 1 \end{bmatrix} \begin{bmatrix} S_x & 0 & 0 \\ 0 & S_y & 0 \\ 0 & 0 & 1 \end{bmatrix}$$

When scaling is effected with respect to some fixed point $(x0\ y0)$, translate point $(x0\ y0)$, to origin, perform scaling, translate the point back to its original position. Hence the final scaling matrix can be obtained by multiplying the three matrices as follows:

$$\begin{bmatrix} 1 & 0 & 0 \\ 0 & 1 & 0 \\ -x_0 & -y_0 & 1 \end{bmatrix} \times \begin{bmatrix} S_x & 0 & 0 \\ 0 & S_y & 0 \\ 0 & 0 & 1 \end{bmatrix} \times \begin{bmatrix} 1 & 0 & 0 \\ 0 & 1 & 0 \\ x_0 & y_0 & 1 \end{bmatrix} = \begin{bmatrix} S_x & 0 & 0 \\ 0 & S_y & 0 \\ (1-S_x)x_0 & (1-S_y)y_0 & 1 \end{bmatrix}$$

2.10.3 ROTATION

Any point can be effectively rotated in relation to a fixed point. We consider clockwise rotation to be negative and anticlockwise rotation to be positive. Refer to Figure 2.24.

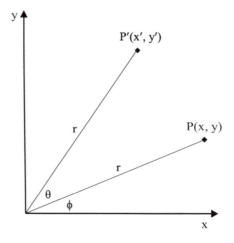

FIGURE 2.24   Rotation of a point P to P' about the z-axis

From the figure,

$$X = r\cos\phi$$

$$Y = r\sin\phi$$

$$X' = r\cos(\theta + \phi) \tag{2.4}$$

$$= r[\cos\theta\cos\phi - \sin\theta\sin\phi]$$

$$= (r\cos\phi)\cos\theta - (r\sin\phi)\sin\theta$$

Also

$$X' = X\cos\theta - Y\sin\theta$$

$$Y' = r\sin(\theta + \phi)$$

$$Y' = r[\sin\theta\cos\phi + \cos\theta\sin\phi] \tag{2.5}$$

$$Y' = X\sin\theta + Y\cos\theta$$

Equations (2.4) and (2.5) can be written in matrix form as (for rotation of a point about the Z-axis):

$$\begin{bmatrix} X' & Y' & 1 \end{bmatrix} = \begin{bmatrix} X & Y & 1 \end{bmatrix} \begin{bmatrix} \cos\theta & \sin\theta & 0 \\ -\sin\theta & \cos\theta & 0 \\ 0 & 0 & 1 \end{bmatrix}$$

2.10.3.1   Concatenation Rule

Sequences of transformation can be combined into one transformation by the concatenation process.
When three transformation matrices are to be concatenated then the following rule is followed:
$A \times B \times C = A \times (B \times C) = (A \times B) \times C$
where A, B and C are transformation matrices.

Example 2.3: *Find the final position of the line having the end points (3, 5) and (10,5) when it is translated by three units in x-direction and then rotated by 30° in clockwise direction.*

Solution: Translation matrix when line is translated by 3 units in *x*-direction is given by

$$[T_1] = \begin{bmatrix} 1 & 0 & 0 \\ 0 & 1 & 0 \\ 3 & 0 & 1 \end{bmatrix}$$

Rotation matrix when the line is rotated by 30° in clockwise direction.

$$[R_1] = \begin{bmatrix} \cos(-30^\circ) & \sin(-30^\circ) & 0 \\ -\sin(-30^\circ) & \cos(-30^\circ) & 0 \\ 0 & 0 & 1 \end{bmatrix}$$

$$= \begin{bmatrix} 0.866 & -0.5 & 0 \\ 0.5 & 0.866 & 0 \\ 0 & 0 & 1 \end{bmatrix}$$

Concatenating the matrix $[T_1]$ and $[R_1]$ we have resultant matrix R as

$$[R] = [T_1][R_1]$$

$$= \begin{bmatrix} 1 & 0 & 0 \\ 0 & 1 & 0 \\ 3 & 0 & 1 \end{bmatrix} \times \begin{bmatrix} 0.866 & -0.5 & 0 \\ 0.5 & 0.866 & 0 \\ 0 & 0 & 1 \end{bmatrix}$$

$$[R] = \begin{bmatrix} 0.866 & -0.5 & 0 \\ 0.5 & 0.866 & 0 \\ 2.598 & -1.5 & 1 \end{bmatrix}$$

Hence, the final position of point (3, 5) will be

$$\begin{bmatrix} x_1' & y_1' & 1 \end{bmatrix} = \begin{bmatrix} 3 & 5 & 1 \end{bmatrix} \times [R]$$

Similarly, the final position of point (10, 5) will be

$$\begin{bmatrix} x_2' & y_2' & 1 \end{bmatrix} = \begin{bmatrix} 10 & 5 & 1 \end{bmatrix} \times [R]$$

2.10.4 REFLECTION

This method may be used to create a mirrored image of an item. All reflections are made with respect to a single axis, thus the name "axis of reflections."

When reflecting along the *x*-axis, the *x*-coordinate of a point is preserved but the *y*-coordinate is inverted (changes sign). When the reflection axis is the *y*-axis, the *y*-coordinate of the reflection does not change while the *x*-coordinate flips sign.

Reflection about the *x*-axis: Reflection of Point *P* about the *x*-axis is *P'* (refer to Figure 2.25).

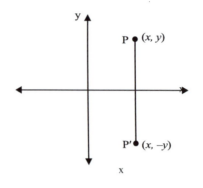

FIGURE 2.25   Reflection about the *x*-axis

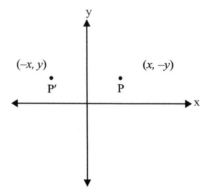

FIGURE 2.26   Reflection about the *y*-axis

$$\text{Reflection matrix is given by } \left[R_x \right] = \begin{bmatrix} 1 & 0 & 0 \\ 0 & -1 & 0 \\ 0 & 0 & 1 \end{bmatrix}$$

Hence if after reflection, coordinates are (X', Y'), then $[X'\ Y'\ 1] = [X\ Y\ 1] \times [R_x]$

Reflection about the y-axis (refer to Figure 2.26):

$$\text{Reflection matrix is given by } \left[R_y \right] = \begin{bmatrix} -1 & 0 & 0 \\ 0 & 1 & 0 \\ 0 & 0 & 1 \end{bmatrix}$$

Hence to find coordinates of point P' i.e., (x', y') about the *y*-axis:

$$\begin{bmatrix} x' & y' & 1 \end{bmatrix} = \begin{bmatrix} x & y & 1 \end{bmatrix} \times \begin{bmatrix} -1 & 0 & 0 \\ 0 & 1 & 0 \\ 0 & 0 & 1 \end{bmatrix}$$

2.10.4.1   To Find Reflection Matrix when the Axis of Reflection Is the Line Passing through Origin

Refer to Figure 2.27.

The equation of the line passing through origin is $y = mx$, where m is the slope

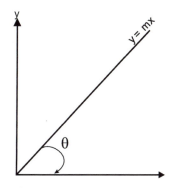

FIGURE 2.27   Axis of reflection passing through origin

($m = \tan \theta$).
The following steps should be taken:

(1) Rotate the line that is the axis of reflection $y = mx$, in a clockwise direction by angle $\theta = \tan^{-1}(m)$ to align it with the x-axis. Rotation matrix is given by $[A_1]$

$$[A_1] = \begin{bmatrix} \cos(-,) & \sin(-,) & 0 \\ -\sin(-,) & \cos(-,) & 0 \\ 0 & 0 & 1 \end{bmatrix}$$

(3) Reflection about the x-axis is obtained. Let $[A_2]$ represent the reflection matrix. Then

$$[A_2] = \begin{bmatrix} 1 & 0 & 0 \\ 0 & -1 & 0 \\ 0 & 0 & 1 \end{bmatrix}$$

(5) Now, the line is rotated by an angle in a counterclockwise manner to regain its original location

$$[A_3] = \begin{bmatrix} \cos, & \sin, & 0 \\ -\sin, & \cos, & 0 \\ 0 & 0 & 1 \end{bmatrix}$$

The resultant reflection matrix $[R]$ is obtained by concatenating $[A_1]$, $[A_2]$, $[A_3]$ as
$[R] = [A_1] \times [A_2] \times [A_3]$

2.10.5   SHEAR

Shape distortion occurs when a tangential force is applied to an item. As a result of the transformation, the item looks to have interior layers that have been made to glide over one another. This process, and the resulting alteration, are both referred to as shearing.

Shearing is a transformation that distorts an item or an image. Two types of shear exist. Refer to Figure 2.28.

(1) *X*-direction shear,
(2) *Y*-direction shear.

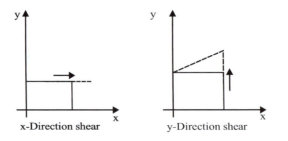

FIGURE 2.28   Shearing

The *x*-coordinate will vary in an *x*-direction shear while the *y*-coordinate stays the same. If Sh_x is the shearing factor in *x*-direction then the basic equations are

$$x1 = x + Sh_x \times y$$

$$y1 = y$$

The *y*-coordinate will change in *y*-direction shear while the *x*-coordinate stays the same. If Sh_y is the shearing factor in *y*-direction then the basic equations are

$$x1 = x$$

$$y1 = y + x \times Sh_y$$

Thus, transportation matrix for *x*-direction shear is

$$\begin{bmatrix} 1 & 0 & 0 \\ Sh_x & 1 & 0 \\ 0 & 0 & 1 \end{bmatrix}$$

Similarly, transformation matrix for *y*-direction shear is

$$\begin{bmatrix} 1 & Sh_y & 0 \\ 0 & 1 & 0 \\ 0 & 0 & 1 \end{bmatrix}$$

Simultaneous shearing, which occurs when shearing occurs simultaneously in the *x* and *y* directions, is illustrated by the homogeneous matrix below.

$$\begin{bmatrix} 1 & Sh_y & 0 \\ Sh_x & 1 & 0 \\ 0 & 0 & 1 \end{bmatrix}$$

Example 2.4: *A line having end (2, 2) and (5, 5) is scaled by 2 units in x-direction and 5 units in y-direction. Find the transformation matrix and the final coordinates of the l ine.*
   Solution: The transformation matrix is given by

$$[T] = \begin{bmatrix} 1 & 0 & 0 \\ 0 & 1 & 0 \\ T_x & T_y & 1 \end{bmatrix} = \begin{bmatrix} 1 & 0 & 0 \\ 0 & 1 & 0 \\ 2 & 3 & 1 \end{bmatrix}$$

Let the new coordinates be (x'_1, y'_1) and (x'_2, y'_2) corresponding to (2, 2) and (5, 5) then:

$$\begin{bmatrix} x'_1 & y'_1 & 1 \end{bmatrix} = \begin{bmatrix} x & y & 1 \end{bmatrix} \times [S]$$

$$\begin{bmatrix} x_1 & y_1 & 1 \end{bmatrix} = \begin{bmatrix} 2 & 2 & 1 \end{bmatrix} \times \begin{bmatrix} 2 & 0 & 0 \\ 0 & 5 & 0 \\ 0 & 0 & 1 \end{bmatrix}$$

$$\begin{bmatrix} x'_1 & y'_1 & 1 \end{bmatrix} = \begin{bmatrix} 4 & 10 & 1 \end{bmatrix}$$

$$\left(x'_1 \quad y'_1 \right) \equiv \left(4, \quad 10 \right)$$

Similarly,

$$\begin{bmatrix} x'_2 & y'_2 & 1 \end{bmatrix} = \begin{bmatrix} 5 & 5 & 1 \end{bmatrix} \times \begin{bmatrix} 2 & 0 & 0 \\ 0 & 5 & 0 \\ 0 & 0 & 1 \end{bmatrix}$$

$$\begin{bmatrix} x'_2 & y'_2 & 1 \end{bmatrix} = \begin{bmatrix} 10 & 25 & 1 \end{bmatrix}$$

Hence,

$$\left[x'_2, y'_2 \right] \equiv (10, \quad 25)$$

Example 2.5: *A line having end points (2, 4) and (6, 10) is rotated by 30° in a clockwise direction. Find the transformation matrix.*

Solution: The transformation matrix in this case is given by the following rotation matrix:

$$[R] = \begin{bmatrix} \cos\theta & \sin\theta & 0 \\ -\sin\theta & \cos\theta & 0 \\ 0 & 0 & 1 \end{bmatrix}$$

$$[R] = \begin{bmatrix} \cos\left(-30°\right) & \sin\left(-30°\right) & 0 \\ -\sin\left(-30°\right) & \cos\left(-30°\right) & 0 \\ 0 & 0 & 1 \end{bmatrix}$$

$$[R] = \begin{bmatrix} 0.866 & -0.50 & 0 \\ +0.50 & 0.866 & 0 \\ 0 & 0 & 1 \end{bmatrix}$$

Example 2.6: *A square with endpoints A(1, 1), B(6, 1), C(6, 6) and D (1, 6) is rotated 50° counterclockwise while point (6, 1) remains stationary. Determine the last coordinates.*

Solution: Since point B(6, 1) is fixed, it is first translation to origin, then rotation is performed and then point B is translated back to its original position. The following steps may be considered.

Step 1: Translation of point B to origin :

$$[T_1] = \begin{bmatrix} 1 & 0 & 0 \\ 0 & 1 & 0 \\ -6 & -1 & 1 \end{bmatrix}$$

Step 2: Rotation by 50° clockwise about origin :

$$[R] = \begin{bmatrix} \cos(-50°) & \sin(-50°) & 0 \\ -\sin(-50°) & \cos(-50°) & 0 \\ 0 & 0 & 1 \end{bmatrix} = \begin{bmatrix} 0.643 & -0.766 & 0 \\ 0.766 & 0.643 & 0 \\ 0 & 0 & 1 \end{bmatrix}$$

Step 3: Translation of fixed point B back to its original position

$$[T_2] = \begin{bmatrix} 1 & 0 & 0 \\ 0 & 1 & 0 \\ 6 & 1 & 1 \end{bmatrix}$$

The resultant transformation matrix is given by $[T]$ where
$[T] = [T_1] \times [R] \times [T_2]$
Hence,

$$[T] = \begin{bmatrix} 1 & 0 & 0 \\ 0 & 1 & 0 \\ -6 & -1 & 1 \end{bmatrix} \times \begin{bmatrix} 0.643 & -0.766 & 0 \\ 0.766 & 0.643 & 0 \\ 0 & 0 & 1 \end{bmatrix} \begin{bmatrix} 1 & 0 & 0 \\ 0 & 1 & 0 \\ 6 & 1 & 1 \end{bmatrix}$$

$$= \begin{bmatrix} 0.643 & -0.766 & 0 \\ 0.766 & 0.643 & 0 \\ -4.624 & 4.953 & 1 \end{bmatrix}$$

The new coordinates are given by

$$[A'] = [A] \times [T]$$

Hence,

$$(x_A, \quad y_A) \equiv (-3.215, \quad 4.83)$$

Similarly,

$$\begin{bmatrix} x_B & y_B & 1 \end{bmatrix} = \begin{bmatrix} 6 & 1 & 1 \end{bmatrix} \times [T] = \begin{bmatrix} 0, & 1, & 1 \end{bmatrix}$$

i.e. $$\begin{bmatrix} x_A & y_A & 1 \end{bmatrix} = \begin{bmatrix} 1 & 1 & 1 \end{bmatrix} \times \begin{bmatrix} 0.643 & -0.766 & 0 \\ 0.766 & 0.643 & 0 \\ -4.624 & 4.953 & 1 \end{bmatrix} = \begin{bmatrix} -3.215 & 4.83 & 1 \end{bmatrix}$$

2.10.6   3-D Transformations

The x, y, and z coordinates of a point are taken into account in 3-D transformations. The transformation matrix $[R_T]$ for translation is provided by

$$[R_T] = \begin{bmatrix} 1 & 0 & 0 & 0 \\ 0 & 1 & 0 & 0 \\ 0 & 0 & 1 & 0 \\ T_x & T_y & T_z & 1 \end{bmatrix}$$

The transformation matrix for 3-D scaling is provided by

$$[R_S] = \begin{bmatrix} S_x & 0 & 0 & 0 \\ 0 & S_y & 0 & 0 \\ 0 & 0 & S_z & 0 \\ 0 & 0 & 0 & 1 \end{bmatrix}$$

Rotation in 3-D can be about the *x, y* or *z* axis

The equations of rotation of a point about the *z*-axis are

$$x' = x \cos_, - y \sin_,$$

$$y' = x \sin_, + y \cos_,$$

$$z' = z$$

Hence $[R_z]$ is given by, $[R_z] = \begin{bmatrix} \cos\theta & \sin\theta & 0 & 0 \\ -\sin\theta & \cos\theta & 0 & 0 \\ 0 & 0 & 1 & 0 \\ 0 & 0 & 0 & 1 \end{bmatrix}$

Similarly, the equations of rotation of a point about the *x*-axis are

$$y' = y \cos\theta - z \sin\theta$$

$$z' = y \sin\theta + z \cos\theta$$

$$x' = x$$

Hence $[R_x]$ is given by

$$[R_x] = \begin{bmatrix} 1 & 0 & 0 & 0 \\ 0 & \cos\theta & \sin\theta & 0 \\ 0 & -\sin\theta & \cos\theta & 0 \\ 0 & 0 & 0 & 1 \end{bmatrix}$$

For rotation about the *y*-axis the equations will be

$$z' = z \cos\theta - x \sin\theta$$

$$x' = z \sin\theta + x \cos\theta \quad y' = y.$$

Hence $[R_y]$ is given by

$$[R_y] = \begin{bmatrix} \cos\theta & 0 & -\sin\theta & 0 \\ 0 & 1 & 0 & 0 \\ \sin\theta & 0 & \cos\theta & 0 \\ 0 & 0 & 0 & 1 \end{bmatrix}$$

In 3-D issues, every object's reflection is acquired with respect to any plane. The plane of reflection may be any conventional plane, such as XY, YZ, ZX, etc. For instance, if the reflection is with regard to the XY plane, the point's z-coordinate is inverted. Consequently, the relevant reflection matrix is

$$\begin{bmatrix} 1 & 0 & 0 & 0 \\ 0 & 1 & 0 & 0 \\ 0 & 0 & -1 & 0 \\ 0 & 0 & 0 & 1 \end{bmatrix}$$

The reflection about any plane may be obtained through the process of concatenation.

Example 2.7: A sphere having centre (10, 10, 10) and radius 8 units is translated by 3 units in x-direction and 5 units in z-direction. Then it is rotated by 45° in a counterclockwise direction about the y-axis. Find the new centre of the sphere.

Solution :

Step 1 : Translation matrix in x and z directions

$$[T_1] = \begin{bmatrix} 1 & 0 & 0 & 0 \\ 0 & 1 & 0 & 0 \\ 0 & 0 & 1 & 0 \\ T_x & T_y & T_z & 1 \end{bmatrix} \times \begin{bmatrix} 1 & 0 & 0 & 0 \\ 0 & 1 & 0 & 0 \\ 0 & 0 & 1 & 0 \\ 3 & 0 & 5 & 1 \end{bmatrix}$$

Step 2: Rotation matrix about the y-axis

$$[R_1] = \begin{bmatrix} \cos\theta & 0 & -\sin\theta & 0 \\ 0 & 1 & 0 & 0 \\ \sin\theta & 0 & \cos\theta & 0 \\ 0 & 0 & 0 & 1 \end{bmatrix} \times \begin{bmatrix} \cos 45^0 & 0 & -\sin 45^0 & 0 \\ 0 & 1 & 0 & 0 \\ \sin 45^0 & 0 & \cos 45^0 & 0 \\ 0 & 0 & 0 & 1 \end{bmatrix}$$

$$= \begin{bmatrix} .707 & 0 & -.707 & 0 \\ 0 & 1 & 0 & 0 \\ .707 & 0 & .707 & 0 \\ 0 & 0 & 0 & 1 \end{bmatrix}$$

Step 3 : The final transformation matrix is obtained as

$$[T] = [T_1] \times [R_1]$$

$$= \begin{bmatrix} 1 & 0 & 0 & 0 \\ 0 & 1 & 0 & 0 \\ 0 & 0 & 1 & 0 \\ 3 & 0 & 5 & 1 \end{bmatrix} \times \begin{bmatrix} .707 & 0 & -.707 & 0 \\ 0 & 1 & 0 & 0 \\ .707 & 0 & .707 & 0 \\ 0 & 0 & 0 & 1 \end{bmatrix}$$

$$= \begin{bmatrix} .707 & 0 & -.707 & 0 \\ 0 & 1 & 0 & 0 \\ .707 & 0 & .707 & 0 \\ -1.414 & 0 & 1.414 & 1 \end{bmatrix}$$

Step 4: The new centre of the sphere can be obtained as

$$\begin{bmatrix} x_1 & y_1 & z_1 & 1 \end{bmatrix} = \begin{bmatrix} 10 & 10 & 10 & 1 \end{bmatrix} \times \begin{bmatrix} .707 & 0 & -.707 & 0 \\ 0 & 1 & 0 & 0 \\ .707 & 0 & .707 & 0 \\ -1.414 & 0 & 1.414 & 1 \end{bmatrix}$$

$$= \begin{bmatrix} -1.414 & 10 & 1.414 & 1 \end{bmatrix}$$

Hence, the new centre is $\begin{pmatrix} -1.414 & 10 & 1.414 \end{pmatrix}$

Example 2.8: State the transformation matrix for reflection about
    (i) X - axis (ii)y-axis
    (iii) Origin (iv) Y = x
    (v) Y = -x
Solution:
For reflection about the x-axis

$$T = \begin{bmatrix} 1 & 0 & 0 \\ 0 - & 1 & 0 \\ 0 & 0 & 1 \end{bmatrix}$$

For reflection about the y-axis

$$T = \begin{bmatrix} -1 & 0 & 0 \\ 0 & 1 & 0 \\ 0 & 0 & 1 \end{bmatrix}$$

(ii) For reflection about origin

$$T = \begin{bmatrix} -1 & 0 & 0 \\ 0 & -1 & 0 \\ 0 & 0 & 1 \end{bmatrix}$$

(iv) For reflection about line y=x

$$T = \begin{bmatrix} 0 & 1 & 0 \\ 1 & 0 & 0 \\ 0 & 0 & 1 \end{bmatrix}$$

(vi) For reflection about line y = -x

$$T = \begin{bmatrix} 0 & -1 & 0 \\ -1 & 0 & 0 \\ 0 & 0 & 1 \end{bmatrix}$$

Example 2.9: A square ABCD having coordinates (1,0), (0,0), (0,1) and (1,1) respectively is rotated by 45° about A (1,0). Determine the new coordinates.
    Solution: Let us attempt this question in a different way. The square ABCD has coordinates in matrix form as.

$$\begin{bmatrix} 1 & 0 & 1 \\ 0 & 0 & 1 \\ 0 & 1 & 1 \\ 1 & 1 & 1 \end{bmatrix}$$

Matrix for rotation in clockwise direction about origin is

$$\begin{bmatrix} \cos(-45°) & \sin(-45°) & 0 \\ -\sin(-45°) & \cos(-45°) & 0 \\ 0 & 0 & 1 \end{bmatrix}$$

We have to rotate square ABCD about point A(1,0). We first translate square ABCD. by Tx= - 1 and $Ty = 0$, i.e.,

$$\begin{bmatrix} 1 & 0 & 1 \\ 0 & 0 & 1 \\ -1 & 0 & 1 \end{bmatrix} \begin{bmatrix} 1 & 0 & 1 \\ 0 & 0 & 1 \\ 0 & 1 & 1 \\ 1 & 1 & 1 \end{bmatrix} = \begin{bmatrix} 0 & 0 & 1 \\ -1 & 0 & 1 \\ -1 & 1 & 1 \\ 0 & 1 & 1 \end{bmatrix}$$

Now we rotate in clockwise $\theta = 45°$

$$\begin{bmatrix} \cos(-45^0) & -\sin(-45^0) & 0 \\ -\sin(-45^0) & \cos(-45^0) & 0 \\ 0 & 0 & 1 \end{bmatrix} = \begin{bmatrix} 0 & 0 & 1 \\ -1 & 0 & 1 \\ -1 & 1 & 1 \\ 0 & 1 & 1 \end{bmatrix}$$

Example 2.10: Determine the proper 2-D transformation that reflects a figure around a given point (0.5, 0.5).

   Solution: Translating given point to origin

$$T = \begin{pmatrix} 1 & 0 & 0 \\ 0 & 1 & 0 \\ -0.5 & -0.5 & 1 \end{pmatrix}$$

Now obtaining reflection of the object about origin

$$M = \begin{bmatrix} -1 & 0 & 0 \\ 0 & -1 & 0 \\ 0 & 1 & 0 \end{bmatrix}$$

Translating point back to original position.

$$T^{1} = \begin{bmatrix} 1 & 0 & 0 \\ 0 & 1 & 0 \\ -_{1}0.5 & -_{1}0.5 & 0 \end{bmatrix}$$

The Transformation can be given as

$$R = TMT - 1$$

$$R_{T} = \begin{bmatrix} -1 & 0 & 0 \\ 0 & -1 & 0 \\ 1 & 1 & 1 \end{bmatrix}$$

2.11 FUNCTIONS OF A GRAPHICS PACKAGE

As discussed earlier, a graphics package is required to digitally synthesise and manipulate visual content on a computer screen. Let us now summarise the major functions of a graphics package.

1. A graphics package is essentially required to generate 2-D and 3-D graphic elements such as point, line, circle polygon, sphere, cube, cylinder and cone, alphanumeric characters and special symbol etc. These basic drawing elements are called primitives. Various standard algorithms are available to generate graphic primitives.
2. It is often required in CAD packages to enlarge a complete drawing or a small part, reduce the size of drawing, translate a view with respect to other views, rotate a section about an axis, take a mirror image of a symmetric part about a reference to complete the object. All this is accomplished with the help of a graphics package.
3. View control is another important function of computer graphics. View control helps the user to see the CAD model from various angles by rotating the model. The CAD model can be viewed at a desired magnification. Sometimes, a user wants to see only a part of the drawing on the screen rather than the complete drawing, this is accomplished using windowing. Hidden lines and hidden surfaces can be removed using graphics so as to get a better view of the 3-D model. Graphics is capable of generating various types of colours and rendering schemes.
4. The user input functions of a graphics package allow users to enter commands and CAD data in the CAD package. The data or commands are entered using the various types of CAD input devices discussed earlier.

2.12 SUMMARY

* Computer graphics is the field of computer science concerned with the presentation of images, animation and drawings.
* GKS, PHIGS and CORE are some of the graphics standards that are used by graphical packages.
* Display devices are the primary output devices used for computer graphics. They are of two types: CRT-based and solid state monitors (flat screens).
* The electron beam scans the phosphor-coated glass screen by using either of the two techniques: Raster scan and random scan.
* In the raster scan technique, the screen is divided into small squares called *pixels*.
* The DDA method and Bresenham's line-drawing algorithm are typical line-drawing algorithms.
* The most popular methods for drawing circles are the midpoint circle algorithm and Bresenham's circle algorithm.
* The Cohen–Sutherland method and midpoint subdivision algorithm are two typical line-clipping algorithms.
* The commonly used transformations used in CAD packages are: translation, scaling, rotation and reflection.

2.13 EXERCISE

1. What are the benefits of CAD? Explain in detail (BT level 1).
2. What are software standards? Explain the graphic kernel system in detail (BT level 1).
3. Explain various types of display devices used for computers (BT level 2).
4. Explain why random scan and DVST is not recommended for a CAD system.(BT level 2).
5. Briefly explain flat panel display (BT level 2).

6. Explain the coordinate representation used in graphics (BT level 2).
7. Explain Bresenham's algorithm for line generation (BT level 2).
8. How can you generate a circle or centre C and radius r using Bresenham's algorithm (BT level 2)?
9. What is transformation? Explain the terms translation, rotation, scaling and reflection. Write their transformation matrix (BTlevel 2).
10. Write 3-D transformation matrix for rotation about the x, y, z-axis (BT level 2).
11. Find the overall transformation matrix for the reflection of a triangular lamina about the line $2y = x + 2$ (BT level 3).
12. Explain the operating characteristics and some applications of plasma panels, liquid crystal displays (LCDs) and digitiser (BT level 2).
13. What image-creating and image-manipulating features does a general-purpose graphics software offer? How is a two-dimensional scene represented in a device's coordinate system (BT level 2)?
14. Write the full form of GKS and IGES. Define IGES (BT level 1).
15. Write the functions of a graphics package (BT level 2).
16. Explain the following terms related to three-dimensional transformation and show the final position graphically in each case (BT level 2).
   (a) Translation
   (b) Rotation

2.14 MULTIPLE-CHOICE QUESTIONS

1. What is computer graphics?
   a. The creation and manipulation of images using computers.
   b. The study of computer systems and architecture.
   c. The development of software programs for computers.
   d. The analysis of algorithms and data structures.
2. Which of the following is not a type of 2-D graphics primitive?
   a. Point.
   b. Line.
   c. Rectangle.
   d. Sphere.
3. Which of the following is a common file format for storing digital images?
   a. MP3.
   b. PDF.
   c. JPEG.
   d. HTML.
4. What is the process of rendering in computer graphics?
   a. Creating a 3-D model from 2-D primitives.
   b. Applying lighting and shading to a 3-D scene.
   c. Converting a digital image to a different file format.
   d. Creating a user interface for a software program.
5. Which of the following is not a common application of computer graphics?
   a. Video game development.
   b. Scientific visualisation.
   c. Financial analysis.
   d. Product design and prototyping.
6. What is a Graphics Kernel System (GKS)?
   a. A standard API for computer graphics programming.

    b. A type of graphics card used in gaming computers.

    c. A type of operating system used for computer graphics.

    d. A software package for creating 2-D graphics.

7. Which of the following is a feature of GKS?

    a. Support for rendering 3-D graphics.

    b. Compatibility with all types of graphics hardware.

    c. Built-in support for graphics file formats.

    d. Support for multiple programming languages.

8. Which of the following is a benefit of CAD data exchange?

    a. Enables collaboration among users of different CAD software programs.

    b. Reduces the need for data backup and storage.

    c. Improves the performance and speed of CAD software programs.

    d. Reduces the complexity and cost of CAD software development.

9. What is the purpose of a neutral file format in CAD data exchange?

    a. To enable data transfer between different CAD software programs.

    b. To provide a backup copy of CAD data for disaster recovery purposes.

    c. To improve the speed and performance of CAD software programs.

    d. To simplify the process of CAD data conversion.

10. Which of the following is a commonly used neutral file format for CAD data exchange?

    a. DXF.

    b. PDF.

    c. MP4.

    d. ZIP.

11. Which of the following is not a challenge in CAD data exchange?

    a. Compatibility issues between different CAD software programs.

    b. Loss of data during file conversion.

    c. Security risks associated with sharing CAD data.

    d. Slow data transfer speeds between different CAD software programs.

12. What is geometric transformation in CAD?

    a. The process of converting CAD data to a different file format.

    b. The process of creating 3-D models from 2-D sketches.

    c. The process of changing the size or shape of a CAD object.

    d. The process of moving, rotating, or scaling a CAD object in 2-D or 3-D space.

13. Which of the following is an example of a 2-D geometric transformation?

    a. Translation.

    b. Extrusion.

    c. Fillet.

    d. Loft.

14. Which of the following is an example of a 3-D geometric transformation?

    a. Rotation.

    b. Trim.

    c. Offset.

    d. Chamfer.

15. Which of the following is not a common type of geometric transformation?

    a. Shear.

    b. Scale.

    c. Sweep.

    d. Divide.

Answers

1. Answer: a. The creation and manipulation of images using computers.
2. Answer: d. Sphere.
3. Answer: c. JPEG.
4. Answer: b. Applying lighting and shading to a 3-D scene.
5. Answer: c. Financial analysis.
6. Answer: a. A standard API for computer graphics programming.
7. Answer: d. Support for multiple programming languages.
8. Answer: a. Enables collaboration among users of different CAD software programs.
9. Answer: a. To enable data transfer between different CAD software programs.
10. Answer: a. DXF.
11. Answer: d. Slow data transfer speeds between different CAD software programs.
    Note: While slow data transfer speeds can be a challenge in CAD data exchange, it is not directly related to the process of converting data between different CAD software programs.
12. Answer: d. The process of moving, rotating, or scaling a CAD object in 2-D or 3-D space.
13. Answer: a. Translation.
14. Answer: a. Rotation.
15. Answer: d. Divide.

3 Curves, Surfaces and Solids

Learning Outcomes: After studying this chapter, the reader should be able

LO 1: To know the important properties for curve design and representation (BT level 1).
LO 2: To understand the different types of curves such as B-spline and Bezier curves (BT level 2).
LO 3: To explain 3-D graphic surfaces such as polygon surface and ruled surface (BT level 2).
LO 4: To understand solid modelling, colour models, shading, etc. (BT level 2).

3.1 INTRODUCTION

When it comes to mechanical engineering, most of the parts have convoluted geometries. As a result, specific methods have been created to accurately represent them and produce photorealistic pictures on computers. These true shapes generated on a computer may be used to derive properties such as surface area, volume, mass and moment of inertia, etc. The model created may be used to instruct computer numerically controlled (CNC) machines to make a physical product.

It is necessary to consider the needs of the designer who will be using these techniques to build models of diverse forms before delving into the mathematical aspects of shape representation. When working on the body of a car or plane, for instance, the designer requires a wider range of tools at their disposal to provide a seamless finish. Simple designs like plane-faced polyhedral and cylinder sections may suffice for modelling refrigerator components.

LO 1. To know the important properties for curve designing and representation

3.2 CURVE REPRESENTATION

As the designer begins to use an interactive shape-modelling package, they try to comprehend the requirements. Thus, the design process becomes iterative. The designer first examines the provided shape to determine how it appears. This requires generating images of approximate shapes to evaluate the design. Making the necessary adjustments within the constrained language of alterations supported by the mathematical shape representations is the second phase. If all goes according to plan, the designer will only have to fiddle with a few of the shape model's parameters to get the effect they want. Therefore, they must be knowledgeable enough with the form representation to make educated guesses about which parameters require adjusting and by how much. A judicious decision needs to be taken so as to vary which parameter is provided in order to get the desired shape. If the curve shape depends on limiting the number of mutable attributes, the designer's work is made simpler, but the number of conceivable shapes is also reduced. On the other hand, if the form of the curve is dependent on a large number of factors, the designer will be able to create more realistic and adaptable simulations of their work. Some representations of shapes may use a flexible set of parameters. That way, the designer may employ as many or as few as necessary to get the desired form.

The curve representations must be mathematically tractable and computationally convenient. Some aspects for our curve representation have been suggested by both user and computer needs. ***Let us enumerate some of the important properties for curve design and representation:***

DOI: 10.1201/9781003350842-3

1. **Control points:** In a predictable manner, the curve's form is determined by these vertices. Thus, finding control points through which a curve must pass is a typical method of interactively modifying the curve's form. Interpolation of the control points is a curve as shown in Figure 3.1.
2. **Axis independence:** Different coordinate systems for measuring the control points must not alter the overall form of the curve. The contour of the curve should remain unchanged even if the control points are rotated, for instance by 45 degrees. Altering the coordinate frame of reference in some mathematical formulations may alter the geometry of a curve.
3. **Local control or global control:** It's up to the designer to decide whether the curve should shift just at the control point or wherever it's being adjusted. The first pattern of action is referred to as "local control," whereas the latter is known as "global control," as shown in Figure 3.2. If the designer is attempting to tweak a specific area of the curve, the global control might get in the way and cause frustration.
4. **Variation diminishing property:** Consider Figure 3.3. Rather than smoothing out minor imperfections, certain mathematical curve representations tend to magnify them. Oscillation of this kind around the points of control is often undesired. Other curves have a tendency to pass through the control points smoothly without oscillations. Such curves are said to possess variation diminishing property.
5. **Versatility:** The mathematical model for curve representation should be such that designers may adjust a curve's adaptability by adding or deleting regulator points. A straight line connecting the two regulator points is one possible solution for a curve with just two of them. Now, depending on where the control point is placed, the curve may take on a variety of new forms.
6. **Order of continuity:** A complicated form is made up of numerous curves that are connected together at each end. Have a look at Figure 3.4. The joint's ultimate form is

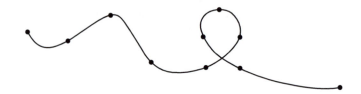

FIGURE 3.1 Control points govern the curve shape

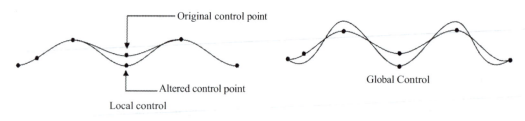

FIGURE 3.2 Local and global control action

Curve with variation diminishing property.

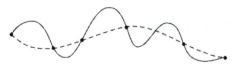

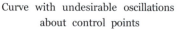

Curve with undesirable oscillations about control points

FIGURE 3.3 Variation diminishing

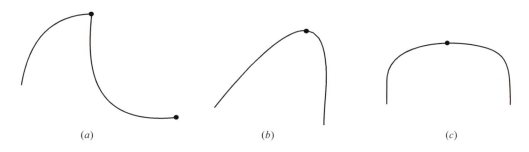

FIGURE 3.4 Order of continuity at joints (*a*) zero-order continuity, (b) first-order continuity (same slope) (*c*) second order continuity (same curvature)

determined by the sequence of continuation. In the case of zero-order continuity, the two curves need to just overlap; in the case of first-order continuity, the intersection must be tangent to both curves. Assuming second-order continuity, the curvature will remain the same.

3.2.1 PARAMETRIC FORM

A curve, in mathematics, is a cubic polynomial function whose first and second derivatives are both continuous across any point on the curve.

Modelling curves and surfaces mathematically in parametric form is easy. A vector may, for example, be used to represent a point on a curve

$$P(u) = [x(u) \ y(u) \ z(u)]$$

Parametric functions in *x*, *y* and *z* trace the outline of a curve or surface when their values are varied within some range (often 0–1). For surfaces, two parameters are needed. Creating a straightforward function that can produce the overall curve form is often impossible. So, the entire shape is defined by a series of functions.

The seamless transition from one segment of piecewise curve to the next depends on the connections made at the control points by enforcing continuity conditions at the control points.

The parametric equations of some of the commonly used curves is given below:

1. **Circle:** A circle is a locus of a point moving in a plane such that its distance from a fixed point (called centre) is constant. It is given by equations

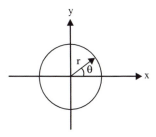

$$x = r \cos\theta$$

$$y = r \sin\theta$$

If the centre is (x_c, y_c, z_c), then the parametric equations of circle become:

$$x = x_c + r \cos\theta$$

$$y = y_c + r \sin\theta \qquad \text{where } 0 \geq \theta \leq 360°$$

$$z = z_c$$

2. **Parabola:** A parabola describes the position of a moving point whose distance from a stationary point (the focus) equals its distance from a stationary line (called directrix). A set of parametric equations representing parabola are

$$x = at^2 \quad y = 2at$$

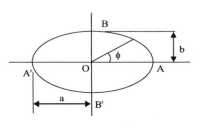

If the coordinates of parabolic vertex are (x_v, y_v, z_v), then the equations become:

$$x = x_v + at^2$$

$$y = y_v + 2\,at$$

$$z = z_v$$

3. **Ellipse:** In geometry, an ellipse is defined as the locus of a moving point in space whose distance from two fixed points (called foci) is always the same and equal to the major diameter. A set of parametric equations representing ellipse is

$$x = a \cos\phi$$
$$y = b \sin\phi$$

If the centre is (x_c, y_c, z_c), then the parametric equations of ellipse becomes:

$$x = x_c + a \cos\phi$$

$$y = y_c + b \sin\phi \qquad \text{where} \qquad 0 < \phi < 360°$$

$$z = z_c$$

4. **Hyperbola:** The loci of a moving point on a hyperbola are those positions where the difference between the distances to the foci, which are fixed, and the point's current location is constant and equal to the hyperbola's transverse axis. Its equations are

$$x = a \cosh\theta$$

$$y = b \sinh\theta$$

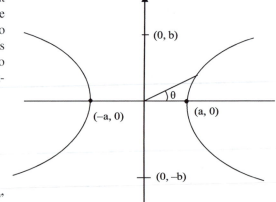

If the axis of hyperbola intersect at (x_v, y_v, z_v), then the parametric equations of hyperbola are

$$x = x_v + a \cosh\theta$$

$$y = y_v + b \sinh\theta$$

$$z = z_v$$

5. **Straight line:** Equations of straight line in parametric form are

$$x = x_0 + (x_1 - x_0)\, t$$

$$y = y_0 + (y_1 - y_0)\, t$$

$$z = z_0 + (z_1 - z_0)\, t$$

where $\qquad\qquad 0 \le t \le 1$

3.2.2 PARAMETRIC CONTINUITY CONDITIONS

To construct a composite curve, the endpoints of many distinct curves must be joined in the right sequence. However, the transition between parametric curves should be smooth. In order to accomplish this condition, we can apply suitable continuity conditions at the end points. Curves are defined using parametric coordinate functions of the sort, $x = f1\,(t)$, $y = f2\,(t)$ and $z = f3(t)$, we can set parametric continuity conditions at the joining points. As already discussed, there are three types of continuity conditions that can be employed: Zero order, first order and second order continuity conditions.

Zero-order continuity exists. C^0 represents the point of intersection between the two curves. In other words, a position vector at the end of one curve is identical to a position vector at the beginning of the connecting curve. Initial-order consistency C^1 identifies an intersection point between two curves that share a tangent, as determined by the equality of the tangent vectors at the endpoints of the two curves. Second order continuity $C2$ means that the two curves have same curvature at the joining points, i.e., both first and second order derivative at the junction of two meeting curves are same. The order of continuity at joints is illustrated in Figure 3.4

3.3 INTERPOLATION AND APPROXIMATION SPLINES

Spline curves are created by providing the coordinates of a group of points known as control points. Either an interpolation strategy or an approximation strategy is used to fit continuous polynomial functions to these control points. If the curve segments of the polynomial spline are fitted such that the curve traverses each of the control points, then the curve is said to be "control-point-robust" as shown in Figure 3.5(a). Interpolation of the control points is the name given to the resulting curve.

However, if the curve approaches the control points without necessarily passing through them, it is deemed to have approached them. Refer to Figure 3.5(b).

Interpolation curves are generally used for generating animation paths, whereas approximation curves are used for structuring object surfaces.

In the next section, Bezier curves and B-splines are explained in detail. Surprisingly effective off-curve control locations are present in each of these curves.

3.4 BLENDING FUNCTIONS

For given control points, either traversing the curve through all the control points (known as interpolation) or passing close to these points might result in a more aesthetically pleasing shape (known

(a) A set of 5 control points interpolated
by piece wise continuous polynomials

(b) A set of 5 control points approximation
by piece wise continuous polynomials

FIGURE 3.5 Interpolation And Approximation

as approximation). Sometimes, it becomes necessary to make a curve using a number of curve segments so as to meet the design criteria. Mathematically, while modelling a curve $F(x)$ with several curve segments, we try to create the curve's equation as the sum of smaller curve segments $P_i(x)$, also known as blending functions. Thus,

$$F(x) = \sum_{i=0}^{n} a_i P_i \quad (x)$$

The blending functions are chosen keeping in mind the type of composition and display required. Hence, polynomials are the most popular blending functions among the designers. Cubic polynomials (having degree 3) have proved to be very useful as they have close resemblance to a mechanical spline used by the draftsmen. Also, they have the required smoothness properties and are suitable to represent three-dimensional (3-D) curves.

A polynomial of degree n has the form:

$$P(x) = a_0 + a_1 x + a_2 x2 + \dots a_{x-1} xn-1 + a_n xn$$

A continuous piecewise polynomial $F(x)$ of degree n is a set of r polynomials $f_i(x)$, each of degree n and having $r + 1$ nodes $n_0, n_1 \dots n_r$ such that

$$F(x) = f_i(x) \text{ for } n_i \leq x \leq n_{i+1}, \text{ for } i = 0, 1 \dots r - 1$$

For the polynomials to match or join together at the nodes, the following condition must be satisfied

$$f_{i-1}(n_i) = f_i(n_i) \text{ for } i = 1, 2, \dots r - 1.$$

But this condition does not impose any restriction on how smoothly the polynomials f_i (x) meet. Thus, there can be sharp contours at the meeting point as shown in Figure 3.6.

Making composite curves from blending functions in parametric form can also be accomplished easily. The curves can be joined by using any one of three: *Continuity of zero order, first order or second order.* Some commonly used blending functions are Lagrange polynomials, Hermite cubic polynomials, B-splines and Bernstein polynomials.

3.5   3-D CURVES (SPACE CURVES)

3-D curves play an important role in the engineering design and manufacturing of automobiles, ships, aircraft, propeller blades, shoes and bottles, etc.

Two techniques are available for obtaining a mathematical curve from data. These curves may be identified as either blended parabolas or cubic spline curves. These techniques are sometimes referred to as the curve fitting

LO 2. To understand the different types of curves

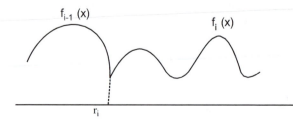

FIGURE 3.6   Sharp contours at the meeting point

method. They are characterised by the fact that the derived mathematical curve passes through each and every data point.

Another option is to build the mathematical description of a space curve ab initio, i.e., from scratch, without having any idea what the form of the curve will be. You may do this in one of two ways. This is the generalisation of Bezier curves to B-spline curves, which is a very useful tool. One distinguishing feature of these two methods is that very few curve points (if any) really go through the control points. These methods are frequently referred as ***curve fairing techniques***.

3.5.1 SPLINE CURVE

Splines are used nowadays in computer graphics packages to design intricate curves and surfaces. Splines are widely used for designing automobiles, aircraft bodies, hulls of ships, etc.

The polynomial components of a spline curve constitute its composite nature. Certain conditions for border continuity are satisfied by these portions. Each section should flow smoothly into the next.

Normally three types of parametric continuity are used. These are:

(1) Zero-order parametric continuity,
(2) First-order parametric continuity,
(3) Second-order parametric continuity.

Cubic splines are often used in drawings for making objects or to specify paths for object motion. Cubic polynomials used to specify cubic splines offer optimal flexibility and speed of computation. Cubic splines are more stable, require fewer computations and save more memory than higher polynomials. Cubic splines provide greater versatility in modelling non-standard curves than polynomials of a lower order. For cubic splines, the set of equations in parametric form can be given as

$$x(t) = a_x + b_x t + c_x t2 + d_x t3$$
$$y(t) = a_y + b_y t + c_y t2 + d_y t3$$
$$z(t) = a_z + b_z t + c_z t2 + d_z t3$$

where $$0 \leq t \leq 1$$

3.5.1.1 B-Spline Curves

These are very commonly used approximating splines having local control. With this method, complex geometric curves are generated with continuity at joints when piecing curves together. The spline function uses mathematical restrictions to restrict the usable curve space to those curves with the necessary joint continuity. The B-spline approach sidesteps this issue by using a collection of blending functions that are only supported on a local scale, while certain spline formulations may provide this capability at the price of local control. Hence, the position of the curve depends only on a few neighbouring control points.

The B-spline curve is given by the expression,

$$P(u) = \sum_{k=0}^{n} P_k, B_k, d(u) \text{ Where } u_{min}, \leq u \leq u_{max} \& 2 \leq d \leq n+1$$

Using this general equation, the coordinates along a B-spline curve may be determined. P_k is the inputted set of control points, which consists of $n + 1$ points in this instance. B and D are portrayed by (B_k, d). Blending spline functions are polynomials of degree $d - 1$, where d may be any positive integer between 2 and $(n + 1)$. Local control of B-splines is achieved by setting blending functions at intervals over the whole u range.

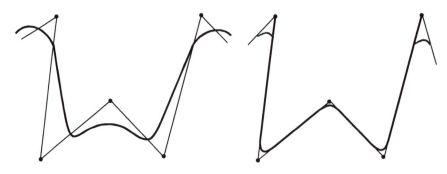

FIGURE 3.7 B-spline methods have local control

Blending functions for B-spline are given by

$$B_{k,1}(u) = \begin{cases} 1 & \text{if } u_k \leq u \leq u_k + 1 \\ 0 & \text{otherwise} \end{cases}$$

$$B_{k,d}(u) = \frac{u - u}{u_{k+d} - u_k} \; B_{k,d-1}(u) + \frac{u_{k,d} - u}{u_{k+d} - u_k} B_{k+d-1}u,$$

In this instance, all blending functions are given across a discrete range of u values, denoted by d. k not vector is the collection of sub-interval terminal values u. Note that in the above expression of $B_{k,d}(u)$, the denominator can become zero. Hence, this formulation adopts the conversion

Refer to Figure 3.7. The main advantage of B-spline curves is local control over the curve shape.

3.5.1.1.1 Properties of B-Spline Curve

1. It follows the shape of control polygon
2. The sum of a B-spline basis function for any parameter value is one. The basis function is either positive or zero.
3. Maximum order of a B-spline curve is one less than the number of control polygon vertices.
4. Clamped B-spline curve $P(u)$ passes through the two end control points.
5. The curve shows convex hull property, i.e., the curve lies within the convex hull of its control polygon.
6. A B-spline curve shows local control due to which one can modify it locally.
7. A B-spline curve shows variation diminishing property, i.e, it does not oscillate, Moreover, a straight line intersects the curve only as many times as it intersects the control polygon.

Use either periodic or non-periodic blending functions with the B-spline. Periodic blending functions characterise non-uniform B-splines. Consequently, given a constant value of n and d, all blending functions will have the shape shown in the following diagram. Each next blending function is only a rotated replica of the last one (Figure 3.8).

3.5.2 BEZIER CURVE

The inventor of this strategy is P. Bezier, who works for the French company Regie Renault. Bezier curves have an advantage over cubic splines because the control point's position can be used to define and modify the curve's direction at the joints. Changing the control points has an impact on the curve's form all along the curve, not only close to the control points. This is a major disadvantage.

3.5.2.1 Properties of Bezier Curve

1. The original and ultimate control locations are both traversed. This curve is only closed if the beginning control point and the end control point coincide as shown in Figure 3.9.

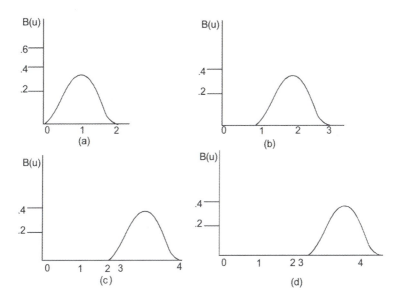

FIGURE 3.8 Priodic B spline blending functions

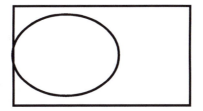

FIGURE 3.9 A closed Bezier curve with first and last control point coinciding

2. The curve is tangent to the corresponding edge of control points at the end points.
3. The Bezier curve will remain in the convex of the polygon. This is called convex hull property.
4. The Bezier curve does not oscillate. This is called variation diminishing property.
5. It requires less memory and fewer calculations than cubic spline curves in terms of computing.
6. **Axis independence:** Regardless of the coordinate system used to determine the positions of the control points, a Bezier curve can be constructed.
7. **Global or local control:** These curves prohibit any kind of regional leadership. This signifies that a change in a single control point affects the whole curve.
8. **Order of continuity:** Zero, first or even higher order continuity may be used to assemble Bezier curves of lesser orders into a more complex and composite curve.

Mathematically, a Bezier curve is represented as

$$P(t) = \sum_{i=0}^{n} B_i J_n, \quad i(t) \tag{3.1}$$

where J_n, $i(t)$ is a blending function, given by the relation
$J_n, i = nC_i t i (1 - t)n{-}i$

and ^nC_i is the binomial coefficient $^nC_i = \dfrac{n!}{i!(n-i)!}$. If the 3-D location of control

point B_i is (x_i, y_i, z_i) Equation (3.1), a vector equation can be expressed by writing equations for x, y and z parameter functions separately as

$$x(t) = \sum_{i=0}^{n} x_i J_{n,} \quad i\left(t\right)$$

$$y(t) = \sum_{i=0}^{n} y_i J_{n,} \quad i\left(t\right)$$

and $z(t) = \sum_{i=0}^{n} z_i J_{n,} \quad i\left(t\right)$

The behaviour of Bezier curves is governed by blending functions. A Bezier curve is shown on xy plane in Figure 3.10. Regarding the z-coordinate, every control point has a value of 0. Creating a regular polygon by connecting four control points generates the curve. It is evident that the intermediate control points determine the values of Bezier curves' initial and terminal slopes.

Example 3.1: *Generate a 3-D Bezier curve using the following control point (5, 4, 2), (6, 2, 3), (5, –2, 4) and (6, –4, 3).*
 Solution There are four control points, hence $n = 3$.
 For x, y and z coordinates, parameter functions can be defined as

$$x(t) = \sum_{i=0}^{3} x_i\ ^3C_i t^i (1-t)^{3-i}$$

$$y(t) = \sum_{i=0}^{3} y_i^3 C_i t^i (1-t)^{3-i}$$

And

$$z(t) = \sum_{i=0}^{3} z_i\ ^3C_i t^i (1-t)^{3-i}$$

and
 Simplifying these equations as follows:

$$x(t) = 5 \times {}^3C_0\, t^0\, (1-t)^{3-0} + 6 \times {}^3C_1\, t^1\, (1-t)^{3-1} + 3 \times {}^3C_2\, t^2\, (1-t)^{3-2}$$
$$+ 6\ {}^3C3\ t^3\ (1-t)^{3-3}$$

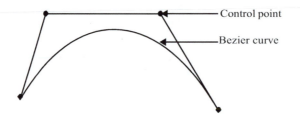

FIGURE 3.10   Bazier curve with four control points used to define it

or
$$x(t) = 5 (1 - t)^3 + 18 t (1 - t)^2 + 9 t^2 (1 - t) + 6 t^3$$

Similarly,

$$y(t) = 4 (1 - t)^3 + 6 t (1 - t)^2 - 6 t^2 (1 - t) + 4 t^3$$

$$z(t) = 2 (1 - t)^3 + 9t (1 - t)^2 + 12 t^2 (1 - t) + 3 t^3$$

Let step size for $t = 0.1$, the corresponding values of $x(t)$ and $y(t)$ are tabulated below:

t	$x(t)$	$y(t)$	$z(t)$	t	$x(t)$	$y(t)$	$z(t)$
0.0	5	4	2	0.8	4.84	−2.592	3.376
0.1	5.19	3.344	2.298	0.9	5.27	−3.344	3.242
0.2	5.2	2.592	2.584	1.0	6	−4	3
0.3	5.09	1.768	2.846				
0.4	4.92	0.896	3.072				
0.5	4.75	0	3.25				
0.6	3.728	−0.288	3.368				
0.7	4.65	−1.768	3.414				

Example 3.2: *Derive a parametric equation of a cubic Bezier curve.*

Solution: For a cubic Bezier curve, $n = 3$. This implies, the curve has four control points say B_0, B_1, B_2 and B_3. Thus, for four control points, a Bezier curve equation can be written in parametric form as

$$P(t) = \sum B_i{}^3 C_i t^i (1-t)^{3-i} \mathfrak{A}$$

$$= (1-t)^3 B_0 + 3t(1-t)^2 B_1 + 3t^2(1-t)B_2 + t^3 B_3$$

$$= \left(1 - t^3 - 3t + 3t^2\right) B_0 + \left(3t^3 - 6t^2 + 3t\right) B_1 + \left(-3t^3 + 3t^2\right) B_2 + t^3 B_3$$

This can be written in matrix form as

$$P(t) = \begin{bmatrix} t^3 & t^2 & t & 1 \end{bmatrix} \cdot [K] \cdot \begin{bmatrix} B_0 \\ B_1 \\ B_2 \\ B_3 \end{bmatrix}$$

where

$$[K] = \begin{bmatrix} -1 & 3 & -3 & 1 \\ 3 & -6 & 3 & 0 \\ -3 & 3 & 0 & 0 \\ 1 & 0 & 0 & 0 \end{bmatrix}$$

3.5.3 HERMITE CURVES

A Hermite curve is an interpolating piecewise cubic polynomial with a defined tangent at each control point. Except for the constraints at its ends, every segment of a Hermite spline is independent from every other segment, allowing for fine-grained control. A Hermite curve section is represented by following set of equations:

$$x(u) = a_x u^3 + b_x u^2 + c_x u + d_x \ y(u) = a_y u^3 + b_y u^2 + c_y u + d_y \ z(u) = a_z u^3 + b_z u^2 + c_z u + d_z$$

If $P(u)$ represents the parametric cubic point function, a vector equivalent of the above three equations can be written as

$$P(u) = au^3 + bu^2 + cu + d \text{ where } 0 \le u \le 1$$

The equation can be written in matrix form as

$$P(u) = \begin{bmatrix} u^3 & u^2 & u & 1 \end{bmatrix} \cdot \begin{bmatrix} a \\ b \\ c \\ d \end{bmatrix}$$

and the derivative of the point function can be expressed as

$$P'(u) = \begin{bmatrix} 3u^2 & 2u & 1 & 0 \end{bmatrix} \cdot \begin{bmatrix} a \\ b \\ c \\ d \end{bmatrix}$$

If P_k and P_{k+1}, are the two control points, then the boundary conditions for the curve section between control points P_k and P_{k+1} is given by

$$P(0) = P_K \quad P(1) = P_{K+1} \quad P'(0) = D P_K \quad P'(1) = DP_{K+1}$$

$$\text{Now } P(0) = \begin{bmatrix} 0 & 0 & 0 & 1 \end{bmatrix} \cdot \begin{bmatrix} a \\ b \\ c \\ d \end{bmatrix}$$

$$P(1) = \begin{bmatrix} 1 & 1 & 1 & 1 \end{bmatrix} \cdot \begin{bmatrix} a \\ b \\ c \\ d \end{bmatrix}$$

$$P'(0) = \begin{bmatrix} 0 & 0 & 1 & 0 \end{bmatrix} \cdot \begin{bmatrix} a \\ b \\ c \\ d \end{bmatrix}$$

And

$$P'(1) = \begin{bmatrix} 3 & 2 & 1 & 0 \end{bmatrix} \cdot \begin{bmatrix} a \\ b \\ c \\ d \end{bmatrix}$$

The above equations can be combined as

$$\begin{bmatrix} P(0) \\ P(1) \\ P'(0) \\ P'(1) \end{bmatrix} = \begin{bmatrix} 0 & 0 & 0 & 1 \\ 1 & 1 & 1 & 1 \\ 0 & 0 & 1 & 0 \\ 3 & 2 & 1 & 0 \end{bmatrix} \begin{bmatrix} a \\ b \\ c \\ d \end{bmatrix}$$

If P_k and P_{k+1} are the two control points, then the boundary condition for the curve section between control points P_k and P_{k+1} is given by

$P(0) = P_k, P'(1) = P_{k+1}$, $P'(0) = DP_k$ and $P'(1) = DP_{k+1}$. Hence, the above matrix equations can also be written as

$$\begin{bmatrix} P_k \\ P_{k+1} \\ DP_k \\ DP_{k+1} \end{bmatrix} = \begin{bmatrix} 0 & 0 & 0 & 1 \\ 1 & 1 & 1 & 1 \\ 0 & 0 & 1 & 0 \\ 3 & 2 & 1 & 0 \end{bmatrix} \begin{bmatrix} a \\ b \\ c \\ d \end{bmatrix}$$

Solving these equations to form polynomial coefficients:

$$\begin{bmatrix} a \\ b \\ c \\ d \end{bmatrix} = \begin{bmatrix} 0 & 0 & 0 & 1 \\ 1 & 1 & 1 & 1 \\ 0 & 0 & 1 & 0 \\ 3 & 2 & 1 & 0 \end{bmatrix}^{-1} \begin{bmatrix} P_k \\ P_{k+1} \\ DP_k \\ DP_{k+1} \end{bmatrix}$$

$$= \begin{bmatrix} 2 & -2 & 1 & 1 \\ -3 & 3 & -2 & -1 \\ 0 & 0 & 1 & 0 \\ 1 & 0 & 0 & 0 \end{bmatrix} \begin{bmatrix} P_k \\ P_{k+1} \\ DP_k \\ DP_{k+1} \end{bmatrix} = M_H \begin{bmatrix} P_k \\ P_{k+1} \\ DP_k \\ DP_{k+1} \end{bmatrix}$$

where M_H is called a Hermite matrix. It is the inverse of boundary constraint matrix. Hermite curves are used for digitising applications.

Substituting the value of coefficients in the initial equation, we get

$$P(u) = \left(2u^3 - 3u^2 + 1\right)Pk + \left(-2u^3 + 3u^2\right)P_{K+1} + \left(-2u^2 + u\right)DP_k + \left(u^3 - u^2\right)DP_{k+1}$$

$$= B_{H0}P_k + B_{H1}P_{k+1} + B_{H2}DP_k + B_{H3}DP_k + 1$$

Where

$$B_{H0}, B_{H1}, + B_{H2}, \text{ and } B_{H3}$$

are the blending function.

3.5.3.1 Comparison of Bezier, B-spline and Hermite curves

1. Both Bezier and B-spline curves have a convex hull defined by control points which are not there in Hermite curves.
2. A Hermite curve interpolates all the control points which is not done by Bezier and B-spline curves.

3. Bezier and Hermite curves can interpolate some control points used to define their shape, but B-spline curves cannot interpolate any control points used to define it.
4. Bezier curves and Hermite curves have zero-order continuity inherent in their representation while B-spline curves make use of second-order continuity. Bezier and Hermite curves can easily achieve first-order continuity.
5. While B-spline and Hermite methods have local control, Bezier curves do not provide local control.

3.6   3-D GRAPHICS SURFACES

A surface is anything that has both length and breadth in 3-D space, such as a thin plate or a huge piece of cloth. A flat 2-D surface is called *plane surface.* In any 3-D graphics computer-aided design (CAD) package graphics scenes comprise different kinds of objects e.g., solid model of various components, assemblies, tools, machines, etc. Objects with attributes derived from many materials may be described using a variety of methods. This chapter discusses several surfaces, including polygonal, quadric and superquadratic surfaces, in addition to blobby objects.

LO 3. To understand 3-D graphics surfaces

Surface is specified by equations having two independent variables or parameters. Like curves, surfaces can also be specified by equations in parametric and non-parametric form. The non-parametric form of equation can be further written in two forms: ***Explicit form*** and ***implicit form***. In explicit form, the z-coordinate of any surface point, indicated by the equation $z = f$, is stated in terms of x and y. (x, y). As a consequence, it is possible to calculate the position of any surface point P $[x, y, f(x, y)]$. In implicit form, an equation of the surface can be written in the form $F(x, y, z) = 0$.

In parametric form, three equations for finding out the coordinates of any point on the surface can be specified in terms of parameters s and t but within parameter range (a, b) and (c, d) respectively as:

$$X = f(s,t)$$

$$Y = g(s, t)$$

$$Z = h(s, t)$$

where $a \leq s \leq b$ and $c \leq t \leq d$

The boundaries of polynomial bivariate (two variables) surface patches, which are used to characterise the coordinates of a point on a curved surface, are determined by parametric polynomial curves. Surfaces may be modelled using a variety of polynomials, similar to how curves are modelled. Currently, the most prevalent kind of polynomial is a cubic in both parameters. This kind of surface is sometimes referred to as a bicubic surface. A governed surface is a surface that results from the linear blending of sections created by two or more curves. Figure 3.11(a), (b) and (c) illustrates a ruled surface.

3.6.1   POLYGON SURFACES

They are a set of surface polygons that enclose the object interior.

It is one of the most frequently used boundary representation techniques for 3-D graphics objects. The boundary representation, often known as the rep method, is a technique for describing a 3-D object as a group of surfaces, utilising linear equations to describe polygon surfaces. Thus, it becomes simpler to enhance the rate at which objects may be shown on a surface. Despite the fact that certain graphics programmes employ other techniques (such as splined surfaces), they eventually treated as polygons.

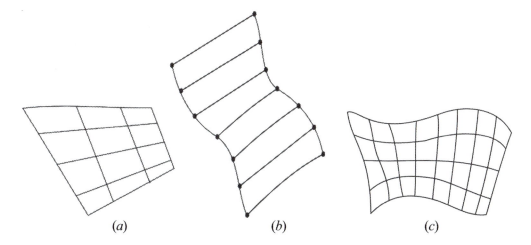

(a)   (b)   (c)

FIGURE 3.11 Ruled surface

Polygon surfaces when used in 3-D CAD packages efficiently define objects with plane surfaces compared to objects with curved surfaces. In the case of curved surfaces like a cylinder or cone the surface is represented as polygon mesh as shown in Figure 3.12.

Polygon surfaces are created using vertex coordinates and attribute parameters. While using a CAD package, as information for each object to be made is input, the data for each polygon are organised into tables. The useful data are subsequently retrieved from these tables for display and modification of the solid models.

There are two major kinds of polygon data tables: Geometric tables and attribute tables. There are various properties, such as vertex coordinates, that may be found in geometric tables that govern the shape and orientation of polygon surfaces. In the characteristics table, surface qualities such as reflectivity, transparency and roughness are documented.

Creating vertex tables, edge tables and polygon tables is a straightforward method for organising geometric data. A table known as the vertex table contains the coordinates for an object's vertices. All vertices of an edge are specified by pointers in the edge table that lead back to the vertex table. The polygon table uses the edge table to identify surface-enclosing edges. This is elaborated in Figure 3.13.

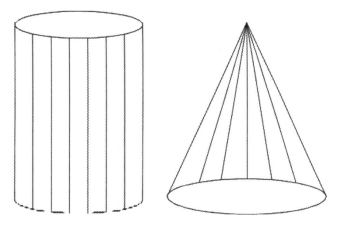

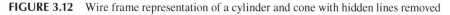

FIGURE 3.12 Wire frame representation of a cylinder and cone with hidden lines removed

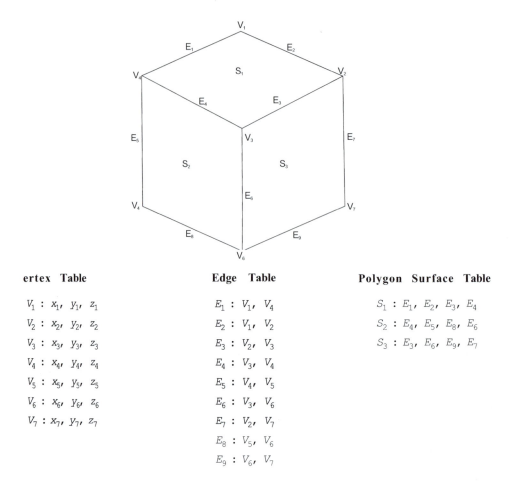

ertex Table	Edge Table	Polygon Surface Table
$V_1 : x_1, y_1, z_1$	$E_1 : V_1, V_4$	$S_1 : E_1, E_2, E_3, E_4$
$V_2 : x_2, y_2, z_2$	$E_2 : V_1, V_2$	$S_2 : E_4, E_5, E_8, E_6$
$V_3 : x_3, y_3, z_3$	$E_3 : V_2, V_3$	$S_3 : E_3, E_6, E_9, E_7$
$V_4 : x_4, y_4, z_4$	$E_4 : V_3, V_4$	
$V_5 : x_5, y_5, z_5$	$E_5 : V_4, V_5$	
$V_6 : x_6, y_6, z_6$	$E_6 : V_3, V_6$	
$V_7 : x_7, y_7, z_7$	$E_7 : V_2, V_7$	
	$E_8 : V_5, V_6$	
	$E_9 : V_6, V_7$	

FIGURE 3.13   Geometric table representation

In order to display 3-D objects, the input data has to be processed through various steps. These include transformation of solid model, conversion of local coordinates to world coordinates then to normalised coordinates and finally to device coordinate system.

As we know that the 3-D object is made up of planes, the information about spatial orientation of individual planes that form the sides of the object is desirable. The equation of plane is given by following expression:

$$Px + Qy + Rz + S = 0$$

A point (x_1, y_1, z_1) lies on the plane and the surface of the model if

$$Px_1 + Qy_1 + Rz_1 + S < 0$$

and if $Px_1 + Qy_1 + Rz_1 + S > 0$, the point does not lie on the surface of the model. In contrast, in a right-handed cartesian system, the parameters $(P, Q, R$ and $S)$ of a plane are determined by selecting their vertices counterclockwise and seeing the surface from the outside in.

Finite element method (FEM) packages like NISA, PRO/MECHANICA and COSMOS discretise the body into small elements called finite elements to determine the stress distribution. This process is called mesh generation or meshing. Meshing can be accomplished using polygon mesh. A polygon mesh may be defined as a collection of vertices, edges and polygons in which each edge

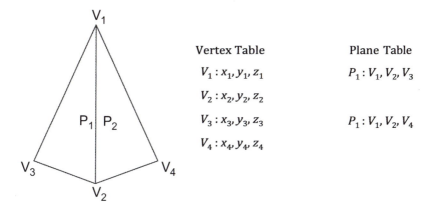

Vertex Table

$V_1 : x_1, y_1, z_1$

$V_2 : x_2, y_2, z_2$

$V_3 : x_3, y_3, z_3$

$V_4 : x_4, y_4, z_4$

Plane Table

$P_1 : V_1, V_2, V_3$

$P_1 : V_1, V_2, V_4$

FIGURE 3.14   Polygon mesh

links no more than two polygons. Also, the mesh elements should not be overlapping. An example of such representation is shown in Figure 3.14.

3.6.2 QUADRIC SURFACES

Quadric surfaces are implicitly defined by the equation $f(x, y, z) = 0$, where f is a quadric polynomial in x, y and z. Spheres, ellipses, toruses, parabolas and hyperbolas are all instances of common quadric surface definitions. The equation used for defining quadric surfaces is given by

$$Ax^2 + By^2 + Cz^2 + 2Dxy + 2Eyz + 2Fzx + 2Gx + 2Hy + 2Jz + k = 0$$

Sphere: In the above equation if $A = B = C = -k = 1$ and $D = E = F = G = H = J = 0$, then the equation becomes

$$x^2 + y^2 + z^2 = 1$$

It is an equation of spherical surface with radius unity and coordinate origin as its centre.
If the radius is r and the origin remains unchanged, the equation becomes

$$x^2 + y^2 + z^2 = r^2$$

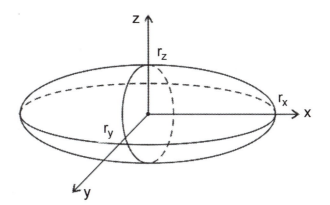

FIGURE 3.15   Ellipsoid

Ellipsoid: Refer to Figure 3.15. The equation of ellipsoid surface is given in cartesian form as

$$\left(\frac{x}{r_x}\right)^2 + \left(\frac{y}{r_y}\right)^2 + \left(\frac{z}{r_z}\right)^2 = 1$$

where r_x, r_y, r_z are the radius along x, y and z directions respectively. Hence an ellipsoid is an extension of a sphere with different radii in three mutually perpendicular directions.

Torus: A torus may be formed by rotating a circle or other conic around a fixed axis. The equation of a torus surface is given by

$$\left\{ r - \sqrt{\left(\frac{x}{r_x}\right)^2 + \left(\frac{y}{r_y}\right)^2} \right\}^2 + \left(\frac{z}{r_z}\right)^2 = 1$$

An advantage of using a quadric surface is its ease of computing. It is easy to test whether a point lies on the quadric surface.

3.6.3 SUPERQUADRIC SURFACES

Superquadrics are a further generalisation of quadric surfaces and provide greater flexibility in generating complicated object shapes. Examples of such surfaces are superellipse and superellipsoid.

Superellipse: The Cartesian equation of a superellipse is given by

$$\left(\frac{x}{r_x}\right)^{\frac{2}{s}} + \left(\frac{y}{r_y}\right)^{\frac{2}{s}} = 1$$

where s is a variable parameter that can be assigned any real value. Various shapes generated on varying the value of s are shown in Figure 3.16.

Superellipsoid: The Cartesian equation of a superellipsoid is given by the expression

$$\left\{ \left(\frac{x}{r_x}\right)^{\frac{2}{s_0}} + \left(\frac{y}{r_y}\right)^{\frac{2}{s_0}} \right\}^{\frac{s_0}{s_1}} + \left(\frac{Z}{r_z}\right)^{\frac{2}{s_1}} = 1$$

For $S_0 = S_1$, we get the ordinary ellipsoid equation in three dimensions.

3.6.4 BEZIER SURFACES

Bezier curves are easily extended into three dimensions to create Bezier surfaces. Two orthogonal sets of Bezier space curves define a Bezier surface. The surface appears as a set of quadrilateral patches or tiles, which can be shaded to yield a realistic image. Control points that define Bezier surface can be manipulated so as to give the surface some aesthetic or engineering properties.

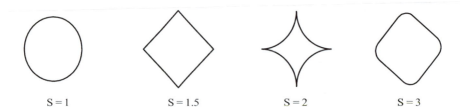

S = 1   S = 1.5   S = 2   S = 3

FIGURE 3.16   Superellipse drawn for various values of s

A Bezier surface can be plotted by using two orthogonal Bezier curves and specifying the input mesh of control points. Hence, a parametric equation of a Bezier surface comprises two parameters (say, s and t) and is formed by the Cartesian product of the two Bezier blending functions. The equation is

$$P(s,t) = \sum_{i=0}^{m} \sum_{j=0}^{n} B_{ij} J_{i'm}(u) J_{i'n}(v)$$

$$= \sum_{i=0}^{m} \sum_{j=0}^{n} B_{ij}\, B_{ij'}{}^{m}C_i\, u^i (1-u)^{n-i}\, {}^{n}C_j\, v^j (1-v)^{n-j}$$

Where $0 \leq u \leq 1$

$$0 \leq v \leq 1$$

By giving a mesh of control points and then applying two sets of orthogonal Bezier curves to the input, it is possible to generate Bezier surfaces. As shown in Figure 3.17(a), there are eight control points for one set of space curves while its orthogonal set has only four control points. The eight control points define a series of four space curves along which parameter u varies from 0 to 1. In orthogonal direction, four control points define a series of eight space curves along which parameter v series from 0 to 1. Hence, the mesh has in all $8 \times 4 = 32$ control points. Figure 3.17(b) shows a Bezier surface defined by a mesh of control points.

Since a Bezier surface is an extension of a Bezier curve, the properties of the surface remain the same as that of the curve. Axis independence, variation diminishing property, alterability and command over continuity of Bezier curves facilitate the creation of animated images. As with the curves, a Bezier surface can also be formed by joining together individual patches using suitable boundary constraints. Continuity at the joints between two patches can be achieved by using zero or first-order continuity. Zero-order continuity may be achieved by matching the control points that define the boundary curves of a particular route with a neighbouring patch.

3.6.5 B-SPLINE SURFACES

A B-Spline surface may be constructed in the same way as a Bezier surface. Multiplication of B-spline blending functions by the Cartesian operator results in a vector point function for the B-spline surface. The equation for the B-spline surface follows:

$$P(U,V) = \sum_{i=0}^{m} \sum_{j=0}^{n} P_{i,j} N_{i,k}(\mathbf{u})\, N_{j,i}(V)$$

Figure 3.18 shows B-spline surface and their mesh of control points.

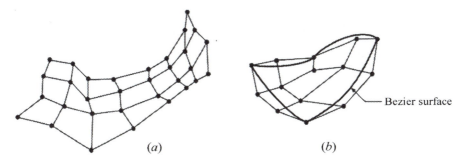

(a) (b)

Bezier surface

FIGURE 3.17 Control points for the Bezier surface

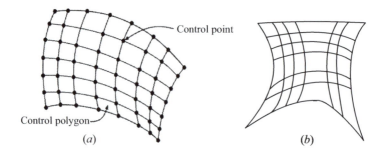

FIGURE 3.18 B-spline surface

3.7 BLOBBY OBJECTS

Some objects do not maintain a fixed shape. They tend to change their shape with a change in environment or under the action of some force. For example, a freely falling droplet of water which may be spherical initially will tend to take on an oval shape under gravity.

When any person flexes his muscles, the shape of the muscles change. Melting substances like ice or wax change their shape till they melt completely. Such objects are said to exhibit "blobbiness" and are called *blobby objects.*

Molecules are typical examples of blobby objects. When considered in isolation a molecule may take a spherical shape. But in actual physics the effect of neighbouring molecules must be considered. Due to attraction or repulsion force, as the case may be, their shape will vary as shown in Figure 3.19.

Various models have been developed to represent blobby objects. One such method is given by Gaussian density functions, where a surface function is given by the expression,

$$f(x, \quad y, \quad z) = \sum_i q_i e^{-p_i r_i^2} - k = 0$$

In this expression $r = \sqrt{x^2 + y^2 + z^2}$, controlling the blotchiness of an object are parameters p and q, while parameter k sets a threshold. To generate dents rather than bumps, the parameter q is given a negative value. Figure 3.20 (a) shows a 3-D Gaussian bump with centre at o height q and standard deviation P.

3.8 FRACTALS

Shapes of manufactured parts and components can be easily described with mathematical equations as they have regular shapes and smooth surfaces. But natural objects such as clouds, snow, mountains, plants and feathers cannot be described by equations. Such objects have irregular and fragmented features and can be described by Fractals geometry methods. Such natural objects have two **basic characteristics:**

(i) *Infinite detail at every point:* If we zoom in on continuous regular shapes repeatedly, we are bound to get a final smooth view. But if we try to zoom in on fractal objects like hills and clouds, the original degree of detail is maintained in the enlarged picture. As the spectator gets closer, the jagged shape of an item against the sky, such as a hill, cloud or tree, stays unaltered. As we move towards a mountain details of boulders become apparent. As

FIGURE 3.19   Variation in shape of molecules with changing molecular force

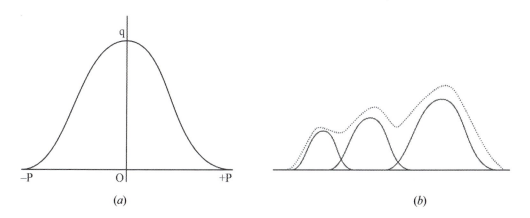

$$(a) \hspace{6cm} (b)$$

FIGURE 3.20   A composite blobby object formed by combining three Guassian bumps

we continue to move closer, smaller details such as outlines to rocks, then stones and then grains appear. It means, on moving closer, the view does not get smoothened.

(ii) ***Self-similarity between the object and object parts:*** Depending on the fractal representation employed, self-similarity of objects may be portrayed in a number of ways. In order to explain fractal objects, an approach that requires repetition of the same activity is used. Theoretically, they may be modelled as processes that continue forever. In practice, however, just a few processes are necessary to create images portraying natural phenomena.

A transformation function is repeatedly applied to points in the same region of space to generate a fractal. If $Pi = (xi, yi, zi)$ is the initial point, then each interaction of the transformation function F with the calculation will increase the granularity:

$$P_1 = F(P_i) \; P_2 = F(P_1) \; P_3 = F(P_2)$$

and so on.

As already discussed, for practical purposes, transformation is carried out a finite number of times only such that objects displayed on screen have finite dimensions. As the number of transformations are increased, more and more details are visible i.e., procedural representation approaches a true fractal.

3.9   SOLIDS

Since the widespread availability of personal computers, CAD software has become the undisputed norm for the design process. Broadly, this representation is called ***geometric modelling.*** Both 2-D and 3-D models qualify as "geometric." A 3-D geometric model can be implicitly classified as

LO 4. To understand solid models

(A) Line model (wire frame model),
(B) Surface model,
(C) Solid model (volume model). Refer to Figure 3.21.

The ***line model*** is commonly referred to as ***wireframe* representation.** The wireframe model representation contains only vertex and edge information. The complete model is constructed by line entity, with the end coordinates of lines having well-defined connectivity relationships. Thus, a line is the smallest drawing entity in a wireframe model. An inherent disadvantage in this type of model is that if the model is complicated. It becomes less distinct and more difficult to comprehend.

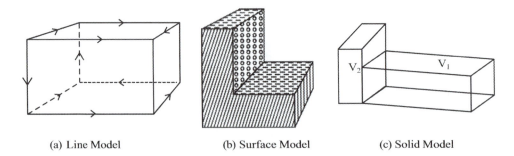

(a) Line Model   (b) Surface Model   (c) Solid Model

FIGURE 3.21   Solid Modeling

It is unusual for a large number of lines from various regions of a sophisticated model to cross. Therefore, a wireframe model cannot correctly depict solids with complicated geometrical features. It cannot also be used to determine mass or moment of inertia, which are volumetric properties. Most solid modelling systems, such as AutoCAD, Pro/E, etc., include a wireframe representation option for solid models (see Figure 3.21(a)).

Surface modelling refers to creating a graphics object model by using surfaces. A surface model is made by joining surfaces to form a completely closed body object. Hence, in surface modelling, the smallest drawing entity is surface. The type of surface used for surface modelling may be plane surface such as the one shown in Figure 3.21(b) or it may be ruled surfaces (rotated curved surfaces), quadric, superquadric surfaces or even more complex ones like Bezier surface, B-spline surface, etc. Unlike wireframe models, surface models are not ambiguous in external shape and give a clear representation of the solid object as far as external views are required. However, these to have some inherent limitations. Surface models cannot give any information on internal shape and features of an object. Hence, interior detailing is not possible. They cannot be used to calculate mass, moment of inertia or centre of gravity of the object. Surface modelling is not suitable where generating NC/CNC part program and tool path generation is required. Surface modelling is more useful in applications such as designing sheet metal components and the modelling of car bodies etc. Design software such as Pro/E, CATIA, SolidWorks, etc. provide easy-to-use surface modelling modules for this purpose.

Solid modelling, also sometimes referred as volume modelling, is the most widely used approach for representing solids as it gives a complete description of the solid. A solid model can be used to generate internal details and cross-sectional views. Hidden line removal is possible using solid modelling. Moreover, solid modelling can be used to calculate mass, centre of gravity, moment of inertia and other geometrical properties. Solid modelling can be used for downstream manufacturing planning applications such as automatic cutting tool path generation, etc. A solid model can be generated by a number of techniques. We study solid modelling in detail in the next section. Refer to Figure 3.21(c).

3.9.1   SOLID MODELLING CHARACTERISTICS

Solid modelling is a tool for generating a 3-D representation of an object. Most of the applications in CAD software contain modules (or tasks) for creating solid part model geometry. These models can be used for many downstream applications such as drafting 2-D drawings, interference studies, mass properties calculation, kinematic analysis, stress analysis, manufacturing, assembly and other applications. The most recent CAD programmes, such as IDEAS, PRO/E, Catia SolidWorks, Solid Edge, etc., are intended to make it simpler to develop and analyse mechanical engineering products using a concurrent engineering method. Packages such as these make it simple for departments within an organisation to communicate and work on solid model and design geometry for a variety of activities.

A CAD solid modelling system should satisfy the following requirements:

(1) **Rigidity:** A solid model should have unchangeable, uniform configuration and shape independent of objects location and orientation.
(2) **Homogeneous:** A 3-D model should have homogeneous interiors and solid boundary.
(3) **Finite Volume:** A solid model must occupy some finite space.
(4) **Finite Description:** A solid model must be of finite size and should have a finite number of faces so that it can be correctly represented by the computer.

While preparing solid models of a component we must keep in mind the final objectives for which the model will be used. For example, the model may be used to calculate mass, volume and surface area of the solid, moment of inertia about various axes or position of its centroid. We may also wish to know how the object will move or deform under specified forces, or how heat transfer can take place when applied to some heat source. To compute mass, the CAD/CAM engineer has to assume an appropriate value for its density; for deformation, value of modules of elasticity is required. Visual effects have to be set based on the optical nature of the material and by the texture of part surface. Thus, we can say that the basic purpose of a solid model is to provide an accurate description of the geometry of the component. In addition, it should be possible to specify various material properties and other visual inputs needed to facilitate the prediction of engineering application, and for appropriate computer graphics visualisation.

3.9.1.1   Constructive Solid Geometry (CSG)

In constructive solid geometry, using Boolean operations, the volume of 3-D primitives that overlap is merged to create a solid entity. The Boolean operations used are union, intersection or difference. The primitives used by CSG are simple 3-D objects such as cones, pyramids, cylinders, blocks, spheres, torus, wedge, etc. Figure 3.22 shows an example for forming new shapes using Boolean operation.

A cone is seen adjacent to a hemisphere in this diagram. As seen in Figure 3.22, the union operation yields a composite object (b). Readymade primitives are provided in most of the packages which can be given suitable dimensions. Otherwise, the primitives themselves can be formed using construction commands like sweep, blend, extrude, revolve and the like. To create a new 3-D

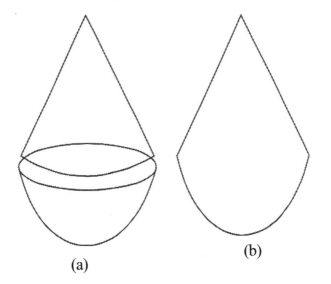

(a)

(b)

FIGURE 3.22 Combining two primitives, a cone and a hemisphere using union operation produces a new object

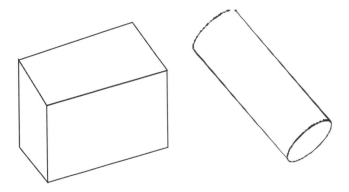

FIGURE 3.23   Constructive solid geometry

solid using the CSG method, two primitives are dragged into a region of space and given a suitable orientation with respect to each other. Then a suitable Boolean operation is used to combine the volumes of two primitives. Now more primitives can be added one by one to this new solid to get the final shape.

Figure 3.23 shows a block and a cylinder.

With a ***union operation*** the result is a single solid object incorporating all the space occupied by each one of the individual components (see Figure 3.24).

With ***difference operation*** the result is a single solid incorporating the space which is occupied by the first component minus the space occupied by the other component (see Figure 3.25).

When two or more primitives are combined with an ***intersection operation,*** the result is a single solid incorporating the space which is occupied by both the primitives (see Figure 3.26).

For a CSG application, the primitives may be provided by the CAD package itself or the primitives may be developed using two common techniques: Sweep and Extrude. Figure 3.27(a) shows extruding a section through a thickness "*d*."

Figure 3.28 shows sweeping a section along a specified path.

A technique called ***ray-casting*** in commonly used to implement CSG operations. In this method, a plane called "firing plane" is assumed, paralleling the display's pixel plane. Boolean operations are performed by sending rays from each pixel point along this firing plane across the items to be merged. This aids in locating the spots where two surfaces meet along each ray's trajectory and organising them according to their distance from the firing plane. The set operation that was

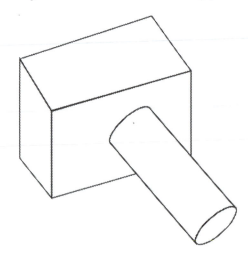

FIGURE 3.24   Union operation

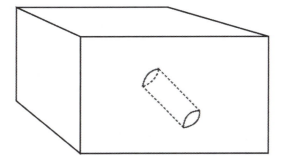

FIGURE 3.25 Union operation

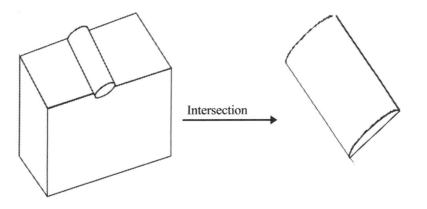

FIGURE 3.26 Union operation

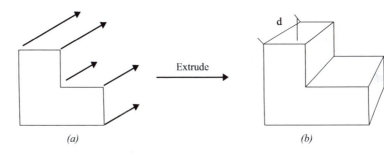

(a) *(b)*

FIGURE 3.27 Extrude operation

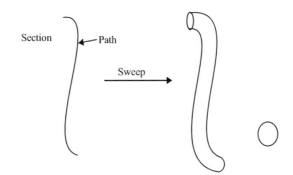

FIGURE 3.28 Sweep operation

previously stated is now responsible for establishing the surface boundaries of the composite objects. Figure 3.29(a) is an illustration of the ray-casting technique used to identify the surface bounds of a CSG object.

The ray-casting technique is also used to determine volume of the solid model as shown in Figure 3.29(b). For this the firing plane can be divided into any large number of small-sized squares with a known area. Once the thickness of the object is determined using ray-casting technique, the volume over the squares can be added to find the total volume.

Using ray-casting, it is possible to find places on the surface of solid objects by projecting an imaginary ray from each pixel on the screen. Using this technique, it is possible to decide whether or not a pixel has to be set bright, the value on a greyscale or the colour to be given to that pixel. The technique has also been successfully used to deal with a group of overlapping objects, such as models of machine tool assemblies, etc. to solve the visible surface problem. According to the technique, that surface is visible which is nearest to the screen. For example, the single ray shown in Figure 3.29, first intersects object at 1 and A, then object 2 at B, then again object 1 at C and object

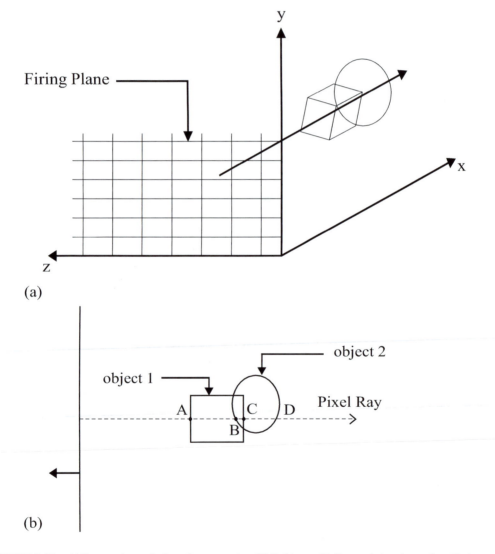

(a)

(b)

FIGURE 3.29   (a) Ray casting technique for generating CSG objects. (b) Determining the surface limits and volume using ray casting technique

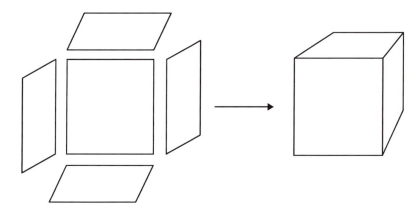

FIGURE 3.30 Boundary representation technique

2 at D. The distance from the screen to the intersected surfaces are computed. Then the pixel is set to the colour of the surface nearest to the screen.

3.9.1.2 Boundary Representation: (B-rep)

Refer to Figure 3.30. B-rep is another method for generating a solid model in which a solid is described by the elements which form its boundary. B-rep is done by a set of surfaces that enclose the object's interiors. The graphics systems store all object descriptions as a set of polygon surfaces. Linear equations are used to describe the surfaces mathematically. This facilitates and accelerates object rendering and presentation. A polygon representation may precisely define the surface features. In other applications, wireframe representation may be used.

The coordinates of the model have to be arranged using an appropriate data structure. Different types of data structure used to store the coordinates are enumerated below:

1. Edge is a function of a start vertex and a finish vertex, and surface is the function of a set of n edges, i.e., $E = f(V_s, V_f)$ and $s = f(E_1, E_2, E_3E_n)$.
2. A surface is a function of a set of n vertices, and an edge is a function of a start vertex and a finish vertex, i.e., $S = f(V_1, V_2, V_3 .... V_n)$ and $E = f(V_s, V_f)$.
3. A surface is a function of n vertices, and an edge in a function of two intersecting surfaces, i.e., $S = f(V_1, V_2, V_3 .... V_n)$ and $E = f(S_1, S_2)$.

Often, a more sophisticated data structure such as *linked list* is a more practical choice.

3.9.1.3 Sweep Representation

Create a new object by dragging an existing one along a preset route across space. This technique may be used to create symmetrical 3-D objects in a variety of orientations. For example, a simple sweep can be created by a 2-D cross-section being swept along normal to plane of cross-section area. It is known as ***translational sweep*** or extrusion. Figure 3.31 illustrates a translational sweep.

Rotational sweep is created by rotating a cross-section about an axis. Figure 3.32 illustrates rotational sweep.

The object of the sweep may or may not be a 2-D slice. A solid sweep may assist in modelling and recognising the area swept away by a robot end effector following a specified trajectory or by a machine tool cutting head. Any axis may be picked in the event of a rotating sweep. If the axis is perpendicular to the cross-sectional plane, a 2-D shape may be generated. Nevertheless, a 3-D object is formed if the depth of the cross-section is adequate. More advanced applications of sweep include: Change in cross-section shape or size from one end of sweep to the other, sweep along some non-linear curve function, etc.

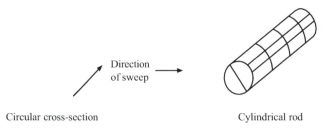

FIGURE 3.31   A cylindrical rod constructed from translational sweep of circular cross-section

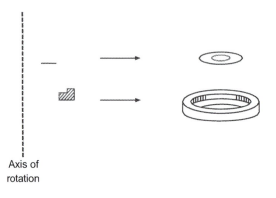

FIGURE 3.32   A washer created by rotational sweep

3.9.1.4   Spatial Partitioning Representation

This is another technique for representing the solids in which a solid is further subdivided into a number of closely spaced, non-intersecting smaller solids or cells. These cells may or may not be of same type as the original solid. In fact, they may vary in size, type and orientation. Depending upon the way a solid must behave in order to perform the desired task, there are two main methods by which spatial-partitioning representation is accomplished: Cell decomposition and spatial-occupancy enumeration.

3.9.1.5   Cell Decompositioning

It is one of the most commonly used techniques of spatial partitioning. It decomposes the solid into a set of primitive cells that are parameterised (varying in a few parameters). Cell decomposition makes use of bottom-up construction in which complex shapes are created from simple primitives by sticking them together but the cells must not intersect while sharing a single point, edge or face. Cell decomposition has potential use in finite element analysis in which the system to be analysed is descretised or divided into smaller elements called finite elements, with the condition that the elements should not overlap each other. An example of cell decomposition being used to generate a solid is shown in Figure 3.33. The solid in Figure 3.33(b) is created by sticking primitives in figure 3.33(a) at flat faces.

3.9.1.6   Spatial Occupancy Enumeration

It is technique of spatial partitioning representation analogous to cell decomposition, but the difference is that in spatial occupancy enumeration, the solid is subdivided into exactly identical cells arranged in a fixed regular grid. These cells or volume elements are called *voxels*. Various solid shapes such as cube, pyramid, prism, etc. can be used as voxels but the most commonly used type is the cube. Representation of a solid as regular array of cubes is known as *cuberille*. Spatial occupancy enumeration is an approximation technique.

For creating a solid model using spatial occupancy enumeration, a CAD engineer has to control the presence or absence of a cell at various locations of the model so as to give it a shape as close as possible to the real object. For example, if a sphere is approximated by cubic cells, the true shape

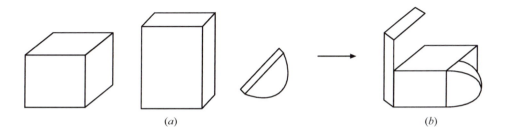

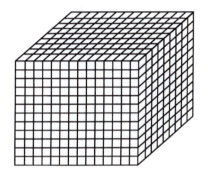

FIGURE 3.33 Cell decomposition technique

FIGURE 3.34 A world formed by cubic cells using spatial occupancy enumeration

of sphere cannot be achieved. This is an obvious disadvantage of spatial occupancy enumeration although the shape can be improved by reducing the size of cell and increasing the number of cells. It is easy to determine whether a cell lies inside or outside a solid. Parts with orthogonal walls as surface boundaries can be accurately modelled using cubic cells as shown in Figure 3.34.

3.9.2 Concept of Hidden Line and Surface Removal

A common requirement of CAD packages in solid modelling is to hide the portion of a line or surface that lies behind another surface or solid object. This process is called hidden line or hidden surface removal. The lines in the backdrop are shown as dotted or dashed lines or should be completely omitted. Hence, need arises to identify hidden portions of lines. One possible approach is to identify the hidden lines by comparing each line to each surface and clip the hidden portion by some clipping algorithm. The sweeping object might be a 2-D slice, but it could also be something else altogether. A solid sweep may assist in modelling and identifying the area cleared by a robot end effector following a predetermined trajectory or by a machine tool cutting head. Any axis may be selected for rotational sweeps. A 2-D form is generated if the axis is parallel to the section plane. Nevertheless, a 3-D object is produced if the cross-section is sufficiently deep, as shown in Figures 3.35.

Another situation may be to have lines intersecting a surface as shown in Figure 3.35. In such a case, line will have less depth than the surface boundary at one intersection while the other intersection will have greater depth than the surface boundary. In this case, the line will intersect with the surface at some point which can be calculated using plane equation. Then, the hidden portion of the line can be obscured. A popular algorithm for hidden line or surface elimination is the Z-buffer algorithm.

3.10 HALF-SPACE

When the 3-D Euclidean space is cut in half by a plane, each of the resulting halves are called a half-space. It may be any of the two halves that a hyperplane creates in an affine space. To put it

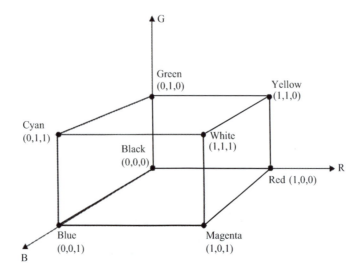

FIGURE 3.35   Hidden line and surface removal

another way, the points that are not incident to the hyperplane are split into two convex sets (i.e., half-spaces) such that any subspace from a point in one set to a point in the other set intersects the hyperplane. There are two basic kinds: Open and closed halves. When a hyperplane is subtracted from an affine space, two open sets are left behind, one of which is an open half-space. The union of an open half-space with its defining hyperplane produces a closed half-space. Assuming a 2-D space, we call a half of that space a half-plane.

3.11   COLOURS

According to the system's capabilities and the designer's objectives, the user is provided with a variety of colour and brightness level options. Unlike random scan displays, which only show a few colours, the raster scan technology has an unrivalled depth of colour representation. These colours are given some codes, usually positive integers. For CRT monitors, these colour codes are then converted into intensity level settings for the electron beam. For other output devices like a colour plotter or printer, the codes could control inkjet deposits or pen selections.

In a raster system some memory storage is provided corresponding to each pixel in the frame buffer. This memory storage per pixel decides the number of colour choices available (refer Table 3.1). Colour information is stored in frame buffer in either of two ways:

1. Colour codes are directly stored in the frame buffer.
2. You may use constant values as an index into a separate database containing colour codes using constant values. Preferred is a minimum of three bits per pixel so that a wider spectrum of colours may be represented. Each of the three-bit places in an RGB monitor is utilised to control the intensity level (on or off) of the accompanying electron gun.

3.11.1   COLOUR MODELS

A colour model is a technique for creating a large colour palette using just three or four primary colours. The first may be additive, whereas the second may be subtractive.

Figure 3.36 shows a unit cube representation of Red-Green-Blue (RGB) and Cyan-Magenta-Yellow (CMY) models.

TABLE 3.1

Eight Colour Codes for Three-Bit per Pixel Frame

Colour Code	Stored Colour Values in Frame Buffer Corresponding to:			Displayed Colours
	Red	Green	Blue	
0	0	0	0	Black
1	0	0	1	Blue
2	0	1	0	Green
3	0	1	1	Cyan
4	1	0	0	Red
5	1	0	1	Magenta
6	1	1	0	Yellow
7	1	1	1	White

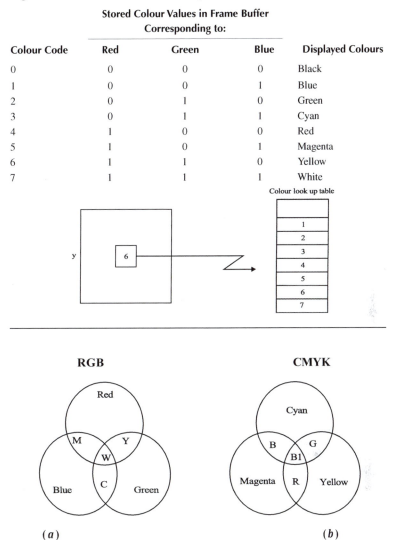

FIGURE 3.36   Difference between RGB and CMY model.

3.11.2 GREYSCALE

With monitors having no colour capabilities, Greyscale (or different shades of grey) are used for display of primitives. Specifying greyscale levels using integers between 0 and 1, which are subsequently converted to binary codes and saved in raster files (refer Table 3.2).

3.12 SUMMARY

- Control points govern the shape of the curve in a predictable way.
- If a small shift in control point changes the shape of the curve only in the nearby region, it is said to possess local control but if the shape of the curve changes throughout it is said to possess global control.

TABLE 3.2

Intensity Codes for a Four-Level Greyscale System

Intensity Levels	Colour (Binary	Codes Codes)	Display Greyscale Colour
0.00	0	0	Black
0.33	0	1	Dark grey
0.67	1	0	Light grey
1.0	1	1	White

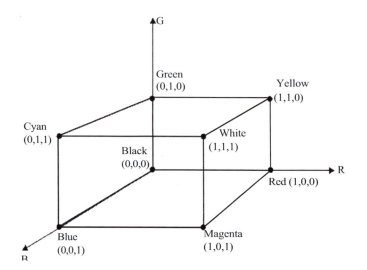

FIGURE 3.37   Unit cube representation of RGB and CMY models

- Interpolation happens when a curve is traced such that it contacts each control point, whereas approximation occurs when the curve is traced without hitting any control points.
- Spline curves are used to create intricate curves and surfaces and have found application in designing automobile and aircraft bodies.
- A Bezier curve passes through first and last control points. This curve shows axis independence and global control.
- Computer graphics make use of graphics surfaces such as quadric surfaces such as sphere, ellipsoid, torus and superquadric surfaces such as superellipse, superellipsoid.
- Flexible bodies which tend to change their shape under some external influence is shown using blobby objects.
- 3-D objects can be created in computer graphics using line model, surface model or solid model.
- Solid models can be generated using two techniques: Constructive solid geometry and boundary representation.
- Monitors with no colour capabilities make use of grey scale while colour monitors use additive (RGB) or subtractive (CMY) colour models.

3.13   EXERCISE

1. What are the important properties for curves designing (BT level 2)?
   Or
   List and explain basic properties of space curves.

2. Differentiate between interpolation and approximation method for generating control points of splines (BT level 4).
3. Briefly describe 3-D curves (BT level 2).
4. Explain Bezier curves. What are their properties (BT level 2)?
5. Discuss various types of quadric and superquadric surfaces available in the graphics packages. What do you understand by the term blobby objects? How do you model them (BT level 2)?
6. What are the essential properties of a CAD solid model (BT level 1)?
7. What are the applications of solid models (BT level 1)?
8. Describe the "ray casting technique" for generating CSG objects (BT level 2)?
9. Explain the colour system used in raster scan display device. Explain various colour models. What is grey scale (BT level 2)?
10. Why do you prefer Bezier form of cubic curves over the Hermite form for interactive computer graphics (BT level 4)?
11. How are approximation splines and interpolation splines defined? Determine the Hermite spline blending functions and then sketch the resultant curves. Do any limitations exist while using Hermite splines? How is it eliminated (BT level 2)?
12. Explain constructive solid geometry in depth and explain your ideas using illustrations, modelling of 3-D objects with translational, rotational, and other forms of symmetry. Provide logical explanations and examples (BT level 2).

3.14 MULTIPLE-CHOICE QUESTIONS

1. Which of the following is a commonly used curve representation method in CAD?
   a. B-spline
   b. Vector graphics
   c. Pixel-based images
   d. ASCII text
2. Which of the following is a benefit of using parametric curves in CAD?
   a. Allows for precise control over the shape and size of curves
   b. Requires less computational resources than other curve representation methods
   c. Provides higher image quality than other curve representation methods
   d. Supports a wider range of file formats than other curve representation methods
3. Which of the following is a commonly used spline type in CAD?
   a. Hermite spline
   b. Bezier spline
   c. Catmull-Rom spline
   d. All of the above
4. Which of the following is not a commonly used curve representation method in CAD?
   a. Fourier transform
   b. NURBS
   c. Conic sections
   d. Elliptic curves
5. Which of the following is not a commonly used surface representation method in 3D graphics?
   a. Polygon meshes
   b. NURBS
   c. Bezier curves
   d. Fourier series
6. Which of the following is a benefit of using parametric surfaces in 3D graphics?
   a. Allows for precise control over the shape and size of surfaces

   b. Requires less computational resources than other surface representation methods
   c. Provides higher image quality than other surface representation methods
   d. Supports a wider range of file formats than other surface representation methods

7. Which of the following is a commonly used surface type in 3D graphics?
   a. Plane
   b. Sphere
   c. Cone
   d. All of the above

8. Which of the following is not a commonly used surface modeling technique in 3D graphics?
   a. Extrusion
   b. Sweeping
   c. Filleting
   d. Pixelation

Answers

1. Answer: a. B-spline
2. Answer: a. Allows for precise control over the shape and size of curves
3. Answer: d. All of the above
4. Answer: a. Fourier transform
5. Answer: d. Fourier series
6. Answer: a. Allows for precise control over the shape and size of surfaces
7. Answer: d. All of the above
8. Answer: d. Pixelation

4 Finite Element Method

Learning Outcomes: After studying this chapter, the reader should be able:

LO 1: To understand finite element modelling and analysis (BT level 2).
LO 2: To understand the basic steps in the finite element method (BT level 2).
LO 3: To understand two-dimensional problems in finite element stress analysis (BT Level 2)

4.1 INTRODUCTION

Sometimes, when considering a system as a whole, its behaviour is difficult to conceptualise. In contrast, by disassembling the system into its component elements, its evaluation becomes far less intimidating. Due to this, it is easy to comprehend and integrate the behaviour of each individual component into an explanation of the whole system's behaviour. This concept is the basis for the finite element method (FEM).

LO 1. To understand Finite element modeling and analysis

Development in the theory of the FEM started in the early 1940s when a need was felt for improved aircraft structural analysis. By the 1960s, engineers utilised FEM for a variety of analyses, such as stress, fluid flow and heat transfer, among others. In the 1960s, FEM was utilised to address non-linear problems. Fast development in the field of computer hardware and software led to development of application software that can be used for FEM-based analysis. Examples of such software are NISA, ANSYS, NASTRAN, Hypermesh, COSMOS, Pro/E, etc. This software is used extensively to solve complex, real life, design and analysis problems. In fact, FEM is now an imperative part of computer-aided engineering (CAE). It is a method for mathematical solution of a wide range of engineering problems. Today, the technique has found wide acceptance in the automobile industry for deformation and stress analysis of automobile bodies and optimising the weight, magnetic flux, thermal flux, fluid flow, acoustics, radiation analysis, seepage, etc.

4.2 PROCEDURE FOR FINITE ELEMENT ANALYSIS

Consider a car's piston as an example. During normal operation, pistons in internal combustion engines are subjected to a variety of forces and stresses. These include impact loads, friction forces, cylinder wall responses caused by thermal expansion of the piston, etc. Because of

LO 2. To understand Basic steps in finite element method

these pressures, the piston body may acquire an atypical stress pattern. It is feasible to determine the nature of the stress distribution using a finite element analysis technique in which the whole piston body is divided into smaller pieces called finite elements. This material may have a cuboid, tetrahedral, prismatic or hexahedral shape. These components' four corners (or nodes) are connected together. To determine the stress at these sites, it is necessary to create element matrices. Using a global stress matrix, the stress distribution across the piston's whole body is then mapped.

After analysing the stress distribution over the piston's body, it is feasible to optimise piston design by increasing wall thickness in areas with higher stress accumulation.

After conducting a comprehensive examination of the stress distribution over the piston's body, piston designs may be optimised by increasing wall thickness where stress is anticipated to be greatest.

Any analysis to be performed by using the FEM can be divided into following steps:

1. Discretisation,
2. Choosing the solution approximations,
3. Forming the element matrices and equations,
4. Assembling the matrices,
5. Finding the unknowns,
6. Interpreting the results.

1. **Discretisation:** In this step the entire body to be analysed is divided into smaller elements or finite elements. These elements are connected to each other through nodes. The elements should not overlap each other. Dividing the body into elements and nodes is called *mesh generation* or *meshing*. Figure 4.1 shows a cantilever beam. The finite element mesh generation is shown in Figure 4.2. The cantilever is divided into six small elements. These elements have a cubic shape. The corner points of the elements are called nodes. The finite elements are numbered from 1 to 6. The elements are interconnected by nodes where the elements meet and move in unison.

In this case the cantilever is discretised into six elements only. But for better estimation of stress distribution in the cantilever, the number of field elements should be higher. The higher the number of finite elements, the better is the estimation of field variables.

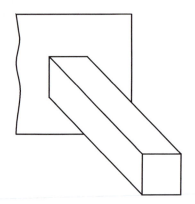

FIGURE 4.1   Cantilever beam

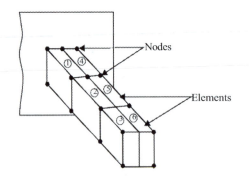

FIGURE 4.2   Mesh creation for a finite element model

The finite elements are categorised by:

(a) Family,
(b) Order,
(c) Topology.

The geometric and displacemental characteristics of an element are referred to as its "element family." In general, one should use the simplest element type that will model the problem. It is also important to consider the type of output that is needed. Beam, Plane Stress, Axis Symmetrical Solids, Thin Shells and Solids are the most widely used structural model families.

Beam elements are used to predict overall deflection and bending moment but cannot be used to find local stress concentration at the point of application of loads. Utilising thin shell elements in buildings with thin walls, such as sheet metal components, might be advantageous. Solid elements give a more realistic view but increase the calculation work.

The arrangement of the components is also a categorisation. Orders of elements that may be used to interpolate the strain between nodes include linear, parabolic and cubic equations. Each edge of a linear element has two nodes, but each edge of a parabolic element has three and each edge of a cubic element has four.

The topology of an element describes its overarching form, such as a triangle or a square. The element's family determines the topology. Since the quadrilateral element has more degrees of freedom, it can better reflect the genuine displacement function of a structure, it is preferable to the triangle element when building structural models. See Figure 4.3 to get an idea of different types of elements.

Elements also contain different numbers of degrees of freedom at each node. Elements used to model two dimensional problems may only contain two degrees of freedom at each node as the node is free to move in two directions only. In general, the maximum number of degrees of freedom at each node is six, i.e., three translational and three rotational, although not all elements will use all six.

2. **Choosing the approximate solution:** The analysis is initially restricted to a single field element by finding the values of field variables at the nodes of these elements. The values of the field variables on the entire element domain can be found out by extrapolating the values at the nodes and approximating the solution. This can be done by assuming the polynomial expressions as these are easy to differentiate or integrate.

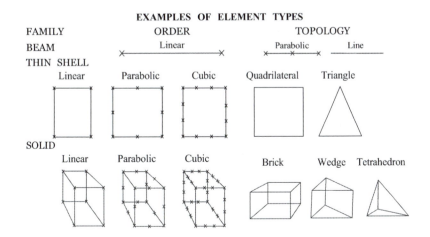

FIGURE 4.3 Different types of finite elements

3. **Forming the element matrix/equations:** The analysis of a single element is done by applying equations of equilibrium to that element. These equations can then be expressed in form of a matrix called element matrix. Such element matrices can be generated for each of the element.

4. **Assembling the matrices:** The element matrices of all the elements are combined or assembled to form the global stiffness matrix, which represents the entire body or contanium. The boundary condition can then be applied to the global stiffness matrix. This will reduce the size of the global matrix.

5. **Finding the unknown field variables:** The unknown field variables can be found out from the global stiffness matrix by using Gauss elimination approach. The value of field variables can thus be known at the nodal points, which can ultimately be used to find the values of field variables over the entire element domain.

6. **Interpreting the results:** Once the value of field variables is obtained from the above analysis, the conclusions are drawn and appropriate modifications are incorporated into the original design in order to improve the design. For example, in the case of stress analysis of a piston, wall thickness can be increased at the sites where the stress concentration is more and probability of failure is high. This last step is important as it needs detail knowledge of design.

4.2.1 Types of Finite Element Analysis

The FEM has been adopted to solve a wide range of engineering design analysis problems. It has been used to solve static and dynamic analysis problems, linear and nonlinear analysis problems, thermal analysis, fluid flow and magnetic field analysis.

Structural analysis in used to find stress distribution in buildings, bridges, machine tool beds, columns, guideways, etc. When the loads acting on the body are not varying, this kind of study is known as static analysis when the loads acting on the body remain constant over time, while dynamic analysis is used when the loads vary over time. Until the forces acting on a body reach a steady state, the type of response is called transient response analysis.

Linear analysis is conducted when structural properties, such as stiffness, are maintained constant during the whole investigation. Non-linear analysis refers to the study of events whose features vary over time.

Thermal analysis is used to find temperature distribution, thermal stresses, etc.

In all these types of analysis, basically the FEM approach is divided into two subgroups:

1. Finite Element Modelling,
2. Finite Element Analysis.

Finite Element Modelling includes mesh generation that comprises of generating finite elements and nodes, application of loads and deciding the material properties, etc.

Finite Element Analysis comprises forming element matrices, assembling the element matrices and applying boundary conditions to find the unknowns. The results can also be analysed using graphical tools, so that the design engineer can take more constructive decisions.

A number of software packages is available for carrying out finite element modelling and analysis. Examples of such software are COSMOS, ANSYS, NISA, PRO-MECHNICA, HYPERMESH, etc. In such packages, the processes carried out before the finite element analysis are called as **preprocessors**, while the processes carried out after finite element analysis are called **postprocessors**.

Various steps involved in solving a problem by the FEM can be expressed by the flow chart in Figure 4.4.

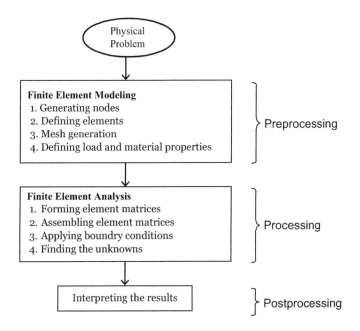

FIGURE 4.4 Steps in finite element method

4.3 TYPES OF FORCES

In finite element structural analysis problems, basically three types of forces are considered:

(A) Body force,
(B) Traction force.
(C) Point force.

Body forces are the forces which are distributed uniformly over the body and are expressed as force per unit volume. An example of such a force is weight per unit volume, which is a vector quantity and is given by vector f as

$$f = \begin{bmatrix} f_x & f_y & f_z \end{bmatrix}^T = \begin{bmatrix} f_x \\ f_y \\ f_z \end{bmatrix}$$

Traction forces are the forces acting on the surface of the body and are expressed as force per unit area. Examples of such forces are frictional resistance, surface drag, viscous force, pressure, etc. In a one-dimensional problem, surface traction can be expressed as force per unit length. The surface traction T can be given by its component values at points on the surface by

$$T = \begin{bmatrix} T_x & T_y & T_z \end{bmatrix}^T$$

Point force is a force applied by some external means and is acting at a point. It is expressed in absolute units. A load P acting at a point on a body can be represented by its three components as

$$P_i = \begin{bmatrix} P_x, & P_y, & P_z \end{bmatrix}^T$$

These forces acting on a body of volume V and surfaces S are shown in Figure 4.5.

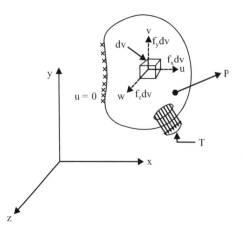

FIGURE 4.5 A three-dimensional body with body force, traction force and point load. Note that boundary is constrained for some region where displacement is specified ($u = 0$)

4.4 PRINCIPLE OF MINIMUM POTENTIAL ENERGY

When an elastic body is applied to an external load, it gets deformed and an internal energy called strain energy is developed in it. Let us consider an elastic spring which, when loaded by an external force P, gets expanded by an amount U. Let the spring have stiffness K. The strain energy developed in the spring is given as

$$\text{Strain Energy } (SE) = \frac{1}{2} \times \text{ Force } \times \text{ displacement}$$

$$= \frac{1}{2} \times (KU) \times U$$

$$= \frac{1}{2} KU^2$$

Due to this external force P, the work potential developed is given by:

$$\text{Work potential} = W = -P \times U$$

The principal of minimum potential energy states that at equilibrium, the total energy associated with the body is minimum. The required condition can be derived as

Total energy $E = SE + W$

$$\text{Total energy } E = \frac{1}{2} KU^2 - P \times U$$

For minimising E put $\dfrac{dE}{dU} = 0$

$$\frac{dE}{dU} = KU - P = 0$$

$$KU = P$$

This equation can be expressed in matrix form as

$$[K] \times [U] = [P]$$

In this equation $[K]$ is called **stiffness matrix,** $[U]$ represents the **displacement matrix** and $[P]$ represents the force matrix. It may be noted that the size of the displacement matrix and force matrix are the same and both are column matrices. Thus, it is clear that the **stiffness matrix** is a **square matrix.**

In this chapter we restrict our study to one-dimensional and two-dimensional stress analysis problems. Hence the name, each node in a one-dimensional problem may only move along a single axis. Each node in a two-dimensional problem has two degrees of freedom and may move in just one of two possible directions.

4.4.1 ONE-DIMENSIONAL PROBLEMS

Coordinates and shape functions: Consider a one-dimensional element shown in Figure 4.6. The location of any point on the element is expressed with reference to a datum. This can be simplified by defining natural or intrinsic coordinate system. Natural coordinate x is expressed as

$$\xi = \frac{2\left(x - x_1\right)}{\left(x_2 - x_1\right)} - 1$$

Hence, any point on the element in Figure 4.6 can be expressed in terms of natural coordinate ξ. From the above expression for node 1, $x = x_1$ and $\xi = -1$. For node 2, $x = x_2$ and $\xi = 1$. Thus, over the entire length of element ξ varies from -1 to 1. This co-ordinate system is used to define "**shape functions**" which are used in interpolating the displacement field.

By interpolating using a linear distribution, the unknown displacement at any location inside an element may be determined. The $N1$ and $N2$ shape functions are utilised for linear interpolation are defined as

$$N_1 = \frac{1-\xi}{2} \text{ and } N_2 = \frac{1+\xi}{2}$$

The shape function is a significant parameter because the displacement of any point over an element may be defined in terms of the nodal displacement and the form function. Any modification to the element's position is reflected by the phrase,

$$U = N_1\, q_1 + N_2\, q_2 \text{ (4.1)}$$

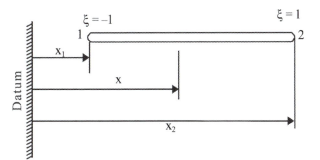

FIGURE 4.6 One-dimensional element in x and y coordinates

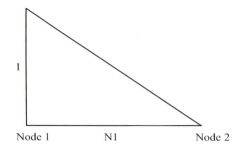

FIGURE 4.7   Shape function.

This can be represented in matrix form as

$$U = N q$$

Where $N = [N_1 \qquad N_2]$ and $q = [q_1 \qquad q_2]T$

U is displacement of point on the element and q_1, q_2 are nodal displacements.
Equation (4.1) is called displacement function and q is referred to as element displacement vector.
It may be observed that

at node 1, $\xi = -1$, therefore $N_1 = 1$ and $N_2 = 0$. At Node 2, $\xi = 1$, therefore $N_1 = 0$ and $N_2 = 1$.
   Thus, N_1 varies from 1 to 0 over an element. (Figure 4.7)

Similarly, N2 varies from 0 to 1 over an element. (Figure 4.8)
   It can be observed that distance of any point on the element can be expressed in terms of shape function as

$$X = N_1x_1 + N_2x_2 \tag{4.2}$$

   It is clear from Equations (4.1) and (4.2) that both displacement as well as geometry of the element can be expressed in terms of shape function. Such elements are called isoparametric elements.

4.4.2   ELEMENT STRAIN DISPLACEMENT MATRIX

Consider a very small element of length dx. Let dU be the small displacement in the element as a result of application of load. Thus, strain over the element is given by

$$\varepsilon = \frac{dU}{dx}$$

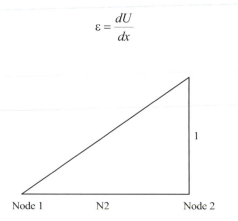

FIGURE 4.8   Shape function.

We know the u and x are both dependent on ξ, therefore using the chain rule of differentiation, the above expression can be written as

$$\varepsilon = \frac{dU}{d\xi} \times \frac{d\xi}{dx} \tag{4.3}$$

But

$$U = N_1 q_1 + N_2 q_2$$

$$U = \frac{1-\xi}{2} q_1 + \frac{1+\xi}{2} . q_2 \tag{4.4}$$

Therefore $\dfrac{dU}{d\xi} = \dfrac{-q_1 + q_2}{2}$

Also $\xi = \dfrac{2(x - x_1)}{(x_2 - x_1)} - 1$

Therefore $\dfrac{d\xi}{dx} = \dfrac{2}{(x_2 - x_1)} = \dfrac{2}{le} \tag{4.5}$

Where le = length of the element.

Therefore, substituting the values from (4.4) and (4.5) in (4.3) we get

$$\varepsilon = \frac{-q_1 + q_2}{2} \times \frac{2}{le} = \frac{-q_1 + q_2}{le}$$

The above equation can be written in matrix form as

$$\varepsilon \, E = Bq \text{ and is called element strain displacement matrix (4.6)}$$

$$\text{where } B = \frac{1}{le}\begin{bmatrix} -1 & 1 \end{bmatrix}$$

$$\text{and } q = \begin{bmatrix} q_1 \\ q_2 \end{bmatrix}$$

It can be observed that B is a constant matrix, hence there is constant strain within the element. Stress developed within the element can be found by using Hook's Law as

$$\sigma = E \, B \, q$$

where E is Young's Modulus of elasticity.

The above expression gives inference that the stress developed within the element is also constant.

4.4.3   ELEMENT STIFFNESS MATRIX

For linear elastic materials, the strain energy per unit volume in the body is given by:

$$S\,E = \frac{1}{2} \times \text{ stress } \times \text{ strain}$$

$$= \frac{1}{2} \sigma^T \varepsilon$$

and total strain energy *TSE* is given by

$$TSE = \frac{1}{2}\int_v \sigma^T \varepsilon \, dv$$

Substituting the value of stress as $\sigma = EE$ and $dV = A \, dx$, the above expression becomes

$$TSE = \frac{1}{2}\int_{le} (E\varepsilon)^T \varepsilon \, A \, dx$$

But from Equation (4.6), $E = Bq$

$$\therefore TSE = \frac{1}{2}\int_{le} (EBq)^T B q \, Adx$$

$$= \frac{1}{2}\int_{le} Eq^T B^T B q \, Adx$$

$$= \frac{1}{2}q^T \left(B^T BEA \int_{le} dx \right) q$$

Substituting the value of B in above expression

$$TSE = \frac{1}{2}q^T \left(\frac{1}{le}\begin{Bmatrix} -1 \\ 1 \end{Bmatrix}\frac{1}{le}\begin{bmatrix} -1 & 1 \end{bmatrix} EA \, le \right) q$$

$$= \frac{1}{2}q^T \left(\frac{EA}{le}\begin{bmatrix} 1 & -1 \\ -1 & 1 \end{bmatrix} \right) q$$

The above equation is of the form $TSE = \frac{1}{2}q^T Keq$

where $Ke = \frac{EA}{le}\begin{bmatrix} 1 & -1 \\ -1 & 1 \end{bmatrix}$ is called element ***stiffness matrix***

4.4.4 ELEMENTAL BODY FORCE MATRIX

The potential energy due to body force is given by the expression $PE_B = \int_{le} U^T fA \, dx$
    where f = Body force per unit volume
    A is the cross-sectional area and
    U is the displacement of a point on the body.
    Now Equation (4.1) substituting $u = N_1 q_1 + N_2 q_2$

$$P.\,E_B = \int_{le} (N_1 q_1 + N_2 q_2) fA \, dx$$

$$= fA\int_{le} N_1 q_1 dx + fA\int_{le} N_2 q_2 \, dx \qquad (4.7)$$

$$= fAq_1\int_{le} N_1 dx + fAq_2\int N_2 \, dx$$

We already know that

$$\int N_1 \, dx = \int \frac{1-\xi}{2}dx$$

and

$$\xi = \frac{2(x - x_1)}{x_2 - x_1} - 1 \Rightarrow \frac{d\xi}{dx} = \frac{2}{le}$$

$$dx = \frac{le}{2} d\xi$$

$\therefore$

$$\int N_1 dx = \int_{-1}^{1} \frac{1 - \xi}{2} \times \frac{le}{2} d\xi$$

$$= \frac{le}{2} \left[\frac{\xi}{2} - \frac{\xi^2}{4} \right]_{-1}^{1} = \frac{le}{2}$$

Likewise, $\int N_2 dx = \dfrac{le}{2}$

$\therefore$ From Equation (4.7) potential energy due to body force is P given by

$$P.\, E_B = f\, A\, q_1 \frac{le}{2} + f\, A\, q_2 \frac{le}{2}$$

This equation can be written in matrix form as

$$P.\, E_B = q^T f_e$$

$$\text{Where } q^T = \begin{bmatrix} q_1 & q_2 \end{bmatrix}$$

and $f^e = \dfrac{fAle}{2} \begin{Bmatrix} 1 \\ 1 \end{Bmatrix}$, is called element body force matrix.

Note that the body force is distributed equally over the two nodes.

4.4.5 ELEMENTAL TRACTION FORCE MATRIX

The potential energy due to traction force is given by

$$P.E_T = \int_{le} U^T T\, dx = \int (N_1 q_1 + N_2 q_2) T\, dx$$

$$= T\, q_1 \int N_1 dx + T q_2 \int N_2 dx = q_1\, T \frac{le}{2} + q_2\, T \frac{le}{2}$$

$$= q^T T_e \text{ (Matrix form)}$$

where $T_e = \dfrac{Tle}{2} \begin{Bmatrix} 1 \\ 1 \end{Bmatrix}$, is called elemental traction force matrix.

Again, it can be noted that the traction force is distributed equally over the two nodes. The expression for total potential energy for the element can be written as

$$P.E = \frac{1}{2} q^T K_e q - q^T f^e - q^T T^e - u_i P_i$$

When using principal of minimum potential energy, differentiating with respect to qt and equating to zero, it can be written as

$$Kq = f e + T_e + P_i$$

The above equation defines the forces acting on the element which can also be written in matrix form as

$$[K] [Q] = [F]$$

where $[K]$ is called the global *stiffness matrix*
$[Q]$ is called the global *displacement matrix*
and $[F]$ is called the global *force matrix*.

4.4.6 GLOBAL STIFFNESS MATRIX

The global stiffness matrix which represents the entire contanium can be generated by assembling the element stiffness matrix for each element. This procedure of assembling the element stiffness matrix can be understood by taking example of a stepped bar as shown in Figure 4.9.

The bar is discretised into three elements numbered (1), (2) and (3). A node has been provided at each step as well as at the two extreme ends of the bar.

We have already proved that element stiffness matrix for an element is given by

$$Ke = \frac{EA}{le}\begin{bmatrix} 1 & -1 \\ -1 & 1 \end{bmatrix}$$

Since there are four nodes, the order of global stiffness matrix will be 4×4.

Hence, a stiffness matrix for element 1 having nodes 1 and 2 can be written in form of 4×4 matrix as

$$Ke_1 = \frac{E_1 A_1}{le_1}\begin{bmatrix} & 1 & 2 & 3 & 4 \\ 1 & -1 & 0 & 0 \\ -1 & 1 & 0 & 0 \\ 0 & 0 & 0 & 0 \\ 0 & 0 & 0 & 0 \end{bmatrix}_1 \text{GLOBAL D.O.F.}$$

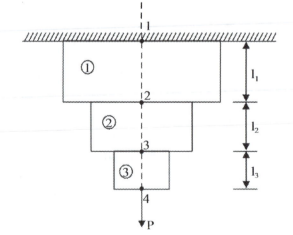

FIGURE 4.9 Global stiffness matrix.

Likewise, stiffness matrix for element 2 having nodes 2 and 3 can be written as

$$Ke_2 = \frac{E_2 A_2}{le_2} \begin{bmatrix} 0 & 2 & 3 & 4 \\ 0 & 1 & -1 & 0 \\ 0 & -1 & 1 & 0 \\ 0 & 0 & 0 & 0 \end{bmatrix}$$

Stiffness matrix for element 3 having nodes 3 and 4 becomes

$$Ke_3 = \frac{E_3 A_3}{le_3} \begin{bmatrix} 0 & 0 & 0 & 0 \\ 0 & 0 & 0 & 0 \\ 0 & 0 & 1 & -1 \\ 0 & 0 & -1 & 1 \end{bmatrix}$$

Now global stiffness matrix k is given by

$$K = Ke_1 + Ke_2 + Ke_3$$

$$K = \begin{bmatrix} \dfrac{A_1 E_1}{le_1} & \dfrac{-A_1 E_1}{le_1} & 0 & 0 \\ \dfrac{-A_1 E_1}{le_1} & \dfrac{A_1 E_1}{le_1} & 0 & 0 \\ 0 & 0 & 0 & 0 \\ 0 & 0 & 0 & 0 \end{bmatrix} + \begin{bmatrix} 0 & 0 & 0 & 0 \\ 0 & \dfrac{A_2 E_2}{le_2} & \dfrac{-A_2 E_2}{le_2} & 0 \\ 0 & \dfrac{-A_2 E_2}{le_2} & \dfrac{A_2 E_2}{le_2} & 0 \\ 0 & 0 & 0 & 0 \end{bmatrix} + \begin{bmatrix} 0 & 0 & 0 & 0 \\ 0 & 0 & 0 & 0 \\ 0 & 0 & \dfrac{A_3 E_3}{le_3} & \dfrac{-A_3 E_3}{le_3} \\ 0 & 0 & \dfrac{-A_3 E_3}{le_3} & \dfrac{A_3 E_3}{le_3} \end{bmatrix}$$

$$K = \begin{bmatrix} \dfrac{A_1 E_1}{le_1} & \dfrac{-A_1 E_1}{le_1} & 0 & 0 \\ \dfrac{-A_1 E_1}{le_1} & \dfrac{A_1 E_1}{le_1} + \dfrac{A_2 E_2}{le_2} & \dfrac{-A_2 E_2}{le_2} & 0 \\ 0 & \dfrac{-A_2 E_2}{le_2} & \dfrac{A_2 E_2}{le_2} + \dfrac{A_3 E_3}{le_3} & \dfrac{-A_3 E_3}{le_3} \\ 0 & 0 & \dfrac{-A_3 E_3}{le_3} & \dfrac{A_3 E_3}{le_3} \end{bmatrix}$$

4.4.7 GLOBAL FORCE MATRIX

If f is the body force acting per unit volume and T is the traction force per unit length, global four matrix for the stepped bar shown in Figure 4.9 will be a 4×1 matrix that can be written as

$$F = \begin{bmatrix} \dfrac{f_1 A_1 le_1}{2} + \dfrac{T le_1}{2} + R_1 \\ \dfrac{f_1 A_1 le_1}{2} + \dfrac{f_2 A_2 le_2}{2} + \dfrac{T le_1}{2} + \dfrac{T le_2}{2} \\ \dfrac{f_2 A_2 le_2}{2} + \dfrac{f_3 A_3 le_3}{2} + \dfrac{T le_2}{2} + \dfrac{T le_3}{2} \\ \dfrac{f_3 A_3 le_3}{2} + \dfrac{T le_3}{2} + P \end{bmatrix} = \begin{bmatrix} F_1 + R_1 \\ F_2 \\ F_3 \\ F_4 \end{bmatrix} \quad (\text{assumption})$$

Note that the body force (*fAle*) and traction force (*Tle*) acting over each element is divided into two equal parts, one part each being applied at each of the two nodes of the element.

Here f_1, f_2, f_3 represent body force per unit volume of elements 1, 2 and 3 respectively.

R_1 is the reaction force at node 1 and T is the traction force.

Now using equation $[K][Q] = [F]$ for the stepped bar shown in Figure 4.9

$$F = \begin{bmatrix} \dfrac{A_1 E_1}{le_1} & \dfrac{-A_1 E_1}{le_1} & 0 & 0 \\[2ex] \dfrac{-A_1 E_1}{le_1} & \dfrac{A_1 E_1}{le_1} + \dfrac{A_2 E_2}{le_2} & \dfrac{-A_2 E_2}{le_2} & 0 \\[2ex] 0 & \dfrac{-A_2 E_2}{le_2} & \dfrac{A_2 E_2}{le_2} + \dfrac{A_3 E_3}{le_3} & \dfrac{-A_3 E_3}{le_3} \\[2ex] 0 & 0 & \dfrac{-A_3 E_3}{le_3} & \dfrac{A_3 E_3}{le_3} \end{bmatrix} \begin{bmatrix} Q_1 \\ Q_2 \\ Q_3 \\ Q_4 \end{bmatrix} = \begin{bmatrix} F_1 + R_1 \\ F_2 \\ F_3 \\ F_4 \end{bmatrix}$$

Applying boundary condition $Q_1 = 0$, and solving the above matrix for Q_1, Q_3 and Q_4 using the Gauss elimination method, the first row and first column of the above matrix can be eliminated to solve the remaining matrix. Let the above equation be written as

$$\begin{bmatrix} K_{11} & K_{12} & K_{13} & K_{14} \\ K_{21} & K_{22} & K_{23} & K_{24} \\ K_{31} & K_{32} & K_{33} & K_{34} \\ K_{41} & K_{42} & K_{43} & K_{44} \end{bmatrix} \begin{bmatrix} Q_1 \\ Q_2 \\ Q_3 \\ Q_4 \end{bmatrix} = \begin{bmatrix} F_1 + R_1 \\ F_2 \\ F_3 \\ F_4 \end{bmatrix}$$

Then by using the Gauss elimination approach, the remaining matrix is

$$\begin{bmatrix} K_{22} & K_{23} & K_{24} \\ K_{32} & K_{33} & K_{34} \\ K_{42} & K_{43} & K_{44} \end{bmatrix} \begin{bmatrix} Q_2 \\ Q_3 \\ Q_4 \end{bmatrix} = \begin{bmatrix} F_2 \\ F_3 \\ F_4 \end{bmatrix}$$

The three equations in matrix form can be solved to find the value of displacement at nodes 2, 3 and 4 (i.e., Q_2, Q_3 and Q_4 respectively).

The strain in any element can be found out using expression

$$E = B\,q$$

$$\varepsilon = \frac{1}{le}\begin{bmatrix} -1 & 1 \end{bmatrix}\begin{bmatrix} Q_x \\ Q_y \end{bmatrix}$$

Stress in the element *i* given by

$$\sigma = E\varepsilon = EBq$$

$$= \frac{E}{le}\begin{bmatrix} -1 & 1 \end{bmatrix}\begin{bmatrix} Q_x \\ Q_y \end{bmatrix}$$

where E = Young's modulus of elasticity, Q_x and Q_y are the displacement at the two extreme nodes of the element.

Once the value of Q_2, Q_3 and Q_4 have been calculated, the value of reaction R acting at node 1 can be calculated by using the first row of equation $[K][Q] = [F]$

$$K_{11}\,Q_1 + K_{12}\,Q_2 + K_{13}\,Q_3 + K_{14}\,Q_4 = F_1 + R_1$$

4.4.8 STEPS FOR SOLVING ONE-DIMENSIONAL PROBLEMS

1. Discretise the body.
2. Consider the forces acting on the body. In cases where the body is vertical, the body force must be considered while it can be neglected in cases of a horizontal body. The traction force is only considered when its value is given.

    Note: (A) Whenever the point force is acting over the continuum, a node must be provided at the point of application of force while discretisation.

    (B) Whenever the element has varying cross-sectional area, the discretisation has to be effected by dividing the body into elements with constant cross-sectional area.
3. Form element stiffness matrix for each element.
4. Assemble element stiffness matrices to form the global stiffness matrix.
5. Use the Gauss elimination approach to solve displacement at the nodes.
6. Find strain and calculate stress developed in the elements.

4.5 TWO-DIMENSIONAL PROBLEMS

The finite element analysis of two-dimensional trusses is presented in this section. A two-dimensional truss is shown in Figure 4.10.

LO 3. To understand 2D problems in finite element stress analysis

All loads and reactions must be considered to function purely at the joints when resolving a truss problem. In addition, it is expected that frictionless pin joints connect all of the truss members at their terminals. Each member of the truss can be considered as a finite element and each joint can be considered as a node.

Using the finite element method, one may calculate displacement at joints (nodes), stress in each element, response force calculations, etc. In the global coordinate system, each node has two degrees of freedom, one in each of the global x and y directions.

4.5.1 LOCAL AND GLOBAL COORDINATE SYSTEMS

Unlike one-dimensional structures, two-dimensional trusses, also called plane trusses, have members with various orientations. The finite element approach may be used to estimate the displacement of joints (nodes), the stress in each element and the computing of reaction forces, among other things. Every point in the global coordinate system has two degrees of freedom in relation to the global x and y axes.

A truss element is shown in Figure 4.11 with respect to the local and global coordinate system.

In the local coordinate system, the axis passes through the element running along its length. In the figure it is represented by x'. The nodes at the two extreme ends of this member are numbered 1 and 2 with respect to this x' axis.

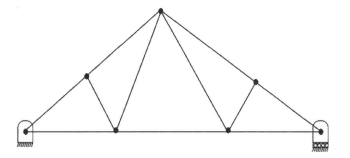

FIGURE 4.10 A two-dimensional truss

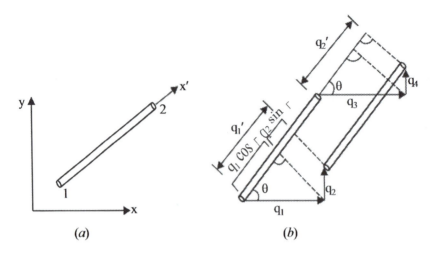

FIGURE 4.11   Two-dimensional truss element. (a) In local co-ordinate system. (b) In global co-ordinate system

From the figure, it can be observed that

$$q_1' = q_1 \cos \theta + q_2 \sin \theta \qquad\qquad (4.8)$$

$$q_2' = q_3 \cos \theta + q_4 \sin \theta \qquad\qquad (4.9)$$

where q'_1 and q'_2 are the displacement of nodes 1 and 2 in a local coordinate system and q_1, q_2, q_3 and q_4 are the displacement of nodes in global coordinate system.

It is known that the direction cosines l and m are defined as $l = \cos \theta$, $m = \sin \theta$. Therefore, the above equations can be written as

$$q_1' = q_1 \times l + q_2 \times m$$

$$q_2' = q_3 \times l + q_4 \times m$$

Now these equations can be written in matrix form as

$$\begin{bmatrix} q_1' \\ q_2' \end{bmatrix} = \begin{bmatrix} l & m & 0 & 0 \\ 0 & 0 & l & m \end{bmatrix} \begin{bmatrix} q_1 \\ q_2 \\ q_3 \\ q_4 \end{bmatrix}$$

$$i.e. \quad q' = L \quad q$$

where $l = \begin{bmatrix} l & m & 0 & 0 \\ 0 & 0 & l & m \end{bmatrix}$ is called a transformation matrix.

To determine direction cosines l and m, consider an element of length le as shown in Figure 4.12.

$$\text{Then } l = \cos \theta = \frac{x_2 - x_1}{le}$$

$$m = \sin \theta = \frac{y_2 - y_1}{le}$$

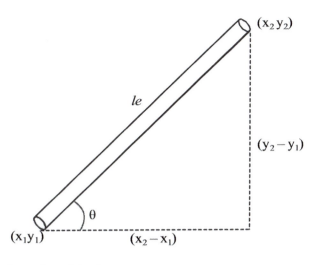

FIGURE 4.12 Direction cosines of the element

Note that θ is the angle between local x' axis and global x axis at node 1 of the element. Angle θ is positive in anticlockwise direction.

4.5.2 ELEMENT STIFFNESS MATRIX

The truss element in a local coordinate system is a one-dimensional form. Because of this discovery, we may use previously published one-dimensional element results. This indicates that the local coordinate system truss element stiffness matrix is given by

$$K = \frac{EA}{le}\begin{bmatrix} 1 & -1 \\ -1 & 1 \end{bmatrix}$$

where E is the Young's modulus and A is the element cross-sectional area.

To generate element stiffness matrix in global coordinates, consider the strain energy in the element. Strain energy in local coordinates is given by

$$SE = \frac{1}{2}q'^T K' q'$$

Substituting $q' = Lq$ in the above equation, we get

$$SE = \frac{1}{2}q^T \begin{bmatrix} L^T & K' & L \end{bmatrix} q$$

Strain energy in global coordinates is written as

$$Ue = \frac{1}{2}q^T K q$$

where K is element stiffness matrix in global coordinates. Hence,

$$K = LT\,K'L$$

i.e. $K = \begin{bmatrix} l & 0 \\ m & 0 \\ 0 & l \\ 0 & m \end{bmatrix} \times \frac{EA}{le}\begin{bmatrix} 1 & -1 \\ -1 & 1 \end{bmatrix} \times \begin{bmatrix} l & m & 0 & 0 \\ 0 & 0 & l & m \end{bmatrix}$

$$K = \frac{EA}{le} \begin{bmatrix} l^2 & lm & -l^2 & -lm \\ lm & m^2 & -lm & -m^2 \\ -l^2 & -lm & l^2 & lm \\ -lm & -m^2 & lm & m^2 \end{bmatrix}$$

The above expression gives the element stiffness matrix for a plane truss in a global coordinate system.

4.5.3 STRESS AND STRAIN CALCULATION IN TRUSS ELEMENTS

Strain in a truss element is given by change in length per unit original length.

$$\text{i.e. } Strain\,\varepsilon = \frac{q_2' - q_1'}{le}$$

$$\text{In matrix form } \varepsilon = \frac{1}{le}\begin{bmatrix} -1 & 1 \end{bmatrix}\begin{bmatrix} q_1' \\ q_2' \end{bmatrix}$$

But $q' = Lq$

$$\text{Therefor } \varepsilon = \frac{1}{le}\begin{bmatrix} -1 & 1 \end{bmatrix}Lq$$

$$\varepsilon = \frac{1}{le}\begin{bmatrix} -1 & 1 \end{bmatrix}\begin{bmatrix} l & m & 0 & 0 \\ 0 & 0 & l & m \end{bmatrix}q$$

$$\varepsilon = \frac{1}{le}\begin{bmatrix} -l & -m & l & m \end{bmatrix}q$$

Strain in a truss element is given by change in length per unit original length.

Example 4.1: *The figure shows stepped bar bearing a load of 500 N. Use the principal of minimum potential energy to determine the displacement at the nodes. Find the strain in each of the elements. (Length and area of cross section are indicated in Figure 4.13.)*
    Solution:
    Discretisation: Discretising the complete part into elements (say (1) and (2)) (Figure 4.14 and
        Figure 4.15) let $l_1 = l_2 = l$

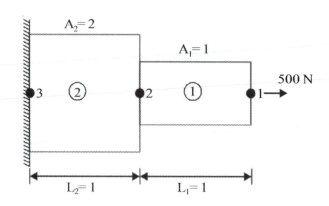

FIGURE 4.13 Stepped bar

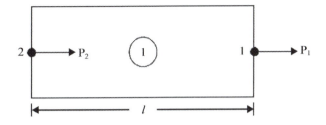

FIGURE 4.14　Element 1

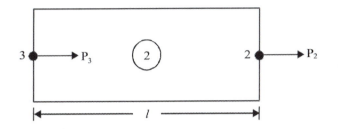

FIGURE 4.15　Element 2

- Let A_1 = area of element (1) and A_2 = area of element (2)

Let displacement of node 1 = x_1
and displacement of node 2 = x_2

- Let P_1 and P_2 represent external forces acting at nodes 1 and 2 respectively.

1 and 2 are local nodes of element (1) Let stiffness of element (1) = k
　Then

$$\text{Stress = Young's Modulus} \times \text{Strain}$$

$$\text{or } \frac{\text{Force}}{\text{Area}} = E \times \frac{\Delta l}{l} \Rightarrow \text{Force } = E \times \text{ Area } \times \frac{\Delta l}{l}$$

Applying the above equation for nodes (1) and (2)
　For node (1):

$$\frac{EA_1}{l} \times \Delta l = P_1$$

$$\text{or } \frac{EA_1}{l}\left(x_1 - x_2\right) = P_1 \tag{4.10}$$

$$\text{For node }(2): \ \frac{EA_1}{l}\left(x_2 - x_1\right) = P_2 \tag{4.11}$$

Writing equations (4.10) and (4.11) in matrix:

$$\frac{EA_1}{l}\begin{bmatrix} 1 & -1 \\ -1 & 1 \end{bmatrix}\begin{bmatrix} x_1 \\ x_2 \end{bmatrix} = \begin{bmatrix} P_1 \\ P_2 \end{bmatrix}$$

Here $\dfrac{EA_1}{l}\begin{bmatrix} 1 & -1 \\ -1 & 1 \end{bmatrix}$ is called element stiffness matrix $\begin{bmatrix} x_1 \\ x_2 \end{bmatrix}$ is called displacement matrix

$\begin{bmatrix} P_1 \\ P_2 \end{bmatrix}$ represents the force matrix

Analysing element (2):

Displacement of node (2) = x_2
Displacement of node (3) = x_3
P_2 and P_3 are the forces acting on nodes (2) and (3) respectively.

Note: For element (2), global node (2) is local node (1) and global node (3) is local node 2.
Hence,
For node (1) (i.e., global node (2))

$$\frac{EA_2}{l}\left(x_2 - x_3\right) = P_2 \tag{4.12}$$

For node 2 (i.e., global node (3))

$$\frac{EA_2}{l}\left(x_3 - x_2\right) = P_3 \tag{4.13}$$

Writing Equations (4.12) and (4.13) in matrix form

$$\frac{EA_2}{l}\begin{bmatrix} 1 & -1 \\ -1 & 1 \end{bmatrix}\begin{bmatrix} x_2 \\ x_3 \end{bmatrix} = \begin{bmatrix} P_2 \\ P_3 \end{bmatrix}$$

Now, the equation for global node (1) can be written as

$$\frac{EA_1}{l}\left(u_1 - u_2 + ou_3\right) = P_1 \tag{4.14}$$

Equation for global node (2) can be written as

$$\frac{EA_1}{l}\left(x_2 - x_1\right) + \frac{EA_2}{l}\left(x_2 - x_3\right) = 2P_2$$

But $A_2 = 2A_1$

$$\therefore \quad \frac{EA_1}{l}\left(x_2 - x_1\right) + \frac{E(2A_1)}{l}\left(x_2 - x_3\right) = 2P_2$$

$$\Rightarrow \quad \frac{EA_1}{l}\left(-x_1 + 3x_2 - 2x_3\right) = 2P_2 \tag{4.15}$$

Similarly, the equation for global node (3) can be written as

$$\frac{2A_1E}{l}\left(0x_1 - x_2 + x_3\right) = P_3 \tag{4.16}$$

$$\frac{A_1E}{l}\left(0x_1 - 2x_2 + 2x_3\right) = P_3$$

Equations (4.14), (4.15) and (4.16) can be written in matrix form as

$$\frac{EA_1}{l}\begin{bmatrix} 1 & -1 & 0 \\ -1 & 3 & -2 \\ 0 & -2 & 2 \end{bmatrix}\begin{bmatrix} x_1 \\ x_2 \\ x_3 \end{bmatrix} = \begin{bmatrix} P_1 \\ 2p_2 \\ P_3 \end{bmatrix}$$

Applying boundary conditions
   (*i*) Node (3) is fixed, therefore displacement at node (3) = x_3 = 0. Now P_1 = 500
P_2 = 0 (No force acting at node (2))
P_3 = R (Reaction force)
Thus, we have

$$\frac{EA_1}{l}\begin{bmatrix} 1 & -1 & 0 \\ -1 & 3 & -2 \\ 0 & -2 & 2 \end{bmatrix}\begin{bmatrix} x_1 \\ x_2 \\ 0 \end{bmatrix} = \begin{bmatrix} 500 \\ 0 \\ R \end{bmatrix}$$

By applying elimination approach, the third row and third column can be eliminated

$$\therefore \quad \frac{EA_1}{l}\begin{bmatrix} 1 & -1 & 0 \\ -1 & 3 & -2 \\ 0 & -2 & 2 \end{bmatrix}\begin{bmatrix} x_1 \\ x_2 \\ 0 \end{bmatrix} = \begin{bmatrix} 500 \\ 0 \\ R \end{bmatrix}$$

Hence, the equation reduces to the form

$$\frac{EA_1}{l}\begin{bmatrix} 1 & -1 \\ -1 & 3 \end{bmatrix}\begin{bmatrix} x_1 \\ x_2 \end{bmatrix} = \begin{bmatrix} 500 \\ 0 \end{bmatrix}$$

The nodal displacements x_1 and x_2 at nodes (1) and (2) respectively can be calculated from the above equation.
   To determine strain (E) in elements (1) and (2):

Strain in element (1) = $\varepsilon_1 = \dfrac{x_1 - x_2}{l}$

Strain in element (2) = $\varepsilon_2 = \dfrac{x_2 - x_3}{l}$ to determine stress(es) in elements (1) and (2): Stress in element (1) = $\sigma_1 = E \times E_1$
   Stress in element (2) = $\sigma_2 = E \times E_2$

Example 4.2: *For the axially loaded member shown in Figure 4.16, determine the nodal displacements:*
   Given that:

   Area of aluminium rod = 39 × 10−4 m2
   Area of brass rod = 13 × 10−4 m2
   Modulus of Elasticity, E_{Al} = 70 GPa
   Modulus of Elasticity, E_{Brass} = 100 GPa
   Axial load, P_2 = 280 kN
   Axial load, P_3 = 100 kN

SOLUTION:

Step 1: Discretise the bar into two elements as shown in Figure 4.16.
Step 2: The element stiffness matrixes are

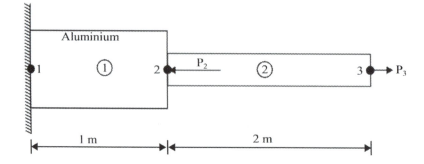

FIGURE 4.16 axially loaded member

$$k_1 = \frac{E_1 A_1}{l_1}\begin{bmatrix} 1 & -1 \\ -1 & 1 \end{bmatrix} = \frac{70 \times 10^9 \times 39 \times 10^{-4}}{1}\begin{bmatrix} 1 & -1 \\ -1 & 1 \end{bmatrix}$$

$$= 2.73 \times 10^8 \begin{bmatrix} 1 & -1 \\ -1 & 1 \end{bmatrix}$$

$$k_2 = \frac{E_2 A_2}{l_2}\begin{bmatrix} 1 & -1 \\ -1 & 1 \end{bmatrix}$$

$$= \frac{100 \times 10^9 \times 13 \times 10^{-4}}{2}\begin{bmatrix} 1 & -1 \\ -1 & 1 \end{bmatrix}$$

$$= 0.65 \times 10^8 \begin{bmatrix} 1 & -1 \\ -1 & 1 \end{bmatrix}$$

Step 3: Assemble element stiffness matrixes k_1 and k_2 to form global stiffness matrix k

$$k = \begin{bmatrix} k_1 & -k_1 & 0 \\ -k_1 & k_1 + k_2 & -k_2 \\ 0 & -k_2 & k_2 \end{bmatrix}$$

Step 4: Applying $[F] = [k][x]$

$$10^8 \begin{bmatrix} 2.73 & -2.73 & 0 \\ -2.73 & 2.73 + 0.65 & -0.65 \\ 0 & -0.65 & 0.65 \end{bmatrix}\begin{bmatrix} x_1 \\ x_2 \\ x_3 \end{bmatrix}\begin{bmatrix} 0 \\ -280 \times 10^3 \\ 100 \times 10^3 \end{bmatrix}$$

The boundary condition is $x_1 = 0$, using the elimination approach the above matrix equation will reduce to

$$10^8 \begin{bmatrix} 3.38 & -0.65 \\ -0.65 & 0.65 \end{bmatrix}\begin{bmatrix} x_2 \\ x_3 \end{bmatrix}\begin{bmatrix} -280 \times 10^3 \\ 100 \times 10^3 \end{bmatrix}$$

On solving we get $x_2 = 0.66$ mm and $x_3 = 0.57$ mm. Hence, the nodal displacement is given by $x_1 = 0$, $x_2 = -0.66$ mm and $x_3 = 0.57$ mm.

Example 4.3: *Consider the bar shown in Figure 4.17. An axial load of 15 kN is applied as shown in the Figure 4.17.*

(1) *Determine the displacement at each node.*

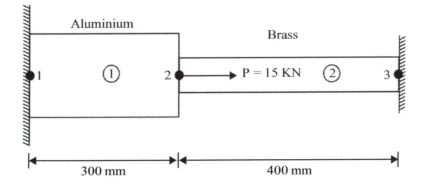

FIGURE 4.17 Stepped bar of Aluminium and Brass

(2) *Determine the stress in each element and the reaction at the fixed ends.*

The area of cross-section and Young's modulus are given in the following table.

Material	Area of Cross-Section	Young's Modulus
For aluminium section	600 mm2	70 GPa
For brass section	300 mm3	83 GPa

SOLUTION:

Step 1: Discretising the bar into two elements with one node each at the fixed ends and one node at the change in cross-section.

Step 2: The element stiffness matrices are

$$k_1 = \frac{E_1 A_1}{l_1}\begin{bmatrix} 1 & -1 \\ -1 & 1 \end{bmatrix} = \frac{70 \times 10^3 \times 600}{300}\begin{bmatrix} 1 & -1 \\ -1 & 1 \end{bmatrix}$$

$$k_2 = \frac{E_2 A_2}{l_2}\begin{bmatrix} 1 & -1 \\ -1 & 1 \end{bmatrix} = \frac{83 \times 10^3 \times 300}{400}\begin{bmatrix} 1 & -1 \\ -1 & 1 \end{bmatrix}$$

The global stiffness matrix that is assembled from k_1 and k_2 is

$$\text{The global load vector is } F = \begin{bmatrix} 0 \\ 15000 \\ 0 \end{bmatrix}$$

Step 3: We know that $[F] = [K] \times [x]$

$$\therefore \quad 10^3 \times \begin{bmatrix} 140 & -140 & 0 \\ -140 & 202.25 & -62.25 \\ 0 & -62.25 & 62.25 \end{bmatrix}\begin{bmatrix} x_1 \\ x_2 \\ x_3 \end{bmatrix} = \begin{bmatrix} R_1 \\ 15000 \\ R_3 \end{bmatrix}$$

where R_1 and R_3 are reactions at nodes (1) and (3) applying boundary conditions
$x_1 = 0$ and $x_3 = 0$

By the method of elimination of rows and columns for $x_1 = 0$ and $x_3 = 0$, the above matrix is reduced to the form

$$103 \times [202.25] \times [X_2] = [15000]$$

$\therefore x_2 = 0.0742$ mm

Hence the nodal displacement matrix is

$$[x] = \begin{bmatrix} 0 \\ 0.0742 \\ 0 \end{bmatrix}$$

The displacement at nodes (1) and (3) is zero while at node (2) it is 0.0742 mm.

Step 4: Stress calculation force in element (1), $F_1 = k_1(x_2 - x_1) = \dfrac{E_1 A_1}{l_1}(x_2 - x_1)$

Stress in element (1)

$$\sigma_1 = \frac{E_1}{l_1}(x_2 - x_1) = \frac{70 \times 10^3}{300}(.0742 - 0)$$

Stress in element (2)

$\sigma_1 = 16.8$ MPa (tensile)

$$\sigma_2 = \frac{E_2}{l_2}(x_3 - x_2) = \frac{83 \times 10^3}{400}(0 - .0742)$$

$\sigma_2 = -15.39$ MPa $= 15.39$ MPa (Compressive)

Step 5: To find reactions at fixed ends:

$$10^3 \times \begin{bmatrix} 140 & -140 & 0 \\ -140 & 202.25 & -62.25 \\ 0 & -62.25 & 62.25 \end{bmatrix} \begin{bmatrix} 0 \\ 0.0742 \\ 0 \end{bmatrix} = \begin{bmatrix} R_1 \\ 15000 \\ R_3 \end{bmatrix}$$

$\therefore$ Reaction at node (1) (R_1):

$$R_1 = 10^3 \times \begin{bmatrix} 140 & -140 & 0 \end{bmatrix} \times \begin{bmatrix} 0 \\ 0.0742 \\ 0 \end{bmatrix}$$

$R_1 = -10.388 \times 10^3$ N $= -10.388$ kN

Reaction at node (3) (R_3):

$$R_3 = 10^3 \times \begin{bmatrix} 0 & -62.25 & 62.25 \end{bmatrix} \times \begin{bmatrix} 0 \\ 0.0742 \\ 0 \end{bmatrix}$$

$$R_3 = -4618.95\,\text{N} = -4.618\text{kN}$$

Example 4.4: *Consider the metaphorical step ladder (Figure 4.18). As an example, suppose we apply a load of P = 200 kN. Determine the node displacements, element stresses, and support responses. Use elimination approach for boundary conditions. Take E = 2 × 105 N/mm2.*

Solution:

Step 1 Discretisation of the bar.

We discretise the bar into two elements as shown in the Figure 4.19.

Step: Element stiffness matrix.

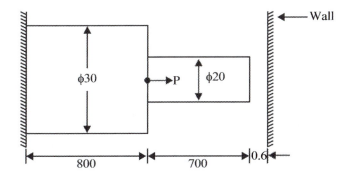

FIGURE 4.18   Metaphorical step ladder

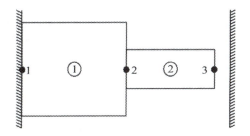

FIGURE 4.19   Two elements of the step ladder

For element (1) k_1

$$k_1 = \frac{E_1 A_1}{l_1}\begin{bmatrix} 1 & -1 \\ -1 & 1 \end{bmatrix} = \frac{2 \times 10^5 \times \frac{\pi}{4}(30)^2}{800}\begin{bmatrix} 1 & -1 \\ -1 & 1 \end{bmatrix}$$

$$= 10^5\begin{bmatrix} 1.766 & -1.766 \\ -1.766 & 1.766 \end{bmatrix}$$

For element (2) k_2,

$$k_2 = \frac{E_2 A_2}{l_2}\begin{bmatrix} 1 & -1 \\ -1 & 1 \end{bmatrix}$$

$$= \frac{2 \times 10^5 \times \frac{\pi}{4} \times 20^2}{700}\begin{bmatrix} 1 & -1 \\ -1 & 1 \end{bmatrix} = 10^5 \times \begin{matrix} & 2 & 3 \\ & \begin{bmatrix} 0.897 & -0.897 \\ -0.897 & 0.897 \end{bmatrix} \end{matrix}$$

Assemble matrix k_1 and k_2 to form global stiffness matrix k_G

$$[k_G] = 10^5\begin{bmatrix} 1.766 & -1.766 & 0 \\ -1.766 & 1.766 + 0.897 & -0.897 \\ 0 & -0.897 & 0.897 \end{bmatrix}$$

$$[k_G] = 10^5\begin{bmatrix} 1.766 & -1.766 & 0 \\ -1.766 & 2.663 & -0.897 \\ 0 & -0.897 & 0.897 \end{bmatrix}$$

Step 3: In this problem, we should first determine whether due to action of load P, contact occurs between the bar and the wall. To do this, assume that the wall does not exist, then find the displacement of node (3).

We know that

$$[K] \times [x] = [F]$$

$$10^5 \begin{bmatrix} 1.766 & -1.766 & 0 \\ -1.766 & 2.663 & -0.897 \\ 0 & -0.897 & 0.897 \end{bmatrix} \times \begin{bmatrix} x_1 \\ x_2 \\ x_3 \end{bmatrix} = \begin{bmatrix} R_1 \\ 200,000 \\ 0 \end{bmatrix}$$

Where R_1 is reaction at node (1)

In this case, the boundary condition is $x_1 = 0$. Hence using elimination approach

$$10^5 \begin{bmatrix} 2.663 & -0.897 \\ -0.897 & 0.897 \end{bmatrix} \times \begin{bmatrix} x_2 \\ x_3 \end{bmatrix} = \begin{bmatrix} 200,000 \\ 0 \end{bmatrix}$$

Solving the above set of matrices, we get

$x_2 = 1.132$ mm and $x_3 = 1.131$ mm

So, using the assumption that there is no wall to the right and node (3) is free to move under acting load, we get the displacement of node (3) = 1.131 mm.

But actually node (3) is not allowed to move more than 0.6 mm to its right due to presence of a wall. Hence, the actual boundary conditions are

$x_1 = 0$

and $x_3 = 0.6$ mm

Hence, solving for nodal displacements again, using $[k] [x] = [F]$, we get

$$10^5 \begin{bmatrix} 1.766 & -1.766 & 0 \\ -1.766 & 2.663 & -0.897 \\ 0 & -0.897 & 0.897 \end{bmatrix} \times \begin{bmatrix} 0 \\ x_2 \\ 0.6 \end{bmatrix} = \begin{bmatrix} 0 \\ 200,000 \\ 0 \end{bmatrix}$$

On solving, we get $x_2 = 0.953$ Hence the nodal displacements are

$x_1 = 0$, $x_2 = 0.953$ mm and $x_3 = 0.60$ mm Nodal displacement matrix is

$$[x] = \begin{bmatrix} 0 \\ 0.953 \\ 0.60 \end{bmatrix}$$

Step 4: Stress calculation: Stress in element (1)

$$\text{Force} = \frac{E_1 A_1}{l_1} (x_2 - x_1)$$

$$\therefore \quad \text{Stress, } \sigma_1 = \frac{E_1}{l_1}(x_2 - x_1) = \frac{2 \times 10^5}{800}(0.953 - 0) = 237.5 \text{N} / \text{mm}^2 \text{ (Tensile)}$$

Stress in element (2)

$$\sigma_2 = \frac{E_2}{l_2}(x_3 - x_2) = \frac{2 \times 10^5}{700}(0.60 - 0.953) = -43.143 \text{N} / \text{mm}^2$$

$$\sigma_2 = 100.857 \text{N} / \text{mm}^2 \text{ (Compressive)}$$

Step 5: Reaction calculation :

$$10^5 \times \begin{bmatrix} 1.766 & -1.766 & 0 \\ -1.766 & 2.663 & -0.897 \\ 0 & -0.897 & 0.897 \end{bmatrix} \times \begin{bmatrix} 0 \\ 0.7510 \\ 0.60 \end{bmatrix} = \begin{bmatrix} R_1 \\ 200,000 \\ R_3 \end{bmatrix}$$

$\therefore$ Reaction at node (1), R_1:

$$R_1 = 10^5 \begin{bmatrix} 1.766 & -1.766 & 0 \end{bmatrix} \begin{bmatrix} 0 \\ 0.953 \\ 0.60 \end{bmatrix}$$

$R_1 = -1.6829 \times 10^5$ N $= -168.29$ kN
Reaction at node (3), R_3:

$$R_3 = 10^5 \begin{bmatrix} 0 & 0.897 & 0.897 \end{bmatrix} \begin{bmatrix} 0 \\ 0.953 \\ 0.60 \end{bmatrix}$$

$R_3 = 1.2118 \times 10^5$ N $= 139.304$ kN

Example 4.5: *For the bar in Figure 4.20, determine the nodal displacements, element stresses and support reactions. The cross-sectional areas are 250 mm2 and 400 mm2. Youngs modulus E = 200 × 109 N/m2.*

Solution:
$E = 200 \times 109$ N/m2 $= 200 \times 103$ N/mm2
Step 1: Discretisation of the bar
The stepped bar is discretised into three elements and four nodes as shown in Figure 4.21.
Step 2: Element stiffness matrix for element (1)

$$k_1 = \frac{E_1 A_1}{l_1} \begin{bmatrix} 1 & -1 \\ -1 & 1 \end{bmatrix} = \frac{200 \times 10^3 \times 250}{150} \begin{bmatrix} 1 & -1 \\ -1 & 1 \end{bmatrix}$$

$$= 3.33 \times 10^5 \begin{bmatrix} 1 & -1 \\ -1 & 1 \end{bmatrix}$$

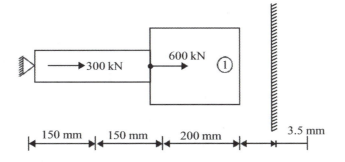

FIGURE 4.20   Stepped bar

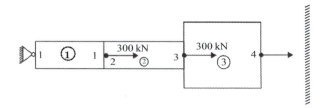

FIGURE 4.21   Three elements of stepped bar

For element (2)

$$k_2 = \frac{E_2 A_2}{l_2}\begin{bmatrix} 1 & -1 \\ -1 & 1 \end{bmatrix}$$

$$= \frac{200 \times 10^3 \times 250}{150}\begin{bmatrix} 1 & -1 \\ -1 & 1 \end{bmatrix} = 3.33 \times 10^5 \begin{bmatrix} 2 & 3 \\ -1 & 1 \end{bmatrix}$$

For element (3),
$$k_3 = \frac{E_3 A_3}{l_3}\begin{bmatrix} 1 & -1 \\ -1 & 1 \end{bmatrix}$$

$$= \frac{200 \times 10^3 \times 400}{200}\begin{bmatrix} 1 & -1 \\ -1 & 1 \end{bmatrix} = 4 \times 10^5 \begin{bmatrix} 1 & -1 \\ -1 & 1 \end{bmatrix}$$

Step 3: Assemble matrix k_1, k_2 and k_3 to form global stiffness matrix k_G

$$[K_G] = 10^5 \begin{bmatrix} 3.33 & -3.33 & 0 & 0 \\ -3.33 & (3.33 + 3.33) & -3.33 & 0 \\ 0 & -3.33 & (3.3314) & -4 \\ 0 & 0 & -4 & -4 \end{bmatrix}$$

Step 4: In this problem, we should first determine whether due to the action of loads, contact occurs between the bar and the wall or not. To find this, assume that the wall does not exist, then find the displacement of node (4).
We know that $[K_G][x] = [F]$

$$10^5 \begin{bmatrix} 3.33 & -3.33 & 0 & 0 \\ -3.33 & 6.66 & -3.33 & 0 \\ 0 & -3.33 & 7.33 & -4 \\ 0 & 0 & -4 & -4 \end{bmatrix}\begin{bmatrix} x_1 \\ x_2 \\ x_3 \\ x_4 \end{bmatrix} = \begin{bmatrix} R_1 \\ 300 \\ 400 \\ 0 \end{bmatrix}$$

Where R_1 is reaction at node (1).
Applying the boundary condition i.e., $x_1 = 0$ and using the elimination approach, the above matrix equation is reduced to the form

$$10^5 \begin{bmatrix} 6.66 & -3.33 & 0 \\ -3.33 & 7.33 & -4 \\ 0 & -4 & 4 \end{bmatrix}\begin{bmatrix} x_2 \\ x_3 \\ x_4 \end{bmatrix} = \begin{bmatrix} 300 \\ 400 \\ 0 \end{bmatrix} \times 10^3$$

On solving, we get $x_2 = 2.1$ mm, $x_3 = 3.3$ mm and $x_4 = 3.3$ mm.
Thus, the displacement of node (4) towards the right is only 3.3 mm. Under the action of loads, the bar will not touch the wall as the gap is 3.5mm. Hence, no reaction will develop at this end.

$$\text{Nodal displacement matrix is } \begin{bmatrix} 0 \\ 2.1 \\ 3.3 \\ 3.3 \end{bmatrix}$$

Step 5: Element stress calculation.
   Stress in element (1),

$$\sigma_1 = \frac{E}{l_1}(x_2 - x_1) = \frac{200 \times 10^3}{150}(2.1 - 0) = 2.8 \times 10^3 \text{ N} / \text{mm}^2$$

Stress in element (2),

$$\sigma_2 = \frac{E}{l_1}(x_3 - x_2) = \frac{200 \times 10^3}{150}(3.3 - 2.1) = 1.6 \times 10^3 \text{ N} / \text{mm}^2$$

Stress in element (3),

$$\sigma_3 = \frac{E}{l_3}(x_4 - x_3) = \frac{200 \times 10^3}{200}(3.3 - 3.3) = 0$$

Step 6: To find the support reaction at node (1)

$$R_1 = \begin{bmatrix} 3.33 & -3.33 & 0 & 0 \end{bmatrix} \begin{bmatrix} 0 \\ 2.1 \\ 3.3 \\ 3.3 \end{bmatrix} = -6.993 \times 10^5 \text{ N}$$

Example 4.6: *Consider the three-bar truss with pin joints as shown in Figure 4.22. It is given that E = 200 GPa and area of cross-section for all the three elements is 350 mm2. Treating each member as one-dimensional linear elements, determine:*

   (a) *Stiffness matrix for each element,*

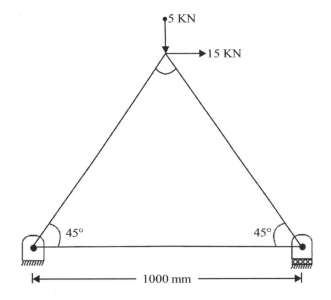

FIGURE 4.22   Three bar truss

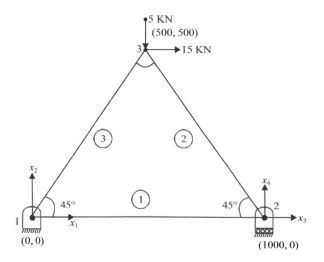

FIGURE 4.23   Three elements of three bar truss

(b) *Global stiffness matrix for the entire truss,*
(c) *Displacement at nodes,*
(d) *Stress in each member,*
(e) *Reaction at supports.*

Solution: (a) Discretising the truss into three elements and three nodes. Figure 4.23

(a) Generating a tabular form to represent coordinates of the nodes
(b) Generating an element connectivity table to represent relation between local nodes and global nodes

Element	Local	Node
	1	2
1	1	2
2	2	3
3	3	1

Note: The user may choose how components are interconnected. As an alternative to the above definition, element (2)'s connectivity may also be written as 3-2. When computing direction cosines, however, the selected connection approach must be accounted for. The angle that the element makes with the x axis at local node (1) is used to determine direction cosines for a particular element.

Hence, using the element connectivity table, we obtain the direction cosines table:

Element	θ	$L = \cos \theta$	$M = \sin \theta$
1	0°	1	0
2	135°	−0.707	0.707
3	225°	−0.707	−0.707

(For example, for element (3), the local node (1) is global node (3). The angle made by element (3) with the x axis at global node 3 is 225°. Hence, $l = -0.707$ and $m = -0.707$). For element 1, the element stiffness matrix can be written as, k_1

$$k_1 = \frac{EA_1}{l_e} \begin{bmatrix} l^2 & lm & -l^2 & -lm \\ lm & m^2 & -lm & -m^2 \\ -l^2 & -lm & l^2 & lm \\ -lm & -m^2 & lm & m^2 \end{bmatrix}$$

For element (1) $l = 1$, $m = 0$, $A = 350$ mm2, $le = 1000$ mm,
$E = 200\ GPa = 200 \times 103$ N/mm2

$$\therefore\quad k_1 = \frac{200 \times 10^3 \times 350}{1000} \begin{bmatrix} 1 & 0 & -1 & 0 \\ 0 & 0 & 0 & 0 \\ -1 & 0 & 1 & 0 \\ 0 & 0 & 0 & 0 \end{bmatrix}$$

$$k_1 = 70 \times 10^3 \begin{bmatrix} 1 & 0 & -1 & 0 \\ 0 & 0 & 0 & 0 \\ -1 & 0 & 1 & 0 \\ 0 & 0 & 0 & 0 \end{bmatrix}$$

Similarly for element (2), $l = -0.707$, $m = 0.707$, $le = 707.11$ mm
$E = 200 \times 103$ N/mm2, $A = 350$ mm2

$$\therefore\quad k_2 = \frac{200 \times 10^3 \times 350}{707.11} \begin{bmatrix} 0.5 & -0.5 & -0.5 & 0.5 \\ -0.5 & 0.5 & 0.5 & -0.5 \\ -0.5 & 0.5 & 0.5 & -0.5 \\ 0.5 & -0.5 & -0.5 & 0.5 \end{bmatrix}$$

$$= 99 \times 10^3 \begin{bmatrix} 0.5 & -0.5 & -0.5 & 0.5 \\ -0.5 & 0.5 & 0.5 & -0.5 \\ -0.5 & 0.5 & 0.5 & -0.5 \\ 0.5 & -0.5 & -0.5 & 0.5 \end{bmatrix}$$

Similarly, for element (3)

$$k_3 = 99 \times 10^3 \begin{bmatrix} 0.5 & 0.5 & -0.5 & -0.5 \\ 0.5 & 0.5 & -0.5 & -0.5 \\ -0.5 & -0.5 & 0.5 & 0.5 \\ -0.5 & -0.5 & 0.5 & 0.5 \end{bmatrix}$$

(b) Now, the stiffness matrices of the constituent parts are merged to generate the stiffness matrix of the structure. This is accomplished by adding the stiffness contributions of the constituent parts while keeping in mind their interdependence,

$$K_G = 10^3 \begin{bmatrix} (70+49.5) & 49.5 & -70 & 0 & -49.5 & -49.5 \\ 49.5 & 49.5 & 0 & 0 & -49.5 & -49.5 \\ -70 & 0 & (70+49.5) & -49.5 & -49.5 & 49.5 \\ 0 & 0 & -49.5 & 49.5 & 49.5 & -49.5 \\ -49.5 & -49.5 & -49.5 & 49.5 & 49.5+49.5 & -49.5+49.5 \\ -49.5 & -49.5 & 49.5 & -49.5 & -49.5+49.5 & +49.5+49.5 \end{bmatrix}$$

$$K_G = 10^3 \begin{bmatrix} 119.5 & 49.5 & -70 & 0 & -49.5 & -49.5 \\ 49.5 & 49.5 & 0 & 0 & -49.5 & -49.5 \\ -70 & 0 & 119.5 & -49.5 & -49.5 & 49.5 \\ 0 & 0 & -49.5 & 49.5 & 49.5 & -49.5 \\ -49.5 & -49.5 & -49.5 & 49.5 & 99.0 & 0 \\ -49.5 & -49.5 & 49.5 & -49.5 & 0 & 99 \end{bmatrix}$$

(c) A modification must be made to the stiffness matrix K_G for the structure shown above because to boundary conditions. Because joint 1 is a hinge fixed joint, node (1) has no freedom of movement ($x1 = x2 = 0$). Joint 2 is a roller joint, hence its motion is limited to the x-axis alone ($x4 = 0$), with no y-axis mobility. To use the elimination approach, we first eliminate the rows and columns of the preceding K matrix that correspond to the degrees of freedom 1, 2 and 4. The simplified equations for finite elements are as follows:

$$10^3 \begin{bmatrix} 119.5 & -49.5 & 49.5 \\ -49.5 & 99 & 0 \\ 49.5 & 0 & 99 \end{bmatrix} \begin{bmatrix} x_3 \\ x_5 \\ x_6 \end{bmatrix} = \begin{bmatrix} 0 \\ 15 \times 10^3 \\ -5 \times 10^3 \end{bmatrix}$$

Solving the above equations yields the displacement as

$$\begin{bmatrix} x_3 \\ x_5 \\ x_6 \end{bmatrix} = \begin{bmatrix} 0.143 \\ 0.22 \\ -0.12 \end{bmatrix} \text{mm}$$

The nodal displacement matrix for the entire structure can therefore be written as

$$[X] = \begin{bmatrix} 0 & 0 & 0.143 & 0 & 0.22 & -1.12 \end{bmatrix}^T \text{mm}$$

(d) Stress in each element can be determined using formula

$$\sigma_1 = \frac{200 \times 10^3}{1000} [-1 \quad 0 \quad 1 \quad 0] \times \begin{bmatrix} x_1 \\ x_2 \\ x_3 \\ x_4 \end{bmatrix}$$

$$= 20[-1 \quad 0 \quad 1 \quad 0] \times \begin{bmatrix} 0 \\ 0 \\ 0.143 \\ 0 \end{bmatrix} = 28.6 \text{N} / \text{mm}^2$$

∴ Stress in element (1)

$$\sigma_1 = \frac{200 \times 10^3}{1000} [-1 \quad 0 \quad 1 \quad 0] \times \begin{bmatrix} x_1 \\ x_2 \\ x_3 \\ x_4 \end{bmatrix}$$

$$= 20[-1 \quad 0 \quad 1 \quad 0] \times \begin{bmatrix} 0 \\ 0 \\ 0.143 \\ 0 \end{bmatrix} = 28.6 \text{N} / \text{mm}^2$$

Stress in element (2)

$$\sigma_2 = \frac{E}{le}\begin{bmatrix} -l & -m & l & m \end{bmatrix} \times \begin{bmatrix} x_3 \\ x_4 \\ x_5 \\ x_6 \end{bmatrix}$$

$$= \frac{200 \times 10^3}{707.1}\begin{bmatrix} 0.707 & -0.707 & -0.707 & 0.707 \end{bmatrix} \times \begin{bmatrix} 0.143 \\ 0 \\ 0.22 \\ -0.12 \end{bmatrix}$$

$$\sigma_2 = -40.35 \text{N} / \text{mm}^2$$

Stress in element (3)

$$\sigma_3 = \frac{E}{le}\begin{bmatrix} -l & -m & l & m \end{bmatrix} \times \begin{bmatrix} x_5 \\ x_6 \\ x_1 \\ x_2 \end{bmatrix}$$

$$= \frac{200 \times 10^3}{707.1}\begin{bmatrix} 0.707 & 0.707 & -0.707 & -0.707 \end{bmatrix} \times \begin{bmatrix} 0.22 \\ -0.12 \\ 0 \\ 0 \end{bmatrix}$$

$$= 20.00 \text{N} / \text{mm}^2$$

As a last step, we must determine the reactions of individuals giving assistance. Calculate the reaction forces along d.o.f. 1, 2 and 4 (corresponding to fixed supports). To get these values, the formula $R = KQ - F$ is utilised. In this connection, only the rows of K that include the support d.o.f.s should be used. $F = 0$ for these degrees of freedom. Given this, we get at:

$$\begin{bmatrix} R_1 \\ R_2 \\ R_4 \end{bmatrix} = 10^3 \begin{bmatrix} 119.5 & 49.5 & -70 & 0 & -49.5 & -49.5 \\ 49.5 & 49.5 & 0 & 0 & -49.5 & -49.5 \\ 0 & 0 & -49.5 & 49.5 & 49.5 & -49.5 \end{bmatrix} \times \begin{bmatrix} 0 \\ 0 \\ 0.143 \\ 0 \\ 0.22 \\ -0.12 \end{bmatrix}$$

On solving, we get

$$R_1 = -27.0875 \times 10^3 \text{N} = -27.0875 \text{kN}$$

$$R_2 = -4.99 \times 10^3 \text{N} = -4.990 \text{kN}$$

$$R_4 = 9.99 \times 10^3 \text{N} = 9.99 \text{kN}$$

Node	x	y
1	0	0
2	1000	0
3	500	500

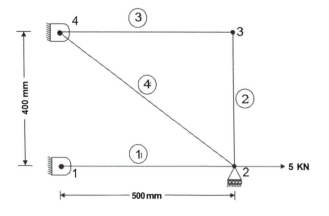

FIGURE 4.24   Four bar truss

Example 4.7: *For the four-bar truss shown in Figure 4.24, determine displacement at the nodes and the stress in each member. Area of cross-section of each member is 150 mm2. Take E = 300 GPa.*

Solution: Discretise the truss into four elements numbered from (1) to (4) as shown in figure. Taking nodes at the end points of the bar, we get four nodes, one each at the intersection. Being a two-dimensional problem, each node will have two degrees of freedom one each in x and y direction as shown in Figure 4.25. Also, taking node (1) as origin we can write coordinates for remaining nodes.

   (I) Nodal coordinates:

Node	x	y
1	0	0
2	500	0
3	500	400
4	0	400

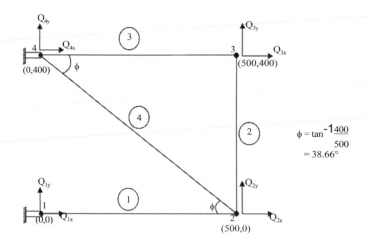

FIGURE 4.25   Four elements of the truss

(II) Element connectivity table:

Element	Node 1	Node 2
1	1	2
2	2	3
3	3	4
4	4	2

(III) Direction cosine table:

Element	Angle θ at Node 1	le	$L = \cos\theta$	$M = \sin\theta$
1	0	500	1	0
2	90°	400	0	1
3	180°	500	−1	0
4	321.34° (360 − 38.66)	640.31	0.78	−0.62

Element stiffness matrix k is given by

$$k = \frac{EAe}{le}\begin{bmatrix} l^2 & lm & -l^2 & -lm \\ lm & m^2 & -lm & -m^2 \\ -l^2 & -lm & l^2 & lm \\ -lm & -m^2 & lm & m^2 \end{bmatrix}$$

Taking the value of l and m for each element from the above table, we get element stiffness matrix of four elements as

$$\text{For element}\,(1): k_1 = \frac{300\times10^3\times150}{500}\begin{bmatrix} 1 & 0 & -1 & 0 \\ 0 & 0 & 0 & 0 \\ -1 & 0 & 1 & 0 \\ 0 & 0 & 0 & 0 \end{bmatrix}$$

$$= 90\times10^3\begin{bmatrix} 1 & 0 & -1 & 0 \\ 0 & 0 & 0 & 0 \\ -1 & 0 & 1 & 0 \\ 0 & 0 & 0 & 0 \end{bmatrix}$$

$$\text{For element}\,(2): k_2 = \frac{300\times10^3\times150}{400}\begin{bmatrix} 0 & 0 & 0 & 0 \\ 0 & 1 & 0 & -1 \\ 0 & 0 & 0 & 0 \\ 0 & -1 & 0 & 1 \end{bmatrix}$$

$$= 112.5\times10^3\begin{bmatrix} 0 & 0 & 0 & 0 \\ 0 & 1 & 0 & -1 \\ 0 & 0 & 0 & 0 \\ 0 & -1 & 0 & 1 \end{bmatrix}$$

$$\text{For element}(3): k_3 = \frac{300 \times 10^3 \times 150}{400} \begin{bmatrix} 1 & 0 & -1 & 0 \\ 0 & 0 & 0 & 0 \\ -1 & 0 & 1 & 0 \\ 0 & 0 & 0 & 0 \end{bmatrix}$$

$$= 112.5 \times 10^3 \begin{bmatrix} 1 & 0 & -1 & 0 \\ 0 & 0 & 0 & 0 \\ -1 & 0 & 1 & 0 \\ 0 & 0 & 0 & 0 \end{bmatrix}$$

$$\text{For element}(4): k_4 = \frac{300 \times 10^3 \times 150}{640.31} \begin{bmatrix} 0.61 & -0.48 & -0.61 & +0.48 \\ -0.48 & 0.38 & 0.48 & -0.38 \\ -0.61 & 0.48 & 0.61 & -0.48 \\ 0.48 & -0.38 & -0.48 & 0.38 \end{bmatrix}$$

$$= 70.28 \times 10^3 \begin{bmatrix} 0.61 & -0.48 & -0.61 & 0.48 \\ -0.48 & 0.38 & 0.48 & -0.38 \\ -0.61 & 0.48 & 0.61 & -0.48 \\ 0.48 & -0.38 & -0.48 & 0.38 \end{bmatrix}$$

Global stiffness matrix $[K_G]$ can be obtained by assembling element stiffness matrices k_1, k_2, k_3 and k_4.

$$K_G = 10^3 \begin{bmatrix} 90 & 0 & -90 & 0 & 0 & 0 & 0 & 0 \\ 0 & 0 & 0 & 0 & 0 & 0 & 0 & 0 \\ -90 & 0 & 132.87 & -33.73 & 0 & 0 & -42.87 & 33.73 \\ 0 & 0 & -33.73 & 155.37 & 0 & -112.5 & 33.73 & -42.87 \\ 0 & 0 & 0 & 0 & 112.5 & 0 & -112.5 & 0 \\ 0 & 0 & 0 & -112.5 & 0 & 112.5 & 0 & 0 \\ 0 & 0 & -42.87 & 33.73 & -112.5 & 0 & 155.37 & -33.73 \\ 0 & 0 & 33.73 & -42.87 & 0 & 0 & -33.73 & 42.87 \end{bmatrix}$$

Using the principle of minimum potential energy, we know that $[K][x] = [F]$ Hence

$$10^3 \begin{bmatrix} 90 & 0 & -90 & 0 & 0 & 0 & 0 & 0 \\ 0 & 0 & 0 & 0 & 0 & 0 & 0 & 0 \\ -90 & 0 & 132.87 & -33.73 & 0 & 0 & -48.87 & 33.73 \\ 0 & 0 & -33.73 & 155.37 & 0 & -112.5 & 33.73 & -42.87 \\ 0 & 0 & 0 & 0 & 112.5 & 0 & -112.5 & 0 \\ 0 & 0 & 0 & -112.5 & 0 & 112.5 & 0 & 0 \\ 0 & 0 & -42.87 & 33.73 & -112.5 & 0 & 155.37 & -33.73 \\ 0 & 0 & 33.73 & -42.87 & 0 & 0 & -33.73 & 42.87 \end{bmatrix} \begin{bmatrix} Q_{1x} \\ Q_{1y} \\ Q_{2x} \\ Q_{2y} \\ Q_{3x} \\ Q_{3y} \\ Q_{4x} \\ Q_{4y} \end{bmatrix} = \begin{bmatrix} 0 \\ 0 \\ 5000 \\ 0 \\ 0 \\ 0 \\ 0 \\ 0 \end{bmatrix}$$

Since nodes (1) and (4) have hinge support
$Q_{1\,x} = Q_{1y} = Q_{4x} = Q_{4y} = 0$
Since node (2) has roller support, $Q_{2y} = 0$
Therefore, by applying elimination approach, the above equations can be reduced to the form

$$10^3 \begin{bmatrix} 132.87 & 0 & 0 \\ 0 & 112.5 & 0 \\ 0 & 0 & 112.5 \end{bmatrix} \begin{bmatrix} Q_{2x} \\ Q_{3x} \\ Q_{3y} \end{bmatrix} = \begin{bmatrix} 5000 \\ 0 \\ 0 \end{bmatrix}$$

On solving, we get

$Q_{2\,x} = 0.037$ mm

$Q_{3\,x} = 0$

$Q_{3\,y} = 0$

The nodal displacement matrix can be given by

$[x] = [\,0\ 0\ 0.037\ 0\ 0\ 0\ 0\ 0\,]^T$

Stress in each element can be determined using relation

$$\sigma = \frac{E}{le}\begin{bmatrix} -l & -m & l & m \end{bmatrix} \times [x]$$

Stress in element (1):

$$\sigma_1 = \frac{300 \times 10^3}{500}\begin{bmatrix} -1 & 0 & 1 & 0 \end{bmatrix} \times \begin{bmatrix} Q_{1x} \\ Q_{1y} \\ Q_{2x} \\ Q_{2y} \end{bmatrix}$$

$$= 600\begin{bmatrix} -1 & 0 & 1 & 0 \end{bmatrix} \times \begin{bmatrix} 0 \\ 0 \\ 0.037 \\ 0 \end{bmatrix}$$

$$= 22.2\text{N} / \text{mm}^2$$

Stress in element (2):

$$\sigma_2 = \frac{300 \times 10^3}{400}\begin{bmatrix} 0 & -1 & 0 & 1 \end{bmatrix} \times \begin{bmatrix} 0 \\ 0 \\ 0 \\ 0 \end{bmatrix}$$

$$= 0$$

Similarly, $\sigma_3 = 0$ and $\sigma_4 = 0$.

Example 4.8: A truss carries a downward load of 100 kN as shown in Figure 4.26. Treating members as one-dimensional line elements, determine the stress in each element.

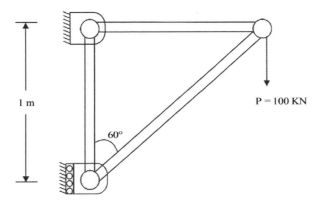

1 m

60°

P = 100 KN

FIGURE 4.26 Three bar truss

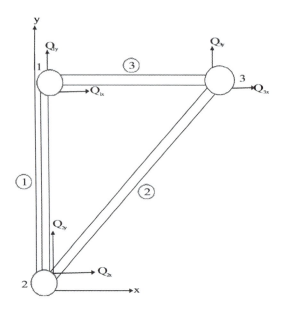

FIGURE 4.27   Three elements of a truss

Take E = 200 GPa and area of cross-section = 500 mm² for all members.
Solution: Discretising the truss into three elements and three nodes as shown in Figure 4.27, let us consider origin at node (2).

(i) Nodal coordinates are:

Node	x	y
1	0	1
2	0	0
3	1.732	1

(iii) Direction cosine table:

Element	Angle θ at Node 1	le (mm)	$l = \cos\theta$	$m = \sin\theta$
1	2700	1000	0	−1
2	300	2000	0.866	0.5
3	1800	1732	−1	0

Note: That θ is the angle that vector 1 → 2 for a particular element makes with the x axis.
Now writing element stiffness matrix:
For element (1):

$$kl = \frac{200 \times 10^3 \times 500}{1000} \begin{bmatrix} 0 & 0 & 0 & 0 \\ 0 & .75 & 0 & -.75 \\ 0 & 0 & 0 & 0 \\ 0 & -.75 & 0 & .75 \end{bmatrix}$$

For element (2):

$$k2 = \frac{200 \times 10^3 \times 500}{2000} \begin{bmatrix} .75 & .433 & -.75 & -.433 \\ .433 & .25 & -.433 & -.25 \\ -.75 & -.433 & .75 & .433 \\ -.433 & -.25 & .433 & .25 \end{bmatrix}$$

For element (i):

$$k3 = \frac{200 \times 103 \times 500}{1732} \begin{bmatrix} 1 & 0 & -1 & 0 \\ 0 & 0 & 0 & 0 \\ -1 & 0 & 1 & 0 \\ 0 & 0 & 0 & 0 \end{bmatrix}$$

Thus

$$k1 = 100 \times 10^3 \begin{bmatrix} 0 & 0 & 0 & 0 \\ 0 & .75 & 0 & -.75 \\ -0 & 0 & 0 & 0 \\ 0 & -.75 & 0 & .75 \end{bmatrix}$$

$$k2 = 50 \times 10^3 \begin{bmatrix} .75 & .433 & -.75 & -.433 \\ .433 & .25 & -.433 & -.25 \\ -.75 & -.433 & .75 & .433 \\ -.433 & -.25 & .433 & .25 \end{bmatrix}$$

$$k3 = 57.74 \times 10^3 \begin{bmatrix} 1 & 0 & -1 & 0 \backslash \\ 0 & 0 & 0 & 0 \\ -1 & 0 & 1 & 0 \\ 0 & 0 & 0 & 0 \end{bmatrix}$$

Global stiffness matrix is obtained by assembling k1, k2 and k3. Thus,

$$KG = 10^3 \begin{bmatrix} 57.74 & 0 & 0 & 0 & -57.74 & 0 \\ 0 & 75 & 0 & -75 & 0 & 0 \\ 0 & 0 & 37.5 & 21.65 & -37.5 & -21.65 \\ 0 & -75 & 21.65 & (75+12.5) & -21.65 & -12.5 \\ -57.74 & 0 & -37.5 & -21.65 & (57.74+37.5) & 21.65 \\ 0 & 0 & -21.65 & -12.5 & 21.65 & 12.5 \end{bmatrix}$$

$$KG = 10^3 \begin{bmatrix} 57.74 & 0 & 0 & 0 & -57.74 & 0 \\ 0 & 75 & 0 & -75 & 0 & 0 \\ 0 & 0 & 37.5 & 21.65 & -37.5 & -21.65 \\ 0 & -75 & 21.65 & 87.5 & -21.65 & -12.5 \\ -57.74 & 0 & -37.5 & -21.65 & 95.24 & 21.65 \\ 0 & 0 & -21.65 & -12.5 & 21.65 & 12.5 \end{bmatrix}$$

Nodal force matrix is

$$F = 10^3 \begin{bmatrix} 0 \\ 0 \\ 0 \\ 0 \\ 0 \\ -100 \end{bmatrix}$$

Using the equation [K] [X] = [F]

$$KG = 10^3 \begin{bmatrix} 57.74 & 0 & 0 & 0 & -57.74 & 0 \\ 0 & 75 & 0 & -75 & 0 & 0 \\ 0 & 0 & 37.5 & 21.65 & -37.5 & -21.65 \\ 0 & -75 & 21.65 & 87.5 & -21.65 & -12.5 \\ 0 & 0 & -37.5 & -21.65 & 95.24 & 21.65 \\ 0 & 0 & -21.65 & -12.5 & 21.65 & 12.5 \end{bmatrix} \begin{bmatrix} \theta_{1x} \\ \theta_{1y} \\ \theta_{2x} \\ \theta_{2y} \\ \theta_{3x} \\ \theta_{3y} \end{bmatrix} = 10^3 \begin{bmatrix} 0 \\ 0 \\ 0 \\ 0 \\ 0 \\ -100 \end{bmatrix}$$

Applying boundary conditions $\theta 1x = \theta 1y = \theta 2x = 0$
This gives

$$87.5\,\theta_{2y} - 21.65\,\theta_{3x} - 12.5\,\theta_{3y} = 0 \quad -\text{(i)}$$

$$-21.65\,\theta_{2y} + 95.24\,\theta_{3x} + 21.65\,\theta_{3y} = 0 \quad -\text{(ii)}$$

$$-12.5\,\theta_{2y} + 21.65\,\theta_{3x} + 12.5\,\theta_{3y} = -100 \quad -\text{(iii)}$$

Solve (i), (ii) and (iii) to find the unknown variables. stress in element is given by

$$\sigma = \frac{E}{le}\begin{bmatrix} -I & -m & 1 & m \end{bmatrix}\{\theta\}$$

4.6 SUMMARY

- Stress analysis using the finite element method involves the following steps: Discretisation of body, choosing an approximate solution, forming element stiffness matrix, assembling the matrix, finding the unknowns and interpreting the results.
- According to the principle of minimum potential energy $[K] \times [u] = [P]$ where $[K]$ is called stiffness matrix, $[u]$ is the displacement matrix and $[P]$ is the force matrix.

Element stiffness matrix $K_e = \dfrac{EA}{l_e}\begin{bmatrix} 1 & -1 \\ -1 & 1 \end{bmatrix}$, element body force matrix $f_e = \dfrac{f\,Ale}{2}\begin{Bmatrix} 1 \\ 1 \end{Bmatrix}$,

element fraction force matrix $= \dfrac{Tle}{2}\begin{Bmatrix} 1 \\ 1 \end{Bmatrix}$

In two-dimensional problems, $[K] = \dfrac{EA}{le}\begin{bmatrix} l^2 & lm & -l^2 & -lm \\ lm & m^2 & -lm & -m^2 \\ -l^2 & -lm & l^2 & lm \\ -lm & -m^2 & lm & m^2 \end{bmatrix}$ where l and m are the

direction cosines.

4.7   EXERCISE

1. What is the advantage of using the finite element method (FEM) for engineering analysis problems (BT level 1)?
2. Explain the concepts of the FEM and finite element analysis (FEA) (BT level 2).
3. Explain post processing as applied to finite element method (BT level 2).
4. Discuss different types of elements used in FEM (BT level 2).
5. What are different types of errors in finite element method solutions (BT level 1)?
6. Derive an expression for stiffness matrix of one-dimensional truss element (BT level 3).
7. Consider the bar shown in Figure 4.28. Determine the displacement at the nodes, element stresses and support reactions. Young's modulus of the material is $E = 200$ GPa. Area of cross-section of the bar is 250 mm^2 (BT level 2).
8. Consider the bar shown in Figure 4.29 and determine the nodal displacements, element stresses and support reactions.

	Steel	Aluminium	Brass
Area of cross section (mm^2)	200	350	350
Young's Modulus of Elasticity (GPa)	200	70	85

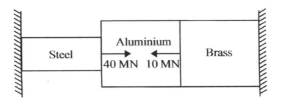

FIGURE 4.28   Straight bar

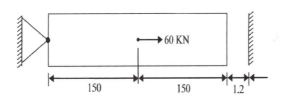

FIGURE 4.29   Stepped bar of steel, aluminium and brass

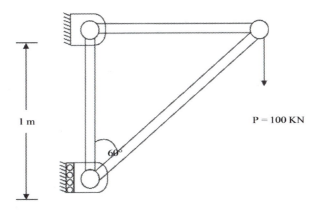

FIGURE 4.30   Three bar frame

9. Figure 4.30 shows a frame carrying a downward load of 100 kN. Treat each member as one-dimensional line elements. Determine
(a) Displacement at nodes,
(b) Stress in each element.
(c) Reactions at supports (BT level 2).

Take area of cross-section as 500 mm^2 and Young's modulus (E) = 200 GPa.

4.8 MULTIPLE-CHOICE QUESTIONS

1. What is the Finite Element Method (FEM)?
   a. A method for modeling 2D and 3D surfaces in CAD
   b. A method for simulating the motion of particles in physics simulations
   c. A method for approximating solutions to differential equations by dividing the solution domain into smaller, simpler elements
   d. A method for interpolating between discrete data points in graphics applications
2. What is the goal of using FEM in engineering analysis?
   a. To obtain exact solutions to differential equations
   b. To minimize the computational resources required to solve differential equations
   c. To approximate the behavior of real-world systems and structures
   d. To simplify the modeling process by using pre-defined templates
3. Which of the following is not a step in the FEM process?
   a. Defining the geometry of the model
   b. Assigning material properties to the model
   c. Meshing the model into smaller elements
   d. Solving the differential equations analytically
4. Which of the following is a common use of FEM in engineering applications?
   a. Designing user interfaces for software applications
   b. Optimizing marketing strategies for products
   c. Simulating the behavior of structures under various loads and stresses
   d. Creating artistic renderings of 3D models
5. What is a two-dimensional problem?
   a. A problem that can be solved in two minutes or less
   b. A problem that involves only two variables
   c. A problem that can be visualized in two dimensions (e.g. on a plane or on a graph)
   d. A problem that involves two separate, unrelated sub-problems
6. Which of the following is an example of a two-dimensional problem?
   a. Calculating the trajectory of a rocket in space
   b. Modeling the behavior of a fluid flowing through a pipe
   c. Designing a bridge to withstand a variety of weather conditions
   d. Predicting the outcome of a political election
7. What is the advantage of using a two-dimensional model in engineering and physics simulations?
   a. It is simpler and faster to solve than a three-dimensional model
   b. It can capture more complex behaviors and interactions than a three-dimensional model
   c. It is easier to visualize and communicate the results of the simulation to others
   d. It is less expensive to compute and requires less computational resources than a three-dimensional model

Answers

1. Answer: c. A method for approximating solutions to differential equations by dividing the solution domain into smaller, simpler elements
2. Answer: c. To approximate the behavior of real-world systems and structures
3. Answer: d. Solving the differential equations analytically
4. Answer: c. Simulating the behavior of structures under various loads and stresses
5. Answer: c. A problem that can be visualized in two dimensions (e.g. on a plane or on a graph)
6. Answer: b. Modeling the behavior of a fluid flowing through a pipe
7. Answer: a. It is simpler and faster to solve than a three-dimensional model

5 Introduction to CAM

Learning Outcomes: After studying this chapter, the reader should be able:

LO 1: To understand role of computer-aided manufacturing (CAM) (BT level 2).

LO 2: To define CAM (BT level 1).

LO 3: To understand numerical control, its need, suitability, historical developments and future trends (BT level 2).

5.1 INTRODUCTION TO COMPUTER-AIDED MANUFACTURING (CAM)

Computer systems are used in computer-aided manufacturing (CAM) to turn computer-aided design (CAD) models into numerical control (NC) code for machine equipment. The term **"computer-aided manufacturing"** (CAM) is often used to refer to the process of employing NC computer software programs to write complicated instructions (code) that drive computer numerically controlled (CNC) machine equipment to manufacture physical products (Figure 5.1). CAM's capabilities are reliant on high-quality components from a variety of industries.

LO 1. To understand role of Computer Aided Manufacturing (CAM).

CAM may be used to build a production plan in the following areas: tooling design, CAD model preparation, NC programming, Coordinate Measuring Machine (CMM) inspection programming, machine tool simulation and post-processing. Direct numerical control (DNC), tool management, CNC machining and CMM execution are examples of procedures used in a manufacturing environment to implement the plan.

5.1.1 APPLICATIONS OF CAM

CAD has shown steady progress over the last few decades. No physical prototypes are needed at any stage of the process, from the conception of the basic design through the generation of the production-necessary Bill of Materials.

CAM takes this one step further. Using CAM software, data from CAD software may be immediately converted into a set of production instructions, eliminating the requirement for a hand-drawn paper design defining the procedures necessary to manufacture the finished product.

Machine-aided manufacturing (MAM) software converts CAD-created 3-D models into a machine-understandable language, often G-Code. Simply explained, G-code is a programming language that CNC machines can interpret. G-code enables the operator to deliver exact instructions to the machine, hence enabling the machine to make many identical items.

Modern numerically controlled machine tools may be networked to form a "manufacturing cell," or a set of machines that collaborate to execute a single production process. Each machine tool (welders, mills, drills, lathes, etc.) in the cell is responsible for a distinct step in the production process, and the product is passed through the cell sequentially, just as it would in a factory.

All equipment in a single cell may be controlled by a single computer, which serves as the "controller." This controller may be programmed with G-code instructions to run the cell with little human monitoring.

DOI: 10.1201/9781003350842-5

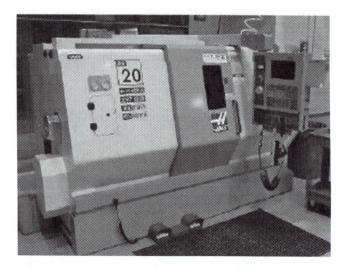

FIGURE 5.1   A CNC machining centre

5.1.2   Benefits of CAM

CAD and CAM enable manufacturers to reduce labour costs and boost output. There is little margin for error. CAM software provides several other benefits. The removal of paper drafts as a mechanism of translating CAD models into production instructions enables quick iteration on product design, with new instructions supplied straight to machine equipment for instant satisfaction.

Several CAM programs can perform simple tasks such as reordering components to decrease the requirement for human interaction even more. Many numerically controlled machine tools may also connect with their operators by text message or e-mail to report the problem and seek more instructions.

CAM software is reflective of a wider trend toward increased mechanisation. One of the numerous benefits of CAM is the ability to establish a precise and effective production plan.

The extensive usage of CAM software indicates a growing tendency toward mechanisation. In addition to its many other advantages, CAM enables the creation of a thorough and efficient production plan.

Advanced CAM systems that combine product lifecycle management may give manufacturing planning and production personnel with data and process management benefits (PLM). Integrating CAM and PLM with DNC systems allows the management and delivery of files to CNC machines on the shop floor.

5.1.3   Limitations of CAM

Unfortunately, the use of CAM has a number of limitations. Initial investment in the required infrastructure might be fairly expensive. In addition to numerically controlled machine tools, CAM requires a full suite of CAD/CAM software and hardware, as well as qualified operators, to produce design models and convert them into production instructions.

In addition, the field of computer-assisted management is riddled with incoherence. Every CNC machine tool uses G-code, but there is no agreement on how the code should be written. Since the code is utilised by such a wide variety of machine tools, manufacturers often create their own versions to control their devices. The conversion of 3-D CAD models to G-code may be difficult. Since CAD systems tend to save data in their own proprietary format, transferring data from CAD to CAM software and then into whatever form of G-code the manufacturer employs may be challenging (much as word processor apps do).

5.2 COMPUTER-AIDED MANUFACTURING (CAM) DEFINED

With the advancement of computer technology, computers have been implemented in almost every kind of industry including the manufacturing sector.
CAM may be defined as any support that can be provided by computers in
manufacturing a given product. Computers may play a direct role or indirect
role in manufacturing a given product.

LO 2. To define Computer Aided Manufacturing (CAM).

The direct role refers to computerised operation and control of a manufacturing process. For
example, consider a lathe machine being controlled by a computer. A number of process parameters
may be monitored. With machining specifications already stored in computer memory in the form
of a program, suitable actions may be initiated by the computer for the purpose of regulating the
machining operation. It involves the use of computer software to develop part programs for machining and other processing applications.

The indirect role of computer in manufacturing refers to:

- Computer-aided process planning,
- Computer-aided NC part programming,
- Computer-aided material requirement planning and manufacturing planning,
- Computer-aided material handling and storage,
- Computer-aided inspection and quality control, etc.

In today's highly competitive business environment, it becomes essential to provide high quality,
customised products in the shortest possible time to the customers. This demands improvement in
manufacturing processes and hence adopting CAM becomes important. Some advantages of CAM
are enumerated as follows:

- Use of CAM reduces manufacturing lead time.
- CAM increases flexibility in manufacturing.
- The scrap produced during machining is reduced as the part programs are made by using
  part geometry generated in the design phase.
- Computer control of manufacturing equipment improves plant productivity.
- Computer-controlled machines have self-diagnostics and monitoring features so they
  require less maintenance and have less breakdown compared to conventional machines.
- Computer control of manufacturing equipment makes it more reliable.
- Use of CAM also lends greater design freedom as any modifications made in design
  can be easily translated into machining specification while working in a computerised
  environment.
- CAM improves responsiveness to a customer's special request. Highly customised parts
  can be made in small batches with ease using computer-controlled machines.

CAM is a part of automation. Hence the chapter will not be complete if we do not study automation.

5.3 NUMERICAL CONTROL (NC) SYSTEM

What is NC: NC of machine tools may be defined as a method of programmable automation in which various the functions of machine tools
are controlled by numbers, letters and some symbols. The numbers, let-

LO 3. To understand Numerical control

ters and symbols are encoded in an appropriate format to define a program of instructions
called the part program for a particular component or job. When the job is changed, the part
program is also changed. Thus, NC machines are automatically operated by commands that are
received by their processing equipment.

The Electronics Industries Association defines NC technology as "a system in which actions are controlled by direct injection of numerical data at some point" (EIA). The system must automatically understand a portion of this data.

An NC machine will activate its various drives to the given degrees and in the defined sequence in response to a set of numerical instructions (the program). Each and every activity involves the creation of an individual component program. It instructs the machine to do a certain job.

5.3.1   Suitability of NC Technology

NC machines have been found suitable where:

1. Parts are made in small batches.
2. Components have complex shapes.
3. A large number of operations have to be performed on the component in its machining.
4. Much metal needs to be removed.
5. Repetition, close tolerances and high accuracy is desired.
6. There is a possibility of change in design.
7. Parts are crucial and expensive and even a small mistake can turn it into scrap.
8. Fixturisation and setups are numerous and costly.

One or more of the above considerations would justify the processing of a part using an NC machine.

5.3.2   Need for NC Systems

NC systems have become very popular in industry these days. This is because even highly skilled workers cannot ensure accuracy and quality on conventional machine tools, whereas on an NC machine even a semiskilled worker can ensure virtually zero rejection. An NC machine operator need not be a highly skilled worker. However, proficient machine programmers are needed to implement NC technology successfully. Wherever high accuracy is desired, at the same time, change in the type of jobs is too frequent, implementing an NC system is the only answer.

5.3.3   Advantages of NC Systems

NC technology brings the following advantages:

1. **Better control of cutting tool:** The fundamental advantage of an NC machine is the precise and improved control of the cutting tool, which is very difficult to do manually. For circular or parabolic tool motion, for example, it is important to govern the tool's x- and y-axis movements simultaneously. This would be difficult for a conventional machine to do, but an NC machine could do it repeatedly with an accuracy of microns.
2. **Flexibility in manufacturing:** An NC machine can easily adapt to design changes in parts by making the corresponding changes in the part program. Also, it can easily adapt to changes in production schedule, thus providing greater flexibility in manufacturing.
3. **Cost of production:** NC machines help in lowering the cost of production due to following reasons:
   - *Reduced fixturisation:* Because positioning of tools with respect to workpiece is done by NC program rather than a fixture or a jig.
   - *Reduced non-productive time:* Because of fewer setups, less setup time, less work handling time and automatic tool changes, etc.
   - *Reduced human error:* NC control minimises human interference, hence the chances of human mistakes are low.

- NC machining centres can perform the machining operations of several conventional machines simultaneously, thus reducing the number of machines required to manufacture a product and also lead time in manufacture. This results in a lower cost of production and greater machine utilisation.
4. Greater accuracy uniformity and productivity.
5. Setup time is reduced.
6. Reduced scrap.
7. Fewer and simpler jigs and fixtures as positioning is done by machine itself.
8. Reduction of direct labour.
9. Accurate costing and scheduling.
10. Reduced workpiece handling.
11. Increased productivity.
12. It is easy to make design changes. It especially proves to be useful in making prototypes.
13. Simplified inspection, as accuracy is maintained due to cutter diameter compensation.
14. *Precision:* NC machines enhance the machining precision. Precision largely depends on human skill. Due to the reduced human role in machining, NC machines guarantee higher precision and consistent quality for whole of its batch.
15. Greater safety due to automatic door closing, etc.

These advantages have made NC technology very popular in industry.

5.3.4   DISADVANTAGES OF NC TECHNOLOGY OVER CONVENTIONAL MACHINES

1. **Cost factor:** NC machines involve higher investment cost compared to conventional machine tools. The cost involved in establishing and running an NC manufacturing setup could be several times more than for their conventional counterparts. The NC technology is sophisticated and complex. It requires higher initial investment as well as higher investment for maintenance. The cost of maintenance includes wages of highly skilled workers and expensive spares. Control systems are also costly.
2. **Training of machine operators and part programmers:** An NC manufacturing facility requires training of operators both for software and hardware. NC is essentially an application of digital technology to control a machine. Hence part programmers need to be trained to write instructions in desired programming languages for machines on the shop floor. This factor is important for successful adoption and growth of NC technology.
3. Danger of loss in flexibility of the machine if the tape or control malfunctions.

5.4   HISTORICAL DEVELOPMENTS

The concept of NC evolved during the Second World War to fulfil need for advanced manufacturing techniques for complex aircraft parts.

The initial work for development of NC was carried out by the US Airforce and the aerospace industry. After the Second World War, in 1940, the US Airforce felt that there were many important parts and components that were required only in small quantity. Also, the curved surfaces could not be accurately machined using master templates. So, a need was felt to develop machine tools and equipment which could ensure quality in production of intricate parts and curved surfaces.

Pearsons Corporation in Transverse City, Michigan, was among the first to initiate research on NC and John Pearsons and Frank Stulen led the project. The initial NC concept that evolved, made use of x, y, z-position coordinates data on punched cards to specify the surface contours of helicopter blades. Subsequently, Servomechanisms Laboratories at Massachusetts Institute of Technology (MIT) was awarded a contract to develop a prototype of a numerically controlled machine tool. The first numerically controlled machine tool was developed by retro-fitting. A conventional tracer mill was used for this purpose, and NC equipment was incorporated into it at MIT in March 1952. During the same period, Alfred Herbert Ltd and Airframe Industries started developing their own prototypes. Ferranti Ltd developed a continuous path control system. The US Airforce funded the projects at MIT for development of part programming languages that could be used to control NC machine tools. This led to development of a programming language named APT or automatically programmed tools which has simple English-like statements as its instructions.

In the 1960s, Japan and Russia also made rapid advances in NC technology. The machine tool manufacturers also started gradually initiating their own research and development projects to introduce commercial NC machines. Today, NC machines are used to make simple as well as complex shapes. They are used for non-machining operations as well, like drafting, spot welding, flame cutting, tube bending, etc.

5.5   FUTURE TRENDS

The future factories will be automated factories. They will make use of CAD and CAM technologies for product design and manufacturing. Even non-manufacturing operations like production scheduling, inventory control, production planning, etc. will be integrated with management information systems to form a computer-integrated manufacturing (CIM) facility.

In the future, organisations will compete on the overall efficiency of its *supply chain*. A supply chain is a network of facilities that includes all the elements involved in fulfilling customer requests. It includes the supplier, the manufacturer, distributor, retailer and customer. Supply chain management involves management of all these elements of the supply chain. Material, information and funds flow takes place across the entire supply chain. Information technology will play a very important role in connecting various elements of the supply chain.

Product development will be done in a CIM environment. The principles of **concurrent engineering** are rapidly being adopted. Advancements in computer hardware and software will booster the CAD/CAM environment, CNC machine tools, robots and machining centres will be used to make products of high accuracy and quality. Such machine tools with integrated computer-aided process planning software material requirement planning automatic material handling systems can improve responsiveness and flexibility of the factories to a great extent.

New emerging technologies like rapid prototyping, nanotechnology, virtual manufacturing micromachining, etc. will reduce product lead time.

Artificial intelligence will be extensively used to develop expert systems, machine vision, voice recognition systems, pattern recognition systems, etc.

5.6   SUMMARY

1. CAM refers to direct or indirect use of computers for manufacturing.
2. Automation makes use of mechanical, electronic computer technology to make a complete system.
3. Three types of automation are: fixed, programmable and flexible automation.
4. NC is a form of programmable automation.
5. NC is suitable when parts are to be made in small batches.
6. NC gives better control of a cutting tool.
7. Use of NC improves flexibility in manufacturing.
8. Implementing NC involves high initial investment and operator training cost.
9. MIT has played a major role in initial development of NC technology.
10. CAD systems and CAM systems can be integrated to form CAD/CAM systems.
11. Integrating business functions to CAD/CAM leads to the concept of CIM.

5.7   EXERCISE

1. Define CAM (BT level 1).
2. Explain the direct and indirect role of computers in manufacturing (BT level 2).
3. What is numerical control (BT level 1)?
4. Under what conditions is it suitable to use NC technology (BT level 2)?
5. State advantages of using NC systems (BT level 1).
6. What are the disadvantages of using NC technology over conventional machines (BT level 2)?
7. State the historical developments that led to advancements in NC technology (BT level 1).

5.8   MULTIPLE-CHOICE QUESTIONS

1. What is CAM?
   a. Computer-Aided Marketing.
   b. Computer-Aided Manufacturing.
   c. Computer-Aided Management.
   d. Computer-Aided Modelling.
2. What is the purpose of an NC system?
   a. To create digital designs for manufacturing.
   b. To control the movement of machines in manufacturing processes.
   c. To monitor and optimise production workflows.
   d. To automate marketing campaigns.
3. What is the main benefit of automation in manufacturing?
   a. Reduced cost of raw materials.
   b. Increased flexibility in production schedules.
   c. Improved efficiency and productivity.
   d. Enhanced product quality and consistency.
4. What is the difference between a CNC machine and a conventional machine?
   a. A CNC machine is manually operated, while a conventional machine is fully automated.
   b. A CNC machine is controlled by a computer program, while a conventional machine is controlled by a human operator.
   c. A CNC machine is faster and more accurate than a conventional machine.
   d. A CNC machine is more expensive than a conventional machine.
5. Which of the following is a common application of NC systems?
   a. Generating toolpaths for 3-D printing.
   b. Creating digital designs for marketing campaigns.
   c. Controlling the movement of robots in a warehouse.
   d. Programming the movement of machine tools in a manufacturing process.
6. Which of the following is not a common application of CAM?
   a. Programming and controlling robotic machines in manufacturing.
   b. Generating toolpaths for CNC machines.
   c. Creating digital designs for 3-D printing.
   d. Developing marketing campaigns for new products.
7. Which of the following is a benefit of using CAM in manufacturing?
   a. Improved efficiency and accuracy in manufacturing processes.
   b. Reduced complexity and variability in product designs.
   c. Increased flexibility in production schedules and workflows.
   d. Lower costs for raw materials and labour.
8. Which of the following is a common CAM software tool used in manufacturing?
   a. Microsoft Excel.
   b. Adobe Photoshop.

   c. Autodesk Fusion 360.
   d. Google Drive.
9. Which of the following is a type of CAM operation used in machining processes?
   a. Drilling.
   b. Painting.
   c. Folding.
   d. Writing.

Answers

1. Answer: b. Computer-Aided Manufacturing.
2. Answer: b. To control the movement of machines in manufacturing processes.
3. Answer: c. Improved efficiency and productivity.
4. Answer: b. A CNC machine is controlled by a computer program, while a conventional machine is controlled by a human operator.
5. Answer: d. Programming the movement of machine tools in a manufacturing process.
6. Answer: d. Developing marketing campaigns for new products.
7. Answer: a. Improved efficiency and accuracy in manufacturing processes.
8. Answer: c. Autodesk Fusion 360.
9. Answer: a. Drilling.

6 Features of NC and CNC Machines

Learning Outcomes: After studying this chapter, the reader should be able:

LO 1: To know Basic components of NC machines (BT level 1).
LO 2: To understand Various classifications of NC systems (BT level 2).
LO 3: To understand the coordinate system used in various NC machines (BT Level 2).
LO 4: To compare ordinary and NC machine tools (BT level 4).
LO 5: To understand direct numerical control (BT level 2).
LO 6: To understand computer numerical control and its features (BT level 2).
LO 7: To understand adaptive control (BT level 2).

VIDEO 3

6.1 FEATURES OF NC MACHINES

Numerical control (NC) is a form of programmable automation. The basic components of an NC machine are:

LO 1. To know Basic components of NC machines

1. Machine Control Unit (MCU),
2. Part program,
3. Processing equipment or machine tool.

Machine control unit: It is the brain of an NC machine. Every NC machine is fitted with a machine control unit (MCU) which is not found in conventional machines. The MCU consists of necessary hardware and software that reads and interprets the part program in order to obtain the mechanical action of machine tools or other engineering equipment.

The MCU is usually housed in a separate cabinet placed close to the machine or it can be like a pendant that can swing around. The MCU can control the tool path, spindle speed, feed rate, depth of cut and other machining parameters. A schematic diagram of an MCU is given in Figure 6.1.

Although most modern MCUs are based on microprocessors, they initially made use of a punched tape and tape reader to transfer the part program.

Part program: The part program is a program of instructions that defines the cutting tool path, spindle speed, feed rate, tool changes, coolant on/off and several other functions of a machine tool that can be automatically controlled. The commands also define the position of the machine tool spindle or the cutting tool with respect to the worktable on which the workpiece is fixtured.

There are several media which the part program can be entered into the MCU. Initially, for several decades a one-inch-wide punched tape was used. It is a long strip of paper, mylar, mylar-coated aluminium, reinforced paper or plastic. It contains a part program in the form of holes. Nowadays,

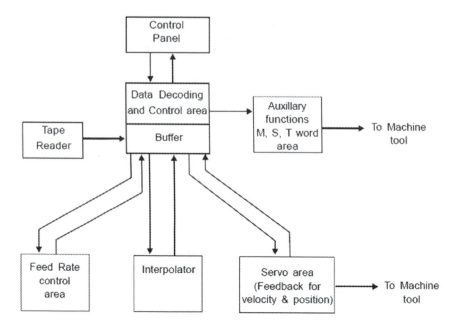

FIGURE 6.1 Schematic diagram of machine control unit

the common media to transfer a part program to an MCU of an NC machine are magnetic cassettes and floppy discs. The part program can also be saved directly into the machine memory. An NC machine does not have an onboard computer, but they are usually equipped with memory to store part programs.

In the case of punched tape, holes are punched in the tape using a tape-punching machine called a flexowriter. This machine works on the principle of a typewriter. There are eight columns of holes that run along the length of the tape. The diameter of the holes is $0.072^{+0.001}_{-0.002}$ inch. The presence or absence of a hole in a certain position represents one bit of information and the entire collection of holes constitutes the part program. There is another column of smaller holes between the third and the fourth columns. These are feed holes of diameter $0.046^{+0.002}_{-0.001}$ inch and get engaged in the sprocket in order to feed the tape to the tape reader.

The punched tape with the component software is coiled onto and read by an electromechanical tape reader. Numerous techniques have been developed to identify the tape's hole pattern while developing the tape reader. These techniques include the photoelectric method, electrical contact fingers and the vacuum method.

Photoelectric technique: A light head is placed on one side of the tape while the photoelectric cells are placed on the other side. Light that enters the holes of the tape activates the cells. The hole tracks on the tape resemble an array of photoelectric cells.

Electrical contact fingers: The reading head consists of a series of eight mechanical fingers or thin brushes that protrude through holes in the punched tape. When the finger completes an electrical contact on the other side of the tape due to presence of a hole, bit information is generated.

Vacuum method: The reading head is made up of suction sensors that indicate the presence or absence of holes. When the reading head encounters a hole, the vacuum is broken and bit information is generated.

It is important to understand how instructions are formed.

- Bit is an abbreviation for "binary digit," the popular term for a binary digit. The value of a column or row may be either zero or one, depending on whether or not it has a gap.
- A row of bits forms a character. A character may be a letter, a number or some symbol.

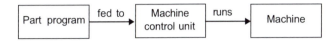

FIGURE 6.2   A typical NC system

- A few characters combine to form an NC-word. Examples of NC words are *n*-word, *g*-word, *x*-word, etc.
- A collection of words form a block. A block forms a complete NC instruction. To separate blocks, an end-of-block (EOB) symbol is used.
- A number of blocks together form a complete part program.

The tape reader reads the data from the tape in pieces. Consequently, it reads just one set of instructions at a time. If the tape reader cycle time is larger than the machine cycle time, the tape reader will not function (i.e., the time taken to read the block is more than the time taken to execute it by the machine), the machine can make indentations on the workpiece due to tool stopping after executing each block. Such machine action can spoil the workpiece. To avoid this phenomenon, a buffer is provided in the MCU (refer to Figure 6.2). Hence, a number of blocks are read in one time and stored in the buffer while the machine executes the block one by one. In the meantime, subsequent blocks are read. And as soon as the buffer is empty, the new set of blocks is loaded in the buffer to be executed later. Hence, chances of the workpiece indentation due to the tool stopping after executing each block is eliminated.

RAM (random access memory) and ROM (read-only memory) are the two most prevalent computer storage types. RAM is temporary storage. When the machine's power is switched off, it vanishes. ROM is non-volatile memory. It stores information permanently (even after the machine is switched off). It may be read repeatedly until the data is intentionally erased.

ROM is used to store information used for repetitive functions such as online help, operating instructions and default parameters, etc. All this information is stored in ROM at the time of manufacturing the machine in the factory. This information remains available to the machine even if power is removed or the machine is down. For this reason, the crucial information is stored in ROM.

RAM is used to temporarily store data. For example, part programs are stored in RAM. Hence, the machine should be equipped with enough RAM to store and process the longest possible programs. Sometimes extendable RAM is provided which means empty slots are available in the MCU.

Since NC machines do not have onboard computers, codes for cutting a component must be created on a separate computer. The machine then obtains the coded program through media such as punch tape, magnetic tape, floppy disc, etc.

6.1.1   Processing Equipment or Machine

This is another important component of NC equipment, because this is the component that performs useful work. For example, in an NC lathe, the processing equipment is the usual lathe machine (excluding MCU) which performs the actual machining operation.

6.2   CLASSIFICATION OF NC SYSTEMS

NC technology is an expensive technology. Hence, it is very important to understand the exact requirement to manufacture a particular component. Different types of NC machines are used to manufacture diverse components. The cost will also vary from machine to machine depending upon the features incorporated in the machine.

LO 2. To understand Various classifications of NC systems

NC machines are broadly classified as follows:

(1) Based on the type of control system:
   (A) Open-loop control NC,
   (B) Closed-loop control NC.

(2) Based on the type of motion control:
    (A) Point-to-point NC,
    (B) Straight-cut NC,
    (C) Contouring NC.
(3) Based on the number of axes:
    (A) 2-axis NC,
    (B) 3-axis NC,
    (C) 4-axis NC,
    (D) 5-axis NC.
(4) Based on the type of power drive:
    (A) Hydraulic NC,
    (B) Pneumatic NC.
(5) Electric NC.

6.2.1 CLASSIFICATION BASED ON THE TYPE OF CONTROL SYSTEM

The NC machine's drive mechanism is capable of both open-loop and closed-loop setups. There are really two primary kinds of control systems: Open loop and closed loop. The machine table positions in an NC machine are specified by data from the tape reader received by the MCU and corresponding to the machine tool's axis. Each axis is equipped with a driving device, such as a stepper motor, DC servomotor or hydraulic actuator.

6.2.1.1 Open-Loop Numerical Control System

An open-loop control system is referred to as "control system without feedback" or "non-feedback control system." In open-loop systems, the control action does not depend on the desired result. The output of the system is not compared to any standard. A system with an open loop consists of a controller and the process it governs. The controller gets some kind of input and then transmits its decision to the controlled object. A block diagram of an open-loop system is shown in Figure 6.3.

In an NC machine, the MCU acts as the controller while the control process may be the positioning of slides, cutting tool speed, feed, etc. Hence, in an open-loop NC machine, the MCU does not make use of feedback signals to indicate the table position to the control unit. Most of the open-loop NC machines make use of a stepper motor. Figure 6.4 shows the block diagram of an NC system.

The main advantage of an open-loop NC system is that it is simple, economical, requires less maintenance and calibration is easy.

```
        I/P    ┌────────────┐  fed to  ┌────────────┐   O/p
        ──────▶│ Controller │─────────▶│ Controlled │──────▶
               └────────────┘          │  process   │
                                       └────────────┘
```

FIGURE 6.3   Block diagram of an open-loop system

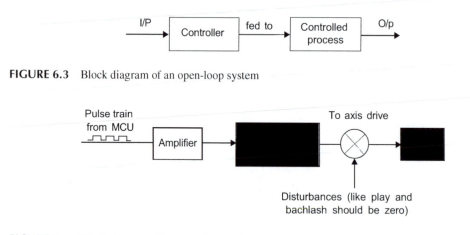

FIGURE 6.4   Block diagram of an open-loop NC system

But there are also some disadvantages associated with it. Optimisation is not possible in open-loop NC systems, these are slow, less accurate and less reliable.

6.2.1.2 Closed-Loop Numerical Control System

Closed-loop control systems may also be referred to as "feedback control systems." The value of a closed-loop control system's feedback loop determines the system's reaction. An error signal is generated when a comparator compares the output to the input it was supposed to use as a standard. The error signal is received by the controller, which then adjusts the output until the desired value is obtained. Therefore, the phrase "closed-loop system" is used to refer to any system with feedback mechanisms. The block diagram of a closed-loop system is shown in Figure 6.5.

In a closed-loop NC system, the actual position and velocity of the axes are measured and compared with their intended values. The difference between them is the result of an incorrect input to the controller for the driving motor. The control operation eliminates the error totally or reduces it to an acceptable level. Figure 6.6 depicts a closed-loop control system that functions via negative feedback.

The feedback signal is generated by a sensor. Typically, rotary or linear transducers are utilised as sensors. It is possible to connect rotary transducers directly or indirectly through gears to the lead screw. One end of linear transducers is attached to the machine tool's frame, while the other end is coupled to the moving slide.

The main advantage of a closed-loop system is that it is more reliable and faster compared to an open-loop system. It can handle a number of variables simultaneously. Also, optimisation is possible.

6.2.2 Classification Based on the Type of Motion Control

In a typical NC machine, the workpiece remains stationary while the tool moves. In a milling machine, for instance, the workpiece is allowed to move relative to the cutting tool. However, from a programmer's point of view, this aspect hardly makes any difference as only relative motion between the tool and the workpiece is important. While writing programs, it is always assumed that

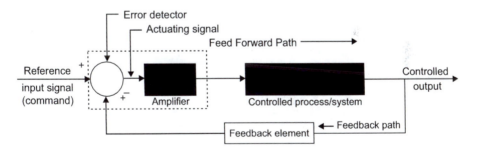

FIGURE 6.5 Block diagram of a closed-loop system

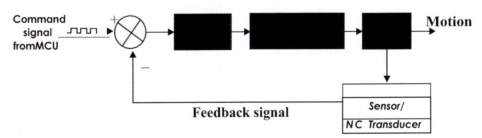

FIGURE 6.6 Closed-loop numerical control system

the tool moves with respect to workpiece. For the second type of machine, the workpiece automatically moves in the opposite direction so as to produce the desired relative motion.

Based on the type of motion control, NC machines are classified as:

1. Point-to-point NC,
2. Straight-cut or axial, cut NC,
3. Contouring NC.

6.2.2.1 Point-to-Point NC

A machine with such a control would simply move the instrument to the designated locations in the designated sequence. This sort of control is appropriate for discrete machining operations, such as drilling and punching, in which the tool's location at the time of cutting is crucial. The travel speed between the selected locations is fixed and cannot be altered. If several holes are to be made, it hardly makes any difference as to how the tool shifts from one hole position to another. After the hole-making operation is over, the tool simply retracts and moves to another location for making the next hole. The path or speed of movement of the tool between subsequent holes is not important.

This is the simplest and least expensive type of control. In point-to-point machines, a high level of control would be unnecessary because machining is not done between subsequent joints. Figure 6.7 illustrates point-to-point control.

6.2.2.2 Straight-Cut/Axial-Cut NC

A NC straight-cut control allows you to specify the speed of the cutting tool along any primary axis. Therefore, subtractive operations in three dimensions are possible (x, y, z). This machine's inability to simultaneously travel in both directions is a significant disadvantage. Therefore, it cannot slice at an angle. To create an angle cut, it is required to rotate the work such that the cutting direction is perpendicular to one of the axes.

Machines for axial cutting with direct control at each cutting point. An example of a straight-cut NC operation is end-milling the sides of a rectangular block. Such an operation is illustrated in Figure 6.8.

6.2.2.3 Contour-Cutting NC/Continuous-Path NC

This variant is the most adaptable, but also the most expensive. It permits simultaneous operation of the instrument along many axes. As seen in Figure 6.9, if a complex form can be approximated by a sequence of small straight-line segments, it is possible to manufacture it within the tolerance range.

This cut is contoured. In addition, NC permits various cutting operations, such as point-to-point and axial. Milling and turning operations often use contour control.

Now the question arises that how does the contouring machine trace its tool path, while moving over a specified profile? This movement is achieved by a technique called *interpolation*. Using this

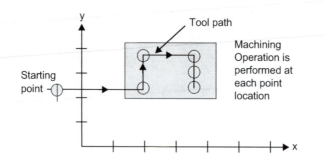

FIGURE 6.7 Point-to-point control in NC

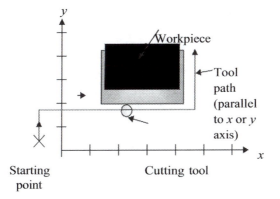

FIGURE 6.8   Straight-cut control in NC

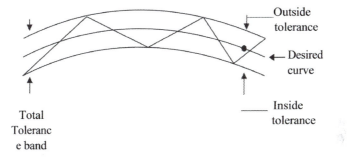

FIGURE 6.9   Straight line approximation of a curve

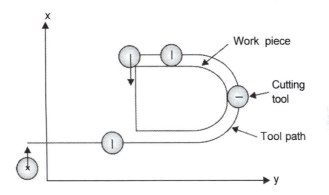

FIGURE 6.10   Contouring control in NC

technique, a large number of very closely spaced points are calculated which can fairly approximate the desired curve.

For example, if the cutter has to trace a parabola (Figure 6.10), a large number of closely spaced points are calculated on this profile, which are then joined by small straight lines. The profile generated by these small straight lines approximates a parabola. It is important to note that a large number of points need to be calculated on the profile so that we can get a smooth curve. It is not possible to manually calculate such a large number of points. Consequently, a number of mathematical subroutines or interpolation algorithms have been developed to solve the vast array of challenges that occur while generating a continuous, smooth route using a contouring-type NC system. Techniques of interpolation may be classed as linear, circular, helical, parabolic or cubic. (We discuss interpolation in more detail later.)

Mathematically, the three types of control can be distinguished in the following manner. Consider the movement of the worktable in XY plane. With point-to-point control, any point (x, y) in the xy plane can be accessed by the machine.

In the case of straight-cut control, apart from x and y, $\dfrac{dx}{dt}$ and $\dfrac{dy}{dt}$ are also controlled, but only one at a time, the other being zero.

With contouring control both $\dfrac{dx}{dt}$ and $\dfrac{dy}{dt}$ are controlled simultaneously. A proper ratio of $\dfrac{dx}{dt}$ and $\dfrac{dy}{dt}$ is maintained for executing motion along slant lines. Since a curve is approximated by small straight-line segments, the ratio of $\dfrac{dx}{dt}$ and $\dfrac{dy}{dt}$ is continuously updated so as to approximate the curve within a desired tolerance band.

Contouring control in two and three axes is most common. Some machines have the capability of controlling motion in five axes simultaneously. These machines can machine virtually any type of surface accurately. Such machines are however very expensive.

6.2.3 CLASSIFICATION BASED ON DRIVES USED IN NC MACHINES

Based on the type of drive system used, NC machines have been classified as: Hydraulic drive NC, Pneumatic drive NC and Electric drive NC. The electric drive NC may either comprise of stepper motor, or AC servomotor or DC servomotor. Various types of drives are discussed as follows:

Hydraulic servomotors are variable speed motors. They produce more power compared to electric servomotors. Such motors are used on large capacity machines. These motors are controlled by an electronic or pneumatic control system which regulates the amount of fluid to the drive. These motors are rarely used but these do find application in dedicated machine tools requiring high rotational speeds, e.g., up to 25,000 rpm. In this case the cutter spindles are driven by turbines which in turn operate with oil or fluid under high pressure.

Pneumatic drives are not popular in NC machines as air is highly compressible. This drive is not very accurate and takes less load as compared to hydraulic servomotor.

Leakage of working fluid is also a serious problem.

Stepper motors: These are used for precise positioning of objects or machine slides without using a feedback control system. The stepper motor is powered by an electrical pulse train generated by the machine's brain. The number of pulses causes the motor shaft to revolve, while the pulse frequency determines the shaft's angular velocity. A stepper motor rotates a precise angular distance, i.e., one step for each pulse it receives. Each pulse turns the shaft by a fraction of one revolution, called the *step angle*. The angle, a, is determined by the relation,

$$a = \frac{360}{np}$$

where n = is the number of phases

$$P = \text{number of poles}$$

Hence, for $n = 4$ and $p = 6$ the step angle, $a = 15°$. The angle of rotation will then be given by number of pulses multiplied by $15°$.

Stepper motors are less expensive and easy to control. However, there are certain limitations with these motors. They produce less power, the maximum being around 5 kW typically. They are noisy. Sometimes, they may miss one or two steps when working under overload. This effects the accuracy of the machine. The number of pulses per second restricts the RPM. For example, for a typical value of 8000 pulses per second, the maximum RPM is only 2400 for a 1.8° step angle (8000/200 × 60 = 2400).

Hence, stepper motor motors are used on light duty machinery where high precision is not required. Such motors are commonly used in open-loop control system.

6.2.3.1 Basic Length Unit (BLU)

Let (x_1, y_1) and (x_2, y_2) be the coordinates of two points in mm and the speed of tool motion along the axes be V m/min, then

Travelling time (in seconds) along x-axis $= \dfrac{(x_2 - x_1) \times 60 \times 10^{-3}}{V}$,

Travelling time (in seconds) along y-axis $= \dfrac{(y_2 - y_1) \times 60 \times 10^{-3}}{V}$,

Incremental position commands in x-direction $= \dfrac{(x_2 - x_1)}{BLU}$,

Incremental position commands in y-direction $= \dfrac{(y_2 - y_1)}{BLU}$,

Where $BLU = \dfrac{Lead\,screw\,pitch\,(mm)}{Steps\,per\,revolution\,of\,stepper\,motor}$

Also, linear velocity of stepper motor, V is given by the expression

$$V = \text{pulse frequency} \times \text{BLU} \times 60 \text{ mm/min}$$

Example 6.1: *An NC machine uses a 200 pulses/revolution encoder and a 10 teeth/inch lead screw for its axis control. Determine the BLU of the machine.*

Solution: Pitch of lead screw $= \dfrac{1}{10}$ inch $= \dfrac{25.4}{10}$ mm = 2.54 mm

$$BLU = \dfrac{Lead\,screw\,pitch\,(mm)}{Steps\,per\,revolution\,of\,stepper\,motor}$$

$$BLU = \dfrac{2.54}{200} = 0.0127\,mm$$

Example 6.2: *An NC machine has a resolution (BLU) 0.01 mm. To move the cutter from coordinates (1, 1) to (3, 4) (both coordinates in mm) at 18 mm/min, how many pulses and at what rate would the controller send to the x and y servo motors?*

Solution: Given cutter feed rate is 18 mm/min.

$$\text{BLU} = 0.01 \text{ mm}$$

Thus, rate at which pulses are generated by the controller $= \dfrac{18}{0.01} = 1800$ pulses/min.

Distance to be covered in x-direction = 3 − 1 = 2 mm. Distance to be covered in y-direction = 4 −− 1 = 3 mm.

Thus, number of pulses sent to x-servo motor $= \dfrac{2}{0.01} = 200$

Number of pulses sent to y-servomotor $= \dfrac{3}{0.01} = 300$

Example 6.3: *The worktable in an NC positioning system is driven by a lead screw with a 4 mm pitch. The lead screw is rotated by a stepping motor that has 250 step angles. The worktable is programmed to move a distance of 100 mm from its present position at a travel speed of 300 mm/min.*

   (i) *How many pulses are required to move the table the specified distance?*
  (ii) *What is the pulse rate to achieve the desired table speed?*

Solution: Given pitch = 4 mm, step angle $= \dfrac{360}{250} = 1.44°$.

$$BLU = \frac{Pitch}{Steps\,per\,revolution} = \frac{4}{250} = 0.016\,mm$$

(i) Pulses required to move the table through 100 mm

$$= \frac{100}{0.016} = 6250$$

Frequency of pulses required to achieve a travel speed of 300 mm/min $= \dfrac{300}{0.016} = 18,750 \text{ pulses/min.}$

DC motors are commonly used for stepless control of speed. These are variable speed motors and rotate in response to the applied voltage. Controlled rectification using thyristors has been used to convert AC to DC and obtain the desired speeds. Recently, microprocessor-based servo amplifiers have also been used as power sources of the main spindle motor of up to 250 kW ratings. In DC servomotors, the speed is controlled by varying the voltage magnitude.

AC induction motors are also used for stepless control. These are also variable speed motors, but the speed is varied by varying the frequency of AC supply. These are more reliable and easily maintained because of the absence of brushes. AC servos can produce more power than DC servos. Larger machines use induction motors rather than stepper motors.

In most of the cases of NC and CNC machines, the spindle is driven by an AC or DC servomotors. The speed of these motors is infinitely variable by means of a techogenerator.

6.2.4 Classification Based on Axis of Machine Movement

In NC and CNC technology, an axis is any direction of movement of machine slides such as X, Y and Z axis. The number of axes which can be simultaneously and independently controlled by the MCU, is used to classify a machine. Therefore, the machines are classified as two, three, four or five axis machines.

For example, a simple CNC lathe is a two-axis machine, where the two axes refer to the tool movement in two orthogonal directions: One along the axis of the job and the other perpendicular to it. If a lathe has two tool turrets, both working independently, then it is a four-axis machine. The MCU is capable of controlling four axes simultaneously in this case. Obviously, the simplest machine is a two-axis machine.

A machine such as a milling machine can have several axes, all of which may not be controlled by the MCU. Such axes are adjusted manually and are useful for proper positioning of the job. These axes are not counted while specifying a machine. For example, there can be a three-axis miller having six degrees of freedom.

6.3 COORDINATE SYSTEM USED IN NC MACHINES

The purpose of a coordinate system in an NC machine is to provide a means of positioning the tool with respect to the workpiece.

Various NC machines have different coordinate systems. Let us discuss coordinate system used in some common machines like NC lathe, drilling machine and milling machine.

6.3.1 NC LATHE

A lathe is provided with two feed axes. These are called x and z axes in radial and axial directions respectively. Note that it is a convention to use part diameter (and not radius) as the x value, in the part program.

6.3.2 NC MILLING MACHINE

An NC milling machine has three linear axes: The x, y and z axis. In addition, these machines may have the capacity to control one or more rotational axis. The rotational axes are called a, b and c axis and specify angles about x, y and z axis respectively. Refer to Figure 6.11.

The right-hand rule is used to determine the positive and negative directions of angular motion. According to the rule, when the thumb is directed in the positive linear axis direction, "the fingers of the right hand are curled in the positive rotational direction" *(x, y* or *z).* Figure 6.11 illustrates this.

6.3.3 NC DRILLING MACHINE

An NC drilling machine uses a coordinate system similar to that of a milling machine. However, there are no rotational axes, a, b or c. The x and the y axis are defined in the plane of the table while the z-axis is perpendicular to this plane. The spindle axis is colinear with the z-direction.

In NC machines, there are two methods of giving coordinates of various points. These are:

(1) Absolute coordinate system,
(2) Incremental coordinate system.

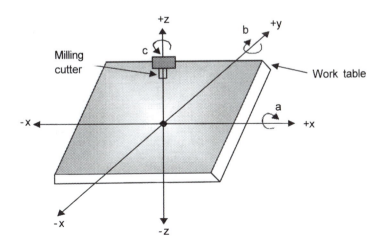

FIGURE 6.11   Coordinate system for NC milling machines

Depending upon the type of NC machine, the part programmer can use either of the two coordinate systems.

6.3.4 Absolute Coordinate System

In this system, tool locations are always defined with reference to a fixed origin, also called a zero point. This origin serves as a datum point from which all the distances are measured parallel to each axis of the system. The location of origin is decided by the user before starting the machining operation. The location of origin can be decided in two ways depending upon whether the location of origin is fixed at certain point or whether it can also be changed. These two types of origin are called fixed origin and floating origin.

Fixed origin: Is always located at the same position on the machine table. Normally, its position is lower-left corner (south-west corner) of the machine tool table such that all the measurements are positive with respect to origin.

Floating origin: This system allows the machine operator to have a zero point at any position on the machine table. This feature is more common in modern NC machines. The location of origin "0" is stored in the MCU memory and the control can be returned to it simply by pressing the zero button.

Refer to Figure 6.12(a) and (b), which shows rectangular plates drilled with five holes. To drill the holes, both fixed origin and floating origin can be used.

It is noteworthy that in an absolute coordinate system all the dimensions are independent of each other. Thus, even if one dimension is measured incorrectly by mistake, the other dimensions remain unaffected and can be measured correctly.

6.3.5 Incremental Coordinate System

In this system, the next tool position is defined with respect to the previous tool position (see Figure 6.12(b). In the previous example, if the tools starts from point P and drills hole in the sequence 1, 2, 3, 4, 5, then the coordinates of:

(A) Point 1 (with respect to point P) is (20, 10),
(B) Point (2) (w.r.t. to point 1) is (40, 0),
(C) Point 3 (w.r.t. point 2) are (0, 20),
(D) Point 4 (w.r.t. point 3) are −40, 0),
(E) Point 5 (w.r.t. point 4) are (20, −10).

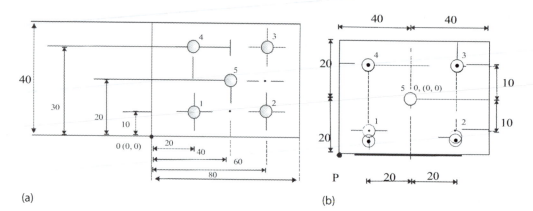

(a)   (b)

FIGURE 6.12   (a) Absolute coordinate system with fixed origin. (b) Absolute coordinate system with floating origin

From the above discussion, we can conclude that:

1. In absolute dimensioning if a dimension has to be changed in the part program, it is easy, as all the measurements are independent of each other.

However, in an incremental system, program editing is difficult as each dimension depends on its previous dimension. Also, if there is an error in one dimension, the same error is passed on to all the subsequent dimensions.

2. An absolute system has slower operation as each time the control has to come back to the origin, whereas incremental systems are comparatively faster.
3. Most of the engineering drawings are made in an absolute system hence the programs can be made directly in an absolute system. However, if we wish to use an incremental coordinate system, all the dimensions need to be converted into incremental form.

6.4 DRAWBACKS OF NC MACHINES

Some of the inherent technical disadvantages of conventional NC machines are as follows:

Machine control unit: The control of an NC machine is hard wired which makes any change in the controller very difficult because of limitations of its basic, configurations as shown in Figure 6.13.
Punched tape: The tape which is usually made of paper gets damaged on repeated use. The stronger tapes like mylar-reinforced paper and mylar-coated aluminium are very expensive.
Tape reader: The tape reader is the least reliable hardware component of the system and fails frequently.
Part programming mistakes: Mistakes like syntax error and numerical error are very common during preparation of programs. This makes the tape preparation a lengthy and tedious task.
Non-optimal speeds and feeds: NC control cannot optimise cutting speed, feed rate or other machining parameters during the machining operation. Hence, the part programmer must decide the cutting parameters carefully. But this reduces productivity.
Management information system: A conventional NC machine cannot provide any information like the number of components manufactured or number of machine breakdowns, etc. which may be desired by the management.

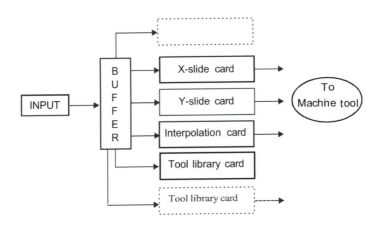

FIGURE 6.13 Hardwired numerical control

Due to such problems in the NC technology, machine tool manufacturers started work on developing further advancements.

6.5 COMPARISON OF ORDINARY AND NC MACHINE TOOLS

- An NC machine is incorporated with an MCU. This MCU has both hardware as well as software to read and interpret the part program. The machine reads the part program and performs the machining operation accordingly. An ordinary machine does not have an MCU. The movement of slides is controlled manually.

  LO 4. To compare ordinary and NC machine tools

- Processing equipment of a machine is the unit that performs useful work. This unit is common in both NC and ordinary machines.
- Circular and parabolic interpolation is quite easy to perform on an NC machine by using software interpolators. Hence, contour shapes can be achieved easily. On ordinary machines, these operations are very difficult to perform.
- In an NC machine, feedback control is possible, whereas on ordinary machines feedback control is not possible.
- In NC machines, there are two methods of giving coordinate points: Absolute coordinate system and incremental coordinate system. The origin may be fixed or floating type.

In ordinary machines, floating origin cannot be used.

- An NC machine may have storage memory associated with it, but an ordinary machines does not have a memory associated with it.
- An NC machine usually has an automatic tool changer (ATC) to change the tools whereas an ordinary machine does not make use of an ATC. The tool has to be changed manually.
- Sophisticated NC machines may have automatic doors which if left open would not start the machining operation, whereas an ordinary machine does not have such facilities.

Advantages of NC machines over conventional machine tools:

- Greater accuracy,
- Improved product quality,
- Lower tooling cost due to omission of expensive jigs and fixtures,
- Lower lead time and setup time,
- Less idle time and better machine utilisation,
- Greater productivity,
- Operator errors are reduced,
- Less scrap or rework.

6.6 APPLICATIONS OF NC SYSTEM

The numerical control has been used for both machine tool and non-machine tool applications. The machine tool applications include:

1. NC lathe,
2. NC milling machine,
3. NC drilling,
4. NC boring,

   5. NC cylindrical grinder,
   6. NC horizontal/vertical machining centre,
   7. Welding machines,
   8. Thermal cutting machines (e.g., laser cutting, plasma arc cutting),
   9. Press for sheet metal bending,
  10. Punch presses.

The non-machine tool applications include but are not limited to:

1. Drafting machines,
2. Coordinate measuring machines,
3. Filament winding machines,
4. Cloth cutting machines,
5. Riveting machines.

6.7   METHODS OF IMPROVING ACCURACY

Different methods and techniques have been adopted from time to time to improve the accuracy of NC machines:

1. Closed-loop systems with feedback sensors improve the accuracy of slide movement.
2. Ball screws are now being used in place of lead screws which eliminates back lash friction and play.
3. Use of software interpolators and the corresponding programs improve the accuracy of machining complicated profiles and intricate shapes.
4. Use of incremental dimensioning method and floating zero also improves the accuracy while drilling a number of holes.
5. Important part programming features such as cutter diameter compensation, dwell programming, subroutines, parametric programming and canned cycles all lead to the improvement of accuracy.
6. Machine can now perform real-time diagnosis of the component being machined as well as various parts of the machine itself. This leads to improvement of accuracy of the component being manufactured, and reduced maintenance and breakdown of machine itself.
7. Adaptive control feature of the machine tool also helps in improving accuracy as various machining parameters are optimised.
8. NC machine accuracy has been improved over a period of time by minimising tool deflection, vibration and chatter.
9. Accuracy of the machine has also been improved by minimising thermal deflection of the machine tool. This has been achieved by providing large heat removing surfaces, use of low friction bearings and symmetrical distribution of heat sources.

6.8   METHODS OF REDUCING PRODUCTION TIME

The total machining time of a job comprises of actual cutting time, idle and reverse motion time, workpiece loading and unloading time and tool changing time.

The actual cutting time can be slightly reduced by optimising cutting speed, feed and depth of cut, etc. But the production time can be considerably reduced by reducing idle and reverse motion time, workpiece loading and unloading time and tool changing time.

Idle and reverse motions are those during which cutting does not take place. In the turning process, a majority of motions are of this type. In drilling and milling idle time is also substantial. This can be reduced by increasing the traverse velocity.

Loading and unloading time can be reduced by automating the process using suitable jigs and fixtures.

Tool changing time can be reduced by using automatic tool changer.

6.9 DIRECT NUMERICAL CONTROL (DNC)

In the late 1960s attempts were made to use a computer as the controller of an NC machine. This resulted in development of DNC technology. A central computer serves as the brains of a network of devices (Figure 6.14). Therefore, the unstable tape and tape reader are excluded from the control unit. Instead, the computer transmits the software of the component to the

LO 5. To understand Direct numerical control

MCU. This core computer's storage capacity is often vast, and it may be a mainframe. The mainframe computer stores the control signals for each NC machine and sends them to the respective machines after processing.

The main parts of a DNC system are:

1. Central computer,
2. Bulk memory to store NC programs,
3. Telecommunication lines,
4. Machine tool.

The main advantage of DNC over NC is that it omits the most unreliable components of NC i.e., the tape and the tape reader.

The major disadvantage of DNC machines is that if the mainframe computer, breaks down for any reason, all the connected NC machines stop working.

As the cost of computers started falling, a dedicated computer began to be used as the controller for each machine. This resulted in development of CNC machines.

6.10 COMPUTER NUMERICAL CONTROL (CNC)

Simply explained, a CNC machine is an NC machine with an integrated computer that serves as the machine's primary control unit (MCU). The adaptability of this machine exceeds that of an NC machine. Contrary to what would be expected, a CNC machine is not subject to the same limita-

LO 6. To understand Computer numerical control and its features

tions as an NC machine. Minimal electronic equipment is needed for control. Generally, software is used to do the basics. That is why it is sometimes termed as softwired control (see Figure 6.15).

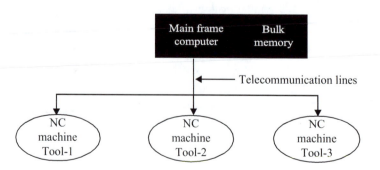

FIGURE 6.14 Schematic of DNC system

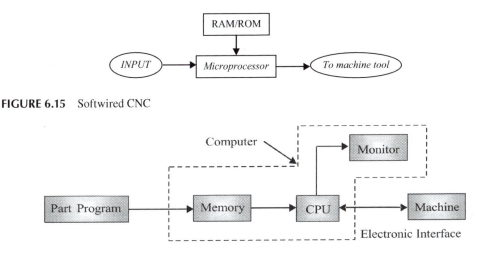

FIGURE 6.15   Softwired CNC

FIGURE 6.16   General configuration of a CNC system

The transition from wired to wireless networks has increased industrial agility and efficiency. CNC machines have the advantage of being able to read, store and alter component programmes, as opposed to their NC equivalents. RAM stores part programmes, while ROM stores control programmes for slide movement, interpolation, etc. On CNC machines, graphical capabilities, diagnostic procedures and system troubleshooting are also accessible. With this, operating and maintaining CNC equipment is much simplified.

NC and CNC machines seem to be almost identical. The only discernible distinction is that CNC machines have a display (CRT) whereas NC machines do not. Figure 6.16 is a simplified block diagram of a CNC system. Thanks to the monitor's continuous status updates, the machine operator may continue a conversation with the machine.

There are several types of CNC machines available today. CNC lathe (turning centre) and CNC milling machines are the most prevalent kinds of CNC machines (horizontal and vertical machining centres).

6.10.1   FEATURES OF CNC SYSTEM

Let us discuss some features of CNC technology that are beyond what is normally found in a conventional hardwired MCU of NC machines. These are:

1. Control system features,
2. Memory features,
3. Programming features,
4. Programmable logic control features,
5. Diagnostic features.

Let us discuss these features one by one.

1. **Control system features:** CNC control is essentially microprocessor-based control. The control may have single or multiple microprocessors. In cases of multiple microprocessors, each takes care of a particular function. Normally, 16- and 32-bit microprocessors are used. The commonly used microprocessors are INTEL 8086, INTEL 80186, MOTOROLA 68000 and TEXAS TMS 900.

Both hardware and software have modular construction. This implies that a specific module is used to serve a specific purpose. This is advantageous in the sense that if failure of one module takes place, it can be replaced or improved easily without effecting the other parts of the control. This improves flexibility and accuracy.

In CNC control there are special programs called executive programs that contain the intelligence needed to carry out different tasks in a CNC systems. For example, the executive program may show an error if you try to operate the machine without closing the door or if the pneumatic pressure is not sufficient to operate the machine. The executive program is usually resident in EPROM (erasable programmable read only memory).

2. **Memory features:** Refer to the following table for memory features:

Memory Type	Features	Design Applications
1. EPROM	Non-volatile, widely used storage	Used for executive program
2. Dynamic RAM	Semiconductor memory	Used for storing part programs
CMOS RAM	Fast access and volatile	
Bubble memory	Non-volatile but lower speed than semi-conductor memory	
3. Magnetic tape, compact disc, floppy disk	Permanent memory, non-volatile	Used for offline data storage

3. **Programming features:** The CNC programming languages usually have the following features:

- Absolute and incremental programming.
- Diameter and radius programming.
- Linear, circular, parabolic and helical interpolation.
- Multiple part program storage capacity.
- **Sequence number search:** If modifications have to be done randomly in various lines, etc. in a lengthy program, you make use of sequence number search in order to reach that block instantaneously.
- **Dwell programming:** If you wish to measure dimensions while the machining is still going on, tools like drilling cutter, end milling cutter, etc. are allowed to dwell (i.e., rotate at one single position) for some time. Dwell position also gives the operator some time to remove the chips.
- **Tool length and diameter compensation:** Due to repeated use, the cutting tool becomes worn and there may be considerable difference between the actual size of the cutter and its original size. If you continue to use the undersized cutter, extra material will be left on the workpiece. Hence, in order to ensure accurate tool path definition, the machine operator should enter the actual tool dimensions into the MCU. Compensations are than automatically made in the computed tool path.

Tool length sensors are nowadays being used to measure cutter length. This measured value is used to correct the programmed tool path.

- **Subroutines/microprogramming:** This feature is used when an operation has to be performed repeatedly. The frequently used machining cycles are saved as subroutines or functions in the memory that can be called by a part program. Hence, there is no need to repeat the same code again and again in the part program.
- **Parametric programming:** CNC programs are written in terms of variables like length, depth, diameter, etc. such that if there is change in value of any one variable, the corresponding change in value of other variables is automatically reflected.

- **Canned cycles:** Also called fixed cycles, these are routines used to remove bulk material in machining operations mostly during rough machining cycles. A canned cycle generates multiple tool movements through a single block. Hence, only one block with a G code can be used instead of two or more blocks for programming the motion.
    4. **Programmable logic controller (PLC):** It is a software-oriented interface between the CNC system and the machine tool to control functions such as coolant on/off, pallet operation, spindle speed functions and tool functions.

A PLC has memory capacity like 4 kB, 7 kB, etc. It has a high-speed microprocessor to execute sequence programming. It incorporates software, timers and counters to transfer data between the MCU and machine tool.

5. **Diagnostic features:** Modern CNC machines possess online self-diagnostic capability which monitors certain aspects of the machine tools and MCU to detect malfunctions or signs of impending malfunctions. A message is displayed on the controller's CRT monitor when the breakdown is about to occur or has already occurred. Hence, corrective action can be taken immediately as this feature can indicate which part of the machine has failed.
   - The machine can perform real time diagnostics of power supply, voltage level, etc.
   - Online diagnosis of the part program's syntax and parity check can be performed.
   - Offline diagnosis helps to ascertain in which part of the machine the breakdown has occurred.

6.10.2   SOME MODERN FEATURES OF CNC

1. **Advanced hardware architecture:** Modern CNC makes use of advanced electronics. Due to very large-scale integration (VLSI), the number of IC chips being used in a control circuit has reduced. This has resulted in improved reliability.
2. **Software modularity:** The CNC machine makes use of modular software, so that in future, if there is a need to change any module, suitable changes can be incorporated easily.
3. **Adaptive control:** The modern CNC tries to optimise the machining process by measuring certain output process variables (like force, torque, cutting temperature, vibration amplitude) and using these to control speed and/or feed. The concept involved in adaptive control is to maximise the material removal rate by varying cutting speed and feed so as to maintain process variables like tool temperature or vibrations within specified limits.
4. **Conversational programming:** The operator can interact with the machine and can get suitable guidance from the software itself while preparing the part program.
5. **Programming flexibility:** Most of the CNC machines can work with a number of programming languages. They can perform a number of mathematical operations at high speed. Such machines can generate complex profiles.
6. **Colour graphics:** The CNC machine computer is capable of colour graphics display. Hence the MCU computer can show tool, workpiece and machining operation, etc. using various colours.
7. The CNC can select suitable cutting speed and feed automatically depending on information provided in the part program.
8. Some modern CNC machines can automatically select cutting tools and proper sequence of tooling.
9. The CNC computer can simulate the machining process and can show the final shape of the finished components after machining.

10. **Background programming:** This feature is provided in the machines which perform long machining operations continuously. In such machines, the computer memory is bifurcated into two parts such that while one program is being used for machining, the new programs can be entered in the other part of the memory.

Some standard CNC controllers are

1. Acramatic,
2. Allen Bradley,
3. Anilan,
4. Cincinnati,
5. Deckel CNC,
6. Emco-Turn,
7. FANUC,
8. Heidenhein,
9. Mazak,
10. Philips,
11. Sinumerik.

Among these, FANUC controls are the most popular. CNC controls popular in India are:

1. FANUC (developed in Japan),
2. HINUMERIC (developed by Hindustan Machine tools, HMT),
3. Anilan Crusade,
4. Allen Bradley,
5. Electrameric.

11. **Tool changing devices :** A complex object may need the use of several instruments. When necessary, the tools of a manual machine are replaced manually. In contrast, tool changes on a CNC machine are executed through part program. The numerous instruments are kept in a tool magazine or a tool drum. If a replacement is necessary, the drum will move to an empty position, approach the old tool and then extract it from the spindle. To change tools, it rotates into position, inserts the tool into the spindle and retracts. The technique outlined below is common for a milling machine's automatic tool changing (ATC). When a new tool is required, the lathe's tool magazine must be repositioned. Modifying the instrument physically is unnecessary. The drums or magazines are accurately indexed so as to provide the desired tool to the ATC mechanism. 8/16/24 bit magazines are quite common, but ATCs with much larger capacity like 100/200/500 are also available. Tool changing time is of the order of a few seconds. This saves time and thus, increases productivity.

12. **Work handling devices:** A number of machining centres have several linear or rotary pallets. By shifting or rotating, these pallets may readily change positions on the machine's table. The other pallets may be used to clamp and unclamp materials while the front pallet is used for machining. This results in less time spent on setup and material handling, which increases production.

13. **Feed drive:** A very important element of the feed drive system on a CNC machine is the recirculating ball screw transmission (see Figure 6.17). This consists of a lead screw and a split nut. As in manual machines, the feed motor rotates the screw to which the nut is attached. The nut moves longitudinally, giving the required feed motion. In order to minimise frictional losses, recirculating balls are used between the nut and the lead screw. The

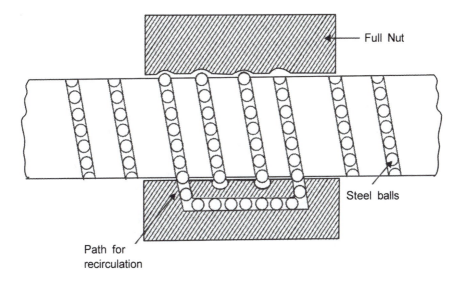

FIGURE 6.17   Recirculating ball screw

friction is greatly reduced because rolling friction is much less than sliding friction. The two halves of the nut are preloaded with respect to each other. This reduces the back lash to a great extent, thus ensuring high accuracy in the movement of the slides. This is the major advantage of the ball screw transmission system. Now, such a system is invariably used in all CNC machines.

To ensure that there is no collision between the tool and the chuck, limit switches are used which automatically stop the feed motion beyond a certain limit. Sometimes, the feed drive is coupled through a slipping clutch which stops the drive immediately in case of any collision, thus minimising the damage.

14. Sophisticated CNC machines have automatic doors. The door is actuated usually by the double acting pneumatic cylinder. Again, as a safety measure, the machine does not execute a program if the door is left open. Even the spindle does not rotate. However, usually the provision is made for slow rotation, say 100 rpm of the spindle even if the door is not closed. This is required for tool offsetting, where measurement is to be taken when the tool just touches the job. Unless the spindle rotates, it is difficult to realise that the tool has just touched the job. With a rotating spindle, a thin layer of chip is removed the moment the tool touches the job. The tool can be made to approach the job in small steps of accuracy of the order of microns. Also, unless the door is open, the operator cannot access the job. Hence, for the operator's convenience, the machine allows slow spindle rotation with its door open.
15. In a manual lathe, the spindle is normally driven by a three-phase AC motor. The motor rotates with a constant velocity. The spindle speed selection is obtained through the gear box. Depending on the design of the gear box, a number of different fixed speeds can be chosen. Intermediate speeds are not available. However, in case of NC and CNC machine, the spindle is driven by AC or DC servomotors whose speed is infinitely variable by means of a technogenerator. The programmer can choose any spindle speed within the available speed range. A typical speed range is 100 rpm to 5000 rpm. Speed outside this range is usually not required.

6.10.3   Difference between NC and CNC Machines

Let us try to compare NC machines and CNC machines.

NC Machines	CNC Machines
1. NC machines are hard wired. The program is read using tape and tape reader.	1. CNC machines are soft wired. The controller is computer based.
2. The tape and the tape reader are the most unreliable components.	2. The tape reader is omitter, since it makes use of microprocessor based control.
3. Part programming mistakes are common due to use of punched tape.	3. Part programming mistakes are not there.
4. The control system does not present opportunity to make changes in speeds and feeds during cutting process.	4. Speed, feed and depth of cut can be varied while machining thus giving high productivity.
5. Since the controller is hard wired, it cannot be altered or improved easily.	5. Since the controller is softwired, various new features such as interpolation algorithms etc. can be added over a period of time.

6.11   ADAPTIVE CONTROL

The concept of adaptive control came into being because of the increasing complexity of parts to be machined and ever-increasing sources of variability in machining. The following are the sources of variability in machining:

LO 7. To understand Adaptive control

1. **Tool wear** leads to increase in cutting forces.
2. **Variation in workpiece rigidity** due to improper setup or fixturisation.
3. **Air gaps** may appear in the cutter path due to typical workpiece geometry. In such air gaps, the feed rate should be increased to save time.
4. **Workpiece hardness may vary at different sections** due to which cutting speed or feed should be varied accordingly.
5. Sometimes, the geometry of cut may also vary in the form of changing depth of cut and width of cut. In such cases feed rate can be adjusted to accommodate for variability.

Under such machining conditions, an adaptive controller is most suitable.

Adaptive control is a further extension of computer numerical control. It refers to a control system that measures certain machining process variables (like torque, force, spindle deflection, temperature, vibration amplitude, power) and uses them to control machining parameters like cutting speed and feed so as to achieve higher machining efficiency. The performance and efficiency in machining is usually judged by metal removal rate and cost per volume of metal removed. The optimum value of machining parameters is maintained to achieve high machining efficiency.

Adaptive control determines the proper speed and/or feed during machining as a function of variations in some factors like workpiece material hardness, depth of cut, etc. Adaptive control has the capability to respond to and compensate for these variations during the process. NC machines lack such capabilities.

Adaptive control systems for machine tools have been classified into two categories. These are:

1. Adaptive control with optimisation (ACO),
2. Adaptive control with constraints (ACC).

ACO makes use of index of performance (IP) which is indicative of overall system performance. Factors like production rate or cost per volume of material removed can be used as an index of performance. An adaptive controller aims at optimising the index of performance by varying speed or feed in the machining operation.

$$IP = f\left(\frac{MRR}{TWR}\right)$$

MRR is material removal rate of a machining operation.

TWR is the tool wear rate of the machining operation.

In ACC-based adaptive controllers, constraints limits are imposed on measured process variables. Cutting speed or feed is regulated so as to maintain measured process variables within the constraint limit values.

6.11.1 Advantages of Adaptive Control of Machining

1. Increased production rates compared to conventional machines or NC machines.
2. Increased tool life due to efficient use of cutting tool. Cutter is uniformly loaded. It is never severely loaded.
3. Parts are protected against possible damage.
4. There is less operator intervention.
5. Part programming becomes easier as selection of feed, etc. is left to the controller.

6.12 PROGRAMMABLE LOGIC CONTROLLER (PLC)

A programmable logic controller (PLC) is a digitally operated electric device that uses an internal programmable memory to store instructions for implementing specific functions such as logic, sequencing, timing, counting and arithmetic and to control different types of machines or processes through digital or analogue input/output modulus. All the logic and sequencing functions can be implemented by means of a PLC. Now, instead of using discrete components such as relays, switches, counters and other separate elements to construct a sequence controller, a PLC can be used. A PLC is a piece of computer hardware that may be designed to replicate the behaviour of discrete logic and sequence elements, such as the relays, timers, counters and other hardwired components present in conventional control systems.

6.12.1 Advantages of PLC

(i) Programming the PLC is easier than wiring the relay control panel.
(ii) A PLC can be reprogrammed. On the other hand, conventional controls must be rewired and are often scrapped instead.
(iii) PLCs occupy less space than relay control panels.
(iv) Maintenance of the PLC is easier.
(v) PLCs have greater reliability.
(vi) The PLC can be interfaced to the plant computer systems more easily than the relays.

6.12.2 Components of PLC

The basic components of PLC are:

(i) *Input Module.* It receives input signals to the PLC. These are the signals from limit switches, push buttons, sensors and other on/off devices. Both the input and output modules are the connections to the industrial process that is to be controlled.
(ii) *Output module.* It sends the output signals from the controller to operate motors, valves and other devices to actuate the process.

(iii) *Processor.* The processor is the Central Processing Unit (CPU) of the PLC. It executes the various logic and sequencing functions on the inputs and determines the appropriate output signals. The processor in a PLC is a microprocessor similar to one used in personal computers.

(iv) *Memory.* Sufficient memory is attached to the processor so that it can store programs of logic, sequencing and other input/output operations. The memory of a typical PLC may range from 1 kB to 48 kB.

(v) *Power Supply.* A power supply of 11 V AC is typically used to drive a PLC even through components of the industrial process that are regulated may have a higher voltage and power rating than the controller itself.

(vi) *Programming device.* A PLC is programmed by means of a programming device. This device is usually detachable from the PLC so that it can be used for multiple PLCs. Various types of programming devices are commercially available. These include teach pendent type devices, similar to the one used by robot systems, and special PLC programming keyboards and CRT displays.

The schematic block diagram of PLC is shown in Figure 6.18.

First, the inputs to the processor retrieves and saves samples from the PLC in its memory. The command program is then executed. Using the input values stored in memory and control logic, the output values are computed. The output module receives updated output values. The phrase "scan" refers to the repetitive process of receiving data (input), executing the control software, and adjusting the output (output revision). How long it takes to perform a scan, also known as the scan time, is determined by the number and complexity of control activities to be conducted in each cycle.

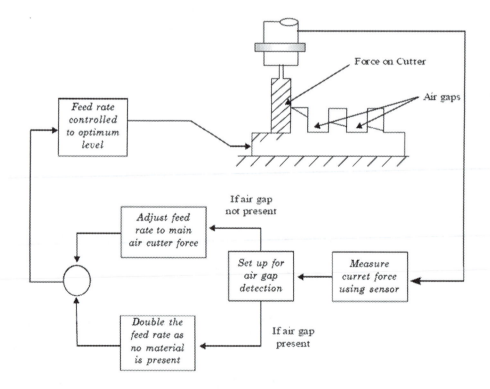

FIGURE 6.18   Schematic block diagram of PLC

6.12.3 FUNCTIONS OF PLC

As discussed earlier, the primary function of a PLC is *sequencing* and *logic control*, but it may have some additional facilities as well such as *arithmetic* functions, *matrix* functions and *analogue control*. Arithmetic functions include addition, subtraction, multiplication and division. These capabilities enable the implementation of more advanced control algorithms. A number of PLCs provide matrix operations on previously stored values.

Some PLCs are equipped with a Proportional-Integral-Derivative (PID) control algorithm. Approaching analogue control systems with digital computers, such as PLCs and computer process controllers. It can be understood that the evolution of PLCs is tending to merge with conventional computers.

6.13 SUMMARY

1. An NC machine has three basic components: MCU, part program and processing equipment.
2. Initially, punched tape and a tape reader were used to read part programs which were later replaced by memory.
3. Photoelectric technique, electric contact fingers and vacuum method were developed to read program from punched tapes.
4. An NC machine may have open-loop control or closed-loop control.
5. Depending upon the type of motion control, an NC machine can be classified as point-to-point, straight-cut and contouring NC.
6. An NC machine can make use of hydraulic, pneumatic or electric drives. But a pneumatic drive is not preferred due to inherent disadvantages.
7. NC machines make use of an appropriate coordinate system to position the tool with respect to work piece.
8. A CNC machine has a dedicated computer as compared to an NC machine.
9. DNC makes use of a single, high-capacity computer to control a number of machines.
10. CNC machines make use of a recirculating ball screw compared to an ordinary lead screw.
11. Adaptive control tries to optimise the machining process by controlling certain process variables like temperature, spindle deflection, etc.

6.14 EXERCISE

1. Define an NC system (BT level 1).
2. What is CAM? What is its future scope in India (BT level 1)?
3. State the suitability of NC technology. What are its advantages and disadvantages (BT level 1)?
4. Explain the working of basic components of NC machine with schematic diagrams (BT level 2).
5. What are the disadvantages of punched tape and tape reader? What are various methods of reading punched tape (BT level 1)?
6. Explain the working of machine control unit in detail (BT level 2).
7. Give classification of NC machine based on: (BT level 3)
    (i)   Type of control system,
    (ii) Type of motion control,
    (iii) Type of power drive used,
    (iv) Axis of machine movement.
8. Explain the coordinate movement, NC lathe, milling and drilling machine (BT level 2).
9. Differentiate between absolute and incremental coordinate system (BT level 4).

10. What is fixed origin and floating origin (BT level 1)?
11. What are the drawbacks of NC machines (BT level 1)?
12. Differentiate between ordinary and NC machine tools (BT level 4).
13. Propose some methods to improve the accuracy of machine tools (BT level 4).
14. What is direct numerical control and computer numerical control (BT level 1)?
15. State some features of modern CNC machines (BT level 1).
16. Differentiate between NC and CNC machines (BT level 4).

6.15   MULTIPLE-CHOICE QUESTIONS

1. What is the cylindrical coordinate system?
   a. A coordinate system that uses polar coordinates to define locations.
   b. A coordinate system that uses three axes, X, Y, and Z, to define locations.
   c. A coordinate system that uses only two axes, X and Y, to define locations.
   d. A coordinate system that uses a combination of Cartesian and polar coordinates to define locations.
2. What is the absolute coordinate system?
   a. A coordinate system that uses the machine's origin point as the reference point for all movements.
   b. A coordinate system that uses the last programmed point as the reference point for all movements.
   c. A coordinate system that uses a preset reference point for all movements.
   d. A coordinate system that uses a combination of absolute and incremental movements to define locations.
3. What is the incremental coordinate system?
   a. A coordinate system that uses the machine's origin point as the reference point for all movements.
   b. A coordinate system that uses the last programmed point as the reference point for all movements.
   c. A coordinate system that uses a preset reference point for all movements.
   d. A coordinate system that uses a combination of absolute and incremental movements to define locations.
4. What is the main advantage of NC and CNC machines over conventional machines?
   a. Higher accuracy and precision.
   b. Lower cost of raw materials.
   c. Greater flexibility in production schedules.
   d. Faster production speeds.
5. What is Direct Numerical Control (DNC)?
   a. A system that controls multiple machines from a central computer.
   b. A system that uses numerical data to control a machine's movement directly.
   c. A system that allows machines to communicate directly with each other.
   d. A system that uses a combination of manual and automated controls to operate machines.
6. What is a punch tape in DNC?
   a. A type of tape that contains numerical data used to control machines.
   b. A type of tape used to punch holes in materials.
   c. A type of tape used to hold material in place during machining.
   d. A type of tape used to mark reference points on materials.
7. What is a Remote Job Entry (RJE) system in DNC?
   a. A system that allows machines to communicate directly with each other.

b. A system that allows a central computer to control multiple machines.

c. A system that allows users to submit jobs to a central computer from a remote location.

d. A system that uses numerical data to control a machine's movement directly.

8. What is a Distributed Numerical Control (DNC) system?

a. A system that controls multiple machines from a central computer.

b. A system that uses numerical data to control a machine's movement directly.

c. A system that allows machines to communicate directly with each other.

d. A system that allows operators to manually input data into a machine.

9. What is the purpose of DNC?

a. To reduce the time required to manually program machines.

b. To improve the accuracy of machine movements.

c. To increase the productivity of machines.

d. All of the above.

Answers

1. Answer: a. A coordinate system that uses polar coordinates to define locations.

2. Answer: a. A coordinate system that uses the machine's origin point as the reference point for all movements.

3. Answer: b. A coordinate system that uses the last programmed point as the reference point for all movements.

4. Answer: a. Higher accuracy and precision.

5. Answer: a. A system that controls multiple machines from a central computer.

6. Answer: a. A type of tape that contains numerical data used to control machines.

7. Answer: c. A system that allows users to submit jobs to a central computer from a remote location.

8. Answer: c. A system that allows machines to communicate directly with each other.

9. Answer: d. All of the above.

7 NC Part Programming

Learning Outcomes: After studying this chapter, the reader should be able

LO 1: To understand manual part programming (BT level 2).
LO 2: To understand computer-aided part programming using APT programming language (BT level 2).

7.1 INTRODUCTION

The numerical control (NC) part program is a sequence of instructions which have to be executed by the Machine Control Unit (MCU). These instructions describe the work that has to be done by the machine tool and make the machine operate in a particular manner. The instructions are suitably coded in a format such that they can be easily interpreted by the MCU. The NC part program for a particular machine consists of instructions that define the cutting tool path and other information (like spindle speed, feed, depth of cut, etc.) which is necessary for a machining operation.

LO 1. To understand Manual part programming

A part program may be prepared manually without any help of the computer. This is called manual part programming. When NC part programming is accomplished with the help of some computer software, it is called computer-aided part programming.

We have already discussed in the previous chapter that a complete NC instruction is called a block. Various blocks are separated using an end of block (EOB) symbol. These blocks consist of NC-words. An NC-word is a complete unit of information in itself. Various NC-words used in part programming language are discussed below:

7.2 NC-WORDS USED IN PART PROGRAMS

1. N-Word.

Also called a sequence number, it is used to identify a block. When a part program is run, the block being executed is highlighted and can be identified by its sequence number.

An N-word is given for the programmer's convenience and can be omitted. The sequence numbers can be given in ascending or descending order. Some gap is recommended between sequence number of consecutive blocks (e.g., N10, N20, N30 …). This allows for future editing. For example, in case a new block has to be incorporated in the program, the entire sequence need not be changed. A sequence number consists of character "N" followed by digit numbers.

2. G-Word.

The controller must receive this word, often known as a "preparatory word," before receiving the subsequent commands. G01 is used in a continuous system to prepare the NC controller for linear interpolation. It utilises G02 to interpolate a circle in a clockwise direction.

DOI: 10.1201/9781003350842-7

3. X, Y and Z-words.

Also known as coordinates, they are used to give coordinate positions of the tool.

- X, Y and Z are absolute axis movements.
- U, V and W or I, J and K are relative or incremental movements.
- a, b and c are used to specify angular positions about x, y and z axis respectively.
- Different NC systems use different formats for writing X, Y, Z-words. For example, X 5.285, or Y −6.420. Some formats omit decimal points in writing the coordinate. For example, in such format the above X and Y words will be written as X 5285 or Y −6420. For positive coordinates, the plus sign is optional, while for negative coordinates the minus sign is mandatory.

4. F-word.

Also known as feed rate word, it is used to specify the feed rate in a machining operation. Units for the feed rate may be mm/min, mm/rev, inch/min or inch/rev as determined by the G-codes G94 and G95.

5. S-word

Also known as cutting speed word, it is used to specify the cutting speed of a machining process. i.e., the rate at which the spindle rotates, e.g., S1000 signifies that the rotating speed of spindle is less than 1000 rpm.

6. T-word.

A T-word is used for tool selection in machines having a tool turret or tool magazine. It is used when a cutting tool has to be changed. Each tool in the tool magazine is identified by a unique number. The tool corresponding to the T-word is automatically loaded in the cutting position by appropriate movements of the tool magazine or tool turret. For example, T01, T02, T03 represent the tool selection words.

7. M-words.

Also known as miscellaneous words, these are used to specify certain miscellaneous functions which may be available on the machine tool. For example, coolant ON/OFF, start spindle clockwise/counterclockwise, rewind the tape are some of the miscellaneous functions. The M-word is the last word in the block.

8. EOB.

Also known as end of block, it is used to identify the end of a complete instruction. When the control encounters EOB, it comes to know that this is the end of the current instruction.

7.3 FORMATS FOR WRITING PART PROGRAMS

Various standard formats have been developed to write NC part programs. Three formats are most commonly used. These are:

1. Word address format,
2. Tab sequential format,
3. Fixed block format.

These formats use different methods of writing the words in a block of instruction.

1. Word Address Format.

In this format, a letter precedes each word, hence identifying the function of numerical data followed and addressing the data to a specific location in the controller memory. There is a standard sequence in which NC words should be written. The sequence is

N- word
G-word
X- word
Y-word
Z-word
F-word
S-word
T-word
M-word
EOB

For example, in word address format, a typical instruction block will be written as:

N50	G81	X50	Y20	G600	S1000	T02	M08	EOB
N60	X100	EOB						

- In this format, since each NC word is prefixed by a corresponding letter, the words can be written in any sequence.
- If NC word numerical data remains unchanged then it need not be repeated in the subsequent block.

2. Tab Sequential Format.

In this format, the NC words are written in fixed standard sequence (as discussed previously), each word being separated by processing tab key.

- Since the words are written in the standard sequence, address letter (N, G, X, Y, ... etc.) are not required.

- If the numerical data of a word remains the same as in the previous block, it need not be repeated in the subsequent block.

For example, if the previous command in word address format is to be written in tab sequential format, it would become:

50 Tab 81 Tab 50 Tab 20 Tab 600 Tab 1000 Tab 02 Tab 08 Tab EOB. 60 Tab 100 Tab Tab Tab Tab Tab Tab EOB (carriage return) respectively.

3. Fixed Block Format.

- NC words in this format should be written in a standard sequence.

- Address letters are not required.
- Even if the numerical data of the words remain same as in the previous block, it must be repeated in the subsequent block.
- The characters within each NC word must be of the same length and format. Consider the previous example, the same block can be written in fixed block format as follows:

50	81	50	20	600	1000	02	08	EOB
60	81	100	20	600	1000	02	08	EOB

In this chapter, we use word the address format to write the part programs.

7.4 LIST OF COMMONLY USED G-WORDS

G-Word	Function
G00	Rapid traverse or rapid positioning in point-to-point mode linear interpolation
G01	
G02	Circular interpolation (clockwise). Circular interpolation (counterclockwise). Dwell (for a specified time
G03	period)
G04	
G10	
G17	Input cutter offset data
G18	
G19	*XY* plane selection (milling operation) *XZ* plane selection (milling operation) *YZ* plane selection (milling
G20	operation) Input values in inches
G21	
G27	
G28	Input values in millimetres. Reference point return check. Return to reference point. Thread cutting (in
G32	turning)
G40	
G41	
G42	Cancel cutter offset compensation. Cutter offset compensation (left). Cutter offset compensation (right). Tool length compensation + direction. Tool length compensation − direction
G43	
G44	
G49	Tool length compensation cancel

G50	To specify location of coordinate axis system origin relative to starting point of cutting tool in lathes
G90	Absolute dimension programming
G91	Incremental dimension programming
G92	Specify location of coordinate system axis system origin relative to starting point of cutting tool in milling and drilling machines and some lathes
G94	Feed rate in mm per min or inches per min for milling or drilling operation
G95	Feed rate in mm per revolution for milling or drilling operation
G98	Feed rate in mm per min for turning operation
G99	Feed rate in mm per revolution for turning operation

List of Commonly Used M-Words

M-Word	Function
M00	Program stop
M01	Optional program stop
M02	End of program, machine stop
M03	Spindle start (in clockwise direction)
M04	Spindle start (in counterclockwise direction)
M05	Spindle stop
M06	Tool change
M07	Coolant on (in flood mode)
M08	Coolant on (in mist mode)
M09	Coolant off
M10	Clamping of fixture, machine slide etc.
M11	Unclamp
M13	Spindle start in CW direction and turn coolant ON
M14	Spindle start in CCW direction and turn coolant ON
M17	Both spindle and coolant off
M30	End of program, machine stop, and rewind tape
M37	Mirror image X-axis
M38	Mirror image Y-axis
M39	Mirror image off
M60	Pallet change
M98	Subprogram call
M99	Subprogram end

7.5   DESCRIPTION OF G COMMANDS

7.5.1   G00 (Rapid Traverse)

Using G00, the tool may be rapidly moved to the desired spot. During rapid traversal, the machine moves at a high, predefined speed. In this instance, the cutting tool is not really slicing through the material; rather, it is being pushed into a desirable position relative to the workpiece. In G00, the rapid traverse rate exceeds the feed rate, allowing for a more effective use of machine time. During fast traversal, the feed rate is fixed by the machine and cannot be altered by the operator. Thus, it may vary depending on the kind of machine tool used.

For example,

$$G00 \ X \ 10.0 \ Y \ 10.0$$

implies rapid traverse of the tool to $X = 10$ and $Y = 10$ coordinates.

7.5.2   G01 (Linear Interpolation)

G01 is used to adjust the feed rate and hence the movement of the cutting tool. Therefore, it is used anytime and genuine material removal is necessary. The programmer must set the component's feed rate in its code.

For example,

$$G01 \ X \ 10.0 \ Y \ 15.0 \ F \ 25$$

implies movement of the tool to $X = 10$ and $Y = 15$ at feed rate 25.

7.5.3 G02 (CIRCULAR INTERPOLATION, CLOCKWISE)

Circular machining in the clockwise direction needs the G02 program. When running this command, the endpoint and radius of the arc, as well as the machining plane (XYZ or ZX), must be specified. To illustrate,

$$G02\ X\ 20.0\ Y\ 20.0\ R\ 15.0\ F\ 25.$$

Makes a tool to move clockwise along arc of radius 15 from current position to $X = 20$, $Y = 20$ at feed rate of 25.

7.5.4 G03 (CIRCULAR INTERPOLATION, COUNTERCLOCKWISE)

If a circular path must be machined in a counterclockwise manner, use the G03 programme.

7.5.5 G04 (DWELL)

The G04 key causes the application to pause for a specified length of time. It permits the tool to be spun at a consistent speed for a specified period of time.

The format of the command is

$$G04\ X(t)$$

where t is the dwell time.

For instance, if a drill or reamer should remain in a hole for five seconds, the directive may be as follows:

$$G04\ X5.0$$

7.5.6 G17, G18 AND G19

In milling operations, G17, G18 and G19 are utilised to choose the XY, XZ and YZ planes, respectively. For instance, G17 G03 X 20.0 Y 20.0 R 15.0 indicates tool movement over a counterclockwise circular arc in the XY plane.

7.5.7 G20 AND G21

Using the G20 and G21 keys, input data may be typed in either inches or millimetres.

7.5.8 G28

With G28, the tool may be directed to a destination from its initial location. This is accomplished by a rapid traversal mode.

7.5.9 G32 AND G78

When cutting straight or tapered threads, the G78 multiple threading cycle is used instead of the G32 cycle, since G32 does not enable immediate return to the beginning point. In contrast to G32, G78 is a canned cycle.

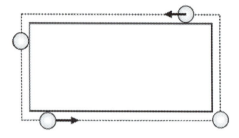

FIGURE 7.1   Cutter radius compensation

7.5.10   G40, G41 AND G42 (CUTTER RADIUS COMPENSATION)

G41 and G42 are employed to deviate the cutter from its intended route by a distance equal to its radius. Figure 7.1 depicts the end machining of the rectangular plate. As opposed to using the plate's edges as the starting point for the cutter's route, as is conventional, the tool's axis should be moved along the dashed path depicted in the image, which is offset from the edges by an amount equal to the cutter's radius. Using cutter compensation and an offset equal to the workpiece's radius, the programmer determines the tool's location in relation to the workpiece. If an offset value equal to the cutter radius is provided, the CNC controller will adjust the tool path automatically. The offset memory includes the necessary offset value. Using G41 for cutting with the left hand and G42 for cutting with the right hand. G40 and G41 are compatible with G00 or G01. With G40, the radius compensation is nullified. It is part of the same sequence as G00 or G01, or the sequence that follows it.

Example 7.1: *Write an NC part program for the end-milling of the plate shown in Figure 7.2 (f =100 mm/min). The plate is 10 mm thick.*

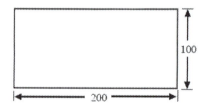

FIGURE 7.2   Job

Solution: Considering that the tool moves on the left side of the workpiece along the dotted path as shown in Figure 7.3.

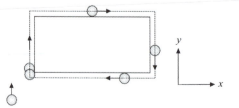

FIGURE 7.3   Cutter radius compensation for the given job.

Program							
N005	G21	G90	G92	G17	X30	Y30	Z10
N010	G00	X0	Y0		Z20	S100	M03
N015	G01	G94 G41	D05		X0	Y100	F100
N020	X200	Y100					
N025	X100	Y0					
N030	X0	Y0					
N035	G00	G40	X30		Y30		
N040	M05	M30					

7.5.11   G43, G44 AND G49

NC and CNC machines have a range of tools stored in the machine's magazine. The magazine has a vast assortment of instruments, including those of various sizes. Consequently, it is necessary to modify their height or length correspondingly. G-codes allow for the use of tool length correction (G43, G44), as well as its cancellation (G49). For example,

G43	T02	H02
G44	T03	H03

The tool number, code number and offset value are stored in a table inside the CNC software. Examine the information in the table below.

Tool Number	Code Number	Offset Value (assumed)
T001	H001	200
T002	H002	150
T003	H003	−100
T004	H004	−300

When the offset value is positive, G43 is utilised, whereas G44 is used when the offset value is negative. At the completion of the programme, the G49 instruction is used to cancel the tool length offset value.

7.5.12   G90 AND G91

In the context of component programming, both absolute and incremental measurement approaches are available. Unlike absolute programming, with incremental programming the beginning point changes with each iteration. Programming for absolute dimension reduction in G90. The language of choice for incremental dimension programming is G91 (Figure 7.4).

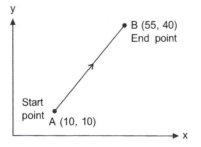

FIGURE 7.4   G 90 and G 91 code.

If G90 is used, the command for defining point B will be:

G90	X 55	Y 40

If G91 is used, command for defining point *B* will be:

G91	X 45	Y 30

7.5.13   G92

This phrase defines the position inside a coordinate system. In milling, drilling and some kinds of lathe machines, it is used to specify the system's origin in relation to the point at which the cutting tool is placed in motion.

For example, G92 *X* 5.0 *Z* 5.0

At the beginning of the part program, the origin of the coordinate system has to be defined. Though the direction of *X*, *Y* and *Z* axis is predefined, the origin can be shifted for the convenience of programming and machining. In the above instruction, the machinist has to move the tool to *X* = 5.0 and *Z* = 5.0 mm, before starting the machining operation. In effect, it defines the origin of the coordinate system.

7.5.14   G94, G95, G98 AND G99

G94 describes the feed rate for drilling and milling operations in millimetres per minute, while G95 does it in millimetres per rotation. The feed rate during a turning operation is stated in either millimetres per minute (G98) or millimetres per rotation (G99).

7.6   DESCRIPTION OF M COMMANDS

7.6.1   M00 (PROGRAM STOP)

Using this command, the present programme execution is abruptly terminated. The spindle, feed and cooling system will be disabled. There is no alarm generated when the chip-protected door is opened. M00 may be used if random quality control inspections are required throughout the course of an activity.

7.6.2   M01 (OPTIONAL PROGRAM STOP)

M01 acts identically to M00 when "Programmed Stop Yes" is enabled through the soft key in the PROGRAM CONTROL menu.

7.6.3   M02 (END OF PROGRAM)

Comparable to the M30 system. Control is lost, the spindle ceases to rotate and the tool is displaced to the right along the *Z* axis.

7.6.4   M03 (SPINDLE START, CLOCKWISE DIRECTION)

By flicking this switch, the spindle is activated in a clockwise direction. Before executing the M03 instruction, you must adjust the spindle speed, close the chip protection door and clamp the workpiece.

7.6.5 M04 (Spindle Start, Counterclockwise Direction)

Used to commence a spindle rotation in a counterclockwise direction. All of the restrictions specified in M03 apply here as well.

7.6.6 M05 (Spindle Stop)

Its role is to stop the spindle spinning. During a turning operation, the M05 may be used to stop the spindle so that the workpiece can be examined, or a new cutting tool can be placed. It is helpful at the end of a program, but that is also when the main spindle goes off.

7.6.7 M06 (Tool Change)

Use the M06 command to swap tools on an NC machine with a tool magazine or tool drum with varying tool capacity. It is coupled with the letter T, which represents a certain musical instrument.

7.6.8 M07, M08 and M09

Push the button to activate the coolant in flood mode (M07), then press the button to activate the coolant in mist mode (M08). In order to disconnect the cooling system, push the M09 button.

7.6.9 M10 and M11

Using the M10 thread, the fixture is clamped in place, and the M11 thread is used to release it.

7.6.10 M13, M14 and M17

Once M13 activates the coolant, the spindle is put in motion counterclockwise. Even when M14 activates the coolant, the spindle starts rotating counterclockwise. M17 turns off the supply of coolant to the spindle.

7.6.11 M30

When the M30 command is sent to a machine, all motors cease rotation, and the control returns to the startup phase.

7.6.12 M37, M38 and M39

With the M37 command, mirroring may be specified relative to the current X position of the tool, and with the M38 command, mirroring can be defined related to the current Y position of the tool. Disabling mirroring is an M39 feature.

7.6.13 M60

The M60 may be used for switching between pallets on an NC/CNC machine that employs several pallets for loading and unloading workpieces.

7.6.14 M98 and M99

The M98 instruction invokes a subroutine or function in a program. This command requires the number of iterations and the name of the subprogram to execute. If you hit M99, the program will instantly revert to its starting state or the block that was chosen.

A subprogram is also sometimes referred as ***subroutine.*** It is placed at the end of the main program. It is used where the repetition of a part program is required to a perform similar operation repeatedly. These subroutines can be called anytime during execution of program with simple instruction code. The subroutines can be nested by calling one subroutine inside another subroutine. However, a subroutine cannot be defined inside another subroutine. This facility saves part programming time and keeps program concise. In the word address format, the subroutine can be added at the end of the program simply by using a sequence number following the main program as if it is a separate and independent program. M98 is used to call the subroutine while M99 is used for return from the subroutine to the main program. The general word address format for subroutine is

$$N......P_{N1} L_{NN} M98$$
$$.........$$
$$N.........M99 P_{N2}$$

Where P indicates the block sequence number when a call for a subroutine has to be made. For example, P150 indicates the call for a subroutine written in N150 sequence number. LNN indicates that the subroutine has to be repeated NN number of times. After execution of the subroutine NN number of times, the control returns to N2 sequence number of the main program using M99.

7.6.15 MACRO

Macros are the subroutines, which are dependent on certain parameters hence are referred as parametric subroutines. As we know that in many machining processes the tool path is similar, but the magnitude may be different as in case of drilling holes of different depths, end milling of rectangular blocks of various lengths and breadths, etc. To avoid rewriting similar statements again and again macros are used. Ready-to-use macros are provided and built in the CNC controller. A macro is written in the same way as a subroutine except that the variable parameter is specified by symbol "*" or number such as #1, #2, #3, etc. Like subroutines, the macros, too, are called from the main program. Thus, by using macros, the programming time and effect can be drastically reduced.

7.6.16 CANNED CYCLE

This too is an important feature in an NC/CNC system and is built in the controller itself. It provides a fixed sequence of operation where tool motions are predefined. Machining operations consist of a number of motions such as rapid traverse, linear interpolation for cutting material at a predefined feed rate and then retracting the tool from the workpiece after cutting is over. These motions and many others can be programmed in a particular sequence at a predefined feed rate by particular preparatory words. Such a built-in facility presents an efficient tool to the programmer to reduce programming time and effort. There are various canned cycles such as turning cycle, milling cycle, drilling cycle, threading cycle and tapping cycle. The preparatory words (G-words) for canned cycles may differ from one another. The part programmer manual supplied by the manufacturer of the controller should be referred for using canned cycles.

The canned cycle uses an additional coordinate word referred to as an R-word which specifies the position of a reference plane above the work surface where the tool should position itself using rapid traverse. After this, the tool performs the cutting operation at the predefined feed rate and again returns to the R-plane using rapid traverse mode after the machining is complete. The R-word is effective only during the typical canned cycle. The canned cycle is cancelled using G80.

Now let us consider the canned cycle for a turning operation. In a turning operation, four steps are followed. First, the tool is fed at a predefined feed rate and depth of cut in X-direction. In the second step it moves in Z direction at a defined feed rate for the material removed. In the third step, it retrieves back in X direction and in the fourth step it moves in Z direction to reposition itself with respect to the workpiece. The third and the fourth step motions are carried in the rapid traverse mode. These four motions can be incorporated in one turning canned cycle thus reducing the programming effort significantly.

7.6.17   TURNING OPERATIONS

Example 7.2: *From a shaft of 25 mm diameter, make a stepped shaft with dimensions as shown in Figure 7.5. Take speed = 3000 rpm and feed = 30 mm/min.*

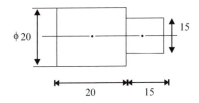

FIGURE 7.5   Job

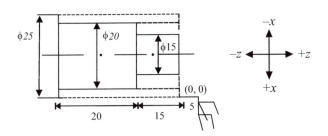

FIGURE 7.6   Job

Solution: Refer Figure 7.6

NC Part Program	Explanation
N01 G21 G90 G92 *X* 5.0 *Z* 5.0	Input values in mm, absolute dimensioning. defining axis of origin
N02 M03 S3000	Spindle start (clockwise)
N03 GOO *X 0.0 Z* 2.0	Rapid traverse of tool to *Z* = 2 mm for clearance
N04 G01 *X* 1.0 *Z* −35.0 *F* 30	Depth of cut = 1.0
N05 G00 *X* 0.0 *Z* 2.0	Tool Retrieves
N06 G01 *X* 2.0 *Z* 35.0	Depth of cut again 1.0 mm
N07 G00 *X* 0.0 *Z* 2.0	Tool retrieves
N08 G01 *X* −2.5 *Z* −35.00	Depth of cut = 0.5 mm
N19 G00 *X* 0.0 *Z* 2.0	Tool retrieves along Z-axis
N10 G01 *X* −3.5 *Z* −15.0	Dept of cut = 1.0, turning for smaller diameter
N11 G00 *X* 0.0 *Z* 2.0	Tool retrieves
N12 G01 *X* −4.5 *Z* −15.0	Turning for smaller diameter
N13 G00 *X* 0.0 *Z* 2.0	Tool retrieves
N14 G01 *X* −5.0 *Z* −15.0	Final cut
N15 G00 *X* 5.0 *Z* 5.0	Rapid traverse to target point
N16 M05 M30	Spindle stop, end of program: Machines stop and tape rewind

Example 7.3: *Prepare part program for obtaining part as shown in Figure 7.7.*

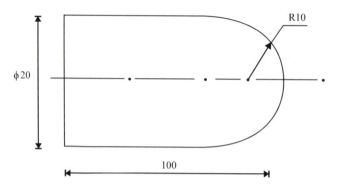

FIGURE 7.7   Part for part program.

Solution:

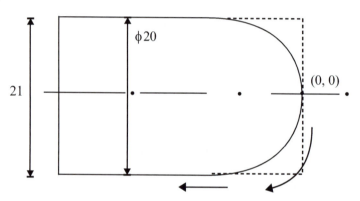

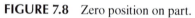

FIGURE 7.8   Zero position on part.

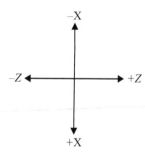

FIGURE 7.9   X and Z axis.

Solution: Refer Figure 7.8 for zero position and Figure 7.9 for X and Z axis.

NC Part Program	Explanation
N05 G21 G90 G92 Z2.0	Input values in mm, absolute dimensioning defining axis origin
N10 G02 X10.0 Z – 10.0 R10.0 F20	Circular interpolation clockwise
N15 G01 X10.0 Z – 100.00 F30	Linear interpolation for turning
N20 G00 X0.0 Z2.0	Rapid traverse to target point
N25 M05 M30	Spindle stop, end of program, machine stop and tape rewind.

7.6.18 MILLING OPERATION

Example 7.4: For the workpiece shown in Figure 7.10, perform the end milling operation to smoothen its edges (remove burrs from the edges). Use an end-mill cutter of 25 mm diameter. Take feed rate of 30 mm per minute. Assume target point to be located at $x = -30$ mm $y = -30$ mm, and $z = +10$ mm. Note that holes are used for locating and positioning the workpiece.

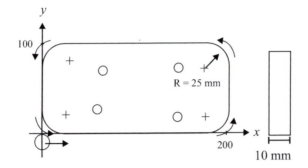

FIGURE 7.10 Job for part program.

NC Part Program	Explanation
N00 G21 G90 G92 X –30.0 Y 0.0 Z 10.0	Input values in mm absolute dimensioning. Defining axis origin
N05 G00 Z –20.0 S800 M03	Rapid traverse of tool to cutter depth, spindle start rotating in clockwise direction
N10 G01 G94 G42 X 175.0 Y0.0 DD4 F 30	Rutter reach the starting position, cutter diameter saved in register no. 4
N15 G01 X 175.00 Y 0.0	Start milling lower edge
N20 G17 G03 X 200.0 Y 25.0 R 25.0	XY plane selection, circular interpolation in anticlockwise direction
N25 G01 X 200.0 Y 50.0	End mill right edge
N30 G17 G03 X 175.0 Y 100.0 R 25.0	XY plane selection, circular interpolation in anticlockwise direction.
N35 G01 X 25.0 Y 100.0	End mill upper edge
N40 G17 G03 X 0 Y 75.0 R 25.0	Circular interpolation in X-Y plane in anticlockwise direction
N45 G01 X 0.0 Y 25.0	End mill left edge
N50 G17 G03 X 25.0 Y 0.0 R 25.0	Circular interpolation in X-Y plane in anticlockwise direction
N55 G00 G40 X 0.0 Y –30.0	Rapid exit from part, cancel offset compensation
N60 M05 M30	Spindle stop, end of program, machine stop and tape rewind

7.6.19 DRILLING OPERATION

Example 7.5: Write an NC part program to drill four holes in a workpiece using a drilling machine as shown in Figure 7.11. The workpiece is a rectangular plate of 200 mm × 100 mm × 15 mm. The diameter of holes is 10 mm. Take feed rate of 0.10 mm per revolution and spindle speed of 800 revolutions per minute. Assume the target point is located at $x = -10$ mm, $y = -10$ mm and $z = 10$ mm. The workpiece surface is fixtured such that its bottom surface is 30 mm above the machine tool table surface so as to provide sufficient clearance beneath the part for drilling through holes (Figure 7.12).

NC Part Program	Explanation
N01 G21 G90 G92 X –10.0 Y –10.0 Z 10.0 EOB	Input values in mm, absolute dimensioning, defining origin of axis
N02 G00 X 20.0 Y 10.0 EOB	Rapid traverse of tool to first hole position i.e., lower left hole
N03 G01 G95 Z –15.0 F 0.10 800 M03 EOB	Drilling lower left hole
N04 G01 Z 10.0 EOB	Taking out drill bit from the hole
N05 G00 X 180.0 Y 10.0 EOB	Rapid traverse to lower right hole position
N06 G01 G95 Z –15.0 F 0.10 EOB N07 G01 Z 10.0 EOB	Drill the hole
	Taking out drill bit from the hole

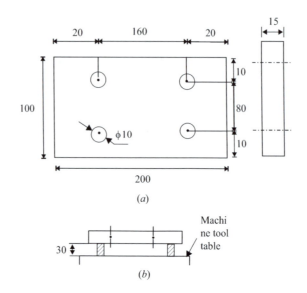

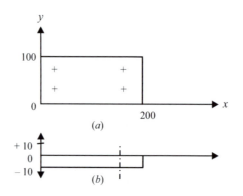

FIGURE 7.11   Workpiece for NC drilling operation

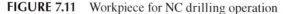

FIGURE 7.12   Front and top view of job.

7.7   COMPUTER-AIDED PART PROGRAMMING

Manual part programming is suitable for only point-to-point jobs like drilling holes and simple turning or milling operations. However, for complicated contouring operations in turning or milling, manual part programming can become quite complicated, tedious and time consuming. For such operations *computer-aided part programming* is recommended.

LO 2. To understand Computer aided part programming using APT programming language

Various part programming languages have been developed over a period of time. Some of them are enumerated below:

1. **APT**

This language also known as Automatically Programmed Tools was developed at MIT, USA. It has provision for both point-to-point (PTP) and continuous path programming for up to five axis machines.

2. **ADAPT**

This language is based on APT. It was developed by IBM and can be used for both PTP and continuous path programming. But it is not as powerful as APT.

3. **EXAPT**

It is also based on APT and was developed in Germany. It optimises cutting speed and feed. It has three versions:

EXAPT I – for drilling and straight cut milling.
EXAPT II – for turning.
EXAPT III – for contouring operations.

In this chapter we only deal with APT in detail.

In computer-aided part programming, a programmer's job is to define the geometry of the work part, to specify tool path and sequence of machining operation in case multiple tools are used.

On the other hand, the computer's job in the first phase is to take the part program as input, translate it into a form understandable by the computer, perform the necessary mathematical calculations and generate cutter location data. In this phase, the output generated is called CLDATA or CLFILE. This file contains universally applicable cutter centre coordinates. The second task of the computer is to convert this generalised cutter location data into appropriate NC codes valid for a particular machine tool. This is called post processing. Figure 7.13 shows steps in computer aided part programming.

7.7.1 APT Programming

There are four types of command statements used in APT language. These are:

1. Geometric statements,
2. Motion statements,
3. Post processor statements,
4. Auxiliary statements (or compilation control statements).

7.7.2 APT Geometric Statements

These statements are used to define the geometry of workpiece in terms of points, lines and surfaces.

The general form of a geometric statement is: Symbol = geometry type/related data

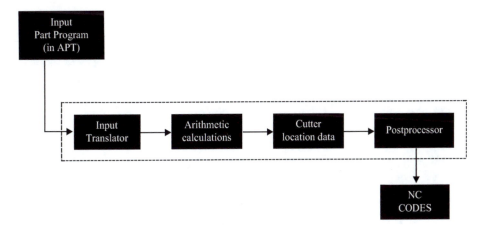

FIGURE 7.13   Computer-aided part programming

Example:

$$P1 = POINT/10.0, 5.0, 8.0$$

i.e., P1 is the point with coordinates (10, 5, 8). Note the punctuation used in the above statement.

- A slash (/) divides a section into two parts. To the left of the slash are the major words like POINT, LINE, PLANE, etc. while to the right of the slash is the related descriptive data.
- A comma is used as separator between data on the right of the slash.
- An equals sign (=), assigns the geometry data to the variable.

Other important geometry statements are LINE, CIRCLE, PLANE, etc. Each of these words can be defined in more than one way. (Refer Figure 7.14 to 7.23)

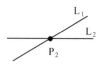

FIGURE 7.14   Specifying a point.

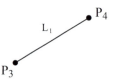

FIGURE 7.15   Specifying a line through two points.

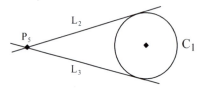

FIGURE 7.16   Specifying a line tangent to circle.

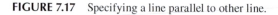

FIGURE 7.17   Specifying a line parallel to other line.

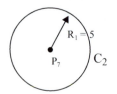

FIGURE 7.18   Specifying a circle through center.

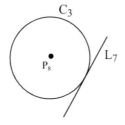

FIGURE 7.19 Specifying a circle tangent to a line.

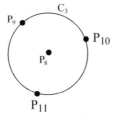

FIGURE 7.20 Specifying a circle through three points.

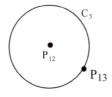

FIGURE 7.21 Specifying a circle through center and one point.

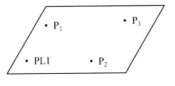

FIGURE 7.22 Specifying planes.

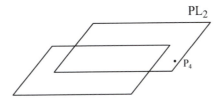

FIGURE 7.23 Specifying parallel planes.

7.7.2.1 Specifying a Point

P1 = POINT/8.0, 3.0, 5.0

P2 = POINT/INTOF, L1, L2

7.7.2.2 Specifying a Line

L1 = LINE/P3, P4

L2 = LINE/P5, LEFT, TANTO, C1 L3 = LINE/P5, RIGHT, TANTO, C1

L4 = LINE/P6, PARLEL, L5
(See Figure 7.17.)
L6 = LINE/P6, PERPTO, L5
C2 = CIRCLE/CENTER, P7, RADIUS, 5
C3 = CIRCLE/CENTER, P8, TANTO, L7
C4 = CIRCLE/P9, P10, P11
C5 = CIRCLE/CENTER, P12, P13

7.7.2.3 Specifying Planes

PL1 = PLANE/P1, P_2, P_3
PL_2 = PLANE/P4, PARLEL, PL1

7.7.2.4 Motion Statements

These commands are for relative motion between the tool and workpiece. Generally, they describe the trajectory of the cutting tool. The general format of motion statements is:

Motion command/descriptive data.

The commonly used words for point-to-point motion statement are:

FROM, GOTO, GODLTA, GOON, GOPAST, GOLET, GORGT, GOUP, GODOWD, GOFWD, GOBACK

These commands are used follows

FROM/ −2.0, −3.0, −10.0
GOTO/ −2.0, −3.0, 0.0

This command instructs the tool to go to point (−2, 3, 0) from its current location.

GODLTA/3, 4, 2 This command instructs the tool to move in incremental mode by 3, 4 and 2 units in x, y and z directions respectively.

Motion statements like GOUP, GODOWD, GOLFT, GORGT, GOFWD, GOBACK can be understood from Figure 7.24:

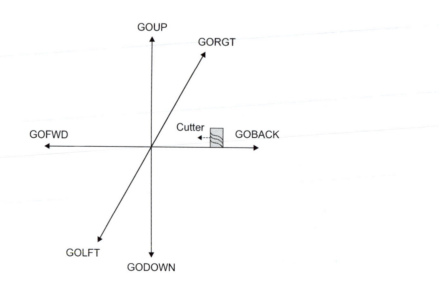

FIGURE 7.24 Use of motion commands

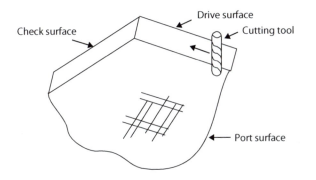

FIGURE 7.25 Drive, part, and check surface.

Contouring motions on the other hand and are somewhat move complicated. Before discussing these commands further, let us understand the concept of derive surface, part surface and check surface.

Refer to Figure 7.25:

Drive surface: This surface is used as a guiding surface for the cutting tool.
Check surface: This surface is used to stop the movement of the tool.
Part surface: This surface either passes through the bottom surface of the cutting tool or is parallel to the bottom surface of the cutting tool.

The check surface should be used in the part program carefully. Four modifier words are used in APT to position the tool with respect to the check surface appropriately. These are TO, ON, PAST and TANTO. Use of the APT modifiers can be understood from Figure 7.26.

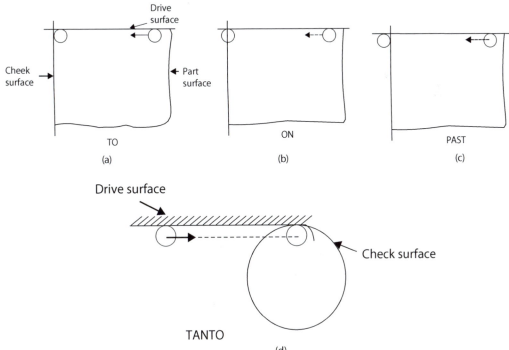

FIGURE 7.26 Use of APT modifiers TO, ON, PAST, TANTO

Note that TANTO is used when the drive surface is tangential to circular check surface.

The three surfaces included in the statement should be specified in the following order: First the drive surface, then the part surface and lastly the check surface.

7.7.2.5 Postprocessor Statements

These are the statements in the APT program that control the machining operation.

Some of the commonly used postprocessor statements are:

COOLNT/ON	=	Turns coolant on
COOLNT/OFF	=	Turns coolant off
SPINDL/	=	Used to specify spindle rpm
FEDRAT/	=	Used to specify feed rate
MACHIN/ RAPID	=	Used to specify the machine tool
END		

7.7.2.6 Auxiliary Statements

These statements are used to specify tolerance, cutter size, part identification and so on. Some of the auxiliary statements are discussed below:

INTOL/ → This is used to specify the maximum allowable tolerance between inside of the curved surface and small straight-line segments used to approximate the curve. For example, INTOL/.002 indicates tolerance as shown in Figure 7.27.

OUTTOL/ → Indicates the maximum allowable tolerance between outside of the actual curved surface and the straight segments used to approximate the curve. This is shown in Figure 7.28 e.g., OUTTOL/.002.

Note that both the inside and outside tolerance can be specified together to indicate allowable tolerance as shown in Figure 7.29.

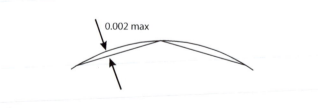

0.002 max

FIGURE 7.27   IN tolerance.

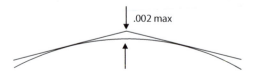

.002 max

FIGURE 7.28   OUT tolerance.

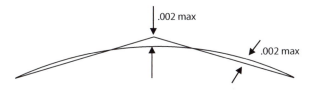

FIGURE 7.29 IN OUT tolerance.

CLPRNT	→	This command also called to take a printout of the cutter location data on the NC tape.
FINI	→	(Finish) this word is used to specify the end of the program.
END	→	This word is used to stop the machine at the end of a section of the program (to change tools manually or some other reason). To continue the program, FROM word is used.
CUTTER/	→	This word is used for offset calculation of the tool path.
e.g., CUTTER/0.800		Indicates that the cutter die, is 0.800 and hence, the tool path must be offset from the part outline by 0.400 mm.

7.7.2.7   Examples of APT Programs

Example 7.6: *Write an APT program to drill holes in a plate as shown in Figure 7.30. Spindle rotates at 500 rpm and required 65 mm feed rate is 0.05 mm per revolution to drill the hole.*

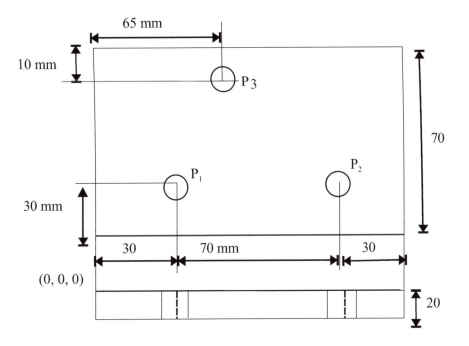

FIGURE 7.30 Workpiece.

Solution:

Program	Explanation
MACHIN/DRILL. 05	Specifies machine identification number
CLPRNT	Used to take printout of cutter location data
UNITS/MM	Specify units
TARGET = POINT/0, −50, −50	Specifies target point i.e., initial point where tool is located
P1 = POINT/30.0, 30.0, 10.0	Define point P1
P2 = POINT/100.0. 30.0, 10.0	Define point P2
P3 = POINT/65.0, 60.0, 10.0	Define point P3
FROM/TARGET	From the initial point i.e., target point, rapidly
RAPID	Rapidly
GOTO/P1	Go to point P1
SPINDL/500, CLW	Spindle RPM is 500 in clockwise direction
FEDRAT/0.05, MMPR	Feed rate is 0.05 mm per rotation
GODLTA/O, 0, −35	Tool goes down by 35 mm with the given feed rate
GODLTA/O. 0, 35	Tool retrieves

Program	Explanation
RAPID	Tool again moves rapidly
GOTO/P2	and goes to point 2
SPINDL/500. CLW	Spindle speed is specified
FEDRAT/0.05, MMPR	Feed rate is specified
GODLTA/O. 0. −35	Tool moves down by (10 + 20 + 5) = 35 mm to drill hole.
GODLTA/O, 0, 35	Tool retrieves
RAPID	Tool again moves in rapid mode
GOTO/P3	Goes to point P3
SPINDL/500. CLW	Spindle speed is specified
FEDRATE/0.05, MMPR	Feed rate is specified
GODLTA/O, 0. −35	Tool moves down by 35 mm to drill hole
GODLTA/O, 0, 35	Tool retrieves
RAPID	Tool again moves in rapid mode
GOTO/TARGET	Goes to target point
SPINDL/OFF	Spindle is off
FINI	End of program

Example 7.7: *For the plate given in Example 7.1 write APT program for end milling of the four edges.*

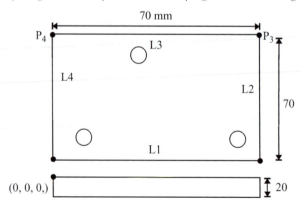

FIGURE 7.31   Part for APT program.

Program	Explanation
MACHIN/MILL, 01	Specify machine identification number
CLPRNT	Have cutter location data
UNITS/MM	Specify units (in mm)
CUTTER/25.0	Specifies cutter diameter
TARGET = POINT/ −50.0, −50.0, 10.0	Specifies initial location on of tool (i.e., centre point of its lower end)
P1 = POINT/O, 0, −25	Defines point P1
P2 = POINT/130, 0, −25	P2
P3 = POINT/130, 70, −25	P3
P4 = POINT/O, 70, −25	P4
L1 = LINE/P1, P24	
L2 = LINE/P2, P3	Defines line L1
L3 = LINE/P3, P4	L2
L4 = LINE/P4, P1	L3
PL1 = PLANE/P1, P2, P3	L4
	Defines plane passing through point P1, P2, P3
FROM/TARGET	From initial target point
GO/TO, L1, PL1, ON, L4	Go to point of intersection of L1, PL1 and on L4 Specifies spindle RPM and direction of rotation
SPINDL/500, CLW	Specifies feed rate
FEDRATE720, MMPM	Tool goes right and with feed rate moves tangential to L1 and Past L2
GORGT/11, PAST. L2	
	Tool goes left tangential to L2 till past L3
GOLFT/L2, PAST, L3	Tool again turns left, moves tangential to L3 past L4
GOLFT/L3, PAST. L4	Tool again turns left, moves tangential to L4 until it is past L1
GOLFT/L4, PAST, L1	
RAPID	Tool enters rapid mode
GOTO/TARGET	Returns to target point
SPINDL/OFF	Spindle is switched off
FINI	End of program

Example 7.8: *For the plate shown in Figure 7.32 write. Write an APT program for end milling of its edges. Thickness of the plate is 20 mm.*

PROGRAM

MACHIN / MILL, 02 CLPRNT
UNITS / MM CUTTER / 25.0
TARGET = POINT/−50.0, −50.0, 10.0
P1−= POINT / 0, 0, −25
P2 = POINT / 120, 0 −25
P3 = POINT / 120, 60, −25
C1 = POINT / 100, 60, −25
P4 = POINT / 88.25, 76.2, −25
P5 = POINT / 20, 20, −25

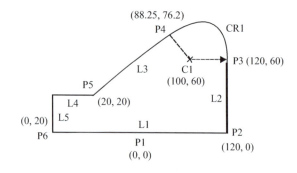

FIGURE 7.32   Workpiece for APT programming.

```
P6 = POINT / 0, 20, –25
L1 = LINE / P1, P2
L2 = LINE / P2, P3
CR1 = CIRCLE / CENTER, C1, TANTO, L2 L3 = LINE / P4, P5
L4 = LINE / P5, P6
L5 = LINE / P6, P1
PL1 = PLANE / P1, P2, P3 FROM / TARGET
GO / TO, L1, PL1, ON, L5 SPINDL / 500, CLW FEDRATE / 50, MMPM GORGT / L1, PAST,
    L2 GOLFT / L2, TANTO, CR1 GOFWD / CR1, PAST, L3 GOFWD / L3, TO, L4 GOFWD
    / L4, PAST, L5
GOLFT/L5, PAST, L1 RAPID GOTO/TARGET SPINDL/OFF
FINI
```

Example 7.9: *Write a part program in APT for end milling of part shown below. Assume suitable tool size, process parameters and any dimension if missing. The thickness of the part is 10 mm.*

SOLUTION:

All dimensions are in mm.
    See figure 7.33.

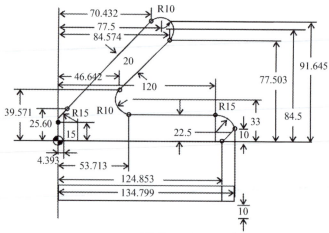

All dimensions are in mm.

FIGURE 7.33   Job for APT program.

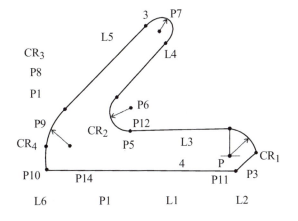

FIGURE 7.34 Points for APT program.

PROGRAM

```
MACHIN/MILLING, 01 CLPRNT
UNITS/MM CUTTER/25.0
TARGET = POINT/–50, –50, 10 P1 = POINT/0, 0, –15
P2 = POINT/124.853, 0, –15
P3 = POINT/134.799, 10, –15
P4 = POINT/120, 22.5, –15
P5 = POINT/53.713, 22.5, –15
P6 = POINT/46.642, 39.571, –15
P7 = POINT/84.574, 77.503, –15
P8 = POINT/70.432, 91.645, –15
P9 = POINT/4.393, 25.60, –15
P10 = POINT/0, 15, –15
P11 = POINT/120, 7.5, –15
P12 = POINT/53.715, 33, –15
P13 = POINT/77.5, 84.5, –15
P14 = POINT/15, 15, – –15 L1 = LINE/ P1, P2
L2 = LINE/ P2, P3 L3 = LINE/ P4, P5
CR1 = CIRCLE/CENTER, P11, TANTO, L3 CR2 = CIRCLE/CENTER, P12, 95
L4 = LINE/ P6, P7 L5 = LINE/ P8, P9
CR3 = CIRCLE/CENTER, P13, TANTO, L5 L6 = LINE/P10, P1
CR4 = CIRCLE/CENTER, P14, TANTO, L6 PL1 = PLANE/ P1, P2, P3 FROM/TARGET
GO/TO, L1, PL1 ON, L6 SPINDL/800, CLW FEDRATE/50, MMPM GORGT/L1, PAST, L2
GOFWD/ L2, PAST, CR1 GOFWD/ CR1, PAST, L3 GOLFT/ L3, TANTO, CR2 GOFWD/
    CR2, TO, L4 GOFWD/L4, TANTO, CR3 GOFWD/ CR3, PAST, L5 GOFWD/ L5, TANTO,
    CR4 GOFWD / CR4, PAST, L6 GOFWD / L6, PAST, L1 RAPID
GOTO / TARGET SPINDL / OFF FINI
```

7.8 SUMMARY

A part program, if made manually without using computer, is called manual part program.

If a part program is made using computers, it is referred to as computer-aided part programming.

NC part programming makes use of following words: N-word, G-word, X, Y, Z-word, F-word, S-word, T-word, M-word, EOB.

An NC part program can be written using any one of the following formats: Word address format, Tab sequential format, Fixed block format.

Examples of computer-aided part programming languages are APT, ADAPT, EXAPT.

APT makes use of geometric, motion, post processor and auxiliary statements.

Motion statements make use of concept of drive surface, check surface and part surface.

Post processor statements control machining operation.

Auxiliary statements specify tolerance, cutter size, part identification, etc.

Part programs can also be generated automatically by using suitable software, defining tool path and machining specifications. etc.

7.9   EXERCISE

1. Explain various words used in NC part programming (BT level 1).
2. Describe various standard formats used to write an NC part program. Which format is most flexible (BT level 2)?
3. Describe computer-aided part programming. What are the common programming languages being used for end-milling, turning, drilling and contouring operations (BT level 2)?
4. Write an APT program for end-milling of a plate shown in Figure 7.35 (BT level 6).
5. Write an APT program for end-milling of edges for plate shown in Figure 7.36 (BT level 6).
6. What is part programming? Discuss the procedure for developing manual part program (BT level 2).
7. Explain the following G-words (BT level 2):
   (a) G00,
   (b) G01,
   (c) G02,
   (d) G04,
   (e) G21,
   (f) G90,
   (g) G98.
8. Explain the following M-words (BT level 2):
   (a) M00,
   (b) M02,
   (c) M04,
   (d) M05,
   (e) M09,
   (f) M13,
   (g) M30.

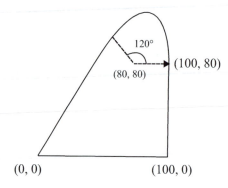

FIGURE 7.35

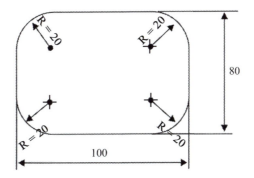

FIGURE 7.36

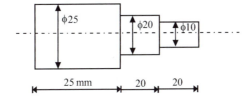

FIGURE 7.37

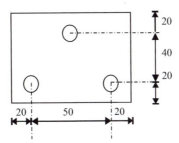

FIGURE 7.38

9. Write a part program for a shaft of 30 mm diameter to make a stepped shaft with dimensions as shown in Figure 7.37. Use appropriate speed and feed when material of the shaft is mild steel (BT level 6).

10. Write a manual NC part program to drill holes in a plate of thickness 10 mm (Figure 7.38). Use appropriate speed and feed rate (BT level 6).

11. Write an address format part program for drilling two similar holes in a rectangular plate of thickness 5 mm at points with coordinates (10, 25) and (55, 60) and also show the part on diagram. Origin and start point is (0, 0). Take spindle speed 1675 rpm and feed 200 mm/min (BT level 6).

12. Write an APT part program for milling a semicircular disc of 5 mm thickness in positions x–y plane with radius 60 mm and centre at (100, 0). Take a spindle speed of 1765 for example and feed 200 mm/min. Given cutter radius 10 mm. Also show the part on diagram with the cutter path (BT level 6).

7.10 MULTIPLE-CHOICE QUESTIONS

1. What is G-code used for in NC part programming?
   a. To specify the tool path for a machine.
   b. To specify the type of material being used.
   c. To specify the cutting speed for a machine.
   d. To specify the feed rate for a machine.
2. Which of the following is a type of programming used in NC part programming?
   a. Macro programming.
   b. Micro programming.
   c. Assembly programming.
   d. Basic programming.
3. What is a work offset in NC part programming?
   a. A reference point used to set the position of the workpiece in relation to the machine.
   b. A code used to specify the cutting speed of the machine.
   c. A code used to specify the type of tool being used.
   d. A code used to specify the feed rate of the machine.
4. What is a tool offset in NC part programming?
   a. A reference point used to set the position of the tool in relation to the machine.
   b. A code used to specify the cutting speed of the machine.
   c. A code used to specify the type of tool being used.
   d. A code used to specify the feed rate of the machine.
5. Which of the following is an advantage of NC part programming?
   a. Reduced setup time.
   b. Increased flexibility.
   c. Improved accuracy.
   d. All of the above.
6. What is the purpose of G-code in CNC machines?
   a. To specify the type of material being used.
   b. To specify the cutting speed of the machine.
   c. To specify the position of the tool and workpiece.
   d. To specify the feed rate of the machine.
7. What is the purpose of M-code in CNC machines?
   a. To specify the type of material being used.
   b. To specify the cutting speed of the machine.
   c. To turn on or off machine functions such as coolant or spindle rotation.
   d. To specify the feed rate of the machine.
8. Which G-code is used to move the tool to a specific position?
   a. G00.
   b. G01.
   c. G02.
   d. G03.
9. Which M-code is used to turn on the spindle?
   a. M01.
   b. M03.
   c. M05.
   d. M08.
10. Which G-code is used to specify a circular motion in a clockwise direction?
   a. G02.
   b. G03.
   c. G04.
   d. G17.

Answers

1. Answer: a. To specify the tool path for a machine.
2. Answer: a. Macro programming.
3. Answer: a. A reference point used to set the position of the workpiece in relation to the machine.
4. Answer: c. A code used to specify the type of tool being used.
5. Answer: d. All of the above.
6. Answer: c. To specify the position of the tool and workpiece.
7. Answer: c. To turn on or off machine functions such as coolant or spindle rotation.
8. Answer: b. G01.
9. Answer: b. M03.
10. Answer: a. G02.

8 System Devices

Learning Outcomes: After studying this chapter, the reader should be able

LO 1: To understand basics of a DC motor (BT level 2).
LO 2: To understand feedback devices used in CNC machines (BT level 2).
LO 3: To know about counting devices (BT level 1).
LO 4: To understand digital to analogue convertor and analogue to digital convertor (BT level 2).

8.1 DC MOTOR

In a manner similar to a DC generator, a DC motor converts electrical energy into mechanical energy. The fundamental concept is that a magnetic field exerts a mechanical force on an electric current-carrying conductor. The direction of the applied force is specified by Fleming's left-hand rule, sometimes known as the motor rule.

LO 1. To understand basics of d.c. Motor.

The essential features of a DC motor are shown in Figure 8.1.

A DC motor requires both the outer, stationary stator and the inner, rotating rotor. At both ends of the rotor's axial shaft are bearings that are shielded by covers that are attached to the stator. This shaft is attached to the load where it protrudes from the end cap at one end.

The stator and the rotor comprise of concentric cylindrical cores. These are made of ferromagnetic material (such as steel). The cylindrical cores are usually fabricated from laminated steel sheets. There is a clearance between the two cylindrical ferromagnetic cores called the *air gap*. There is an electromagnetic field (EMF) present in the air gap. In a combined magnetic circuit, a magnetic flux (f) passes from one core to the other over the air gap. This magnetic flux, in crossing the air gap, generates alternate north and south poles on both stator and rotor. The two cylindrical surfaces (one of stator and other of rotor), just a short distance apart, move relative to one another for electromechanical energy conversion.

Conductors run parallel to the axis of the cylinder near the air gap surface of each or any one of the elements. These conductors are connected suitably to form machine windings.

A DC motor's main field is composed of field poles energised by direct current. Field winding is the process of wrapping wire around field poles. The stator contains both the field poles and the armature, whereas the rotor is the moving component of the machine. The winding over the armature is called armature winding (see Figure 8.2).

The distribution of an odd number of north and south field poles is symmetrical. When a direct current is sent through the armature, it is subjected to a force. The armature is set in motion by a pair of equal and opposing forces of this kind. The coupling or torque (force times the perpendicular distance between their lines of action) is highest when the plane of the coil is parallel to the field; it diminishes as the coil is rotated and vanishes when the coil is perpendicular to the field. This position of the coil is called the "zero-torque position." The coil crosses the zero-torque position due to inertia. Every time the coil crosses the zero-torque position, the commutator reverses the direction of current in the armature, so that the couple on the armature continues to act in the same direction throughout and the coil keeps on rotating continuously. This is how a DC motor works.

DOI: 10.1201/9781003350842-8

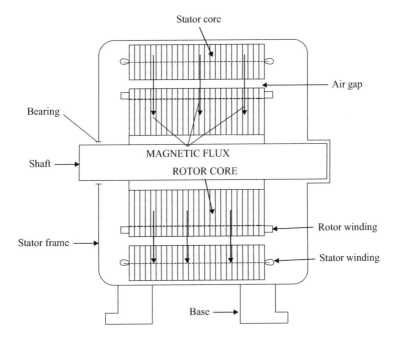

FIGURE 8.1   DC motor

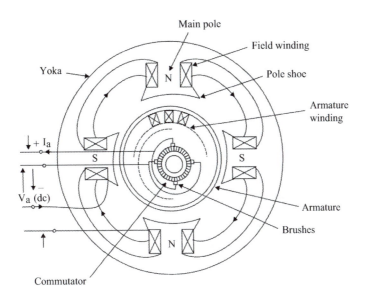

FIGURE 8.2   Cross-sectional view of DC motor

8.1.1   ADVANTAGES OF A DC MOTOR

1. Due to the ease of speed adjustment, DC machines are often used in electromechanical control systems. DC motors have the benefit of being readily modifiable to get the desired speed and torque characteristics. There is considerable flexibility for modifying the tempo while maintaining the same level of effectiveness.
2. The polarity of applied voltage determines the direction of rotation.
3. DC machines are capable of providing large power amplifications.

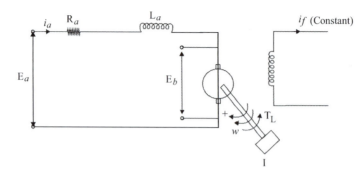

FIGURE 8.3   Schematic diagram of armature-controlled DC motor

4. The capacity of a DC motor to accelerate rapidly from rest makes it excellent for use in servo systems. This kind of motor requires certain physical characteristics, including low inertia and high starting torque. By lowering the armature diameter and extending the armature length to supply the required amount of power, low inertia may be achieved. The field and armature windings of DC motors can be:

- Shunt connected,
- Series connected,
- Compounded,
- Separately excited.

Motors used in industry are generally separately excited. These can be of two types:

1. Armature control with fixed field current (Figure 8.3),
2. Field control with fixed armature current.

8.1.2   ARMATURE-CONTROLLED DC MOTOR

In this motor, speed is controlled by armature voltage E_a, while field current I_f is kept constant. Let E_b be back EMF induced by the rotation of armature windings in the magnetic field. Then E_b is proportional to armature angular velocity (ω) and magnetic flux ϕ. Thus

$$E_b \propto \phi\omega$$

$$E_b = K_1 \phi\omega$$

Where K_1 = Constant

In the operating range, flux ϕ is directly proportional field current I_f.

$$\text{i.e., } \phi = K_2 I_f \ (K_2 = \text{constant})$$

$$\text{Hence } E_b = K_1 K_2 I_f \omega$$

$$E_b = K_b \omega \ (\text{where } K_b = K_1 K_2 I_f)$$

L_a, the self-inductance of the armature owing to flux in the armature (it is quite small and may be neglected). Field wind self-inductance, represented by L_f, is often rather large or shunt and must thus be taken into account).

Circuit equation for armature is

$$E_a - E_b = R_a i_a + L_a \frac{di_a}{dt}$$

$$E_a - K_b \omega = R_a i_a + L_a D i_a = i_a (R_a + L_a)$$

Taking Laplace transform: $E_a - K_b \omega(S) = i_a(S)(SL + R_a)$

$$i_a(S) = \frac{E_a - K_b W(S)}{R_a + SL} = [E_a - K_b \omega(S)] \times \frac{1/R_a}{1 + \frac{SL_a}{R_a}}$$

Let $Z_a = \frac{L_a}{R_a}$

= armature circuit time constant. Hence $i_a(s)$

$$i_a = [E_a - K_b \omega(S)] \times \frac{1/R_a}{1 + \frac{SL_a}{R_a}}$$

$$= [E_a - K_b \omega(S)] \times \frac{1/R_a}{1 + Z_a S}$$

The torque (T) balance for output shaft:

$$T = (ID2 + BD)\,\theta + T_L$$

Taking Laplace $T(S) = (IS2 + BS)\,\theta + T_L(S)$

where I is the moment of inertia of the shaft
B is the damping coefficient
T_L is the load torque

Hence, $T(S) = (IS + B)\omega(S) + T_L(S)$

$$\omega(S) = [T_s - T_L(S)] \times \frac{1/B}{SZ_m + 1}$$

where $Z_m = \frac{I}{B}$ = *mechanical time constant*

The torque developed by the motor is constant also given by

$$T(S) = K_m i_a(S)$$

Using the above equations, the block diagram representation for an armature-controlled DC motor is given in Figure 8.4):

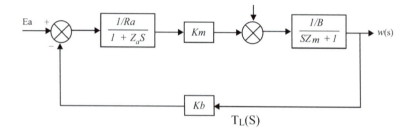

FIGURE 8.4 Block diagram of separately excited armature-controlled DC. motor

8.1.3 FIELD CONTROL DC MOTOR

The current across the motor's armature is kept constant. For a diagram of a field-operated DC motor, see Figure 8.5.

Torque (T) developed by the motor is proportional to magnetic flux (f) and armature current (i_a).

$$i.e., T \alpha \phi i_a$$

$$or \ T = K \phi i_a$$

where constant K for any motor depends upon the total number of armature windings, number of field poles, etc.

In the operating range, flux is directly proportional to field current,

$$\phi \alpha i_f$$

$$\phi = K_1 i_f \ (K_1 = proportionality \ constant)$$

$$Hence \ T = K \phi i_a = K K_1 i_f i_a$$

$$= K_m i_f \qquad (K_1 K_2 i_a = K_m)$$

If the moment of inertia of the armature is I, damping coefficient is B and load torque T_L then the torque equation for armature can be written as

$$T = (ID_2 + BD) \theta + T_L$$

$$= (ID + B) \omega + T_L$$

$$\left(\omega = DQ \right)$$

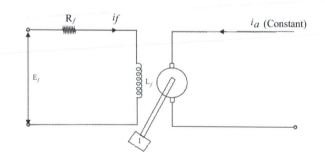

FIGURE 8.5 Circuit diagram of field-controlled DC motor

θ is the angular position of shaft and
ω is the angular velocity of the shaft.

8.2   FEEDBACK DEVICES

NC and CNC machines, mechatronic instruments and robots, etc. incorporate feedback devices in their closed-loop control systems. These are used to
measure parameters such as position, velocity or acceleration which are fed
to the comparator to measure the difference between output and the reference
input. Some of the important feedback devices are linear variable differential transformer (LVDT),
opto-interrupters, optical encoders, synchro, resolver, potentiometer, etc. Let us discuss some of
these feedback devices.

LO 2. To understand feedback devices used in CNC

1. Linear Variable Differential Transformer (LVDT)

This device is used to measure position. The advantage of a LVDT is it is very accurate and is
extremely rugged in nature. It consists of two parts. One part is movable while the other is fixed.
The stationary part consists of primary coils and two secondary coils on either side as shown in the
Figure 8.6.

When the magnetic core is in the middle of the two secondary coils no net EMF is generated. But
when the core is even slightly displaced on either side, net EMF is produced and the voltage generated can be directly calibrated in terms of linear displacement or angular rotation.

2. Opto-Interrupters/Encoder

It consists of light emitter and light receiver (light sensor) with a rotating disk in between the two.
The disk has a black flag as shown in Figure 8.7.

The disk can be mounted on leadscrew of NC/CNC machine. As the leadscrew rotates, the disk
rotates. When the black flag intercepts the path of light, a digital pulse is generated. These pulses
are fed back to the controller of the machine to compare the actual displacement of the slide with
the desired displacement (Figure 8.8).

3. Synchros and Resolver

A synchro is a rotary transducer that converts angular displacement into AC voltage or AC voltage
into angular displacement. A resolver is a type of synchro and is also sometimes called *synchro
resolver*. The major difference between the two devices is that the stator and the rotor winding of
the resolver is displaced mechanically 90° to each other instead of 120° as is the case of synchro. A
schematic diagram of synchro and resolver is shown in Figure 8.9.

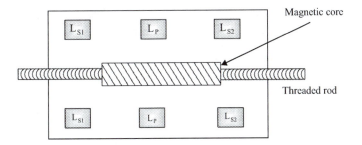

FIGURE 8.6   LVDT

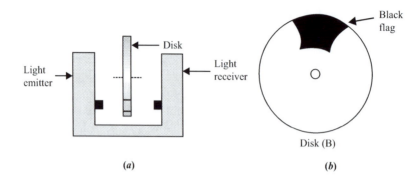

(a)   *(b)*

FIGURE 8.7   Encoder

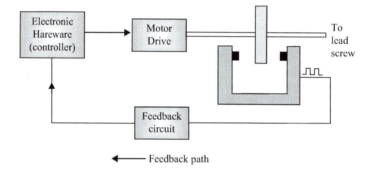

FIGURE 8.8   Schematic block diagram of motor control circuit

In a resolver, when a voltage of $V_0 \sin(w_{ac} t)$ is applied to excite the rotor, the two stator voltages become

$$\text{displacement } [V_{\text{out}} = V_m \sin \theta \sin(\omega_{ac} t)]$$

$$V_{1-3}(t) = V_0 \sin \theta \, \omega_{ac\,t}$$

$$V_{2-4}(t) = V_0 \cos \theta \, \omega_{ac} t$$

where θ is the resolver shaft angle.

4. Inductosyn

This feedback device is commonly used in NC/CNC machines. An inductosyn is shown in Figure 8.10.
It consists of two magnetically coupled elements, one of which moves relative to another.
The stationary element is called the *scale* whereas the moving element is called the *slider*.
On the scale is bonded copper wire track having cyclic pitch $P = 0.1, 0.2$ or 2 mm. The scale has continuous copper wire track which may be of suitable length depending on motion of slide of an NC or CNC machine. The slider consists of two separate tracks of wire of the same pitch as that of scale but separated from one another by a phase of 1/4 of a period (i.e., 90°). Hence when an AC voltage $V_0 \sin(\omega_{ac} t)$ is applied to the scale, the output at the two slider wire tracks is

$$V_1 = V_0 \sin \frac{2\pi x}{P} \sin(w_{ac} t)$$

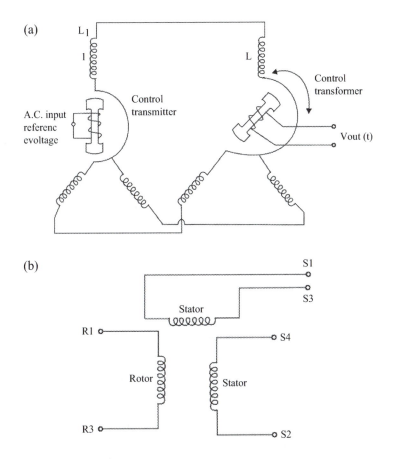

FIGURE 8.9   (a) Schematic of two element synchro system used to measure angular. (b) Schematic electrical circuit of a simple resolver

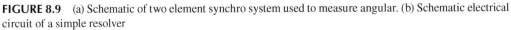

$$V_2 = V_0 \cos \frac{2\pi x}{P} \sin\left(w_{ac}t\right)$$

where P is the wave pitch and x is the linear distance along the scale.

5. Potentiometers

These are the feedback devices used to measure linear or angular position. It is constructed by winding a resistive element in a coil configuration. A potentiometer for measuring linear and angular position is shown in Figure 8.11.

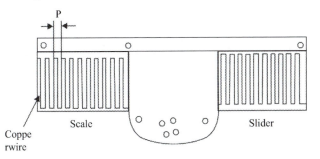

FIGURE 8.10   Schematic of an inductosyn

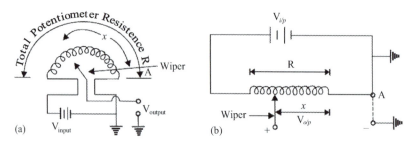

FIGURE 8.11 (a) Potentiometer for measuring linear position. (b) Potentiometer for measuring angular position

When a DC voltage V_{ilp} is applied across entire resistance R the voltage V_{olp} is proportional to linear or rotary distance of sliding contact wiper from reference point A is generated. Output voltage across resistance x is given by

$$V_{olp} = \frac{x}{R} v_{ilp}$$

8.3   STEPPER MOTOR

The increasing trend towards digital control has generated a demand for mechanical devices capable of delivering incremental motions of predictable accuracy. The stepper motor can be considered as a digital device which converts electrical pulses into proportional mechanical movement. It is a special type of motor designed to rotate through a specific angle (called a step angle) for each electrical pulse received by its control unit. Typical step sizes can be an angle of 7.5°, 15° or larger. A stepper motor is used in an open-loop system, hence no feedback is required. It is used where digital control of angular movement of the shaft is desired. The input command is in the form of a train of electrical pulses to turn the shaft through a specific angle.

8.3.1   Advantages

1. It is compatible with digital systems.
2. There is no requirement of feedback hence there is no need to incorporate feedback sensors in such a system.
3. They are relatively inexpensive.

8.3.2   Disadvantages

1. They are not suitable for heavy loads. The allowable speed of a stepper motor is a function of its load torque which strongly depends upon arm position and gripper load. An excessive load on a stepper motor may cause subsequent loss of steps.
2. Stepper motors are limited in resolution and tend to be noisy.

8.3.3   Applications

These are employed for a variety of applications such as:

- **Computer peripherals:** Paper feed motors in printers, positioning of print heads, pens in *XY*-plotters, recording heads in computer disk drives, tape drives, etc.
- For the positioning of cutting tools and worktables in numerically controlled machinery.

- Used in robots to move robot links along various axes. A stepper motor drive is generally used for smaller robots since it cannot deliver large power.

There are two basic types of stepper motor. These are:

- Variable reluctance type,
- Permanent magnet type.

The structure of a variable reluctance motor is as shown in Figure 8.12.

It is observed that both stator and rotor have a toothed structure. Fundamental to the operation of this motor is that the rotor and the stator do not have the same number of teeth. A stator has eight teeth, located at 45° to each other, whereas the rotor has six teeth located at 60° to each other. In addition, each stator has coils wound on it with oppositely placed coils A and A¢ being grouped together and referred to as phase. Hence four phases named A, B, C and D are formed.

A permanent magnet stepper motor is the most commonly used type. It consists of a multiphased stator and permanent magnet rotor as shown in Figure 8.13. The rotor is made of ferrite which is permanently magnetised. Just as with the variable reluctance type, both these structures are also toothed. The major difference between these is that the opposite ends of the rotor are north and south poles of a permanent magnet with teeth at these ends being offset by a half tooth pitch. The left phase is permanently magnetised as south pole and right phase as north pole.

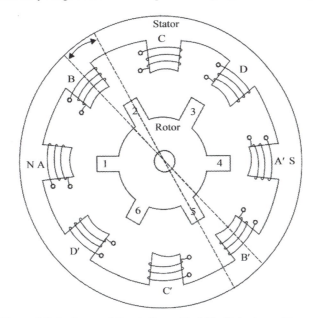

4-Phase, 8-Pole Stator, 6-Tooth Rotor Variable Reluctance Stepper Motor.

FIGURE 8.12   Stepper motor variable reluctance type

FIGURE 8.13   Rotor of permanent magnet stepper motor

The north pole is twisted with respect to south pole structure so that a south pole comes precisely between two north poles. For both type of stepper motors, the stepping angle (a) is given by the relation

$$A = 360°$$

Number of phase × number of poles

$$A = 360$$

$$N \times p$$

Example 8.1: *Find the step angle for a stepper motor having four phases and six poles. Also find the angular rotation when 20 digital pulses are supplied.*
   Solution: Given n = 4, p = 6
   Hence step angle $\alpha = \dfrac{360}{4 \times 6} = 15°$

Angular displacement with 20 digital pulses
Θ = 20 × 15° = 300°

8.4   BASIC DIGITAL LOGIC CIRCUITS

There are some basic operations performed in all digital systems, like computer system, digital control system, etc. These basic logical operations are AND, OR, NOT, NAND, NOR, EX-OR, EX-NOR. These are often called logic gates and are discussed below.

1. OR-Gate

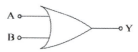

Logic diagram
If *A* and *B* are input and *Y* is the output, then
$Y = A$ OR $B = A \cup B = A + B$
Truth table:

	Input		Output
	A	**B**	**Y**
	0	0	0
	0	1	1
	1	0	1
	1	1	1

2. AND-Gate

$Y = A$ AND $B = A \cap B = A\,B$
Truth table:

A	B	Y
0	0	0
0	1	0
1	0	0
1	1	1

3. NOT-Gate

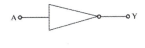

$Y = $ NOT $A = A$
Truth table:

A	Y
0	1
1	0

4. NOR Gate

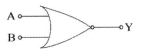

A NOR $B = A \cup B = A + B$
Truth table:

A	B	Y
0	0	1
1	0	0
0	1	0
1	1	0

5. NAND Gate

$Y = A$ *NAND* $B = A \cap B = A\,B$

Truth table:

A	B	Y
0	0	1
0	1	1
1	0	1
1	1	0

6. EX-OR Gate

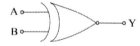

$Y = A$ EX-OR $B = A \oplus B = A\bar{B} + \bar{A} B$
Truth table:

A	B	Y
0	0	0
0	1	1
1	0	1
1	1	0

7. EX-NOR Gate

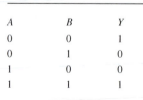

Truth table:

A	B	Y
0	0	1
0	1	0
1	0	0
1	1	1

$Y = $ EX-NOR $B = \overline{AEX - ORB} = A \odot B = AB + \bar{A}\bar{B}$

8.5   COUNTING DEVICES

The counting of events is accomplished by digital devices called counters. For example, the number of persons who have entered a seminar hall can be counted using counters. An appropriate transducer can be used to generate

LO 3. To know counting devices used in CNC machines.

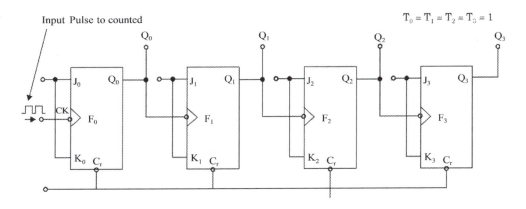

FIGURE 8.14 A four-bit counter using JK FLIP-FLOPS

electrical pulses corresponding to the event (in this case a person entering through the door) and these digital pulses can be counted using a counter. Digital counters are made up of FLIP-FLOPS. A four-bit counter composed of 4, t-type JK FLIP-FLOPS is shown in Figure 8.14.

A four-bit counter can count 24 = 16 digits ranging from 0 to 15. A circuit with n-FLIP-FLOPS has $2n$ possible states. The input i.e., digital pulses to be counted are given at the clock input of F_0 FLIP-FLOP. The output of F_0 i.e., Q_0 is connected to clock input of F_1.

The output of F_1 i.e., Q_1 is connected to clock input of F_2. The output of F_2 i.e., Q_2 is connected to clock input of F_3. The FLIP-FLOPS are cleared by applying logic 0 at the clear input terminal momentarily. But for the normal counting operation it should be maintained at logic 1.

The output Q_0 of F_0 changes at negative edge of each pulse (since $T_0 = 1$). The output Q_1 changes at the negative edge of each Q_0 pulse. The output Q_2 changes at the negative edge of each Q_1 pulse.

At any time, the reading of the counter i.e., Q_3, Q_2, Q_1, Q_0 is the number of pulses counted until that time. The circuit resets itself after counting 16 pulses.

There are different types of counters like:

- Ring counter,
- Twisted ring counter,
- Ripple counters (asynchronous counters),
- Synchronous counters,
- UP/DOWN counters.

In this chapter we do not go into details of these counters.

8.6   ANALOGUE AND DIGITAL SYSTEMS

Electrical signals which are continuous and can have any value in a specific range such signals are referred as *analogue signals*. The electronic circuits used to process these signals are called analogue circuits. The systems which work with analogue signals are called analogue systems. Such systems are incorporated with analogue circuits.

LO 4. To understand digital to analog convertor and analog to digital convertor

There is another class of signals that can have only two discrete values or levels, namely HIGH level and LOW level. Such signals are called digital signals. The systems that work with digital signals are called digital systems. Examples of such systems are digital computers, calculators, watches, telephones, control system of stepping motor controllers, NC and CNC machines, etc. Digital signals are also represented by 0 (LOW) and 1 (HIGH) – 0 and 1 referred as binary digit or bit. A digital system can have only one of the two possible values at a time, either 0 or 1. The two levels are also designated as ON and OFF or TRUE and FALSE corresponding to 0 and 1 respectively.

There are some major advantages of digital systems which are enumerated below:

1. Digital systems are very simple in operation as they work in either one of two states, ON and OFF.
2. Digital technique requires knowledge of binary algebra which is easy to understand.
3. A large number of integrated circuit chips (IC chips) are available because of very large scale integration (VLSI). These are very small in size, reliable, accurate and speed of operation is very high.
4. The effect of noise, ageing, temperature and other disturbances is very small in digital circuits.
5. In digital systems, the display of data and other information is very convenient.
6. Digital circuits have capability of memory and data storage which make them very useful for digital devices like computers and calculators.

Such advantages have led to the use of digital technology in computers, communication and instrumentation. However, it is important to note that the electrical signals are not available in digital form. In fact, these are available in analogue form and need to be converted into digital form to be fed to digital systems. The system used to convert an analogue signal to a digital signal is referred to as analogue-to-digital converter (ADC). The output of the system may again be required in analogue form. Therefore, the digital output signal has to be converted into analogue form. The system used for this purpose is called digital-to-analogue converter (DAC). In microprocessor-based control systems, ADCs and DACs are commonly used and are referred to as peripherals or I/O devices.

8.6.1 DIGITAL-TO-ANALOGUE CONVERTERS

The input to a DAC should be an N-bit binary signal. Such digital signals are available at the output of latches in microprocessor or registers. The analogue output voltage (V_0) corresponding to digital input for an N-bit DAC is given by the relation.

$$V_0 = K(2N - 1\ P_{N-1} + 2N - 2\ P_{N-2} + \dots + 22\ P_2 + 2P_1 + P_0)$$

In the above equation, K is a proportionality constant and

$$P_n = 1 \text{ if the } n\text{th bit of digital input is 1.}$$

$$= 0 \text{ if the } n\text{th bit of digital input is 0.}$$

There are two types of DACs that are being most commonly used.

1. Weighted-resistor DAC,
2. $R - 2R$ ladder DAC.

The circuit diagram of a weighted-resistor DAC is shown in Figure 8.15.

In this circuit, resistance values are weighted in accordance with the binary weights. The switches are thrown to position 1 or 0 for digital inputs corresponding to the specific bit being 1 or 0. The circuit diagram three-bit $R - 2R$ ladder DAC is shown in Figure 8.16.

It uses resistors of only two values i.e., R and $2R$. Input to the network is applied through digitally controlled switches. Such a switch is in position 0 or 1 depending upon the digital input to the bit being 0 or 1.

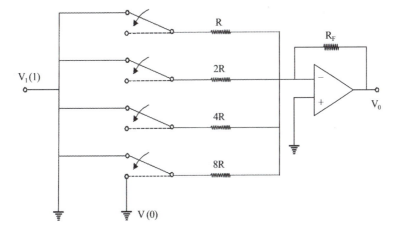

FIGURE 8.15   Weighted-resistor DA

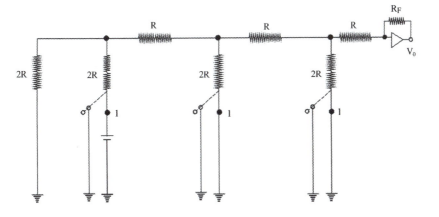

FIGURE 8.16   Three-bit R – 2R ladder DAC

The specifications of DAC given by the manufacturers are: Resolution, linearity, accuracy, setting time and temperature sensitivity.

Resolution: For DAC, the number of bits accepted at the input are defined as its resolution. For example, a three-bit DAC has a three-bit resolution.

Linearity: In a DAC, increments in digital input should be proportional to equivalent increments in analogue output voltage.

Accuracy is the measure of difference between actual output and the desired output. In DAC, it is specified as a percentage of full scale (maximum) output voltage.

Settling time is usually specified by the manufactures. It implies that there should be a limit on frequency at which the digital input can change. If it is operated at too high a frequency, it may not get sufficient time to settle down to final output voltage before being switched on to next digital input.

Temperature sensitivity: Due to resistors, Operational AMPlifier (OPAMP) and temperature sensitivity of input voltage source, the digital input may vary with temperature. It is generally specified as PPM/°C.

8.6.2   ANALOGUE-TO-DIGITAL CONVERTER (ADC)

In an ADC, input is analogue voltage which is continuous in nature. This has to be converted into digital output. The input voltage can have infinite values, whereas output is finite. For N-bit ADC, the output can have only $2N$ values. Hence a three-bit ADC can have eight output voltages and a four-bit ADC can have 16 output voltages. The entire range of analogue voltage has to be divided into various intervals and each interval is assigned a unique digital value. This process is called quantisation. A four-bit ADC can have 16 output values, hence the input analogue voltage should be divided into 16 equal parts as shown in the table below:

Analogue voltage input	Equivalent digital value			
0—V/16	0	0	0	0
V/16—2V/16	0	0	0	1
2V/16—3 V/16	0	0	1	0
3V/16—4 V/16	0	0	1	1
4V/16—5 V/16	0	1	0	0
5V/16—6 V/16	0	1	0	1
6V/16—7 V/16	0	1	1	0
7V/16—8 V/16	0	1	1	1
8V/16—9 V/16	1	0	0	0
9V/16—10V/16	1	0	0	1
10V/16—11 V/16	1	0	1	0
11V/16—12V/16	1	0	1	1
12V/16—13V/16	1	1	0	0
13V/16—13V/16	1	1	0	1
14V/16—15V/16	1	1	1	0
15V/16—16V/16	1	1	1	1
(16V/16 = V)				

Figure 8.17 shows a circuit diagram of three-bit V_0 parallel ADC.

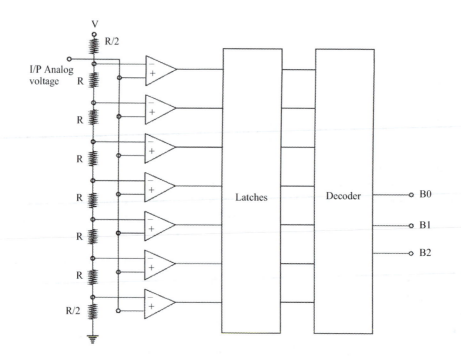

FIGURE 8.17   Three-bit parallel ADC

8.7 SUMMARY

A DC motor works on the principal that a conducting wire, carrying current when placed in magnetic field, experiences mechanical force.

The outer stationary member is called a stator, while inner rotating member is called a rotor.

A DC motor can provide rapid acceleration from a standstill.

Armature winding may be shunt connected, series connected, compounded and separately excited.

A DC motor may be armature control type or field control type.

Feedback devices used in NC and CNC machines are LVDT, opto-interrupters, optical encoders, synchro, resolver, etc.

In a stepper motor, for each digital pulse received, the shaft rotates by a small angle called step angle.

A stepper motor cannot take a heavy load.

Basic logical operations are AND, OR, NOT, NAND, NOR, EX-OR, EX-NOR.

Counting of events is accomplished by digital devices called counters.

Analogue signals can be converted into digital form by using an ADC.

Digital signals can be converted to analogue form using a DAC.

8.8 EXERCISE

1. Explain the working of armature-controlled and field-controlled DC motor using block diagram representation (BT level 1).
2. Describe the working principle of stepping motor. What are its disadvantages (BT level 2)?
3. What are the feedback devices generally used in CNC machines? Explain their working in brief (BT level 1).
4. Describe working and applications of counting devices (BT level 2).
5. State the working principle and applications of: (BT level 1)
   (i)   Digital to analogue convertor,
   (ii) Analog to digital convertor.
6. Explain the construction and working of a DC motor (BT level 1).
7. Explain the mathematical model of an armature-controlled DC motor (BT level 1).
8. Draw a block diagram representation of an armature-controlled and field-controlled DC motor (BT level 3).
9. Differentiate between armature control and field control in DC motors (BT level 4).
10. Discuss construction and working of LVDT (BT level 2).

8.9 MULTIPLE-CHOICE QUESTIONS

1. What is the purpose of a feedback device in a control system?
   a. To measure and provide information about the output of the system.
   b. To measure and provide information about the input to the system.
   c. To control the flow of power to the system.
   d. To regulate the temperature of the system.
2. Which type of feedback device is commonly used in control systems to measure position?
   a. Encoder.
   b. Thermocouple.
   c. Pressure sensor.
   d. Current transformer.
3. What is the purpose of a PID controller in a control system?
   a. To provide power to the system.

b. To measure the input to the system.

c. To regulate the temperature of the system.

d. To control the output of the system based on feedback information.

4. Which of the following is a type of actuator commonly used in control systems?

a. Sensor.

b. Encoder.

c. Servo motor.

d. Transducer.

5. Which of the following is a type of DC motor?

a. Brushless DC motor.

b. Stepper motor.

c. Servo motor.

d. Both a and b.

6. Which of the following is a type of feedback device commonly used in motion control systems?

a. Tachometer.

b. Encoder.

c. Potentiometer.

d. All of the above.

7. What is a stepper motor?

a. A type of DC motor.

b. A type of AC motor.

c. A type of synchronous motor.

d. A type of asynchronous motor.

8. Which of the following is a characteristic of a stepper motor?

a. High torque at low speeds.

b. Low torque at high speeds.

c. High speed and high torque.

d. Low speed and low torque.

Answers

1. Answer: a. To measure and provide information about the output of the system.

2. Answer: a. Encoder.

3. Answer: d. To control the output of the system based on feedback information.

4. Answer: c. Servo motor.

5. Answer: d. Both a and b.

6. Answer: b. Encoder.

7. Answer: c. A type of synchronous motor.

8. Answer: a. High torque at low speeds.

9 Interpolators and Control of NC Systems

Learning Outcomes: After studying this chapter, the reader should be able:

LO 1: To understand interpolators (BT level 2).
LO 2: To understand techniques for linear interpolation (BT level 2).
LO 3: To understand techniques for circular interpolation (BT level 2).
LO 4: To understand control of NC system (BT level 2).

9.1 INTERPOLATOR

In a number of machining situations, a tool has to move along continuous curves, circular paths, arc-shaped trajectories, etc. As opposed to trajectory, numerical control (NC) is discrete, which poses a problem when generating them. So the tool cannot exactly trace the desired path. The NC controller has to calculate a large number of closely spaced points on the cutter path. The points are connected by very small straight lines to form the trajectory as shown in Figure 9.1 for an arc.

LO 1. To understand interpolators.

If these points are very closely spaced, the actual path traced becomes approximately the same as the desired tool path. The minimum distance between the two points that the machine can differentiate is called the *control resolution*. Thus, the accuracy of the machine depends on the control resolution. The process of calculating the points on the trajectory is called *interpolation*.

It is not possible for the part programmer to calculate so many points on the tool trajectory. Therefore, interpolation algorithms or subroutine are made which can calculate a large number of closely spaced points on the trajectory. These programs are called *interpolators*.

Numerous interpolation approaches have been developed to generate smooth, continuous tool trajectories using a contouring-style NC system. These include:

1. Linear interpolation algorithms,
2. Circular interpolation algorithms,
3. Parabolic interpolation algorithms,
4. Helical interpolation algorithms,
5. Cubic interpolation algorithms.

Among these, linear and circular interpolation are the most common and are available on most of the contour cutting machines. Parabolic, helical and cubic are not so common. Interpolation subroutines in the Machine Control Unit (MCU) handle the computations and guidance of the tool.

9.2 LINEAR INTERPOLATOR

It is a program/algorithm which can calculate closely spaced points between the given end points of a line. These points, when joined, form the linear cutter path. It is the preferred approach for creating a straight cutting tool path in

LO 2. To understand linear interpolators.

DOI: 10.1201/9781003350842-9

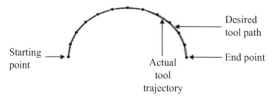

FIGURE 9.1   Interpolator

contouring NC. The lines can be generated both in 2-D and 3-D. For a 2-D line the MCU generates signals for two axes. Whereas in case of a 3-D line, the MCU generates signals along all the three axes. The part programmer is required to specify the end points of the straight line as well as the desired feed rate. The MCU also calculates the tool velocities along all the relevant axes for obtaining the required feed rate along the specified line.

Various interpolation algorithms can be employed to calculate intermediate points on the straight line between the two end points. The following algorithms can be used as linear:

(1) Digital Differential Analyser (DDA) algorithm,
(2) Linear interpolation using slope method.

9.2.1   DDA Algorithm

The inputs for this algorithm are (x_1, y_1) and (x_2, y_2).

The slope of the line $m = \dfrac{y_2 - y_1}{x_2 - x_1} = \dfrac{\Delta y}{\Delta x}$

Hence $\Delta y = m \, \Delta x$

Case 1: If $m < 1$ and +ve

1. Set the left point as the start point,
2. Change in x coordinate is set to unity i.e., $\Delta x = 1$,
3. If (x_i, y_i) is any point on the line, then the coordinates of next point (x_{i+1}, y_{i+1}) can be calculated as follows:

$$\Delta x = 1 \Rightarrow \qquad x_{i1} - x_i = 1$$

$$x_{i+1} = x_i + 1$$

$$\Delta y = m \, \Delta x$$

$$\Delta y = m$$

$$y_{i+1} - y_i = m$$

$$y_{i+1} = y_i + m$$

Note that m can be a real number. Therefore y_{i+1} can also be a real number. In such a case it becomes necessary to round off the value y_{i+1} to the nearest integer as pixels are addressed in integer fashion.

4. If the right point is set as the starting point, the procedure remains the same except that now

$$x_{i+1} = x_i - 1$$

$$y_{i+1} = y_i - m$$

Case 2: If $m > 1$ and $+ve$

1. Set the left point as the start point,
2. Change in y coordinate is set to unity i.e., $\Delta y = 1$,
3. If (x_i, y_i) is any point on the line then the coordinate of next point is found as:

$$\Delta y = 1$$

$$\text{i.e., } y_{i+1} - y_i = 1$$

$$y_{i+1} = y_i + 1$$

$$m = \frac{\Delta y}{\Delta x} = \frac{1}{\Delta x} \quad \left[\because \Delta y = 1 \right]$$

$$\Delta x = \frac{1}{m}$$

$$x_{i+1} - x_i = \frac{1}{m}$$

Or

$$x_{i+1} = x_i + \frac{1}{m}$$

It is necessary to round off the value of x_{i+1} to the nearest integer.

4. If the right point is set as the start point, the procedure remains the same as explained above except,

$$y_{i+1} = y_i - 1$$

$$\text{and} \quad x_{i+1} = x_i - \frac{1}{m}$$

Case 3: If slope of the line is negative and if $|m| < 1$, then follow the procedure for $m < 1$ as explained in Case 1. If $|m| > 1$, then follow the procedure for $m > 1$ as explained in Case 2.

9.3   CIRCULAR INTERPOLATOR

This is an algorithm which generates closely spaced points on the arc or circular profile, which when connected by straight lines approximates a circle. The tool moves from point to point in order to machine a circular cut.

LO 3. To understand circular interpolators.

There can be two types of algorithms used for generating a circle:

(i) Using equation of a circle in cartesian coordinate and polar coordinate,
(ii) Bresenham's circle-generating algorithm.

Using **cartesian coordinate**, form equation of circle with centre (0, 0) and radius r is:

$$x^2 + y^2 = r^2$$

If the centre is (x_c, y_c), the equation is modified as:

$$(x - x_c)^2 + (y - y_c)^2 = r^2$$

Hence $\quad y = y_c \pm \sqrt{r^2 - \left(x - x_c\right)^2}$

If the x-coordinate is varied from $(x_c - r)$ to $(x_c + r)$ then the corresponding y-coordinate can be found out from the above equation. Hence points on the circle can be generated.

The basic disadvantage with the generation of points using the equation is that there is a square root operation in the equation because of which the calculation becomes slow. Secondly, the points will not be spaced evenly on the path of the circle.

Using **polar coordinate** form, equation of circle with centre (x_c, y_c) and radius r is written as:

$$Y = y_c + r \sin \theta$$

$$X = x_c + r \cos \theta$$

Where θ is the angle made with x-axis in an anticlockwise direction. By varying the angle θ from 0 to 360° uniformly, it is possible to generate the points on the circle and hence the problem of uneven spacing will not arise. The only disadvantage with this type of generation is that the trigonometric calculations make the program slow.

The circular interpolator can be modified to generate an ellipse. The equation of ellipse is:

$$\frac{\left(x - x_c\right)^2}{r_x^2} + \frac{\left(y - y_c\right)^2}{r_y^2} = 1$$

where (x_c, y_c) is the centre of the ellipse and r_x, r_y are semi major axis and semi minor axis.

9.4 HELICAL INTERPOLATOR

This is an algorithm that combines the logic of circular interpolation and linear interpolation perpendicular to the plane of the circle to form a helical path. Such an algorithm can be used for machining large internal threads.

9.5 PARABOLIC INTERPOLATOR

This is in less common use. It can make use of parabolic equation $y^2 = 4ax$ or $x^2 = 4ay$ to generate points on a parabolic curve.

9.6 CONTROL OF NC SYSTEMS

We have already discussed that in NC machines, the control system regulates the position and speed of the machine tool's axes. A command signal produced by an interpolator is utilised to drive each axis independently. NC control system can be open-loop type or closed-loop type depending upon customer specifications and economy. An open-loop system uses a stepper motor to drive and move the machine table as illustrated in Figure 9.2.

LO 4. To understand control of NC system.

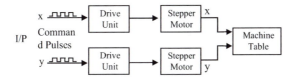

FIGURE 9.2 Schematic representation of open-loop control system for a two-axis NC machine

The command pulses from interpolators are fed to the drive units of the stepper motor. An open-loop system is suitable for a point-to-point (PTP) system such as an NC drill press, punch press, etc.

A closed-loop NC system makes use of a hydraulic drive or motor drive along with feedback elements such as, encoder or resolver. A closed-loop control can be used in PTP, straight cut or contouring NC machines. In a PTP system, a workpiece is mounted on the machine table, which moves relative to the tool. Thus, a PTP system requires control of only the final position of the table. The path and velocity of the table are not significant. The table moves from one point to the next point at high velocity. So, declaration circuits are also incorporated in the PTP NC system to take care of the inertia of the machine table.

In straight cut or contouring NC machines, the tool cuts the material while the machine axes are moving. Therefore, the path followed is significant. The contour shape is determined by the ratio of axial velocities and the position of the tool at the completion of each segment. In a closed-loop system, the command pulses of the interpolator are compared with the signals from the feedback devices (sensors).

9.6.1 Control of Point-to-Point (PTP) Systems

We already know that in a PTP NC system each machine axis is driven independently at the maximum allowable speed. Deceleration circuits are incorporated to take care of inertia-related problems, but the deceleration is accomplished in each axis separately. The path between the points is not significant. A PTP NC system can be based on incremental or absolute programming. The primary control elements in incremental PTP NC systems are the position counters. Each axis of the machine is equipped with a down-counter. Taking into account the dimensions as mentioned in the part program, the down-counter is loaded to a specific axial incremental position in basic length unit (BLUs) which is subsequently decremented by pulses. A pulse corresponds to an axial motion of 1 BLU. Thus, at each instance the contents of the counter represent the distance to the target point.

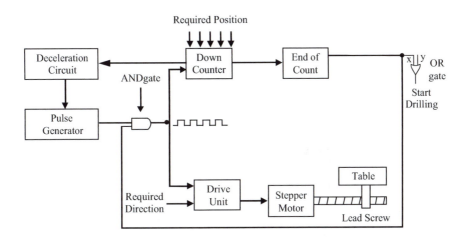

FIGURE 9.3 Absolute closed-loop control

9.6.2 ABSOLUTE CLOSED-LOOP CONTROL

The absolute positioning system makes use of absolute programming and a feedback element. As illustrated in Figure 9.3, the command register is loaded with the desired absolute position of the axis as defined in the dimension word of the part program. Each time a new block is read, the command register is loaded with the corresponding positioning command. The subtractor computes the difference between the desired and actual position. This is called position error. It is fed to the motor through a decelerator. The position register is fed by two alternative sequences of pulses from the feedback element, like the encoder, one for each direction of motion.

9.7   SUMMARY

The process of calculating coordinates of the closely spaced points on the tool trajectory is called interpolation.

The software programs used to calculate a large number of these closely spaced points are called interpolators.

Depending upon the type of trajectory interpolation algorithms may be of any one of the following types:

(a) Linear interpolator,
(b) Circular interpolator,
(c) Parabolic interpolator,
(d) Helical interpolator,
(e) Cubic interpolator.

A linear interpolator makes use of DDA algorithm.

A circular interpolator generates closely spaced points on the arc or circular profile.

Helical interpolation combines circular and linear interpolation techniques to generate a helix.

9.8   EXERCISE

1. What is an interpolator (BT level 1)?
2. Define various interpolation techniques (BT level 1).
3. Elaborate linear interpolation techniques (BT level 2).
4. What techniques are employed for circular interpolation (BT level 1)?
5. Explain the use of interpolators in NC/CNC machines (BT level 2).
6. Discuss the need of interpolators in CAD/CAM (BT level 2).
7. Discuss the DDA interpolator (BT level 2).
8. Write Bresenham's line drawing algorithm (BT level 1).
9. Suggest a circular interpolator that uses the polar coordinate form of equations (BT level 2).
10. Briefly discuss the helical interpolator and parabolic interpolator (BT level 2).
11. Explain with the help of a diagram/table, the principle and working of a circular interpolator (BT level 2).
12. Write a short note on linear versus circular interpolators (BT level 1).

9.9   MULTIPLE-CHOICE QUESTIONS

1. What is the role of an interpolator in an NC system?
    a. To generate the toolpath based on the part program
    b. To control the motion of the machine
    c. To monitor the cutting process and adjust parameters
    d. To provide feedback on the position of the tool and workpiece

2. Which of the following interpolation methods is used to generate a circular toolpath?
   a. Linear interpolation
   b. Circular interpolation
   c. Arc interpolation
   d. Spiral interpolation
3. Which type of interpolation is used to generate a straight line toolpath?
   a. Linear interpolation
   b. Circular interpolation
   c. Arc interpolation
   d. Spiral interpolation
4. Which of the following is a common type of NC system used in milling machines?
   a. Point-to-point system
   b. Continuous path system
   c. Coordinated system
   d. Direct numerical control system
5. Which of the following is a benefit of using a direct numerical control (DNC) system?
   a. Higher accuracy and precision
   b. Reduced setup time
   c. Increased machine speed
   d. All of the above
6. What is a feed rate control in an NC system?
   a. A control that regulates the speed of the spindle
   b. A control that adjusts the speed of the cutting tool
   c. A control that regulates the rate at which the cutting tool moves through the workpiece
   d. A control that adjusts the depth of cut
7. Which of the following is a type of control system used in NC machines?
   a. Open-loop control
   b. Closed-loop control
   c. Hybrid control
   d. Adaptive control
8. What is the purpose of a servo control system in an NC machine?
   a. To control the position of the cutting tool
   b. To control the speed of the spindle
   c. To control the feed rate of the cutting tool
   d. To control the depth of cut
9. What is a tool offset in an NC system?
   a. The distance between the spindle and the workpiece
   b. The difference between the programmed tool position and the actual tool position
   c. The depth of cut for a particular tool
   d. The size of the cutting tool
10. Which of the following is a benefit of using a look-ahead feature in an NC system?
    a. Higher accuracy and precision
    b. Reduced machining time
    c. Increased machine speed
    d. All of the above

Answers

1. Answer: b. To control the motion of the machine
2. Answer: c. Arc interpolation
3. Answer: a. Linear interpolation

4. Answer: c. Coordinated system
5. Answer: b. Reduced setup time
6. Answer: c. A control that regulates the rate at which the cutting tool moves through the workpiece
7. Answer: b. Closed-loop control
8. Answer: a. To control the position of the cutting tool
9. Answer: b. The difference between the programmed tool position and the actual tool position
10. Answer: b. Reduced machining time

10 Computer-Integrated Manufacturing System

Learning Outcomes: After studying this chapter, the reader should be able

LO 1: To understand the concept of group technology, manufacturing cell and composite parts (BT level 2).

LO 2: To understand transfer lines, their configurations, analysis and line balancing (BT level 2).

LO 3: To understand flexible manufacturing system (FMS), benefits and problems in implementing FMS (BT level 2).

LO 4: To understand the concept of computer-integrated manufacturing (CIM), functions and benefits of CIM, its hardware and software requirements (BT level 2).

LO 5: To understand the concept of integrating CAD with CAM (BT level 2):

LO 6 To understand the concept of computer-aided process planning (CAPP) (BT level 2).

10.1 GROUP TECHNOLOGY

When a company manufactures several components, each of which may be available in a vast array of models or variations, it must generate and maintain a dizzying number of drawings, production plans, bills of materials and other administrative papers. This amounts to a big and tedious task if not handled skilfully. Now, if the company gets a new order of a model or component, it is recommended that rather than preparing new designs, engineering drawings and process plans starting from scratch, modifications be made in existing drawings and process plans of similar models already made by the company. Such a practice can save lot of time and effort and lays the foundation of concept called group technology.

LO 1. To understand the concept of group technology.

According to the manufacturing industry's group technology concept, diverse components are divided into smaller batches or groups based on their commonalities in the design and manufacturing process. Such clusters are described using the phrase "part families." Therefore, group technology depends on the concept that many of a company's manufactured products share at least some design or manufacturing features. The parts can be grouped into a part family based on similarity in design attributes such as shape, geometry and dimensions. Parts can also be grouped based on similarity in manufacturing attributes such as processing method, sequence of machining, jigs and fixtures required, etc. Some part families may have similar design as well as manufacturing features.

Components must be identified and coded in order to be organised into component families and used in group technology. The idea is to identify similarities and construct a taxonomy from them. Part classification and coding also facilitates retrieval of designs, process plans, route sheets, etc. from the existing database of company.

While the concept of making part families is at the core of group technology philosophy, it is also one of the most time consuming and difficult tasks. In this chapter, we study two general methods used to make part families. These are:

1. Classification and coding,
2. Product flow analysis.

DOI: 10.1201/9781003350842-10

Examples of some popular coding systems are OPITZ code, MICLASS, DCLASS, KK-3 code, etc. In this chapter, we study the OPITZ code.

10.1.1 OPITZ CODE

It was developed by Professor H. Opitz of Achene Technical University, Germany, and to date remains one of the most popular classification and coding system. OPITZ makes use of following digit and letter sequence for coding:

$$12345 \qquad 6789 \qquad ABCD$$

The first nine digits of the serial number provide information about the product's development. The first five digits, 12345, are known as the form code since they specify the component's basic structural and functional characteristics. The next four digits, 6789, are part of a supplement code that defines the product's characteristics throughout its manufacture. The last four letters are known as *secondary code* and are indicative of the type of manufacturing operation and sequence. The secondary code is often prepared by firms to meet their individual requirements. The interpretation of nine digits can be made from Figure 10.1. The first five digits are used as shown in Table 10.1.

10.1.2 CLASSIFICATION AND CODING

Classification is the process of grouping items into groups based on their common qualities. The features of individual components may be used to classify them into separate categories:

- Design characteristics include major and minor dimensions, basic external or interior shape, length-to-diameter ratio, surface quality, tolerances and the materials used. Such a system is useful for easy design retrieval from a database. It also promotes design standardisation.
- *Manufacturing attributes* refer to manufacturing process, processing equipment required, cutting tools or fixtures required, operation sequence, production time, production rate, etc. Such a system facilitates the retrieval of computer-aided process plans (CAPPs), tooling designs and other production related data from the existing database.
- *Design and manufacturing attributes* aim at combining the functions and advantages of the above two systems into a single classification method.

Coding refers to the process of allotting a unique symbol to the component. Various coding systems have been developed for specific applications.

Example 10.1: *Prepare the form code for the part shown in Figure 10.2.*

Solution: As $L/D = \dfrac{45}{30} = 1.5$ $(0.5 < L/D < 3)$ so the first digit is 1.

The second number is 5 since this component contains threads on one end and steps on the other. Since there is a threaded through-hole, the third number is a 2. Since no surface machining is required, the fourth digit is 0. Since there are no auxiliary holes or gear teeth, the fifth digit is also 0. Hence, the form code for the OPITZ is 15200.

10.1.3 PRODUCT FLOW ANALYSIS (PFA)

PFA is another methodology in GT which uses manufacturing sequence information available on route sheets. The route sheets of components are examined in order to sort through all the components and regroup them by a matrix analysis. New machine cells are formed from the existing

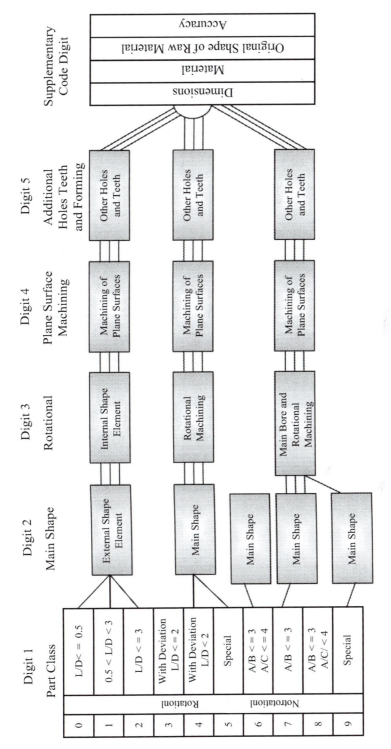

FIGURE 10.1 OPITZ coding system

TABLE 10.1

Coding of First Five Digits of OPITZ Code

Digit 1		Digit 2		Digit 3		Digit 4	Digit 5	
Part class		External shape elements		Internal shape elements		Plane surface machining	Auxillary holes and gear teeth	
						0	No surface machining	0	No auxilary holes
0	L/D < = 0.5	0	Smooth no shape elements	0	No holes no breakthrough	1	Surface pland and /or curved in one around a circle	
1	0.5 < L/D<3	1	Stepped to one end or smooth — No shape elements	1	Smooth or stepped to one end — No shape elements			1	Axial not on pitch circle dia
2	L/D< = 3	2	Thread	2	Thread	2	External plane surface related by graduation around a circle	2	Axial on pitch circle dia
3	Functional groove	3	Functional groove	3	Functional groove	3	External croove and/or slot	3	Radial not on pitch circle dia
4		4	Stepped to both ends — No shape elements	4	Stepped both ends — No shape elements	4	External spline (polygon)	4	Axial and/or radial and/or other direction
5		5	Thread	5	Thread	5	External plane surface and/or slot external spline	5	Axial and/or radial and/or other direction
6		6	Functional groove	6	Functional groove	6	Internal plane surface and/or slot	6	Spur gear teeth
7		7	Functional cone	7	Functional cone	7	Internal spline (polygon)	7	Bevel gear teeth
8		8	Operating speed	8	Operating speed	8	Internal and external polygon and/or slot	8	Other gear theeth
9		9	All others	9	All others	9	All others	9	All others

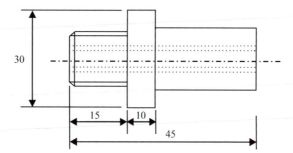

FIGURE 10.2   Component

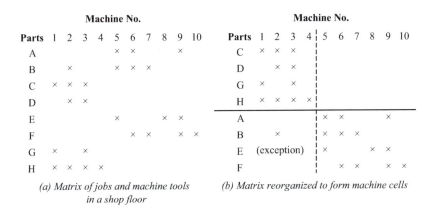

(a) Matrix of jobs and machine tools
in a shop floor

(b) Matrix reorganized to form machine cells

FIGURE 10.3 Schematic to explain PFA

machine layout by analysing the flow of material and then reorganising the machines. The following simple steps can be followed in PFA:

1. Analyse the route sheet of all components to be manufactured.
2. Prepare a matrix as shown in Figure 10.3(a) showing which component gets processed on which machine. Regroup the parts such that each part is included in only one group. The parts which are incompatible to any group can be considered as a separate group.
3. If a machine is required by only one part (or every few parts), or if a machine is required for all the types of parts, then it may be kept out of all the machine cells. (b) shows the regrouping of machine tools to form two machine cells.

10.1.4 Benefits of Group Technology (GT)

Main benefits of group technology are enumerated below:

1. Using the GT concept, new designs can be prepared easily be modifying existing design rather than starting from scratch.
2. Similarly, new process plans can be prepared by editing existing process plans rather than starting from scratch, hence saving time and resources.
3. Standard, optimised process plans can be developed for part families.
4. Standard toolings (jigs, fixtures, templates, etc.) can be developed for part families.
5. Manufacturing lead time is reduced by effective use of GT. Hence, responsiveness to customer requirement increases.
6. GT leads to better utilisation of machines.
7. It simplifies and improves the purchase of raw materials.
8. Reduced material handling requirement and efficient, material flow.
9. Labour and machine specialisation to manufacture particular part families leads to improvement in productivity.

10.1.5 Limitations of GT

1. A lot of time and effort are required initially to make part families.
2. Initial cost of implementation can be high.
3. If the range of products being manufactured by the company changes, GT codes have to be revised.

4. There are a number of GT codes, but no single classification and coding system suits all applications.
5. There is lot of inconvenience for the machine shop to make conversion from conventional layout to group technology manufacturing cells.

10.2   MANUFACTURING CELL (CELLULAR MANUFACTURING)

A manufacturing cell is a self-sufficient manufacturing facility which includes all machines and equipment that are needed to make a part or a subassembly. This concept is also called cellular manufacturing. A manufacturing cell should be well planned and designed in order to operate it profitably. It also takes into account the concept of "group technology," in which similar components are grouped together to capitalise on their common qualities throughout the design and manufacturing stages. Similar components are organised into families. We already know that parts may be similar in terms of:

LO 1. To understand the concept of manufacturing cell and composite part

(A) Design attributes like part geometry, shape, size and weight.
(B) Characteristics of the manufacturing process itself, such as the sequence of the several machining processes required to produce a particular component.

A manufacturing cell may be designed for a particular part family.

10.2.1   Composite Part Concept

This concept is often used for designing a manufacturing cell. A composite part is a hypothetical component that combines the most advantageous characteristics of many current components into a single, more adaptable component. The manufacturing cell would be designed to provide all the machining capabilities to manufacture such a hypothetical part. To manufacture any member of the part family, unneeded operations would simply be omitted.

10.2.2   Classification of Manufacturing Cell

Manufacturing cells can be classified into four categories depending upon the number of machines and the degree to which automatic material handling systems are used.

1. Single manufacturing cell,
2. Group manufacturing cell with manual handling,
3. Group manufacturing cell with semi-integrated handling,
4. Flexible manufacturing cell.

A single manufacturing cell, which comprises a single machine and the jigs, fixtures and other equipment required for its operation, may create one or more component families. In this kind of cell, workpieces that can be entirely machined on a single machine tool, such as a lathe, milling machine or machining centre, may be processed.

To mass produce the same or comparable component families, group production cells with human handling use a number of machines. It is within the purview of the cell operators, who are also accountable for material management. It is widely accepted that the U-shaped arrangement seen in Figure 10.4(a) is the most efficient configuration for these cells.

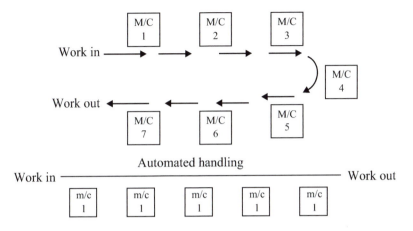

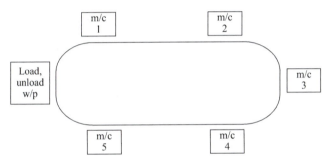

FIGURE 10.4 Manufacturing cell with (a) U-shaped, (b) inline layout for group manufacturing cell with semi-integrated handling

FIGURE 10.5 Loop layout for group manufacturing cell with semi-integrated handling

The group production cell uses semi-integrated material handling systems, such as roller conveyors and flowcharts, to deliver goods from one machine to another. The machines are laid along the conveyor to match the machining sequence. Such as arrangement of machines as shown in Figure 10.4(b) is called inline layout.

If the machining sequence for various parts of a part family varies, a loop layout as shown in Figure 10.5 is considered more appropriate as it allows different machining sequences for different parts in the system.

A flexible manufacturing cell is an automated manufacturing cell. It integrates processing stations (such as CNC machines) with an automated material handling system. Such a system is controlled by a computer.

10.2.3 MANUFACTURING CELL DESIGN

Consider the following considerations while implementing cell-based manufacturing:

1. The amount of work to be performed in the cell would determine the number of machines and other equipment required, as well as the total cost of the cell.
2. Variation in the process routing of the parts belonging to a part family would decide the type of machine arrangement and material handling system required for the cell. For example, for identical process routing, straight line flow is appropriate, but if the variation is significant, U-shaped or loop arrangement would be more suitable.
3. Workpiece factors such as component size, shape, weight, etc. would dictate the size and kind of available machines, material handling equipment and processing equipment.

10.2.3.1   Benefits of Cellular Manufacturing

The benefits of cellular manufacturing are realised in the following fields:

(A) Tooling and fixturisation,
(B) Material handling,
(C) Process planning,
(D) Production and inventory control.

(A) Tooling and Fixturisation

Cellular manufacturing tends to promote standardisation of tooling and fixturisation. Jigs and fixtures are so designed so as to accommodate maximum members of a part family. Due to the similarity of the workpieces produced by each machine tool in a production cell, moving between tasks requires only small modifications. Thus, setup time is saved which in turn reduces the manufacturing lead time and associated cost.

(B) Material Handling

Cellular manufacturing tends to reduce workpart movement and waiting time as an appropriate material handling system is incorporated into the cell. Different types of machine layouts help in the efficient flow of materials through the shop.

(C) Process Planning

In cellular manufacturing, parts are usually classified into part families based on their design and manufacturing attributes. This helps in reducing time for process planning. The process plans can be standardised. Hence, there is no need to start from scratch every time to prepare process plan of a new part.

(D) Production and Inventory Control

With cellular manufacturing, the production scheduling is simplified. It reduces the complexity and size of the scheduling problems as the parts are grouped into families and the machines are grouped in a manufacturing cell. With reduced setup and an efficient material handling system, the work-in-progress and inventory are minimised.

10.3   TRANSFER LINES

LO 2. To understand Transfer lines, their configurations, analysis and line balancing

When some subassemblies or components are to be produced in large volumes, the machines are configured in the required machining sequence to form transfer lines also known as flow lines. Hence, automated transfer lines consist of automated machines or special purpose machines linked together by material handling devices to transfer parts between the machines. Figure 10.6 shows an automated transfer line consisting of a turning centre, two milling machines, one drilling machine and a honing machine. The raw workpiece enters from one end of the line and the finished product leaves the other end of the line.

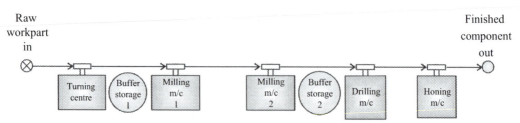

FIGURE 10.6   Configuration of an automated transfer line

A buffer storage may be incorporated between any two machines. A buffer storage is normally used where the machining time of the two consecutive machines is not same. In the above example, buffer stock 1 is maintained between turning centre and milling m/c 1 and buffer stock 2 is maintained between milling m/c 2 and the drilling machine. Sometimes manual machines may also be used in the line when automation is uneconomical. Automated transfer lines are generally installed to manufacture components of mass production.

Some of the advantages of the using transfer for mass production are as follows:

(A) Reduced labour and labour cost,
(B) Higher production rates,
(C) Specialisation of operations,
(D) Integration of operations,
(E) Shorter distance to be moved between two machines, hence reducing manufacturing lead time.

Transfer lines can be arranged in two basic configurations: Inline configuration and rotary configuration.

10.3.1 INLINE CONFIGURATION

In this configuration, the machines are arranged in almost a straight line. If the number of machines is high whereas space is limited, the workflow can take a few 90° turns. Figure 10.6 illustrates an inline configuration. Such as arrangement is preferred for:

(A) Larger workpieces,
(B) A high number of machines,
(C) When buffer storage capacity is required.

10.3.2 ROTARY CONFIGURATION

The machines are arranged in a ring around a dial or table in the centre. Individual workpieces are moved to the appropriate machining or assembly station as the table rotates. Figure 10.7 illustrates a rotary configuration. Such an arrangement is preferred for:

(A) Smaller workpieces,
(B) When the number of machines is less,
(C) When buffer storage capacity is not required.

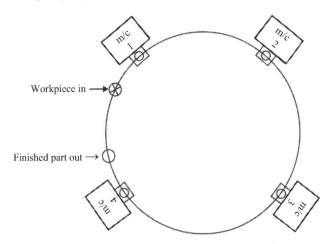

FIGURE 10.7   Rotary configuration for transfer lines

The transfer mechanism used in a transfer line has two basic functions:

(A) To move parts between adjacent machines.
(B) To correctly locate and orient the workpiece with respect to the machine tool.

There are various types of workpart transfer mechanisms which use different methods for transporting the workparts. The methods of workpart transfer can be broadly classified into following four categories:

(A) Continuous transfer method,
(B) Synchronous transfer method,
(C) Asynchronous transfer method,
(D) Pallet fixtures.

Let us discuss these four types of workpart transport systems.

(A) Continuous Transfer Method

The workpieces are moved continuously and at a constant rate. During processing, the machine's workheads must travel along the surface of the workpiece. This method is usually adopted where the weight and size of workhead are small so that there is no inertia problem. A good example of the continuous transfer method can be found in a beverage bottling plant. In the bottling operation, the beverage is discharged into the moving bottles by spouts moving along the bottles.

(B) Synchronous Transfer Method

During this kind of work-past transfer, the machines are immobile. Workpieces must be transported between machines and set up in the precise orientation and position for machining. All the workpieces are moved at the same time. That is why such a system is called synchronous transfer system. Since in this system, the workpieces are transferred with a discontinuous or an intermittent motion, such a method is also called intermittent transfer. This type of workpart transfer method is commonly used in machining and assembly operations, press working operations and progressive dies.

(C) Asynchronous Transfer Method

In this method, each part moves independent of the other parts. The system allows the workpiece to move to the next workstation as soon as processing at the current station is over. Parts are concurrently processed on the assembly line and at the different workstations. This is the most flexible system.

Pallet Fixtures

Sometimes, transfer systems are designed to incorporate pallet fixtures. The workparts can be mounted on pallet fixtures and then transferred between the workstations. The pallet fixtures can be easily transferred, located and clamped in an appropriate position at successive stations. Pallet fixtures are normally designed to carry a variety of similar parts.

10.3.3 Transfer Mechanisms for Automatic Transfer Lines

These are the mechanisms that are used to move materials and components between various process stations. A number of mechanisms has been developed which can be basically classified into two categories:

(A) **Linear transfer mechanisms:** These mechanisms provide linear motion to a workpiece for inline configuration of machines. Examples of linear transfer mechanisms are walking beam systems, roller conveyor systems, chain conveyor systems, etc.

(B) **Rotary transfer mechanisms:** These are the ones which are used to provide rotary motion to the workpiece for rotary configuration of machines. Examples of rotary transfer mechanisms are rack and pinion, ratchet and pawl, Geneva mechanism and cam mechanism.

10.3.4 ANALYSIS OF TRANSFER LINES

The performance of a transfer line can be judged on the basis of three parameters:

(A) Production rate,
(B) Line efficiency i.e., proportion of time the line is operating,
(C) Cost per item produced on the line.

10.3.5 ASSUMPTIONS FOR ANALYSIS OF TRANSFER LINES

In this analysis we assume that:

(A) The transfer system being used is synchronous type.
(B) The transfer line does not possess an internal buffer storage capacity.
(C) When breakdown occurs at any one station of the line, the entire line is shut down.

10.3.5.1 Symbols Used for Analysis

T_C = Average cycle time of transfer line, i.e., the longest processing time at a station of the line plus the time required for the parts to transfer. (The processing time at various stations will be different.) It is the ideal time (with no breakdown) in which process should be completed.

T_P = Average production time, T_P is greater than T_C because of breakdowns of the line. (The line breakdown may take place due to tool failure, limit switch or other electrical malfunctioning, mechanical failure of transfer system, processing machine mechanism, etc.)

T_{bd} = Average breakdown time, is the time required to diagnose the fault and rectify it. Since the line breakdown occurs due to various reasons, the subscript i can be used to specify the reason for breakdown by subscripting the term at T_{bdi}.

N_i = Number of times, the transfer line stops per cycle for reason i.

Hence, total breakdown time = $N_i \times T_{bdi}$

Average production time becomes equal to ideal cycle time plus the total breakdown time, i.e.,

$$T_p = T_c + \Sigma^{N_i}_{T_{bdi}}$$

Production rate (R_p): Considering no breakdown (which is rarely possible)

Ideal production rate: $R_{pc} = \dfrac{1}{T_c}$

Actual production rate: $R_{pa} = \dfrac{1}{T_p}$

Line Efficiency (E_l): It is defined as the proportion of time for which the line is operating,

Line efficiency: $E_l = \dfrac{T_c}{T_p} - \dfrac{T_c}{T_c + \sum N_i T_{bdi}}$

Cost per item (C): This includes:

- Cost of raw material per item (C_r).
- Cost of operating the line. Let C_m be the cost of operating the line per minute. Then total cost of operating the line is equal to $C_m \times T_p$.
- Cost of tooling and fixturisation per item (C_t). Hence total cost per item.

$$C = C_r + C_m \times T_p + C_t$$

Note that this equation does not account for scrap cost, inspection cost and maintenance cost, etc.

10.3.6   Transfer Line Balancing

To "balance" a transfer line is to assign about equal amounts of processing time to each station along the line. If all workstations of a line have equal processing time, there will be perfect balance of the line and there will be no need to maintain buffer between two machines. However, in practical situations it is very difficult to achieve perfect line balancing. If the line is perfectly balanced, we can expect a smooth flow of workpieces between the workstations. When the line is unbalanced, the slowest station determines the overall production rate of the line.

We first discuss the terminology used in line balancing problems.

10.3.6.1   Minimum Rational Work Elements

This can be defined as the smallest individual tasks into which the entire manufacturing process can be subdivided. For example, in piston manufacturing, drilling the gudgeon pin hole can be considered a minimum work element, size turning can be considered another.

Let T_{ei} represent the time required to carry out ith task.

10.3.6.2   Total Work Content

This number represents the sum of all the jobs along the line. Assuming T_{wc} is the amount of time necessary to finish the whole body of work, then,

$$T_{wc} = \sum_{i=1}^{n} T_{ei}$$

where n is the total number of work contents.

10.3.6.3   Workstation Process Time (T_{si})

The workstations of a transfer line may be automatic or manual. One or more distinct jobs may comprise the work performed at a particular station. Hence, workstation process time is the sum of time required for each work element performed at the station. If there are m workstations in a line then,

$$\sum_{j=1}^{m} T_{si} = \sum_{i=1}^{n} T_{ei}$$

10.3.6.4   Procedence Constraints

These constraints refer to the sequence of machining operations to be followed to get a desired output. For example, a threaded hole must be drilled before it can be reamed or tapped.

10.3.6.5   Balanced Delay (*d*)

It is the measure of line inefficiency which results from the idle time of workstation due to inappropriate allocation of work among the stations.

$$d = \frac{mT_c - T_{wc}}{mT_c}$$

10.3.6.6   Precedence Diagram

These diagrams represent the sequence of work elements as suggested by precedence constraints. Work elements are symbolised by nodes. These nodes are connected by arrows to indicate the order in which work elements must be performed.

10.4   FLEXIBLE MANUFACTURING SYSTEM (FMS)

A flexible manufacturing system (FMS) may be described as a network of workstations (typically NC and CNC machine tools), connected by an automated material management and storage system, and controlled by a central computer. Using FMS, several NC/CNC-controlled workstations may simultaneously process various kinds of parts and components. FMS systems are capable of producing different parts without significant downtime for changeover.

LO 3. To understand flexible manufacturing system (FMS), benefits and problems in implementing FMS

10.4.1   FMS Consists of the Following Basic Components

1. Computer-controlled production equipment such as CNC machines,
2. Automated material handling and storage system for transferring parts,
3. Computer control to coordinate monitor and control the activities of CNC machines and material handling system.

10.4.2   FMS Should be Adopted if the Following Conditions Prevail

1. Frequent job changeovers,
2. Short machining time,
3. Small batch production,
4. Increasing part complexity,
5. High precision requirement.

Refer to Figure 10.8. Dedicated equipment like transfer lines are used for low variety but high volume of production. Whereas standalone NC machines are used where high variety but low volume production is desired. FMS is used to fill the gap between dedicated equipment and standalone NC. It is used where medium variety and medium volume of production are desired.

10.4.3   Objectives of FMS

1. Use of NC/CNC technology for medium size production runs.
2. To provide a manufacturing facility that can machine certain types of part families and can easily be reprogrammed for other part families.

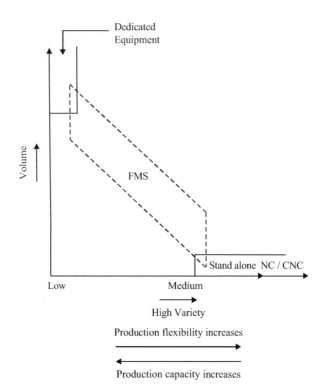

FIGURE 10.8   Application characteristics of an FMS

3. To provide a self-contained manufacturing facility that can automatically schedule, machine and inspect production runs.
4. To provide a supervisory function to computer control and supervise production operation as well as manufacturing equipment.

10.4.4   DIFFERENT TYPES OF FMS DEPENDING ON PERIPHERALS PRESENT

1. Flexible manufacturing module (FMM),
2. Flexible manufacturing cell (FMC),
3. Flexible manufacturing group (FMG),
4. Flexible manufacturing factory (FMF).

Let us discuss these one by one.

10.4.4.1   FMM

It has a single machine, a buffer and a pallet changer (loading and unloading device).
See Figure 10.9.

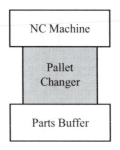

FIGURE 10.9   Schematic diagram of an FMM

Some of the advantages of an FMM over a CNC machine are listed below:

1. A mechanism that loads and unloads components automatically.
2. With little to no downtime, components may be switched out instantly.
3. Remove swarf mechanically.
4. Machining errors are automatically fixed by the machine.
5. Capability to verify parts and adapt to changes.
6. Connectivity between the machine and the computer, for the purpose of transferring data and instructions on the job being done, the tools being used, the machine's current state and any commands that may need to be sent.

10.4.4.2   FMC

It has a group of CNC machines connected by a single automated guided vehicle (AGV). Refer to Figure 10.10.

10.4.4.3   FMG

It consists of two or more cells connected by a single transfer line and controlled by a computer. Refer to Figure 10.11.

10.4.4.4   FMF

It may comprise of several FMGs and FMCs as shown in Figure 10.12.

10.4.5   TYPES OF FLEXIBILITY

Flexibility is the ability to cope up with change. Change may be due to external or internal reasons. An FMS may have following types of flexibility:

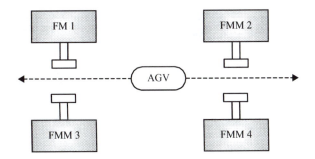

FIGURE 10.10   Schematic view of FMC

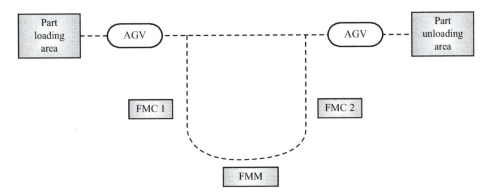

FIGURE 10.11   Schematic view of FMG

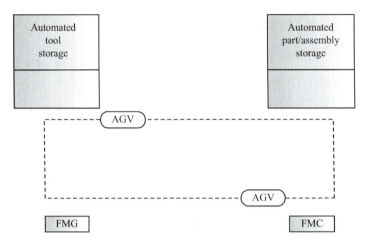

FIGURE 10.12   Schematic view of FMF

1. **Machining flexibility or machine setup flexibility:** Machines should be flexible enough to be able to cut various types of profiles. Example of such a machine tool is a machining centre.
2. **Process flexibility/job flexibility:** This refers to achieving flexibility in a manufacturing system, both at machine level and at system level. At machine level, the machines must be versatile enough to accommodate change in volume and variety of jobs. At systems level, the system must also be versatile enough. An example of such a system is one which is able to machine and transform jobs of various cross-sections.
3. **Transferring flexibility:** This refers to flexibility in transferring various types and sizes of components.
4. **Routing flexibility:** This refers to flexibility in the path chosen to transfer a part. Sometimes the shortest path to transfer the components may be busy. In such a case, the components may be transferred through another route.
5. **Volume flexibility:** The system should have economy of scope and not economy of scale. This implies that, any volume produced should be profitable enough and not a fixed volume only.
6. **Operational flexibility:** This refers to the ability to interchange the order of machining operations on a workpiece while complying with the design constraints.
7. **Actual flexibility:** It is the ability to overcome concrete given changes.
8. **Potential flexibility:** This refers to capability of coping with an undefined universe of change.

As flexibility in a system increases, its design becomes complex, and its cost also increases. Hence, you have to decide, to what extent you have to go for flexibility in your system depending upon your needs and priorities.

10.4.6   DESIGN OF FMS

Implementing a flexible manufacturing system involves high investment. Therefore, an FMS should be carefully planned and designed before implementation. The design of an FMS involves selection of appropriate machine tools, material handling equipment and computer control systems.

1. **Selection of machine tools:** Factors taken into consideration while selecting machine tools for FMS can be:

(A) Shape of the components,
(B) Size of the components,
(C) Variety of the components to be produced,
(D) Material of the component.

The same set of machine tools should be able to machine various shapes and sizes. They should be able to make a variety of components which may be of different materials.

2. **Material handling devices:** Material handling systems can be broadly classified into two categories:
(A) Primary material handling system,
(B) Secondary material handling system.

A primary material handling system helps in the transportation of material and components from machine to machine (e.g., conveyor, AGV, flow cart). Secondary material handling equipment is used for unloading material from the primary material handling equipment and loading it on machine tools in correct orientation. Hence, it must be designed so as to have compatibility with the primary material handling system as well as the computer system.

3. **Computer control systems:** The computer control system to an FMS must be able to serve the following functions:
(A) It should be able to control all necessary machine tool features like:
   - Spindle start clockwise/anticlockwise,
   - Coolant on/off,
   - Clamp/unclamp the workpiece,
   - Machine stop,
   - Workpiece change, etc.
(B) The computer system should have direct numerical control, i.e., it should be able to control a number of machine tools and peripherals, automatic material handling equipment simultaneously.
(C) It should have features for production control, i.e., programs for entry of raw materials and other equipment.
(D) It should have features for tool control. Most of the flexible machines have tool magazines. So the computer control should maintain proper record and information of position of each tool.
(E) It should have features for traffic control in order to avoid collision of automated guided vehicles, robot arms or other material handling systems, etc.
(F) It should maintain information of all the activities going on in the shop floor.

10.4.7 Problems Faced in Implementation of FMS

Implementing an FMS in a company is not an easy task. It requires careful planning, and a number of problems are faced:

1. **Visualisation:** This refers to the planning phase of FMS. The company should be able to visualise to what extent they should go for FMS. There have been cases where a poorly planned FMS has added to a company's woes.
2. **Integration problem:** An FMS is supposed to provide a number of benefits when it is very well knit with other departments of the company. Work in other departments should not suffer due to implementation of FMS.

Characteristics	Job Shop	FMS
Extent of automation	Low	High
Structure	Function oriented	Production oriented
Control of feedback	Manual, partial, unorganised	Computer-aided standardisation
Job process	Serial	Parallel
Detail scheduling	Based on personal knowhow	Based on algorithm
Degree of predetermination	Low	High
Supply of products	Lotwise	Continuous

From the above table we can conclude that there is great contradiction of characteristics and requirements of the job shop and FMS. Hence, turning a job shop into FMS can be very difficult. Integration of various machine tools into one system is a big problem, especially when machine tools are supplied by different suppliers and the compatibility of software with these machine tools and material handling system is not known.

Integrating an FMS is a huge endeavour. Due to the difficulty of merging older systems, it is often laborious to integrate and optimise system components. Existing production methods, such as:

(A) Requirement planning for materials,
(B) Job scheduling,
(C) Tool management,
(D) Material handling to and from the system,
(E) Maintenance.

When an FMS is deployed, these auxiliary duties are likely to be subjected to extreme pressures. Additionally, this may have significant implications for these activities. The result might be a decrease in FMS financing or the termination of another kind of support. If the potential benefits of such resource-intensive projects are to be realised, significant effort is required to meet the urgent requirement of integrating FMS installations into the existing industrial system.

3. **Communication:** There are three criteria that must be met by every FMS communication system:
   A) To allow for the transfer of data between several FMS-connected devices (e.g., part programme files, tool offset tables, robot parameter files, etc.).
   B) To communicate commands to the apparatus (e.g., cycle start, enable operational stop, etc.).
   C) To transmit data about the devices' current states (e.g., device busy, device idle, alarms, etc.). The procedure of communication is made more difficult by the fact that there are still no standardised interfaces for linking machines and their peripherals (like tool magazines) and automated material handling systems.
4. **Financial Justification:** Since implementing an FMS requires huge capital investment, an accurate estimate has to be made as to what extent it can improve the profits of an organisation.

10.4.7.1 Benefits of FMS

Implementing an FMS can have the following benefits:

1. Improved utilisation of equipment,
2. Reduced level of stock and work-in-progress,

3. Shorter lead times,
4. Better product quality,
5. Reduced unit cost of product,
6. More flexible response to customers,
7. Minimisation of direct and indirect labour,
8. Minimisation of special tooling.

(Previously, form tools were used whereas now interpolation software can be used to generate complex profiles.)

10.5 COMPUTER-INTEGRATED MANUFACTURING (CIM)

Computer-integrated manufacturing is an extension of CAD/CAM. It aims at integration of:

LO 4. To understand concept of computer integrated manufacturing (CIM)

Manufacturing and managerial tools like CAD/CAM, flexible manufacturing systems, robotics, material requirement planning, group technology, just-in-time concept, etc.

Other functional areas of organisation including marketing, research and development, finance and personnel, etc. Hence, CIM includes all the engineering functions of CAD/CAM as well as business functions of the firm. Refer to Figure 10.13.

A CIM system combines computer technology with every operational function and information processing function in manufacturing, from order receiving through product design and production to product marketing and distribution. CIM is a larger concept than CAD/CAM since it incorporates a company's commercial activities. Refer to Figure 10.14.

CIM's major objective is to automate and simplify the whole design and manufacturing process using computers for assistance, control and integration at the highest level. The technical backbone of CIM is comprised of distributed data processing, computer networks and database management systems.

10.5.1 BENEFITS OF CIM

1. Reduced labour requirement (for both direct and indirect) design and manufacturing activities,

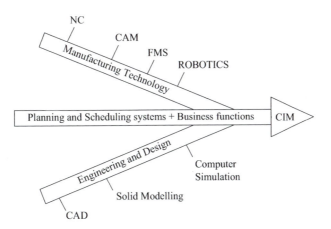

FIGURE 10.13 Integration of technical function in CIM

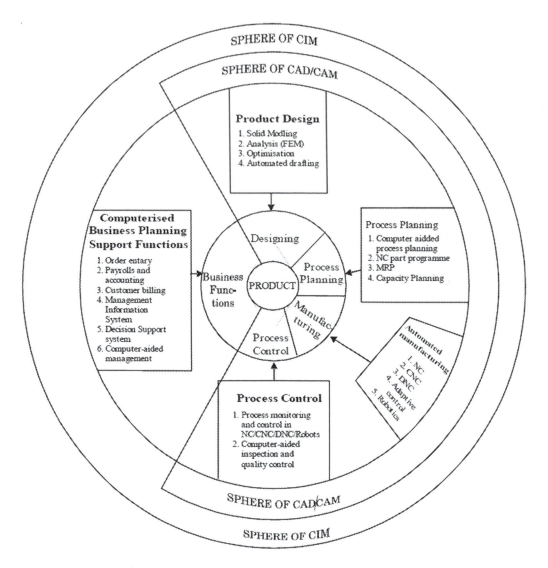

FIGURE 10.14   Scope of a CIM system

2. Reduced lead time in both development and manufacturing of products,
3. Increased flexibility in production capacity and scheduling,
4. Reduced level of inventory in raw materials, work-in-progress and finished goods,
5. Increased utilisation of firms' resources like equipment, labour and other facilities,
6. Improved ability to respond to changes in design of product, demand and supply of product, etc.

To reap these benefits of a CIM system, it should be planned very carefully. The following factors must be considered while planning a CIM system:

1. Availability of resources,
2. Purpose, aim and goal of implementing CIM in the organisation,

3. Availability of emerging technologies,
4. Level of integration desired.

10.5.2 IMPORTANCE OF DATABASE IN A CIM SYSTEM

A database is a central store of information that can be accessed and analysed for diverse reasons by several users.

For the CIM system to be functional, the whole manufacturing organisation must have access to the central database. Products, designs, machine tool information, process plans, materials used, production, finances, orders in hand, marketing, sales, buying and inventories should all be documented as precisely and accurately as possible inside the database. This huge repository of data is stored in the permanent memory of a central computer and is accessed and updated as required by either organisation personnel or the CIM system.

A CIM system also supports the concurrent engineering environment. Concurrent engineering is a concept used for product development activity in an organisation to improve efficiency of product design and reduce the product design cycle time. It brings together representatives from R&D, process planning, manufacturing, materials, quality control, sales and marketing departments to develop the product as a team. Thus, the features desired by each department can be incorporated at the first stage of product development itself. Everyone interacts with each other from the beginning of the product development cycle and performs their tasks in parallel.

CIM requires a massive integrated computer system comprised of computers, machine tools and their controllers for its success. Due to a company's difficulty in integrating different computer and programmed machine types acquired over time from different vendors, industrial communication challenges may arise. Various machine tool manufacturers have been using their own industry standards which makes integrating them in a CIM system a very tough task. Consequently, there has been strong trend towards standardisation to make communication equipment compatible. Various protocols have been developed from time to time. The most commonly followed protocols are:

- Manufacturing automation protocol (MAP),
- Technical and office protocol (TOP) based on ISO/open system interconnect reference model.

10.5.3 HARDWARE, SOFTWARE AND NETWORKING REQUIREMENTS OF A CIM SYSTEM

CIM hardware may comprise:

- Manufacturing equipment such as CNC/DNC/FMS systems or
- Machining centres,
- Robot work cells,
- Material handling and tool handling devices, tool magazines, etc.,
- Automatic storage and retrieval devices,
- Computer-controlled inspection equipment,
- Computers/servers,
- CAD/CAM systems (workstations),
- Printers and plotters,
- Bar code scanners and readers,
- Other peripheral devices.

CIM software may comprise of applications programs to carry out the following functions:

- Management information systems/decision support systems,
- Sales and marketing software,
- Finance software,
- CAD/CAM/CAE packages like IDEAS, PRO/E, Catia, Ansys, DELCAM, NASTRAN, NISA, etc.,
- Computer-aided process planning (CAPP) software,
- Inventory control software,
- Shop floor data collection software,
- Material handling (AGVs) package,
- Production planning and control software,
- Quality management software,
- Networks management,
- Device drivers, etc.

10.5.4 Communication Networking in a CIM System

In order to achieve maximum efficiency from CIM, a high speed and interactive communication network is required.

The following types of communication technology can be adopted according to requirement:

- LAN (local area network),
- WAN (wide area network),
- Intranet.

10.6 CAD/CAM CONCEPT

Initially CAD and CAM developed as two separate fields. CAD application packages were being used for two-dimensional drafting and three-dimensional solid modelling. A manual part program was prepared according to the model. This program was then fed to a CAM system. The CAM system comprises of a machine tool with computer control.

Later on, efforts were directed towards integrating the CAD and CAM activities of an organisation to obtain an integrated CAD/CAM system (Figure 10.15). In this concept, CAD computers are linked to the CNC machines through appropriate interface. The following steps are followed on a CAD/CAM system:

LO 5. To understand the concept of integrating CAD with CAM

1. Part geometry is defined using some interactive graphics design package like IDEAS, Pro/E, SolidWorks and Solid Edge, etc. The geometric, dimensional and material specifications are decided for the part.
2. Next, the tool/cutter path is specified to get the desired component from the workpiece. For this, an appropriate cutting tool is selected from the tool library. Using this tool's dimensions and diameter, the tool offset calculations are made automatically.
3. On the basis of tool path specifications, a part program is made automatically by the software package on giving the appropriate command.
4. This part program is then transferred to the CNC machine using an appropriate interface. Note that there should be complete compatibility between computer-assisted part programming software package and the software of the CNC machine.
5. The CNC machine makes use of computer control to machine the workpiece in order to give it the predefined shape. Usually, closed-loop CNC machines are used to achieve high level of machining accuracy.

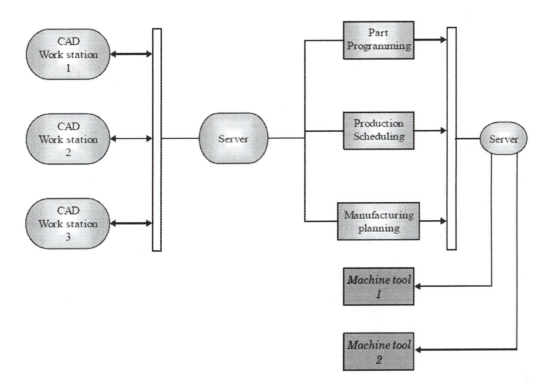

FIGURE 10.15 Information flow chart in CAD/CAM application

10.6.1 DATA EXCHANGE SPECIFICATIONS FOR CAD SYSTEMS

Various CAD systems and CAD application packages are supplied by different vendors. Proper communication and exchange of data between these systems is a significant problem. To overcome this problem, neutral formats have been developed to improve compatibility of these system. Now, the vendors only need to provide translators for their own systems, to preprocess the data into neutral format and to postprocess from neutral format into their own systems. Examples of such neutral formats are:

1. Initial graphics exchange specifications (IGES): Used for 3-D line and surface data.
2. Product data exchange specifications (PDES) is a solid model-based standard.

10.7 COMPUTER-AIDED PROCESS PLANNING (CAPP)

Process planning can be defined as a process of utilising design information to decide a sequence of steps for manufacturing a product. A computer is now used in all the phases of design process and software has been prepared for process planning as well. This is referred as computer-aided process planning (CAPP).

LO 6. To understand the concept of CAPP

In process planning, a detailed strategy and set of instructions for producing a component are developed. In the planning phase, engineering drawings, specifications, lists of components or materials, etc. are used. Listed below are the results of our planning:

1. An outcome of process planning is a collection of machining sequences or routings that describe each stage of the manufacturing process, from work centres and tools to fixtures

and the order in which operations should be executed. This machining sequence is used by the manufacturing resource planning (MRP) system to define production activity processes and resource needs for capacity planning.

2. Procedure diagrams: Work instructions must be detailed and step-by-step, including dimensions relating to individual operations, machining parameters, instructions for machine and tool setup, quality control checkpoints, etc.

The expertise of a manufacturing engineer with production facilities, equipment, capacities, processes and tools serves as the foundation for manual process planning. Process planning is very time-consuming and demands lots of knowledge and experience. Since the engineering industry is now short of such experienced people, their knowledge is being captured in the form of computer algorithms and software programs which can guide less-experienced people for generating the machining sequence, decide tooling, etc.

10.7.1 Types of CAPP

Without the use of CAPP, manufacturers attempted manual process planning by arranging components into families and developing relatively consistent processes for each family. When a new component was introduced to the lineup, personnel were required to manually locate and change the family's process plan. As a consequence, efficiency benefits were realised. CAPP was originally designed to facilitate the electronic storage, retrieval, modification for a new component and printing of finished process plans.

Variant CAPP: The original CAPP approach led to the development of a new computer-aided method dubbed variant CAPP. Group technology (GT) is the basis of variant CAPP's coding and classification approach, enabling the identification of a higher number of component characteristics or factors. Based on these features, the system may choose a basic production approach for the component family.

It does up to 90% of the essential planning and 10% of the remaining time will be spent on changes and revisions to the planner-created process blueprint. The primitive process plans are manually entered into the computer using the super planner idea, which involves the creation of standardised plans based on the accumulated skills and knowledge of several planners and production engineers.

Generative CAPP: During process planning, decisions are governed by predetermined criteria. A process plan is developed with little human interaction based on decision criteria derived from the group technology or features technology code of the component.

Modern CAPP systems are getting more generative, but a system that can produce a whole process plan from component classification and other design data is still under development. This entirely generative system will develop process blueprints using AI and expert-system-like abilities.

Dynamic generative CAPP: Process planning that takes plant and machine capacities, tooling availability, work centre and equipment loads, and equipment condition into consideration (e.g., maintenance downtime). This CAPP system would evolve as the factory's resources and requirements changed. If, for whatever reason, the main machining centre for a particular operation or operations was already at capacity, the generative planning process would evaluate the viability of releasing any further work requiring usage of that work centre, along with alternate processes and associated routings. Using the decision criteria, it is possible to create process designs that reduce the load on the primary facility by transferring part of the work to a secondary route with a less economic impact. A manufacturing resource planning system is required for tracking shop floor status and load data as well as evaluating alternative routings in respect to the schedule.

The phase between design and production in the manufacturing process is called process planning. However, it is a vital component of CAD/CAM integration that is sometimes neglected. Software for CAD generates visual representations of items. For CAM equipment, it is necessary to make fundamental decisions on the equipment to be used, the tooling, and the operation sequence before creating items such as NC part programming. CAPP's objective is just this. Without CAPP, integration of CAD and CAM technologies is impossible. Consequently, CAD/CAM systems that generate tool paths and NC programs include CAPP capabilities to some extent. CAPP systems depend on the graphical information supplied by CAD systems to generate assembly drawings, etc. This graphically oriented data may also be sent to the production function as hardcopy drawings or work instruction displays. The screens at the production workstations in this system give visual representations of the process plans and guide employees sequentially through the assembly process. The screen displays graphical representations of the components to be inserted or assembled, as well as written instructions and warnings, while the worker advances through the assembly process using a footswitch. It is possible to utilise CAPP software to choose tools, feeds and speeds, and to generate NC programmes if NC machining processes are to be used.

10.7.2 Machining Data Selection System in CAPP

While preparing a process plan for manufacturing a component, a number of machining parameters have to be defined. These include but are not limited to:

- Type of machining (milling, turning, drilling, boring, reaming, grinding, tapping, etc.),
- Type of cutting tool (drilling, milling cutter, single point cutting tools, etc.),
- Machining parameters (cutting speed, feed, depth of cut, cutting fluid, jigs, fixtures, etc.).

It is very important to specify all machining parameters accurately in the process plan so that the machining operation can be carried out in the shop floor easily. To define the machining data in the process plan, any one of the following three methods can be used:

1. *Using experience of a highly experienced process planner, foreman or machinist.* But usually there is lack of such highly experienced engineers. Also, this is not a scientific method.
2. *Using a machining data handbook.* Such handbooks provide data often generated by experiments in labs. One such popular handbook is the CMTI handbook. But sometimes, the actual machining conditions may not match with those while performing the experiments. Also, the method of searching for machining data from handbooks is not suitable (or compatible) while working in a computerised environment.
3. *Using a computerised machining database.* To prepare computer-assisted process plans, several databases of machining data are now available in soft form which can be judiciously used to select machining parameters based on workpiece material hardness, geometric shape, tolerances and surface finish, accuracy and precision capabilities of available machines. Such a machining database stored in suitable computer memory, can be easily accessed while preparing computer-aided process plans. Apart from the database, some CAPP software provides machining data based on suitable mathematical models. A common example is that of Taylor's equation which can be used to calculate the cutting speed for tool life. If V is the cutting speed and T is the tool life, then the Taylor equation is:

$$VT^n = C$$

where n and C are constants. But a limitation of using such mathematical models is that not everyone agrees with these equations.

10.7.3   BENEFITS OF **CAPP**

The use of CAPP can yield significant advantages. The following are mentioned as examples:

- Less time spent on process planning, saving on direct labour and materials,
- Less waste, saving on tools and less work in process,
- Less time spent on process planning and production lead time,
- More consistency in process plans; access to up-to-date information in a central database,
- Complete and detailed process plans,
- Better production scheduling and capacity utilisation.

10.8   SUMMARY

- Manufacturing cell makes use of composite part concept.
- Transfer lines are used when the product is to be produced in large volumes (i.e., mass production).
- Buffer storage may be used between two machines in a transfer line to temporarily store parts.
- Transfer line may have inline or rotary configurations.
- Various work part transfer methods are: Continuous transfer, synchronous transfer, asynchronous transfer and pallet fixtures.
- FMS is used for medium volume, medium variety production.
- FMS is of various types: FMM, FMC, FMG and FMF.
- Flexibility is of different types: Machining flexibility, process flexibility, transferring flexibility, routing flexibility, volume flexibility, operational flexibility, actual and potential flexibility.
- A number of problems may be faced while implementing FMS. Hence, it should be designed carefully.
- CIM integrates business functions to CAD/CAM.

VIDEO 4

10.9   EXERCISE

1. What is the concept of composite part? What factors should be taken into consideration for designing a manufacturing cell (BT level 2)?
2. What are transfer lines? Give its classification (BT level 2).
3. What is line balancing? Explain any one method for line balancing (BT level 2).
4. What is a flexible manufacturing system (FMS)? Explain the suitability of FMS (BT level 1).
5. What are various types of flexibility (BT level 1)?
6. Discuss the problems faced in implementing FMS (BT level 2).
7. What is computer-integrated manufacturing? What is its scope (BT level 1)?
8. What are the functions of CIM? State the benefits of CIM (BT level 2).
9. State the hardware and software requirements of CIM. What is the importance of database in a CIM system (BT level 1)?
10. Discuss the CAD/CAM concept (BT level 2)?
11. How can you classify a manufacturing cell? Explain each with the help of a diagram (BT level 4).
12. Discuss "designing a manufacturing cell" (BT level 2).
13. State the benefits of cellular manufacturing (BT level 1).
14. Differentiate between inline and rotary configuration of transfer lines (BT level 4).
15. Discuss: (BT level 2)
    (i)   Continuous transfer method.

     (ii)   Synchronous transfer method.

     (iii)   Asynchronous transfer method.

16. How can you determine line efficiency (BT level 2)?

17. What is balanced delay (BT level 1)?

18. Differentiate between job shop and FMS (BT level 4).

19. Discuss benefits of FMS (BT level 2).

20. Discuss functions of CIM (BT level 2).

21. Discuss the importance of database in a CIM system (BT level 2).

22. Discuss hardware and software requirements of CIM (BT level 2)l.

23. What is CAPP? What are its types (BT level 1)?

24. Explain the concept of mechatronics and MEMS (BT level 2).

25. Define FMS. Name building blocks of FMS and hardware and software components of FMS (BT level 2).

26. Differentiate between FMS and FMC (BT level 4).

27. What is CIM? Mention various elements of CIM. (BT level 1).

10.10   MULTIPLE-CHOICE QUESTIONS

1. What is Computer Integrated Manufacturing (CIM)?
    a. A manufacturing system that uses computer technology to integrate the design, manufacturing, and production processes
    b. A manufacturing system that relies solely on manual labor for production
    c. A manufacturing system that uses robots to perform all manufacturing operations
    d. A manufacturing system that is entirely automated and requires no human intervention

2. Which of the following is a benefit of implementing a CIM system?
    a. Increased production costs
    b. Reduced manufacturing flexibility
    c. Improved product quality
    d. All of the above

3. What is the role of a Manufacturing Execution System (MES) in a CIM system?
    a. To manage and control the manufacturing process
    b. To design and develop new products
    c. To monitor and analyze manufacturing data
    d. To manage and control the inventory of raw materials and finished goods

4. Which of the following is an example of a CIM system component?
    a. Computer-aided design (CAD) software
    b. Computer-aided manufacturing (CAM) software
    c. Programmable logic controllers (PLCs)
    d. All of the above

5. Which of the following is a disadvantage of implementing a CIM system?
    a. High implementation costs
    b. Reduced production efficiency
    c. Increased manufacturing errors
    d. All of the above

Answers

1. Answer: a. A manufacturing system that uses computer technology to integrate the design, manufacturing, and production processes

2. Answer: c. Improved product quality

3. Answer: a. To manage and control the manufacturing process

4. Answer: d. All of the above

5. Answer: a. High implementation costs

11 Automation

Learning Outcomes: After studying this chapter, the reader should be able

LO 1: To know about automation (BT level 1).
LO 2: To understand advantages and disadvantages of automation systems (BT level 2).
LO 3: To know the origin and evolution of automation (BT level 1).
LO 4: To understand application of automation (BT level 2).
LO 5: To understand basic elements of automation (BT level 2).
LO 6: To understand types of automation (BT level 2).
LO 7: To know the current and future trends of automation (BT level 1).
LO 8: To understand hardware components of automation (BT level 2).

VIDEO 5

11.1 INTRODUCTION

Humans have been creating objects for countless aeons. Generally speaking, the vast majority of things were created based on unique specifications. When a tool was required, it was crafted by hand and then utilised to create more. As time progressed, increasingly sophisticated procedures were created to assist humans with manufacturing and production activities. The development of metalworking and weaving techniques, as well as steam and gasoline engines, facilitated the production of a broader variety of goods. In the past, though, items were still created by artisans' expertise in a variety of skills. Large-scale production of goods did not become widespread until the Industrial Revolution and the widespread adoption of electrical energy and machines.

Manufacturing is the process of transforming raw materials into something more valuable and useful. The objective is to increase the value of a raw material by altering its form or qualities. The manufacturing system is the collection of machinery, transportation elements, personnel, storage, computers and other items used for manufacturing.

It is always the goal of an industry to increase output and enhance the quality of the final product. Due to these goals, efforts have been undertaken to replace more and more human activities with those that are powered by machines. Automation is utilised on construction sites. Automation refers to a high level of mechanisation in which the manufacturing processes of a product are carried out by automated means. Logical programming is the substitution of manual command–-response operations with commands and automated tools. Although automation can be utilised in other industries, it is most commonly linked with manufacturing.

LO 1. To know about the Automation.

A computer-controlled automated manufacturing system is a network of material processing units capable of processing a range of part types automatically and simultaneously. In addition to a material transport system, the system is also interconnected by a communication network for integrating all parts of manufacturing. This system is versatile in terms of part routing, part processing, part handling and tool switching. Additionally, an automated production system

 DOI: 10.1201/9781003350842-11

possesses the features listed below: High level of automation, high level of integration and high level of adaptability.

11.1.1 DEFINITION

"Automation" derives from the Greek words "auto" (self) and "matos" (moving). Automation is consequently the mechanism for "self-moving" systems.

Automation refers to a technology that utilises mechanical, electronic and computer systems to regulate processes and production processes. The use of automation technology began when labour and worker tasks were replaced by machines. The technology development process continued to advance until humans began implementing robotic, CAD/CAM and flexible production system technologies to enhance human quality of life and productivity.

11.2 ADVANTAGES AND DISADVANTAGES OF UTILISING AUTOMATED SYSTEMS

Automation has the following advantages:

LO 2. To understand advantages and disadvantages of automation system.

1. To reduce periodic or manual checks.

In certain crucial applications, periodic testing of process variables is required in order to conduct industrial operations. Automation fully lowers the need for human checking of numerous process parameters and establishes automatic working conditions. Utilising closed-loop control approaches, industrial processes automatically modify set variables to predetermined or desired values using automation technologies.

2. To increase productivity.

Automation of manufacturing and other production processes enhances the production rate by increasing output per unit of labour input. Automation of a factory or manufacturing or process facility increases output rates by enhancing production management. This contributes to mass production by substantially lowering assembly time per product while simultaneously improving production quality.

3. To improve product quality.

Due to the fact that automation reduces human involvement, human error is also removed. Automation can ensure uniformity and product quality with a consistent degree of consistency by adaptively controlling and monitoring industrial processes at every stage, from the inception of a product through its final product.

4. To reduce production cost.

The integration of multiple industrial processes with automated technology decreases cycle time, effort and the demand for human labour. This minimises investment costs relative to labour expenses.

5. To increase flexibility.

By making varied use of automation tools, the process can be handled conveniently without any difficult environment, especially in manufacturing processes.

6. To increase the level of security.

By substituting human workers with automatic machines, industrial automation improves the safety of individuals in dangerous working environments. Industrial automation reduces the difficulty of operating complex equipment or processes.

Due to these benefits, there are now fully or partially automated devices in places where only people previously worked, such as in offices, home and road construction, mining, agriculture and other agricultural operations and many businesses.

In addition to these benefits, it is essential that we consider the downsides of adopting and implementing automation in the industrial sector.

1. *Higher start-up cost and the cost of operation.* Investment in automation requires substantial capital expenditures, which are incurred by automated equipment. To design, build and install an automated system can cost millions of dollars.

2. *Higher cost of maintenance.* More maintenance is required than with manually driven devices. Among these are the acquisition of electromechanical devices, such as electromechanically driven valves, sensing devices and intelligent devices. Replacement components for automated systems may be more expensive than those for manual systems.

LO 3. To know origin and evolution of the Automation.

3. *Obsolescence/depreciation cost.* Obsolescence and depreciation are the progressive decline in the value of tangible assets. This phenomenon is characteristic of all equipment and machinery-based physical assets. It is an inevitable result of technological advancement.

4. Not economically justifiable for small scale production.

11.3   ORIGIN, EVOLUTION AND REASON FOR AUTOMATION

Although mechanisation commonly refers to the simple substitution of human labour with machines, automation typically refers to the integration of machines into a self-governing system. Automation, in the sense of making use of machinery or equipment, has been around since at least the 11th century, when miners utilised waterwheels to drain underground tunnels and shafts. The present type of automation may be traced back to the Industrial Revolution, which saw the adoption of automated techniques and technologies to increase production output.

The word "automation" was used about 1946 in the automotive industry to describe the advent of fully automated production lines. The word was first used by D.S. Harder, a manager of engineering at Ford Motor Company at the time. The use of electricity in the 1920s accelerated manufacturing production and altered the dynamics of the factory floor. During the 1930s and 1940s, the industrial application of feedback controllers was a crucial step toward the current automation of manufacturing.

During the 20th century, significant progress was made in a wide variety of fields, including the development of the digital computer, significant strides in the fields of data storage technology and computer programming software, significant strides in the field of sensor technology and a mathematical control theory. All of these advancements have contributed to the growth of automation technology.

Computers are "trained" to simulate human intellect as part of the field of artificial intelligence, which is a subfield of the more sophisticated study of computer science. The ability for learning, language understanding, logical thinking, problem-solving, expert diagnosis and other cognitive abilities are included among these traits. Recent advances in AI research suggest that soon robots and other "intelligent" devices will be able to interact naturally with humans and learn to follow more abstract commands than the specific, step-by-step ones currently required by most programmed machines.

Automation can be adopted for a variety of reasons, with manufacturing costs being a major factor. Under the following situations, automation is always warranted:

Where the environment is extremely hazardous to human health.
Where the procedure is incredibly rapid and complex.
Where automation can generate substantial cost reductions.
Where process control can be made more efficient and streamlined.
Where damage to the work section must be kept to a minimum.

Even in a fully automated production system, humans remain indispensable to the industrial sector. Humans will be necessary to manage and maintain the factory for the foreseeable future, even if they do not directly participate in its industrial processes. The concept of automation is evolving.

LO 4. To understand application of automation.

In manufacturing plants, it has been successfully implemented in the following fundamental areas: Manufacturing processes, material handling, inspection and packaging.

11.4 EXAMPLES OF AUTOMATION

The amount of automatic fractionation in a plant will depend on cost, availability and other constraints. It may be viable and practical to automate all or any portion of a factory, as well as equipment or departments. Depending on the nature of some plants, it may be viable to keep only a portion of them automated.

The following are examples of some automatic machines:

1. Packing machine: Today, many automatic devices for packing factory-made goods are available. The operator loads the finished products, wrapping paper, cartons, etc. into the machine, and the machine wraps the paper, packs the box, etc. There is also, if necessary, a method to manage the count or weight of the items stored in the box or shell, such as the number of cigarettes in the cigarette box, the number of matches in the match box, the number of toffees in the toffee box, etc.
2. Bottle-filling machine: There are numerous varieties of such machines. In these, washing, filling and sealing of bottles with appropriate liquids (sorbet, oil, fruit juice, etc.) are accomplished automatically.
3. Canning machine: Today, all packaging of food and other items is performed by automated machinery. This comprises filling, stamping and packing the box with the necessary items.
4. Office machines: Numerous automated office machines—for writing, duplicating, registering, calculating, etc.—have been developed. In addition to simple addition and subtraction, the computer can also perform other complex calculations. Computers are capable of numerous tasks. In addition to this, automatic machinery for spinning yarn, weaving fabric, cutting and weighing have also been developed. Many types of specialised machines that are employed in different types of businesses are in production today.
5. Automated machines used in metal craft industries: Previously created by hand, gullies and moulds are now manufactured by machines. Wire drawing, extrusions, etc. are all performed by machines. Large numbers of metal sheets, dies, etc. are created and expelled by compressed air.
6. Transfer machines: These are specialist machines that are fully automated. Their integration of indexed or fixed parts in a straight line from one location to the next with automatic machines in their integrated production line results in a very high production rate. These machines are frequently hydraulically or electrically controlled.
7. Numerically controlled machines: In such machines, manual adjustment of the machine slides is replaced by automatic adjustment. The speed of the machine slide has been

replaced with a motor controlled by a "hand wheel" (servomotor). The machine's instructions are printed on punched cards, tape or magnetic tape. The controlling device converts these commands into electrical impulses and transmits them to the servomotor. Upon receiving a signal from this unit, the servomotor turns the machine slides under its control by the amount and in the direction specified by the signal. This machine system constantly displays the real order state of the tables to be compared and makes the necessary adjustments automatically.

11.5 BASIC ELEMENTS OF AUTOMATION

An automated system consists of three basic elements: Power, a programme of instructions and a control system.

Power is necessary to drive the process and operate the controls. Electricity is the primary source of power for automated systems. Alternative energy sources consist of fossil fuels, solar energy, water and wind. In addition, *LO 5. To understand basic elements of automation.* energy is required for the loading and unloading of the work unit, the movement of materials between activities, the activation of control signals, data collecting and information processing.

A programme of instructions specifies the actions carried out by an automated procedure. Each component or product style necessitates at least one processing step. These operations are carried out within a work cycle. A work cycle programme specifies the specific processes that comprise the work cycle. Part programmes are the work cycle programmes. The automated system may need to be programmed to execute distinct work cycles for distinct component or product types. The component software must be coded to accommodate the second pass when required.

The set of instructions is carried out by the system's control element. The control system allows the manufacturing process to accomplish its intended function. The controls of an automated system might be either closed loop or open loop. One definition of a closed loop system is a feedback control *LO 5. To understand basic elements of automation.* system in which the output variable is compared to an input parameter and the resultant difference is used to modify the output so that it once again matches the input. An open-loop control system, in contrast to a closed-loop control system, functions without a feedback loop. In this instance, the controls function without measuring the output variable, therefore there is no comparison between the actual output value and the desired input parameter. The controller is dependent upon a precise model of the influence of its actuator on the process variable.

11.6 AUTOMATION TYPES

Manufacturing automation has spawned three areas of expertise in automation production: Fixed, programmable and flexible automation. These automation types are designed to satisfy the specialised production needs of particular industries.

11.6.1 FIXED AUTOMATION

Fixed automation manufacturing is a system that is commonly referred to as hard automation. In this type of manufacturing, the automated production processes and assembly steps for a specific product are planned out in advance. The order in which production and operations are performed is determined by the configuration of tooling, equipment and machines that are allocated to meet high-volume demands.

The goal of fixed automation systems is to generate products that are similar to one another. When the system is established, often known as "fixed," the product styles either cannot be changed at all or may only be changed with extreme effort. The integration and coordination of the many different sequences of activities that take place throughout the production of a single unit is what contributes to the complexity of the system.

This particular style of production automation may be identified by the significant initial expenditure required for the design and engineering of the equipment. Once built, the equipment has limited adaptability to new product combinations. Automation developed largely to facilitate high rates of production. Fixed automation investments are swiftly amortised because of the exceptionally high demand rates and product quantities for which they are constructed.

11.6.1.1   Examples of Fixed Automation

- Automated assembly machines,
- Web handling and conversion systems,
- Chemical manufacturing processes,
- Material conveyor systems,
- Machining transfer lines,
- Automation processes for paint and coating.

11.6.2   Programmable Automation

By encoding or programming instructions into the system, programmable automation allows for dynamic changes in the setup and operation of machinery. A programmable automation system allows for the development of new programmes for each procedure. In a single production run, items may be made in quantities ranging from the dozens to the thousands.

The initial expenditure in programmable automation is comparable to that of fixed automation for multipurpose machinery. Because of the process's malleability, we may make adjustments to the product's configuration and keep our production numbers low. Programmable automation works effectively for batch manufacturing.

11.6.2.1   Programmable Automation Examples

- Numerically controlled (NC) machine tools,
- Programmable logic controllers,
- Industrial robots.

11.6.3   Flexible Automation

The term "flexible automation" refers to a method of manufacturing that is, as its name indicates, designed to rapidly adapt and respond to changes in production needs, such as changes in the product type and quantity. Computer systems allow humans to command machines through programming or graphical user interfaces (human–machine interfaces). Multiple product varieties can be manufactured at once by modifying the system's settings. Production and supply chain operations are managed by a single computer network. Companies that mass produce a wide range of products in moderate quantities may find the method useful.

Similar to fixed and programmable automation technologies, flexible automation requires a substantial investment to construct a bespoke solution. It's feasible to produce many products at once and at a steady pace. It's easy to make adjustments to new product designs if they're somewhat different. With the use of computer code, the production line may seamlessly move between batches without any interruptions. In addition, the system may be used to roll out a plan for providing customers with individualised items on demand.

11.6.3.1   Flexible Automation Examples

- Robotics,
- Assembly systems,
- Material handling systems.

11.7   CURRENT AND FUTURE TRENDS IN AUTOMATION

As time has progressed, manufacturing companies' goals for automating their processes have broadened beyond only boosting productivity and reducing costs to encompass issues like enhancing product quality and making the production process more flexible. While it's true that automating processes may increase productivity and save expenses, focusing solely on those two goals is shortsighted. It's also important to have a skilled workforce on hand to do routine maintenance. Robots have become increasingly commonplace in industries where accuracy and consistency are paramount, such as the automotive sector, where manufacturing facilities are shipping ever more of them to do routine, repetitive tasks. In modern times in fact, robots have taken over assembly lines. Today's robots operate with greater capabilities, such as enhanced vision systems, increased computational powers and expanded operational capacity.

LO 7. To know current and future trend of automation.

Automation is being used to improve the quality of the manufacturing process, where it can significantly improve quality. The greater emphasis on adaptability and versatility in the manufacturing process is another significant change brought about by automation. Manufacturers are increasingly requesting the capacity to transition from one product to another without having to entirely reconstruct their production systems. Robots will be replaced with "smart or intelligent" robots that will behave and adapt to changing circumstances. They will be capable of multitasking, i.e., they will be able to perform multiple simultaneous tasks. These robots' computer skills will be much improved, and they will be more independent, with the help of Machine Learning (ML) and Deep Learning (DL). The field of industrial automation has come a long way, and it's about to take a giant leap forward toward a more streamlined, effective production facility. Future industrial automation will place a premium on material management, energy efficiency, machinery and equipment use and human resource management.

LO 8. To understand hardware components of automation.

11.8   HARDWARE COMPONENTS FOR AUTOMATION

For automation and process control to be implemented, the control computer must collect data from the process and deliver signals to it. The digital computer operates on digital (binary) data, while at least some of the physical process's data are continuous and analogue. In the computer–process interface, this difference must be accommodated. Sensors, Actuators and Analysers are the components needed to implement this interface.

11.8.1   Sensors

Simply described, a sensor is a device that can detect and validate changes in electrical, physical or other qualities by producing an output. Primarily, the term "industrial automation sensors" are measuring devices that provide a signal in response to changes in a certain physical parameter (input). Sensors are an integral part of industrial automation, playing an important role in the development of smart and highly automated products. Changes in position, length, height, exterior and dislocation may all be detected, analysed, measured and processed using these at industrial manufacturing locations.

The numerous types of sensors used in automation are as follows:

- Temperature sensors,
- Pressure sensors,
- Micro-Electro-Mechanical Systems (MEMS) sensors,
- Torque sensors.

11.8.1.1 Temperature sensors

A temperature sensor is an instrument that measures and transmits temperature data from one device to another. These sensors are used to detect and measure the temperature of a medium, and they are among the most widely used types of sensors. Many different kinds of temperature sensors are used in automated systems, but two of the most prevalent are digital temperature sensors and humidity and temperature sensors.

Temperature sensor applications:

- Exceptional precision and steadiness,
- For measurements in complex industrial applications,
- For measurements in harsh operating environments.

11.8.1.2 Pressure sensors

A pressure sensor is an instrument that detects pressure and converts it into an electronic signal, the quantity of which is proportional to the applied pressure. Turned parts for pressure sensors and vacuum sensors are among the most widely utilised pressure sensors in industrial applications.

- Used to measure pressure below the atmospheric pressure at a certain area.
- Employed in weather instrumentation, aircraft, cars and other gear with pressure capability.
- Pressure sensors can be used to detect factors including fluid/gas flow, velocity, water level and altitude.

11.8.1.3 MEMS Sensors

MEMS sensors for industrial automation translate mechanical signals to electrical impulses. Velocity and Movement Few significant sensors used in industrial automation employ MEMS.

MEMS sensors have diverse applications spanning from industry to entertainment to sports to education.

Used to measure static acceleration (gravity), tilt of an object, dynamic acceleration in an aircraft, shock to an object in a car and vibration of an object.

Used to detect motion, such as when deploying airbags or monitoring nuclear reactors.

11.8.1.4 Torque Sensors

Torque sensors come equipped with the appropriate mechanical stops, improve the capacity for overload and provide extra protection throughout the installation and operating processes. Two of the most important sensors that are utilised in industrial automation are torque transducers and rotating torque.

Torque sensor applications:

- Used for measuring the rotational speed as well as the necessary maintenance needs.
- The amount of torque to be measured, from the standpoint of a quasi-static process.
- Used to measure the greatest rotational speed and oscillating torque.
- Used to quantify mass and the mass moment of inertia.

11.8.2 Actuators

In the automation process, the device that produces the desired effect on the load environment is known as an actuator. In essence, an actuator is a device that transforms any sort of energy into mechanical motion. Typically, it is a device for energy conversion that facilitates the transformation of energy into action. Actuators are made up of two separate components, these are the signal amplifier and the transducer respectively. The amplifier takes the control signal, which has low power, and transforms it into a signal with high power so that it may be supplied to the transducer. The power contained inside the amplified control signal is converted into useful work via the transducer.

When selecting an actuator, the following performance criteria must be present, since they enable a control system to operate as intended.

- Actuators must execute reliably and unaffected by load.
- They must have a durable industrial design that allows them to operate in a variety of conditions without affecting their performance.
- Minimal periodic maintenance is required.
- Actuators must have precise, repeatable positioning.
- An actuator must be able to start and stop without dead time or position overshoot.

An actuator includes:

Energy source: Sources of energy supply actuators with the ability to perform work. For their operation, actuators require electrical or mechanical energy from external sources. Depending on the system of which it is part, the energy accessible to the actuator may be regulated or unregulated.

Power converter: If the energy source connected to the actuators is unregulated, further equipment is required to regulate and convert it into a form suitable for the actuation action. In industrial actuators, hydraulic valves and solid-state power electronic converters are examples of converters.

Controller: In addition to permitting the operation of the power converter, it is the responsibility of the controller to provide actuating signals. In some systems, it provides an interface for the user to provide inputs or check the status of the system.

Load: The mechanical system coupled to the actuator that utilises its motion is referred to as the load. Before coupling an actuator with a load, characteristics such as force/torque and speed are carefully calibrated.

11.8.2.1   Types of Actuators

11.8.2.1.1   Hydraulic Actuators

Hydraulic actuators are extensively utilised in stepper motors and applications requiring clamping, opening, pressing and welding. Utilising hydraulic energy, they facilitate mechanical operation. While the majority of hydraulic actuators are designed to provide linear motion, they can also generate rotating motion. The speed of hydraulic actuators is a significant advantage. When stable yet powerful actuating thrust/forces are required in a small location, these devices are utilised.

11.8.2.1.2   Pneumatic Actuators

Pneumatic actuators are ideally suited for applications requiring extremely accurate motion. They function by utilising a pressurised gas or compressed air to generate linear or rotary mechanical movement. Pneumatic actuators are often encountered in industrial automation equipment, particularly in material handling applications requiring transfer, pick, place or indexing.

11.8.2.1.3   Mechanical Actuators

Mechanical actuators are used in machines to convert rotational motion into linear motion. There are many different types of mechanical actuators, such as rack and pinion systems, pulleys, gears, crankshafts and chains.

11.8.2.1.4   Electrical Actuators

Electrical actuators rely on electricity to function, and they are commonly used in robotics equipment. Electrical actuators can work with the same level of precision as pneumatic actuators, and in many cases, even greater precision. Additionally, they are highly scalable, reprogrammable, and speed and force may even be modified to some extent. Due to this and the fact that they are powered by electricity, electrical actuators are among the most common forms of actuators utilised in industrial settings. Electrical actuators include solenoids with linear motion and electric motors.

11.8.3 ANALYSERS

Once information is detected by an automated system, it must be recorded and evaluated for its content before the system can decide. This duty is carried out by analysers. Computers are the major tool for automaton system analysis. The number of ways in which computers can be programmed to modify data is virtually unlimited. Counters are a common type of analyser utilised by automated systems to determine how many distinct objects are present or move through the system. Counters may be either mechanical or electronic.

11.9 SUMMARY

1. A computer controlled Automated Manufacturing System is a network of material processing units capable of processing a range of part types automatically and simultaneously.
2. A computerised system comprises three fundamental components: Power, a set of instructions and a control system
3. Manufacturing automation has spawned three areas of expertise in automation production: Fixed, programmable and flexible automation.
4. Important automation hardware components include Sensors, Actuators and Analysers.

11.10 EXERCISE

1. Define automation *(BT level 1)*.
2. Explain different types of automation *(BT level 2)*.
3. Compare soft and hard automation *(BT level 4)*.
4. Write about the advantages of automation *(BT level 2)*.
5. Write about the limitations of automation *(BT level 2)*.
6. Explain the working of basic components of automation *(BT level 2)*.

11.11 MULTIPLE-CHOICE QUESTIONS

1. What is automation?
   a. The use of robots to replace human labour.
   b. The use of technology to perform tasks with minimal human intervention.
   c. The use of AI to perform complex tasks.
   d. The use of machines to perform tasks that were previously performed by humans.
2. What is the main advantage of automation?
   a. Reduced costs.
   b. Increased productivity.
   c. Higher quality.
   d. All of the above.
3. Which of the following is an example of automation in the service industry?
   a. Self-driving cars.
   b. Automated assembly lines.
   c. Chatbots for customer service.
   d. Automated stock trading.
4. What is the difference between automation and robotics?
   a. Automation involves the use of machines while robotics involves the use of software.
   b. Automation involves the use of software while robotics involves the use of machines.

    c.   There is no difference between automation and robotics.

    d.   Automation and robotics both involve the use of machines and software.

5. What is the main challenge of implementing automation in a workplace?

    a.   The cost of implementing automation.

    b.   The fear of job loss among employees.

    c.   The difficulty of integrating automation with existing systems.

    d.   The lack of skilled workers to operate and maintain automated systems.

6. Which industry was the first to adopt automation on a large scale?

    a.   Automotive industry.

    b.   Aerospace industry.

    c.   Food processing industry.

    d.   Textile industry.

7. What is the role of artificial intelligence in automation?

    a.   AI is not relevant to automation.

    b.   AI is used to program robots for automation.

    c.   AI is used to optimise and improve automated processes.

    d.   AI is used to replace human workers in automated processes.

Answers

1. Answer: b. The use of technology to perform tasks with minimal human intervention.

2. Answer: d. All of the above.

3. Answer: c. Chatbots for customer service.

4. Answer: b. Automation involves the use of software while robotics involves the use of machines.

5. Answer: b. The fear of job loss among employees.

6. Answer: a. Automotive industry.

7. Answer: c. AI is used to optimise and improve automated processes.

12 Automated Material Handling and Storage

Learning Outcomes: After studying this chapter, the reader should be able

LO 1: To know about the material handling system (BT level 1).
LO 2: To understand different material handling equipment (BT level 2).
LO 3: To understand an Automated Guided Vehicle System (AGVS) and its components (BT level 2).
LO 4: To understand the advantages and disadvantages of AGVS (BT level 2).
LO 5: To explain different types of AGVS (BT level 2).
LO 6: To explain an Automated Storage and Retrieval System (AS/RS) (BT level 2).
LO 7: To analyse AS/RS (BT level 4).
LO 8: To understand automatic identification systems and their types (BT level 2).

12.1 INTRODUCTION

Material handling systems at a warehouse or manufacturing facility can play a crucial role in the storage and movement of materials and products. Material handling is the process of transporting, packing, storing and unpacking a range of products over a short distance at a factory or warehouse.

There are two ways to transport items from one location to another: Manually and with automated technologies. All industrial items are lifted, moved, stored or retrieved manually using human or physical force. In most cases, organisations rely on human labour for manual handling systems. Manual material handling encompasses acts such as lowering, lifting, pulling, pushing, restraining, holding and carrying. In the second scenario, automated material handling devices are utilised. They employ advanced technology to develop computerised systems that require minimal human intervention for moving, locating, retrieving and storing items.

Automated material handling systems are computerised technologies that replace human labour with robot labour. They are utilised for pulling, lifting, pushing, storing and retrieving things and goods. This technology can introduce new levels of productivity and transformation to warehouses and factories. Automated material handling systems guarantee the effective delivery of materials from one location in the manufacturing area to another, whether it be within the same department or bay, at opposite ends of the manufacturing floor or even between buildings.

LO 1. To know about the material handling system.

12.2 MATERIAL HANDLING EQUIPMENT

12.2.1 CONVEYORS

Conveyor systems are widely used in many different sectors to transport items, raw materials, finished goods and other materials from one location to another, usually inside the same building or facility. They are ideal for factories and warehouses that deal with bulky things, sharp objects, raw materials and mass-produced items. Installation of a conveyor system is often costly and restricting.

Material handling, packing and manufacturing all benefit from the use of conveyor systems because of the ease with which they can transfer supplies and goods, as well as the transportation of large items. Conveyors can be either belt or roller or wheel or slat or chain or bucket or trolley or tow or screw or vibrating or pneumatic.

12.2.2 CRANES AND HOISTS

Cranes and hoists are typically employed for vertical movement, i.e., raising and lowering weights, and are therefore overhead machines. There may also be a component of horizontal movement, typically occurring above the factory floor and production equipment. Material is moved in sporadic movements. The primary benefit of cranes and hoists is their ability to carry large objects across overhead areas. Typically, they can only serve a limited area. These systems are ideal for applications with moderate volume.

LO 2. To understand different material handling equipment.

12.2.3 INDUSTRIAL TRUCKS

Industrial trucks are wheeled automobiles. They are more versatile than conveyors since they can move between several locations and are not set in one place. Industrial vehicles are equipped with a variety of attachments. They are appropriate for production on an intermittent basis. The industrial vehicles have flexible pathways and a very large access area at a reasonable cost for hardware. It comprises hand trucks such two-wheeled, four-wheeled, hand lift and forklift, as well as powered vehicles like forklift, tractor-trailer trains, industrial crane trucks and side loaders.

12.2.4 CONTAINERS

The primary purpose of containers is to maintain a unit load. There are either dead containers or live containers. The containers that contain the goods to be transported but do not move themselves are referred to as dead containers, whereas the containers that contain the material to be transported and also move themselves are referred to as live containers.

Figure 12.1 displays a variety of material-handling equipment.

12.3 AUTOMATED GUIDED VEHICLE SYSTEMS (AGVS)

A mobile vehicle that is battery-powered, programmable and autonomously directed is referred to as an automated guided vehicle (AGV). This type of vehicle is used to carry supplies from the warehouse to the shop or assembly line or vice versa without the need for human involvement. The AGVS is a member of a class of exceptionally flexible, intelligent and versatile material handling systems that are used to transport items across the facility between many loading and unloading sites. The AGV is outfitted with automatic guidance technology, which enables it to navigate specified guide paths and come to a halt at predetermined locations.

12.3.1 AGVS COMPONENTS

Vehicle: It is used to transport materials inside the facility without the intervention of a human operator. The components of the vehicle consist of a frame, an electrical system driving unit, an on-board battery charging unit, a precision stop unit, steering, a communication unit, an on-board controller, a safety system and a work platform. Additionally, the vehicle has a safety system to protect the operator.

LO 3. To understand Automated Guided Vehicle System and its component.

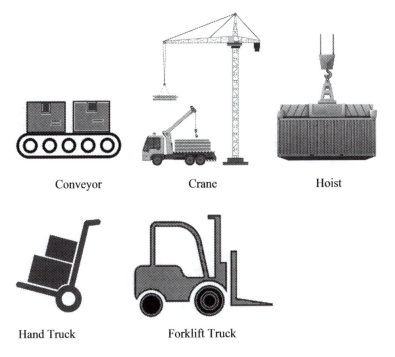

FIGURE 12.1 Material handling equipment

Guide travel: It directs the vehicle along the route. Most AGVs require a guided path to follow. Passive and active tracking are the terms used to describe the procedures used to determine a guiding path. Active tracking utilises inductive principles, whereas passive tracking relies on optical- or metal-detecting methods. Passive approach involves the employment of chemical, paint and adhesive strips or tape; the AGV focuses a beam of light on the reflective tape and measures the amplitude of the reflected beam to follow its journey. Vehicles equipped with metal-detection sensors following stainless steel tape constitute a second passive method. In active mode, a guide wire is utilised. This procedure entails carving a gap in the floor, into which one or more wires are grouted and glued. A live wire is embedded in the guidance path. The AGV's antenna follows the buried wire.

Control unit: It monitors and controls system activities, such as feedback on movements, inventories and vehicle status. The controller is the system's brain, directing the vehicle along the prescribed course and integrating the system. In addition to controlling the AGV system, it integrates with the automatic assembly facility. Typically, the AGV system will consist of three tiers of controller architecture: The vehicle control system, the floor control system and the vehicle on-board processor. There are three varieties of AGVS control systems available:

1. Computer-controlled system,
2. Remote dispatch control system,
3. Manual control system.

In a computer-controlled system, the system controller controls and monitors all exchanges and AGVS vehicle movements. The guide path controller regulates the guide path of the AGVS and transmits the relevant data to the AGVS process controller. The AGVS process controller directly controls the vehicle's movements. Through a remote-control station, a human operator controls the movement of an AGVS in a remote dispatch control system. The control system transmits destination instructions to the vehicle immediately. In a manual control system, the driver loads the vehicle and inputs the desired destination into the vehicle's control panel. The effectiveness of the system is contingent upon the competence of the operator. Interface with a computer: It communicates with other computers and systems, such as the host computer of the mainframe, the automated storage and retrieval system and the flexible manufacturing system.

12.3.2   AGVS Advantages and Disadvantages

Advantages of AGVS:

1. Labour force reduction,
2. Increased levels of both quality and productivity,
3. Professional development opportunities and increased job satisfaction,
4. Reduction in space required,
5. Decrease in the amount of product damage,
6. Strengthening of housekeeping procedures,
7. Simplicity of moving and relocating the item,
8. Compatibility with a variety of other types of automation,
9. Flexibility and adaptability of the system.

LO 4. To understand advantages and disadvantages of AGVS

Disadvantages of AGVS:

1. Only for internal use, cannot be used in the outside world,
2. The need for a floor space that has been specifically planned,
3. If the guidance route bed is unstable, performance will be negatively affected,
4. There must be adequate support from management in order to succeed,
5. It is necessary that each worker contributes equally,
6. Obstacles are brought into existence,
7. Maintenance is essential.

12.3.3   Types of AGVS

There are various types of AGVs that can meet a variety of service needs.

AGVS forklifts: AGVS forklift trucks can pick up and drop off palletised cargo both at floor level and on stands, and the pick-up height and drop-off height can be varied. They are able to automatically pick up and drop off a palletised load. They can place their forks at any height, allowing them to service conveyors or load platforms with varying heights in the material-handling system. Applications of AGVS forklift trucks are relatively recent. Guided forklifts are utilised when the system requires automatic load pick-up and delivery from floor or stand level and the transfer heights at stop sites fluctuate.

LO 5. To explain different types of AGVS

AGVS towing vehicles: These are AGVs without a load-carrying capacity that are equipped with a hitch or tow bar to pull trailers, carts, pallet jacks and wheeled racks. A towing vehicle is a tractor with automatic steering. They are utilised in situations where a large quantity of goods must be transported or in retrofit applications where trailers were once utilised.

Transporters of individual load AGVS: These trucks are designed to transport individual loads. The deck design of unit load transporters can be quite versatile, allowing them to be fitted with rollers, belt conveyors, power lifts, unique fixtures or an on-board robot arm. Over moderate distances, the unit load carrier is able to transport large quantities of cargo while connecting to other automated subsystems in a fully integrated facility. Unit load systems often incorporate automatic product pick-up and delivery, as well as remote management of the system's vehicles. Unit load carriers are typically utilised in warehouse and distribution systems with relatively short guide route lengths and high volumes.

LO 6. To explain Automated Storage and Retrieval System (AS/RS)

AGVS pallet: AGVS pallet trucks are designed to lift, move and transport palletised cargo. They are used for lifting and lowering loads from and onto the floor, hence eliminating the requirement for fixed load platforms. They are mostly utilised for loading and unloading operations at floor level.

12.4 AUTOMATED STORAGE AND RETRIEVAL SYSTEM (AS/RS)

In big manufacturing industries, the number of objects and components is so high that a manual storage and retrieval system is both unreliable and time-consuming. This is because of the sheer number of items and components. Under these kinds of conditions, it is a good idea to make use of the AS/RS. An AS/RS is a complete system that can transport, store, retrieve and report on each and every item in any industrial inventory with the utmost precision down to the minute level. The AS/RS is responsible for regulating inventories in addition to monitoring components and materials that are either in the process of being processed or are in transit.

These automated storage and mechanisation systems accomplish fundamental sets of tasks without human interaction, including:

- The automatic removal of an item from a storage site.
- The transfer of the aforementioned item to a designated processing or interface point.
- An item is automatically stored at a preset location after being received from a processing or interface point.

12.4.1 COMPONENTS OF AUTOMATED STORAGE AND RETRIEVAL SYSTEM

The major components of an AS/RS are:

1. Storage structure,
2. Transport equipment,
3. Pick-up and delivery stations,
4. Storage and retrieval machines,
5. Computer control system.

1. Storage Structure

    It is the rack framework, constructed from steel, that supports the loads and is utilised to hold inventory items. Several rows of storage racks are used to store the materials/items. AS/RS storage structures are significantly taller than typical storage and retrieval systems. The design of AS/RS racks must accommodate integration with storage and retrieval machine guide rails. This structural element is composed of storage spaces, bays and rows.

2. Transport Equipment

    Transport devices, such as AGVs or conveyors, connect the storage structure, in which the materials/items are kept, to the shop floor. The inbound materials and goods are initially sorted and loaded onto pallets. The loaded pallets are then weighed and measured to ensure that they do not exceed the weight and size limits. The accepted loaded pallets are delivered to the automated storage and retrieval system by automated guided trucks or conveyor. The selection of transport devices depends on the required throughput, the type of load to be moved, and the level of plant operating interaction.

3. Pick-up and Delivery Stations

    Pick-up and delivery (P/D) stations are the input/output stations. Typically, they are positioned at the end of the aisles to ease access for the storage and retrieval machinery. The placement and number of P/D stations are determined by the origin and destination of incoming and outgoing loads. The information regarding the pallet's contents is transmitted to the central computer. The central computer assigns the pallet its storage location in storage racks.

4. Storage and Retrieval Machines

A stacker crane refers to a machine used for storage and retrieval. It is used to enter and remove things from inventory. It is distinguished by its capacity to work precisely and safely at high speeds, reach heights of 30 m or more, and function in lanes that are only a few millimetres wide. When the central computer receives a request for the item, it searches its memory for the storage location and instructs the stacker crane to fetch the pallet. The stacker crane is computer controlled and entirely automated.

5. Computer Control System

A computer control system includes two functions: Equipment controls and data control. In addition to inventory control, data automation and network control, this computer control system is frequently linked to an even bigger corporate management information system computer.

12.4.2 AS/RS Advantages and Disadvantages

Advantages of AS/RS:

1. The AS/RS system ensures rapid material movement and distribution.
2. AS/RS automates and centralises the movement of materials, hence reducing the reliance on human judgement.
3. The AS/RS system optimises material circulation and decreases inventory needs.
4. The AS/RS system optimises storage space, consequently decreasing the size of the warehouse.
5. AS/RS facilitates the integration and automation of all industrial functions.

Disadvantages of AS/RS:

1. The initial investment required for the AS/RS is significant.
2. AS/RS requires the utilisation of AGVs or conveyors in order to function properly.
3. Only big manufacturing facilities may make use of the AS/RS.

12.5 ANALYSIS OF AUTOMATED MATERIAL HANDLING AND STORAGE SYSTEM

12.5.1 AGVS Analysis

The decision-making process associated with the system design of AGVS is quite complex. There are two significant difficulties that must be addressed, namely:

Guide path layout,
Number of vehicles required.

1. Guide Path Layout

The design of the guided route for AGVS is one of the most important steps in the design process. The design of flow routes involves a number of key considerations, including the following:

LO 7. To analyze AS/RS

- Which type of guide path layout to use,
- Which flow path to use within the arrangement,
- The total number of load transfer points as well as their specific locations,
- A location for the storage of transfer function stations.

The route is made up of connections and nodes that stand in for various points of interest along the way.

The guide path can be classified into four categories:

- Uni-directional single lane,
- Bi-directional single lane,
- Multiple lanes,
- Mixed.

Vehicle blocking, congestion and unloaded vehicle travel are considerations that depend on the quantity of vehicles and demand for vehicles from different pick-up and delivery sites. Under the aforementioned conditions, simulation is utilised to produce a realistic design.

2. Number of Vehicles Required

The estimation of the number of AGVs necessary for the system is a crucial aspect of its design. Too many vehicles will cause traffic congestion, while too few may result in increased idle time for the system's workstations. Here is a straightforward mathematical study for determining the number of vehicles. These notations are utilised:

D_l = Total average loaded travel distance,
D_e = Total average empty travel distance,
N_{dr} = Number of deliveries required per hour,
T_f = Traffic factor that accounts for blocking of vehicles and waiting of vehicles in line and at intersection. If there is no congestion, the traffic factor is 1. However, when more vehicles are involved, the traffic factor value will certainly be less than 1. Normally, T_f lies between 0.85 and 1,
V = Vehicle speed,
T_{lu} = Loading and unloading time,

The total time per delivery per vehicle (T_d) is given by

$$T_d = \frac{D_l}{v} + T_{lu} + \frac{D_e}{v} \tag{12.1}$$

Equation (12.1) represents the sum of loaded travel time, loading and unloading time and empty travel time.

The number of deliveries per vehicle per hour is given by

$$N_d = \frac{60\ T_f}{T_d} \tag{12.2}$$

Example 12.1: In a XYZ factory with Flexible Manufacturing System, the AGV moves at a speed of 60 m/min and covers an average distance of 180 m to deliver inventory and 120 m for return. If the time required for pick-up and drop is 60 s each, determine the number of AGVs required to meet the demand of 60 deliveries per hour.

SOLUTION:

Given that,
Total average loaded travel distance (D_l) = 180 m,
Total average empty travel distance (D_e) = 120 m,
Number of deliveries required per hour (N_{dr}) = 60,

Vehicle speed (v) = 60 m/min,
Loading and unloading time (T_{lu}) = 60 s = 1 min,
Applying Equation (12.1),

The total time per delivery per vehicle $T_d = \dfrac{D_l}{v} + T_{lu} + \dfrac{D_e}{v}$

$$T_d = \frac{180}{60} + 1 + \frac{120}{60}$$

$$T_d = 3 + 1 + 2$$

$$T_d = 6$$

So, the total time per delivery per vehicle is 6 minutes.
The number of deliveries per vehicle per hour using Equation (12.2) is given by

$$N_d = \frac{60\,T_f}{T_d}$$

Assuming $T_f = 1$

$$N_d = \frac{60}{6}$$

$$N_d = 10$$

In one hour one AGV delivers ten products.

For 60 deliveries per hour, the number of AGVs = $\dfrac{60}{10}$ = 6

So, six AGVs are required to meet the demand of 60 deliveries per hour.

Example 12.2: XYZ industry would like to integrate the AGVS with its flexible manufacturing system. It has to deliver 125 pieces per hour. The AGV moves at a speed of 60 m/min. Average loaded distance travel by one AGV per delivery is 180 m and Average empty distance travel by one AGV per delivery is 140 m. If the time required for pick-up and drop is 60 s each, determine the number of AGVs required to meet the demand. Assume traffic factor as 0.80.

SOLUTION:

Given that,
Total average loaded travel distance (D_l) = 180 m,
Total average empty travel distance (D_e) = 140 m,
Number of deliveries required per hour (N_{dr}) = 55,
Vehicle speed (v) = 60 m/min,
Loading and unloading time (T_{lu}) = 60 s = 1 min,
Traffic factor T_f = 0.80,
Applying Equation (12.1),

The total time per delivery per vehicle $T_d = \dfrac{D_l}{v} + T_{lu} + \dfrac{D_e}{v}$

$$T_d = \frac{180}{60} + 1 + \frac{140}{60}$$

$$T_d = 3 + 1 + 2.34$$

$$T_d = 6.34$$

So, the total time per delivery per vehicle is 6.34 minutes.

The number of deliveries per vehicle per hour using Equation (12.2) is given by

$$N_d = \frac{60 \; T_f}{T_d}$$

Assuming $T_f = 1$

$$N_d = \frac{60 \times 0.80}{6.34}$$

$$N_d = 7.57$$

In one hour one AGV delivers 7.57 = 7 products.

For 55 deliveries per hour, the number of AGVs $= \dfrac{55}{7} = 7.85 = 8$.

So, eight AGVs are required to meet the demand of 55 deliveries per hour.

12.5.2 AS/RS Analysis

1. Storage Space Dimensions

Let l, b and h represent the unit load's length, breadth and height. The length (L), width (W) and height (H) of the AS/RS aisle rack structure are proportional to the unit load dimensions and the number of compartments as follows:

$$L = n_y \, (l + x),$$

$$W = u \, (b + y),$$

$$H = n_z \, (h + z),$$

where n_y and n_z are the number of load compartments along the length and height of the aisle, respectively; x, y and z are the allowances designed into each storage compartment to give clearance for the unit load; and u is the storage depth in unit loads.

One storage aisle's entire storage capacity is stated as follows:

$$\text{Capacity per aisle} = 2 \times n_y \times n_z \quad (12.3)$$

Constant "2" is multiplied because loads are contained on both sides of the aisle.

2. Storage Space Number

AS/RS uses dedicated and randomised storage rules to determine the quantity of available storage spaces. A dedicated storage policy allocates a fixed number of storage slots to a single product. Therefore, the sum of the maximum inventory levels for all goods equals the number of storage slots necessary for the product. In the event of a randomised storage policy, each compartment in the storage aisle has an equal chance of being chosen for a transaction. Similarly, each unit of a particular product has an equal chance of being retrieved during a retrieval process.

3. Number of Storage and Retrieval Machines

The number of storage and retrieval machines can be determined as follows:

$$= \frac{System\ Throughput}{Storage\ and\ Retrieval\ machine\ capacity\ in\ cycles\ per\ hour}$$

System throughput is defined as hourly rate of storage and retrieval transactions that an automated storage system can perform.

12.6 AUTOMATIC IDENTIFICATION SYSTEM

Automatic identification is a procedure that automates the gathering and iden-   *LO 8. To understand*
tification of data in order to store, analyse and classify them. An automatic   *automatic*
identification system normally does not require human interaction. Its objec-   *identification system*
tive is to methodically identify and track a variety of products. They can be   *and its types*
equipment, assets, personnel or inventory. Simply described, it refers to a
range of technologies for autonomously identifying objects. Importantly, it
facilitates a solid materials management process and contributes to the efficiency of the organisation. Because the procedure is automated (rather than relying on pen, paper and people), information is collected rapidly and precisely. Barcodes, handheld and fixed-position scanners and imagers,
radio frequency identification (RFID) tags and readers, and voice recognition, weighing and cubing
devices are the most popular technologies used to identify and capture data. Automatic identification systems provide enterprises with numerous benefits. They provide a much quicker alternative
to human data entry and verification, and a well-designed system is also significantly more accurate.
Due to the fact that automatic identification systems enable real-time monitoring of the number of
units in a facility, they maintain an accurate inventory count. The data linked with an object are
referred to as identifying data. This information may be in the form of photographs, voice record-
ings or fingerprints. This information will be transformed into a digital file prior to being entered
into a computer system. In order to achieve this process, a transducer is used to turn the original
data into a digital file. After entering the database into a computer system, the stored data file is
evaluated by a computer or compared with other files in a database in order to grant access to a
secured system.

The technologies of automatic identification systems comprise of three primary components.
These are as follows: Encoding data entails translating alphanumeric characters into a form that
can be read by a machine. The machine scanner reads the encoded data and converts it to electric
signals. Data decoding—the electrical signals will be translated into digital data, which will subsequently be converted into alphabetic characters.

12.6.1 TYPES OF AUTOMATIC IDENTIFICATION SYSTEM

Various automatic identification and data capturing technologies are as follows:

- Barcodes,
- Radio frequency identification (RFID),
- Biometrics,
- Magnetic stripes,
- Smartcards,
- Voice recognition.

12.6.1.1 Barcodes

The most prevalent automatic identifying technology is barcodes. With the introduction of the
Universal Product Code (UPC) for grocery systems in the early 1970s, barcodes gained prominence.

A barcode consists of printed bars and spaces that correspond to letters or numbers. Barcodes will initially be scanned by barcode readers, which are specialised optical scanners. A barcode is an optical machine that is a readable representation of data or information, and the information it carries pertains to the object to which the barcode is connected. There will be items with barcodes in supermarkets. Using a laser beam, a barcode reader converts the image's information into digital data and sends it to the computer. Moreover, barcodes are typically bidirectional, meaning they can be read from top to bottom, bottom to top, left to right or right to left. Such linear or one-dimensional barcode symbologies as UPC, Code 128, Code 39 and Interleaved 2 of 5 Code use patterns of dark lines and light spaces to encode numeric or alphanumeric data. Matrix or two-dimensional barcode symbologies (such as data matrix and QR code) contain data as a pattern of squares or dots in black and white. Compared to linear barcodes, 2-D symbols can hold far more information in smaller regions.

12.6.1.2 Radio Frequency Identification

Radio frequency identification (RFID) is an emerging technology that delivers tracking information without requiring direct touch with the item being tracked. It is a technique that transfers data between a reader and an electronic tag attached to a specific object via radio waves. This technology is used for identification and data collection. The three components of an RFID system are an antenna, a transceiver and a transponder. RFID systems use a transceiver to transmit digitally encoded data through radio waves through an antenna. The transceiver may be able to both read and write RFID tags, also known as transponders, which are attached to the tracked objects. These tags may contain batteries and actively provide signals to the transceiver, or they may be managed passively by the transceiver. The transceiver is connected to a computer system that interprets and handles the transmitted and received data.

12.6.1.3 Biometrics

Typically, biometrics is used to identify a person by comparing collected biological data with stored data for that individual. Biometrics comprises a range of various ways of personal identification, all of which are primarily employed for security. The biometrics system comprises a scanning device or reader equipped with software that translates scanned biological data, such as fingerprints, into digital representation. Recognition of fingerprints, faces, palm prints and irises are the most common forms of biometric system utilised in the realm of automatic identification systems.

12.6.1.4 Magnetic Stripes

Utilising magnetic stripe technology for security purposes: Magnetic stripe cards are capable of storing data by altering the magnetism of small iron-based magnetic particles on a strip of magnetic material containing magnetic strips. Magnetic stripe information is read by a magnetic stripe reader.

12.6.1.5 Smartcards

Smartcards may be used similarly to magnetic stripe cards in terms of storing personal identification and financial account information, but their underlying technology is significantly different, and their uses are broader. Smartcards feature an embedded microchip with memory for storage, and more sophisticated cards also include a microprocessor that enables the card to make decisions and encrypt data in various ways. This capacity for storage and processing makes smartcards more versatile and secure than magnetic stripe technology. These smartcards have the capacity to store data for identification and application processing.

12.6.1.6 Voice Recognition

Simply put, voice recognition is the technology that allows us to transcribe human speech into text. Essentially, it's a speech-recognition system. A wireless, system-connected device and a wireless headset allow the worker to execute tasks without using their hands or looking at their screen. The worker receives task instructions using a headset. When a person is done with a job, they can affirm it by speaking into the headset. This technique is often used for hands-free shopping and storage.

12.7   SUMMARY

1. Material handling is a crucial activity that assures the safety of both the items and those handling them.
2. Elevators and conveyors are the two most essential types of material handling equipment.
3. AGV systems are material-handling systems that are versatile, dependable, economical to run and simple to integrate with other systems.
4. Automatic identification is a procedure that automates the gathering and identification of data in order to store, analyse and classify it.

12.8   EXERCISE

1. What are the objectives of materials handling system *(BT level 2)*?
2. Explain the importance of material handling *(BT level 2)*.
3. Classify material handling systems *(BT level 4)*.
4. Explain AGV *(BT level 2)*.
5. Describe the different types of AGVS control methods *(BT level 2)*.
6. What is meant by vehicle guidance technology *(BT level 2)*?
7. What are the advantages of AGVs over other material handling systems *(BT level 3)*?
8. Explain "Automatic Identification System" *(BT level 2)*.

12.9   MULTIPLE-CHOICE QUESTIONS

1. What is an automated storage and retrieval system (AS/RS)?
   a. A system that allows forklifts to navigate through a warehouse autonomously.
   b. A system that uses robots to retrieve items from storage and deliver them to a picking station.
   c. A system that automatically tracks inventory levels and generates reorder requests.
   d. A system that uses drones to transport goods from one location to another.
2. Which of the following is an advantage of automated material handling systems?
   a. Reduced costs.
   b. Increased safety.
   c. Improved accuracy.
   d. All of the above.
3. Which type of automated guided vehicle (AGV) is used for handling large and heavy loads?
   a. Unit load AGV.
   b. Tugger AGV.
   c. Assembly line AGV.
   d. Forklift AGV.
4. What is a conveyor system?
   a. A system that uses robots to transport goods between locations.
   b. A system that uses cranes to move heavy items.
   c. A system that uses gravity to move goods from one location to another.
   d. A system that uses a belt or chain to move goods along a path.
5. What is a shuttle system?
   a. A system that uses robotic shuttles to transport goods.
   b. A system that uses shuttles to move goods between different levels of a warehouse.

   c. A system that uses shuttles to move goods between different areas of a warehouse.

   d. A system that uses shuttles to move goods between a warehouse and a transportation vehicle.

6. Which of the following is a disadvantage of automated material handling systems?
   a. High initial investment.
   b. Limited flexibility.
   c. Potential for system downtime.
   d. All of the above.

7. What is a pallet shuttle system?
   a. A system that uses pallets to transport goods between locations.
   b. A system that uses shuttles to move pallets between different levels of a warehouse.
   c. A system that uses shuttles to move pallets between different areas of a warehouse.
   d. A system that uses pallets with built-in motors to transport goods.

Answers

1. Answer: b. A system that uses robots to retrieve items from storage and deliver them to a picking station.
2. Answer: d. All of the above.
3. Answer: a. Unit load AGV.
4. Answer: d. A system that uses a belt or chain to move goods along a path.
5. Answer: b. A system that uses shuttles to move goods between different levels of a warehouse.
6. Answer: d. All of the above.
7. Answer: c. A system that uses shuttles to move pallets between different areas of a warehouse.

13 Automated Inspection System

Learning Outcomes: After studying this chapter, the reader should be able

LO 1: To know about automated inspection systems (BT level 1).
LO 2: To understand off-line and on-line inspection systems (BT level 2).
LO 3: To understand a coordinate measuring machine and its components (BT level 2).
LO 4: To understand the working of coordinate measuring machine (BT level 2).
LO 5: To understand machine vision (BT level 2).

13.1 INTRODUCTION

Inspection is now an integral component of every industrial system. The term inspection refers to the process of checking a product, its components, subassemblies or raw materials to verify if they adhere to the design standards established by the product designer. Through inspection, poor quality is identified, and excellent quality is ensured. The introduction of technologically advanced inspection equipment has assisted in overcoming the limitations of conventional methods. Traditional approaches employed labour-intensive techniques, which increased manufacturing lead time and production expenses. In addition, there is a considerable lag in identifying an out-of-control limit. Automated inspection systems provide the following benefits over manual inspection:

They can rapidly and readily adapt to diverse items and surfaces.
They can be remotely programmed and monitored.
They are available 24 hours a day.
They do inspections faster than human inspectors.
They maintain inspection consistency.
They can conduct inspections under adverse conditions.
They complement rapid manufacturing with rapid inspection.

LO 1. To know about the automated inspection system.

Automated 100% inspection can be incorporated into the production process in order to perform some process-related activity. The acts may consist of one or all of the following: (1) components sorting and/or (2) data feedback to the process. Sorting components involves sorting them into two or more quality categories. The fundamental sorting consists of two levels: Acceptable and unacceptable. Some circumstances call for more than two categories, such as acceptable, reworkable and junk. The feedback of inspection data to the upstream production operation enables the process to be adjusted to minimise unpredictability and increase quality. If inspection measurements reveal that the output is slipping toward one of the tolerance limits (e.g., owing to tool wear), process parameter adjustments can be performed to bring the output closer to its nominal value.

LO 3. To understand Coordinate Measuring Machine and its components.

13.2 OFF-LINE AND ON-LINE INSPECTION

13.2.1 OFF-LINE INSPECTION PROCEDURES

In off-line inspection, the inspection equipment is typically specialised and has no direct interaction with the machine tools. It is understood that off-line inspection occurs after the completion of the

DOI: 10.1201/9781003350842-13

whole machining process. This inspection is conducted at a location distinct from the manufacturing facility. This is utilised if there is more time to check the machined product. Using a coordinate measuring machine, precise off-line inspections of various items are conducted. The downside of off-line inspection is that when poor quality is discovered, the components have already been manufactured. Occasionally, a faulty component may not be included in the sample by default.

13.2.2 On-line Inspection Procedures

This sort of inspection is performed throughout the machining process. There are two different types of on-line inspection. During the manufacturing process, an inspection is conducted, followed by an inspection immediately after the production process. On-line inspections benefit more from automated inspections. Inspection probes are the archetypal forms of on-line inspection. These probes are versatile in their applications.

13.3 COORDINATE MEASURING MACHINE

A coordinate measuring machine (CMM) includes a contact probe and a mechanism for positioning the probe in three dimensions relative to the surfaces and features of a workpiece. To collect dimensions data relevant to the geometry of the component, the x, y and z coordinates of the probe are precisely measured. A CMM is an electromechanical device intended for coordinate metrology. A CMM employs a very sensitive electronic probe to measure a sequence of discrete points based on the geometry of a solid component. These measures are used to verify if the item meets the standards.

Coordinate measuring technology provides solutions for all dimensional measuring jobs and has mostly supplanted conventional inspection measuring instruments. The CMM offers the speed and accuracy to measure items with more repeatability than the conventional approach. Additionally, it boosts productivity while decreasing the likelihood of measurement mistakes. A CMM serves two purposes. It measures the physical geometry and dimensions of an object using the touching probe situated on the machine's axis of motion. In addition, it verifies that the components match the revised design.

13.3.1 Components of CMM

Numerous movable components within a CMM collaborate to enable the machine to evaluate a particular item. There are several varieties of CMMs with varying measurement capabilities, but they always consist of four primary components:

A structure,
A probing system,
A controller,
Software.

13.3.1.1 Structure

The structure forms the foundation of a CMM. It functions as the primary working unit, including the different guideways and probing system. It permits the sensor probe to be moved in the x, y and z directions so that it may be positioned precisely on the component to be measured. Air bearings are given for the motion of the liner in order to decrease vibration. The material utilised to construct this machine has changed throughout time. Initially, CMMs were constructed from steel and granite, but CMM makers today employ ceramic and silicon carbide to construct the machine. Depending on the architecture of the mechanical framework, many types of CMM are available. These are:

1. Cantilever type CMM,
2. Bridge type CMM,
3. Column type CMM,
4. Horizontal arm type CMM,
5. Gantry type CMM.

13.3.1.2 Probing System

The probe is the primary CMM component, as it is the measuring instrument used to measure the object put on the worktable of the machine. These probes interact with an object and measure it according on the coordinate system of the CMM structure. Due to the nature of the probes, their tips are made of a stiff and robust substance. It must also be resistant to changes in temperature so that its dimensions do not vary as the temperature changes. Ruby and zirconia are common materials used. Additionally, the tip may be round or needle-like. Multiple measurement devices on probes transmit point coordinates to the CMM. They function as transducers, translating physical measurements into signals that the machine can understand for CMM analysis. In addition to mechanical probes, several CMM instruments utilise optical lights, lasers or cameras to acquire measurements without touching the workpiece.

13.3.1.3 Controller

The controller regulates the location of the probe and the x–y–z motions of the numerous spindles. In addition, it captures data in the form of measured point sets, which are inputs for CMM software to do additional computations. It permits the changing of running speeds and interprets circulator data. The controller transfers information from the motor's scales and probes

LO 4. To understand working of Coordinate Measuring Machine

to the software, serving as the measurement system's traffic cop. The software system is used for data acquisition, collection and display. It includes a variety of application programs. A variety of application software is available depending on the type of industry.

13.3.2 Working of CMM

There are two primary types of CMM measuring methods. There is a type that uses a contact mechanism (touch probes) to measure a tool's components. The second sort of measuring mechanism employs other techniques, such as cameras or lasers.

The part to be measured is placed on the base of the CMM.

In addition to being positioned above the CMM plate is a moveable gantry with a touching probe.

The probe transmits an electrical signal to the computer upon contact with a portion of the part to be measured.

The acquired data is evaluated for the development of characteristics.

Whether a CMM machine has a camera or laser system, the operation steps are same.

13.3.3 Advantages and Disadvantages of CMM

Advantages:

1. Saves time and preserves process consistency,
2. A high level of precision may be acquired,
3. Extremely accurate,
4. Reduces setup time,
5. Eliminates human error,
6. Less maintenance is necessary,
7. Simple to update,
8. More flexible.

Disadvantages:

1. CMM cannot be relocated from one location to another.
2. Initial cost is substantial.
3. If the probe cannot reach the desired contour shapes, the desired results cannot be achieved.
4. During dimensional examination, the probe may damage soft components composed of rubber and other elastomers.

13.3.4 APPLICATIONS OF CMM

Coordinate measurement devices have applications in the automotive, machine tool, electrical and space industries, among others.

These devices are ideal for testing and inspecting test equipment, gauges and instruments:

CMM is used to do 100% inspections on aviation and space spacecraft.

CMM may be used to determine the component's dimensional accuracy.

CMM may also be used for sorting components for optimal matching within tolerance limitations.

13.4 MACHINE VISION

Visual inspection has been a staple of quality control procedures in the man-   *LO 5. To understand*
ufacturing industry for decades. Internal and exterior examinations of equip-   *machine vision*
ment, such as storage tanks, pressure vessels and pipes, also rely on visual
inspections. Machine vision is becoming increasingly used in production and manufacturing. Deep
learning is offering inspection procedures with quicker, more affordable and better automation.
Since the majority of inspection operations occur at regular intervals, automation is suitable for
this application. Machine vision is a technique and approach used to offer automated image-driven
analysis in applications such as inspection, process control and guiding, and it is widely employed
in today's industries. According to the Automated Imaging Association (AIA), machine vision comprises both industrial and non-industrial applications in which a combination of hardware and software provides operational direction to devices based on the acquisition and processing of pictures.
Machine vision is a fast-advancing technology that may replace or supplement manual inspections,
physical measures, safety monitoring, and facial identification. A machine vision inspection system identifies manufactured product faults, impurities, functional problems and other anomalies.
Machine vision may also verify items for completeness, such as by confirming a match between
product and packaging in the food and pharmaceutical sectors and by examining safety seals, caps
and rings on bottles. Inspection-specific machine vision systems monitor the visual appearance of
the observed material. Using statistical analysis, the system automatically finds probable surface
flaws and categorises them based on similarities in contrast, texture and/or geometry. In terms of
quality and quantity measures, machine vision is superior to human vision due to its superior speed,
precision and repeatability. Machine vision systems are able to identify and analyse item features
that are too tiny for humans to detect. Additionally, machine vision systems can surpass human
visual acuity. Machine vision is capable of seeing in the ultraviolet, x-ray and infrared spectrum
areas. Machine vision systems can check hundreds or thousands of components per minute on production lines.

Advantages of machine vision in automatic inspection:

1. Superior quality,
2. Greater productivity,
3. Decreased machine downtime and setup time,
4. More exhaustive information and stricter process management,
5. The precision and reproducibility of measurements can be significantly improved,

6. Scrap rate decrease,
7. Vastly improved inventory control.

13.4.1 Components of Machine Vision

Lighting, lenses, image sensors, vision processing and communications are the primary components of a machine vision system. Illumination lights the part to be inspected, highlighting its characteristics so they may be captured by camera. The lens collects the picture and transmits it as light to the sensor. A machine vision camera's sensor turns this light into a digital picture, which is subsequently transmitted to the processor for processing. Vision processing is comprised of algorithms that examine a picture, extract the relevant data, do the appropriate inspections and produce a determination. Lastly, communication is often achieved by discrete Input/Output (I/O) signal or data transmitted across a serial connection to a device that is logging or using the information.

13.5 SUMMARY

1. Inspection refers to the process of checking a product, its components, subassemblies or raw materials to verify if they adhere to the design standards established by the product designer.
2. In off-line inspection, the inspection equipment is typically specialised and has no direct interaction with the machine tools.
3. On-line inspection is performed throughout the machining process.
4. A coordinate measuring machine, often known as a CMM, measures the geometry of physical things.
5. A structure, probing system, controller and software are four primary components of a CMM.
6. Machine vision is a fast-advancing technology that may replace or supplement manual inspections, physical measures, safety monitoring and facial identification.

13.6 EXERCISE

1. What is meant by automated inspection *(BT level 2)*?
2. Differentiate between on-line/in-process and on-line/post-process inspection methods *(BT level 5)*.
3. Explain CMM *(BT level 2)*.
4. Describe the advantages of using CMMs over conventional inspection methods *(BT level 2)*.
5. Enumerate the applications in which CMMs become a crucial instrument *(BT level 1)*.
6. Explain machine vision and its application in automated inspection *(BT level 2)*.

13.7 MULTIPLE-CHOICE QUESTIONS

1. Which of the following is a primary goal of automated inspection systems?
   a. To improve inspection speed and accuracy.
   b. To reduce the need for human inspectors.
   c. To eliminate inspection errors.
   d. All of the above.
2. Which type of automated inspection system uses x-rays or gamma rays to detect defects?
   a. Optical inspection systems.
   b. Ultrasonic inspection systems.
   c. Radiographic inspection systems.
   d. Magnetic particle inspection systems.

3. Which type of automated inspection system is commonly used to detect defects in welded joints and castings?
    a. Optical inspection systems.
    b. Ultrasonic inspection systems.
    c. Radiographic inspection systems.
    d. Magnetic particle inspection systems.
4. Which of the following is a disadvantage of automated inspection systems?
    a. They can be expensive to install and maintain.
    b. They may not be able to detect all types of defects.
    c. They require highly trained operators to use them effectively
    d. All of the above.
5. Which type of automated inspection system uses a magnetic field to detect defects?
    a. Optical inspection systems.
    b. Ultrasonic inspection systems.
    c. Radiographic inspection systems.
    d. Magnetic particle inspection systems.
6. Which of the following is an advantage of using automated inspection systems?
    a. They can provide objective and consistent results.
    b. They can improve product quality and reliability.
    c. They can reduce inspection time and costs.
    d. All of the above.
7. Which type of automated inspection system is commonly used to inspect electronic components and printed circuit boards?
    a. Optical inspection systems.
    b. Ultrasonic inspection systems.
    c. Radiographic inspection systems.
    d. Magnetic particle inspection systems.

Answers

1. Answer: d. All of the above.
2. Answer: c. Radiographic inspection systems.
3. Answer: b. Ultrasonic inspection systems.
4. Answer: b. They may not be able to detect all types of defects.
5. Answer: d. Magnetic particle inspection systems.
6. Answer: d. All of the above.
7. Answer: a. Optical inspection systems.

14 Industrial Robots

Learning Outcomes: After studying this chapter, the reader should be able

LO 1: To know the definition of a robot and robot history (BT level 1).
LO 2: To understand robot terminology (BT level 2).
LO 3: To understand various features of robots like manipulator, controller, sensors and power supply unit, etc. (BT level 2).
LO 4: To understand classification of robots based on various criteria (BT level 2).
LO 5: To understand economics of robots (BT level 2).
LO 6: To understand applications of robots in industry (BT level 2).
LO 7: To understand robot programming methods (BT level 2).
LO 8: To understand artificial intelligence for intelligent manufacturing (BT level 2).

14.1 INTRODUCTION TO ROBOTS

Robotics is a form of programmable automation.

Webster's defines a robot as "an automated machine or system that performs duties typically associated with humans or seems to operate with human-like intelligence."

A formal definition of an industrial robot is provided by the Robotics Industries Association (RIA):

> Industrial robots are manipulators that may be taught to do a variety of tasks by manipulating diverse materials, components, tools, and specialised equipment in various ways.

In order for a robot to operate, it needs a certain level of intelligence, which is often given by computer programs embedded into its command and detection hardware. Simply described, an industrial robot is a machine intended for a range of applications.

A computer controls a series of revolute or prismatic joints linking many rigid links on a robotic manipulator. This end is detachable from the base and equipped with a tool for manipulation or assembly. When a joint is moved, the link to which it is connected will shift. A robot's components consist of a mechanical arm (or mainframe), a wrist assembly and a tool. Using this tool, a workpiece inside its work volume may be accessed.

14.2 HISTORY OF ROBOTICS

The Czech word *robota*, from which we get the English word robot, refers to a slave or forced labourer. The Czech author Korel Capek created the word "robot" in his 1921 play *Rossum's Universal Robots* (RUR). Since 1939, when he began his career as a science fiction author, Isaac Asimov produced a variety of robot-centric stories. In his 1942 short story "Runarounder," Asimov coined the word "robotics" for the first time. Asimov established the "Three Laws of Robotics" as follows:

1. A robot must not injure a human being, or, through inaction, allow a human to be harmed.
2. A robot must obey orders given by humans except when that conflicts with the first law.

DOI: 10.1201/9781003350842-14

3. A robot must protect its own existence unless that conflicts with the first or second laws. Over a period of time, a large number of movies has been produced, some picturing robots as friendly servants, others featuring them as predators. Examples of such movies are: *Star Wars*, *The Day The Earth Stood Still*, *Space Odyssey* and *Terminator*, etc.

Initially, the robots developed were of crude design, but fast developments have taken place ever since. Thus, robots can be classified into various generations as follows:

  (i) **First generation robots:** These toys, often referred to as play robots, were popular from the 1960s until the 1980s. They formerly did menial, unskilled tasks such as spray painting and spot welding. In other words, an inefficient kind of control known as "open loop" was utilised.

 (ii) **Second generation robots:** The golden age of these robots was between the early 1980s and the 1990s. Using precise sensors, closed-loop position and velocity control were created.

(iii) **Third generation robots:** These robots are widely used in industry and are equipped with advanced sensing and imaging systems.

 (iv) **Fourth generation robots** are still under development and will include sensors that enable robots to adjust their programming to new environments. Many are now being seen with humanoid characteristics.

  (v) **Fifth generation robots:** It is now the most recent robotics generation. The basic feature is the use of high-level artificial intelligence with automated learning, independent of human involvement, capable of simulating and creating models of performance, reasoning, and behaviour in the most unpredictable and dynamic circumstances. It is anticipated that these robots would excel at imitating humans in two areas: Intelligent decision making and problem solving.

Though, both robots and numerical control (NC) machines are a part of programmable automation, it would be interesting to bring out differences between the two. A robot is lighter and more portable equipment than an NC machine tool. Robot technology is much more advanced compared to NC technology. Unlike an NC machine, a robot makes use of a computer as its controller.

Thus, in the case of robots, on-line programming is possible whereas in NC machines, generally off-line programming is done. Robots are incorporated with advanced sensors and interpolators. Other points of difference are given in the following table.

NC Machines	*Robots*
1. NC machines are fixed in one place.	1. Robots may be fixed or mobile.
2. NC machines are generally used for machining purposes.	2. Robots are used for pick-in-place, assembly, welding, etc.
3. NC machines have a box-type Machine Control Unit (MCU) along with the machine tool hardware.	3. A robot manipulator is mostly in form of an arm.
4. NC machines make use of positioning and velocity sensors.	4. Apart from positioning and velocity sensors, a robot may use a tactile sensor, vision sensor, range sensor, proximity sensor, etc.
5. NC machines do not have load lifting capability.	5. A typical robot can lift as much as 1000 kg load.
6. NC machines acquire more floor space.	6. Robots require comparatively less floor space.
7. NC machines cannot adapt to changes in environment such as temperature change, or dust, etc.	7. Robots can adapt themselves to changes in work environment if they are programmed with judgemental ability.

14.3   ADVANTAGES OF USING ROBOTS IN INDUSTRY

In technically advanced countries such as the USA and Japan, the number of robots being used for industrial and commercial applications has increased rapidly due to the following advantages:

1. **Robots offer reduced cost of production:** When additional benefits are included, the cost of keeping a robot is much less than the average cost of maintaining a human. Robots do not qualify for employment benefits such as paid time off, health insurance or retirement plans since they are not salaried.
2. **Robots can operate in hazardous and hostile environments:** Robots are capable of working in environments that would be uncomfortable or even harmful for humans. Examples include firefighting, working in underground mines, handling radioactive materials, hazardous chemicals and welding, which expose workers to noxious fumes.
3. **Robots offer improved production quality:** Robots allow for more accurate positioning. Also advantageous is the rapid turnaround time. Under certain conditions, welding must be completed before the heat from the operation causes the pieces to distort. Previously unachievable welds are now viable owing to increases in speed and control accuracy. Diecasting is another procedure in which time limitations dictate short casting cycle rates.

The output quality of a company is vital, and robots aid in ensuring that it meets the required level. The robot is assisted by sensors and measuring instruments and hence the final product is produced accurately and meets the prescribed quality standards.

4. **Use of robots results in increased productivity:** Robots can be trained to surpass human labour to some degree. In a straight line, a robot can weld at a rate of 75 centimetres per minute, but a human can only weld at a rate of 25 centimetres per minute. Two regular spray-painting robots can paint a whole automobile, inside and out, with two coats in approximately 90 seconds (wet-on-wet is already in use). A fully human spray-painting workforce could never expect to achieve such efficiency.
5. **Robots enable improved management control in a** Computer Integrated Manufacturing **(CIM) environment:** A record of the work completed by computer-controlled robots may be saved in the robot's or computer's memory. The computer can keep inventory from all warehouse levels. Therefore, a supervisor in the office may determine what is happening in any store by getting the pertinent information from the computer's memory. The manager is not required to make needless journeys between floors. Consequently, operational timeliness, accuracy and supervision are enhanced.
6. **Industrial robots meet occupational safety and health administration standards:** People are renowned for disobeying safety regulations, such as the need to wear protective equipment like helmets and goggles.

Due to these advantages, robots are being increasingly used for industrial applications.

14.4   ROBOT TERMINOLOGY

LO 2. To understand robot terminology.

Some of the terms typically used for robots are discussed in this section.

Accuracy: Accuracy of a robot is a measure of how close the robot end effector can come to the specified coordinates. The degree of accuracy is the difference between the desired position and the actual position reached by the robot arm.

Repeatability: Repeatability of a robot is the degree to which it is able to reproduce the same path/trajectory again and again for the same inputs.

The difference between accuracy and repeatability is understood from the shooter who has to hit at the centre of the target plate. The target plate with bullet marks is shown in Figure 14.1.

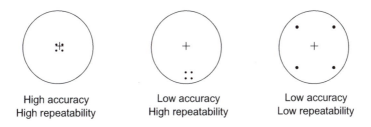

FIGURE 14.1 Accuracy and repeatability

Joints: Comparable to human joints, the components of a robot manipulator may move relative to one another. To elaborate, a junction is the place at which two links meet.

When designing a robot manipulator, you have the option between five unique types of mechanical joints. The straight joint, the right-angle joint, the left angle joint, the rotating joint, the twisting joint and the revolving joint are examples of joints. The joints are shown in Figure 14.2.

Degree of freedom: Degree of freedom refers to the number of movable axes of the of robot arm.

One degree of freedom is associated with each joint.

Payload: It is the maximum load (weight) a robot is able to carry at normal speeds.

This is also sometimes referred as load carrying capacity.

Work volume: Similar concepts are described by the phrase "work envelope." The work envelope is the region within which the end effector of a robot may function. The shapes and dimensions of the work volume are determined by the manipulator's joints and link sizes.

End effector: It refers to the gripper or the tool at the end of the robot arm meant to do some useful work.

Pitch: Up and down motion of end effector about an axis.

Yaw: Side-to-side motion of robot end effect or about an axis.

Roll: Circular motion of end effector about an axis.

Control resolution: This phrase refers to the ability of the robot's controller and positioning system to divide the range of a joint into distinct, controlled places. In other words, it the

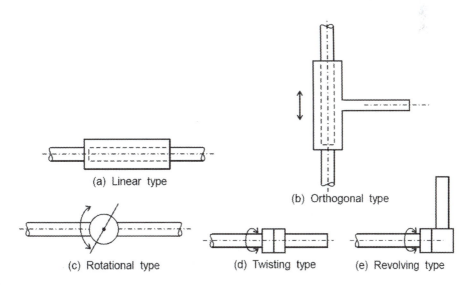

FIGURE 14.2 Joint types

distance between the two closest addressable points. The value of control resolution of a robot arm depends on the capabilities of electromechanical components used and the controller's memory (storage capacity).

14.5 MAJOR FEATURES OF A ROBOT

The major features that are common to almost all types of robots are:

1. Manipulator (or arm),
2. Controller (the brain of robot unit),
3. Sensors,
4. Power supply unit.

Let us discuss each of these one by one.

14.5.1 MANIPULATOR

A manipulator is an industrial robot's mechanical arm. It is comprised of a collection of links linked at different places. There are many sizes and forms of joints and links.

The joints, also sometimes referred to as axes, are generally of two types:

a. **Prismatic:** They produce linear or translational motion. Examples are linear joint and orthogonal joint.
b. **Revolute:** They produce pure rotary motion. Examples are rotational, twist and revolving joints.

The robot has one more degree of freedom per joint. Consequently, the number of joints defines the total degrees of freedom of the robot. Each joint connection comprises an input link and an output link.

The robot manipulator contains three structural elements. The arm, the wrist and the hand (or end effector). A robot may contain hydraulic, pneumatic or electrical actuators to move various mechanical members. The actuators are coupled to mechanical members either directly or indirectly using gears, chains, belts, lead screw or harmonic drive.

14.5.1.1 The End Effector

Like how a human arm's free end has a hand and fingers, a robot's free end contains an end effector.

It is expected that the end effector will perform tasks traditionally performed by the palm and finger arrangement of human hands. These are usually customised to perform specific tasks. Different end effectors are designed for different types of functions and therefore there are large number of different end effectors. End effectors fall into two major categories. These are **grippers** and **tools**.

This is an example of an end effector: The gripper. As part of their duties, robots deliver bottles, boxes and raw materials. Loading and unloading machines, arranging pallets and loading and unloading components from conveyors are further examples.

Tools are a kind of end effector used to manipulate an item, as opposed to just holding it. These instruments include guns for spot welding, spray painting, arc welding and grinding.

The various types of grippers used in industrial robots are mechanical grippers, vacuum cups, magnetic grippers and adhesive grippers.

Mechanical grippers use mechanical fingers activated by simple mechanisms to grasp an object (see Figure 14.3). Use of replaceable fingers allow for wear and interchangeability. One gripper can be removed, and another attached as and when necessary, so that objects of different sizes and shapes can be handled.

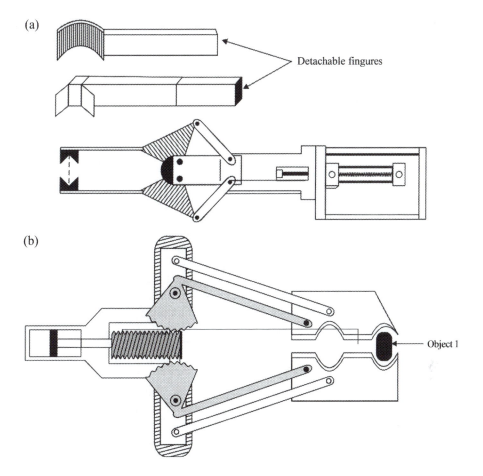

(a)

Detachable fingures

(b)

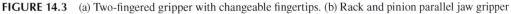

Object 1

FIGURE 14.3 (a) Two-fingered gripper with changeable fingertips. (b) Rack and pinion parallel jaw gripper

Vacuum cups or suction cups are used when objects to be picked are flat, smooth and clean so as to generate satisfactory vacuum. Suction cups are usually made of elastic material such as rubber and plastic. Vacuum pumps are used to remove air between cups and part surfaces. It cannot be used for parts with through holes.

Magnetic grippers are useful in holding ferrous material. Their main advantages are the ability to hold parts with holes. They can also tolerate variation in part size and require only one surface for gripping. They can make use of both permanent magnets and electromagnets. But while parts can be unloaded simply by switching off the electromagnet, for permanent magnet, some special mechanism has to be designed for this purpose.

Adhesive grippers use adhesives to pick up lightweight materials such as cloth, paper, etc. But a disadvantage is that adhesive loses its tackiness on repeated use. Therefore, a special feed mecha-nism has to be incorporated at the robot's wrist to load fresh adhesive material on repeated use.

14.5.2 Controller

There are different types of robot controllers. The less expensive, open-loop control robots can use:

a. Single step sequencer control,
b. Pneumatic logic control,
c. Electronic sequencer control.

Microprocessor-based control is often implemented in the form of feedback loops in close-loop controlled robots:

a. Microcomputer,
b. Minicomputer.

Various functions performed by robot controller are:

a. To start and stop the motion of individual components of the manipulator in a desired sequence and at specified points.
b. To store trajectory motion and sequence data.
c. To make robot interact with the outside world using sensors.

Generally, a digital computer is the preferred controller. It controls the motors that move the robot's joints in order to move the manipulator and end effector. Let's assume something existing at a certain place. A pick-up, transport and placement (PTP) robot would be required to transfer the object from its present position to a predefined location. If the position of the item is known, the controller (computer) estimates how much each joint must move for the end effector to reach the object. Once the end effector is in the correct location, the controller will command it to grasp the object. The controller then instructs the appropriate motors at the joints to move by the required amount in order to reach the desired position. At the last phase, the controller instructs the end effector to place the object in the desired location. Random and unanticipated disturbances may be mitigated by the use of feedback control. A schematic diagram of closed loop (feedback) control is shown in Figure 14.4.

The computer's output is a digital signal, but the majority of motors can only take an analogue signal. Therefore, a digital to analog converter (DAC) is used to interface the computer and the motor drive (or hydraulic and pneumatic drive systems.)

14.5.3 SENSORS

Sensors are the transducers that are used to measure physical variable of interest. These are low power transducers which produce output signal as a measure of the controlled variable. The output signal of a sensor is usually in electrical form (analogue or digital). These are used to inform the robot controller of the status of the manipulator (either continuously or at the end of a desired motion). These are also used for safety monitoring, parts inspection and determining position and related information about objects in the robot cell. The desirable features of a sensor are:

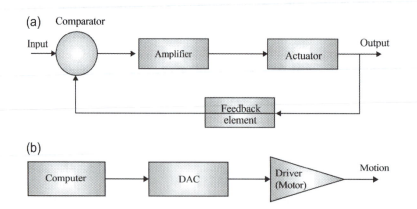

FIGURE 14.4   (a) A closed loop control system. (b) Flow of signal from controller to the drive

- High accuracy and precision over the entire operating range.
- High speed of response to changes in the sensed variables.
- It should be easy to calibrate and operate.
- It should possess a high reliability.

Sensors used in robots may be classified as:

a. Contact sensors: These are the ones that come in contact with some surface to measure a desired physical variable. e.g., tactile sensors and force–torque sensors.
b. Non-contact sensors: These do not need to touch any surface in order to measure the desired parameter. They can sense the parameter from some suitable distance, hence they are called non-contact type, *e.g.,* proximity sensors, range detectors, visual sensors and acoustic sensors.

Tactile Sensors or Touch Sensors: These indicate a physical contact between the end effector carrying the sensor and another object. An example of a tactile sensor is a micro switch. These sensors generate a binary signal indicating whether an object has been touched or not.

These sensors can be used to:

- Signal the robot that a target has been reached.
- Measure objects dimensions during inspection.
- Stop robot motion when its end effector makes contact with an object.

Force and torque sensors: These make use of piezoelectric transducers or strain gauges to measure reaction forces and moments. These are mounted between the end effector (gripper) and the wrist or on load-bearing members of the manipulator. These sensors help robots to perform a number of tasks such as:

- Gripping parts of various shapes and sizes for material handling.
- Assembly work.
- Machine loading and unloading.

Proximity sensors: These can sense and indicate presence of an object within a fixed space near the sensor. These are mounted on the wrist or the end effector as these are main moving parts of a robot. Examples of proximity sensors are eddy current sensors.

By producing an alternating magnetic field at the probe's tip, these devices induce eddy currents in a conductor. These can be used to maintain a fixed distance from a steel plate. A light-based proximity sensor is shown in Figure 14.5. As an object moves closer or away from robot, different sensing elements get activated.

14.5.3.1   Range Detectors

While the proximity sensors can only indicate the presence or absence of an object, there are sensors which can actually measure the distance between the object and the sensors. Such sensors are called range sensors. These sensors can be used to locate the work parts of the robot. Various range detectors have been developed based on different principles.

For example.

a. Range sensors based on supersonic or radar sensing.
b. Optical sensors that can determine distance based on the amount of reflected light.
c. Range sensors based on the triangular principle.

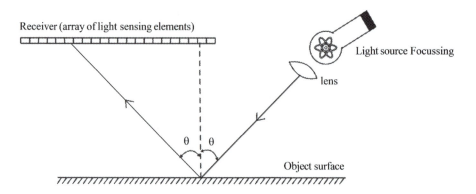

FIGURE 14.5   Schematic diagram for a proximity sensor using light reflected from object surface

From Figure 14.6 $\dfrac{x}{x+r} = \dfrac{q}{P_i}$

$$X = \dfrac{qr}{P_i - q}$$

a. **Infrared sensors** are used to indicate the presence or absence of hot objects and measure temperatures by the infrared light emitted from the surface of an object.
b. **Vacuum switches** are the sensors used to indicate negative air pressure, hence they can be used with vacuum grippers to indicate the presence or absence of an object.
c. **Photometric sensors** are one of the simplest types, they consist of light emitting diode (LED) transmitters and a photodiode receiver that senses light. These sensors can be used to indicate presence or absence of an object.

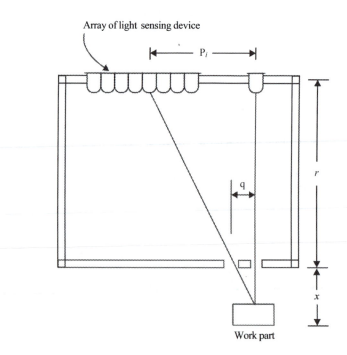

FIGURE 14.6   Schematic diagram of range sensor based on triangular principle

14.5.3.2 Vision Sensors

These can be used to identify objects for pick-and-place purposes, etc. A schematic block diagram of robot vision system is shown in Figure 14.7.

a. The machine vision system consists of a video camera interfaced with a vision computer through a video buffer. The video buffer is also called a frame grabber.
b. The camera signals can be sent to a TV monitor which displays the scene being scanned.
c. A frozen frame of a camera is scanned row by row and the corresponding output signal is stored in digital form in the frame grabber. A video preprocessor is used for initial processing. Hence, the entire burden of processing does not rely on the vision computer which could otherwise make the system slow.
d. The images of the object received from the camera are reduced to silhouettes using a technique called "thresholding." In this technique, the system assumes that the objects of interest will contrast sharply with respect to the background. Thus, all the object intensities are above or below a certain level. This threshold value is used to determine the intensities that should be set as white or black for silhouette formation.

14.5.4 Power Supply Unit

This unit provides the required power to the manipulator's actuators.

The drives in the axes of a robot manipulator convert the computer's electrical orders into mechanical motion. By comparing reference and feedback data, the majority of present-day computer-controlled robots monitor and control the robot's axial movement. The driving motions that occur from the first errors are amplified.

Industrial robots make use of three types of drives. These are:

1. Hydraulic drive,
2. Pneumatic drive,
3. Electric drive.

14.5.4.1 Hydraulic Drives

Due to their small size and enormous power output, they are often used to power strong robots. They may deliver much more angular acceleration than DC motors at the same peak power. As a result of their low time constants, the robot axis is able to operate smoothly.

A hydraulic system has following components (Figure 14.8):

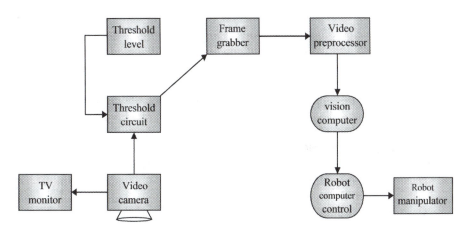

FIGURE 14.7 Block diagram of a robot/machine vision system

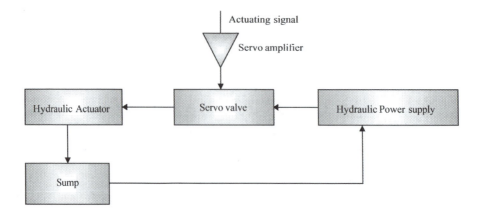

FIGURE 14.8   Hydraulic system for robot

1. Hydraulic power supply for supplying pressurised oil,
2. Servo valve for each axis of motion for synchronising motion of various robot links.
3. Sump or oil tank,
4. A hydraulic actuator for each axis of motion.

There are certain inherent disadvantages of a hydraulic system:

a. The problem of maintenance and leakage of oil from transmission lines and the system components.
b. Oil must be kept clean and protected against contamination.
c. The problem of viscosity variation with oil temperature.
d. The problem of dynamic lag caused by transmission lines.

14.5.4.2   Pneumatic Drives

This type of drive is used in smaller robots. These robots are often only suited for pick-and-place activities with short cycle periods. Allowing sliding joints to move in a translational manner, piston drives may be easily adjusted to operate on compressed air.

Advantages of pneumatic drives:

a. Pneumatic drives are less expensive compared to hydraulic systems because the air used in the activation is exhausted into the surrounding atmosphere and there is no need of extra sump.

Disadvantages of pneumatic systems:

a. Pneumatic pressure is quite low compared to hydraulic pressure, therefore pneumatic drives are restricted to low power applications.
b. The precise control of velocity and position in pneumatic systems is rather difficult as the arm of a pneumatically driven robot may sag and impair the repeatability of the robot.

14.5.4.3   Electric Drives

Electric drives include stepping motors and DC servomotors. Stepping motors are however not appropriate drives for robot arms. They have the following disadvantages:

a. Excessive load on stepping motor might cause a subsequent loss of steps.
b. Stepping motors are noisy.
c. They have limited resolution.

DC servomotors are efficient, robust and provide accurate speed control. This makes them ideal for use in robotics. These are also infinity variable speed motors. In many modern applications AC motors replace DC motors. The reason is that AC motors can produce the same power output with reduced size and higher torque.

14.6 TYPES OF ROBOTS

The classification of robotic systems can be done in different ways.
According to the structure of the manipulator:

LO 4. To understand classification of robots based on various criteria.

a. Cartesian coordinate robots,
b. Cylindrical coordinate robots,
c. Polar coordinate robots,
d. Jointed arm or articulated robots,
e. Selective Compliance Articulated Robot Arm (SCARA).

According to the type of system:

a. Point-to-point robots,
b. Continuous path robots.

According to the type of control loops:

a. Open loop robots,
b. Closed loop robots.

14.6.1 CLASSIFICATION ON BASIS OF STRUCTURE OF MANIPULATOR

a. **Cartesian Coordinate Robots**

Each axis—x, y and z—is composed of two slides that move in opposing directions. Therefore, they are also known as rectilinear robots or x, y and z robots. By altering the relative locations of the three slides, the robot may accomplish tasks inside a cuboidal work envelope. Such robots which are large and give gentry type crane's appearance are called "Gentry Robots."

Advantages

1. Such robots have high rigidity.
2. They have high load carrying capacity.

Limitations

1. The robot is not popular in industry due to its lack of mechanical flexibility.
2. It cannot reach objects on the floor.
3. The speed of operation is slower than that associated with a robot having a rotary base.

Resolution: It has a constant resolution.
Motion: It has three linear motions as shown in Figure 14.9.

b. **Cylindrical Coordinate Robots**

The relevant robots use a vertical column with a slide that may move in both directions along the length of the tube. It is possible to spin the robot arm around the column since it is attached to a slide. In its workstation, the robot is capable of fabricating anything that resembles a cylinder.

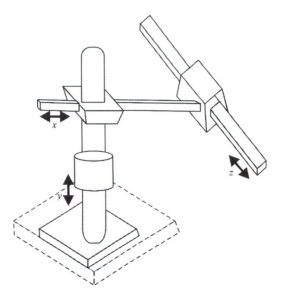

FIGURE 14.9   Cartesian coordinate robot

Advantages

1. More workspace.
2. Maximum and minimum extension is possible.

Limitations

1. 360° rotation is restricted.
2. Good dynamic performance is not achieved by rotary base.

Resolution: It is not constant and depends on the distance between the column and the gripper along horizontal arm.

   Motion: It has two linear and one rotary motion as shown in Figure 14.10.

   c. **Polar Coordinate Robots**

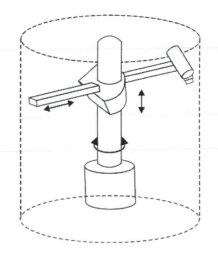

FIGURE 14.10   Cylindrical coordinate robots

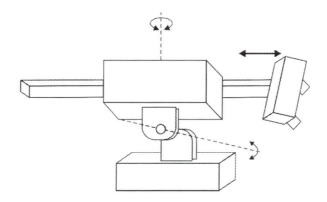

FIGURE 14.11   Polar coordinates robot

On a horizontal pivot, it has an extended telescopic arm that may be raised or lowered. The pivot point is a base that may be rotated. It is commonly referred to as a "spherical coordinate robot" since the robot's arm can move in a spherical coordinate system, which is made feasible by its numerous joints (Figure 14.11).

Advantages

1. It has maximum reach, i.e., the ability of the robot to extend its arm significantly beyond its base.
2. It has better mechanical flexibility.

Limitations

It has low rigidity and load carrying capacity.
Resolution: Very low.
Motion: It has two rotary and one linear motion.

d. **Articulated Robots (Jointed Arm/Revolute Robots)**

As shown in Figure 14.12, the rotating base of these robots is connected to three rigid components that are connected by two swivelling joints. When seeing its design, one is reminded of a human

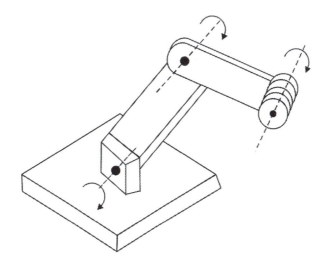

FIGURE 14.12   Jointed arm or articulated manipulator

arm. The gripper is attached to the arm at the wrist, the same as the hand is connected to the fore-arm. The elbow connects the forearm to the upper arm, whereas the shoulder connects the upper arm to the torso.

Advantages

1. Good reach,
2. Ideal for assembly operations.
   Limitations: Mechanical inaccuracy occurs.
   Resolution: It has very low resolution.
   Motion: It has three rotary motions.
   e. **Selective Compliance Articulated Robot Arm (SCARA).**

They are a kind of robot with arms that has moveable joints. These inexpensive devices are used anytime rapid, accurate motion is needed. The capacity of SCARA to insert objects into holes (for mounting resistors, IC chips, etc. on printed circuit board (PCB)) is a significant advantage in assembly operations (see Figure 14.13). A SCARA is designed to be very hard in the vertical plane yet flexible laterally, which facilitates insertion.

14.6.2 CLASSIFICATION ACCORDING TO THE TYPE OF SYSTEM

a. Point-to-Point Robots (PTP Robots)

This technique requires the robot to go to a predefined area where it will stop. To perform the required action, the end effector is used. When a cycle is complete, the robot will go to the next site to repeat the procedure. These robots are used for duties such as manipulating tools and transporting components. These robots have excellent reach and hauling capacity. Spot welding robots are a common kind of these machines. Spot welding is accomplished by adjusting the robot such that the weld location is directly between the electrodes of the gun. The robot will do another round of spot welding at the new site after relocation.

As the robot goes from one site to another, the PTP system is unconcerned about the robot's trajectory or speed. When travelling from one place to another, the shortest path is used. Advanced PTP robots are capable of both linear and non-linear movement.

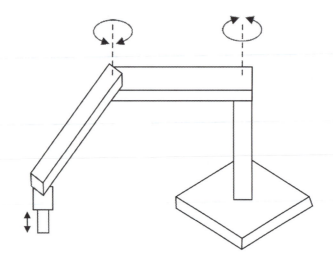

FIGURE 14.13   SCARA robot

A robot system with microprocessor-based control employs command pulses where each pulse causes a motion of 1 BRU in the corresponding axis. Note that one pulse is also equivalent to one bit of information. Examples of such robots are Unimation and Verstran.

b. Continuous Path Robots (CP Robots)

In some applications like spray painting, grinding and arc welding, the robot arm must follow a complex path through space. A CP robot is used in such cases. A CP robot's tool performs the necessary action while the axes of motion (joints) are in motion, much like an arc welder. The arc welding robot aims the welding gun straight forward. For CP robots, it is possible for all axes of motion to be in motion simultaneously and at different rates. Keep in mind that the output quality may suffer as a consequence of the increased pace.

Examples of such robots are PUMA and Maker 110.

c. Trajectory Planning in PTP and CP Robots

Trajectory planning means determination of the actual trajectory, or path along which the robot end effector moves in order to perform a specified task. The path of a robot manipulator is defined by a sequence of points called the "end points" and stored in the robot's computer.

In a PTP robot, the end effector moves in an arbitrary path from one end point to the next end point. These end points in PTP robots are presented in joint coordinates. This means the required position values of each axis are separately given and sent as commands to the corresponding control loop. The controller software program makes use of the data (i.e., joint coordinate values corresponding to various end points) which are obtained by recording the required points of the trajectory with the aid of a teach box.

In CP robots, the trajectory is divided into small sections in order to provide linear motion between closely spaced end points. The trajectory is divided into small linear sections by using interpolation subroutines. (Interpolators are discussed in Chapter 5.) The spacing between points, the linearity obtained and the velocity at which the robot moves all depend upon the computational speed of interpolation algorithms and controller.

14.6.3 ACCORDING TO THE TYPE OF CONTROL LOOPS

A robotic control system may use either open-loop or closed-loop control. In an open-loop control system, the output has no effect on the input. However, a better system is the one in which output is sensed and feedback can be compared with input variables. Such a system is called a closed-loop control system.

Open-loop robots' axes are powered by stepping motors. An electrical pulse is converted into a matching angular motion by the output shaft of a stepping motor spinning across a predetermined angle known as the "stepping angle" (see Figure 14.14).

A stepping motor's dependence on load torque to attain maximum speed is a significant disadvantage. When the load torque rises, the maximum achievable speed falls. Therefore, stepping motors cannot be used in systems with variable load torques, since an unexpectedly large load causes the motor to lose steps, resulting in an undesirable positional error. Industrial robots should not use stepping motors for this reason. The majority of industrial robots in use today operate under a closed-loop control system, which means that the robot's position along each axis of motion is constantly monitored by some kind of feedback mechanism.

The closed-loop control system monitors the position and velocity of each axis and compares them to the predetermined parameters. Error is the departure from the optimal outcome. The control system was designed to eliminate or significantly reduce the frequency of this error.

14.7   ECONOMICS OF ROBOTS

LO 5. To understand Economics of robots.

Before purchasing a robot, certain basic information should be collected. This may include cost of robot installation, production cycle time, benefits and savings resulting from robots.

Most robot users are using robots because of:

1. Reduced labour cost,
2. Elimination of dangerous, dirty and difficult jobs,
3. Increased output rate,
4. Improved product quality,
5. Increased production flexibility,
6. Reduced material waste,
7. Reduced labour turnover,
8. Reduced capital cost.

Management in industry can think of the following advantages of using robots over human labour:

1. Robots do not get tired.
2. They do not seek or obtain paid wages, increment in wages, vacations and other allowances like provident fund, etc.
3. They do not go on strike.
4. Thay do not argue or debate with seniors.

[Thank God, robots are not being used to teach in schools and colleges!]

A robot project may involve various types of costs. These costs can be broadly classified into two categories.

1. **Direct costs:** These include investment cost and operating cost, etc.
2. **Indirect costs:** These include inventory cost, material handling and floor space cost, etc.

14.7.1   INVESTMENT COSTS

These include purchase cost of the robot, engineering and installation cost and cost of tooling, etc.

14.7.2   OPERATING COSTS

These include the cost of direct and indirect (e.g., programmers) labour, training of labour, mainte-nance cost and cost of utilities (e.g., electricity, gas, air pressure) etc.

14.7.3   INVENTORY COST

This includes cost associated with process inventory and finished goods inventory. Technical fac-tors, cost and benefit considerations are important aspects of robot selection and their use. The

FIGURE 14.14   Open-loop robot system

increasing availability, reliability and reducing costs of robots are making them more popular in industry. Robots are making major economic impact on manufacturing operations as the hourly wages are much higher compared to cost of operating a robot per hour.

14.8   APPLICATIONS OF ROBOTS

Robots are being used in dangerous, repetitive and boring tasks. They are being applied to various industrial applications. We shall briefly discuss some of these applications.

LO 6. To understand Applications of robots in industry.

Welding: This is one of the major uses for an industrial robot. Robots can readily and economically perform both spot welding and continuous arc welding.

The type of robots used for spot welding are usually large. They have sufficient payload capacity to use heavy welding gun. Five or six axes are needed to achieve the position and orientation required. Playback robots with point-to-point control are used and are programmed using the lead-through method. Polar coordinate robots and articulated robots are the common configurations used in spot welding operation. The automobile industry is a major user of this type of robots.

Arc welding is also extensively used by the auto industry. In this case, continuous path servo-controlled robots are used. Programming is done by lead-through methods. Cartesian coordinate robots and articulated robots are frequently used in arc welding applications. These robots have five or six axes of motion.

Spray painting: The spray-painting operation should not be performed by human beings as the fine mist of paint can become a cause of health hazards. Hence, robots are used for spray painting. Another advantage of using a robot is that the coating produced will be far more uniform than a human being can ever produce. Numerous robot applications include spray painting of appliances, car bodies, engines, wood products, porcelain coatings on bathroom fixtures, etc.

Other machining operations that an industrial robot can perform include:

- Drilling,
- Grinding,
- Deburring,
- Water jet cutting,
- Laser drilling and cutting.

For operations like drilling and grinding, a powered spindle is attached to the robot's wrist. The spindle rotates the tool such as a drill or grinding wheel. The robot's function is to position and move the tool with respect to workpiece. Similarly in other operations like water jet cutting, laser drilling and cutting, the purpose of a robot is to position the tool with respect to the workpiece.

Material handling and parts transfer: In many applications, robots are required to move parts or objects from one location to another. Often, they are used for machine loading and unloading applications. Sometimes they are required to pick a part from a remote location and place it in a compartmentalised box.

The following points must be considered while designing a robot for material handling applications:

- The objects must be presented to robot in a known position and orientation.
- The end effector must be designed so as to handle the object easily.
- The load carrying capacity of material handling robot must not be exceeded.
- The material handling system should be designed so as to minimise the distance the material has to be moved.
- The robot should be given sufficient degree of freedom for pick-and-place operations. Some material handling operations do not require a high degree of freedom. Others requiring

palletisation operations or picking parts from a moving conveyor require a higher degree of freedom for the robots.
- Usually, PTP robots are used for part handling and transfer applications.

Assembly: Assembly operations are repetitive and monotonous in nature for human beings. Hence, robots are also being used for assembly operations. Robots are being used for the assembly of small electric motors, electrical plugs and switches. In most of these applications it is important that a robot wrist should be compliant. For example, in order to prevent bending of rods or shafts to be inserted into a clearance hole, a force or tactile sensor can be incorporated in the wrist. Alternatively, a remote centre compliance (RCC) device can be used. The action of a remote centre compliance device in a peg hole insertion task is shown in Figure 14.15.

The application of robots is sometimes disadvantageous in assembly because they cannot perform as quickly as fixed automation systems. The assembly applications of a robot are useful only because of their capability to execute programmed variations in the work cycle to accommodate different assembly configurations. To this end, robots are being used extensively for assembling electronic components on PCB.

Inspection: Robots are being used to inspect electronic devices like PCBs. Robots with a comprehensive vision system are also being used for visual inspection. The automobile industry has also been using robots to inspect finished parts or subassemblies to enhance product quality. Sometimes robots can also be used for loading and unloading inspection and testing machines.

Part sorting: Often, robots have been used for the monotonous task of sorting parts like washers and O-rings. This is because sometimes groups of parts are produced in an unsorted manner either to reduce cost or because of tolerance variations that are inherent in the manufacturing process. Sorting robots make use of suitably designed grippers or a vision system to sort parts.

Robots have also found many new fields of application like medical examination and surgery, space exploration, underwater applications mining, firefighting and defence/military applications.

14.9   ROBOT PROGRAMMING METHODS

LO 7. To understand Robot programming methods.

The robot is programmed by entering programming commands into its controller memory by one of the following methods:

Manual method: This method is used for limited sequence robots. The robots are programmed by setting limit switches, ON/OFF switches or stepping switches and

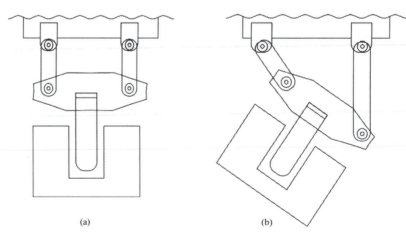

(a)   (b)

FIGURE 14.15   Schematic diagram for remote centre compliance (RCC device being used to insert peg in a hole)

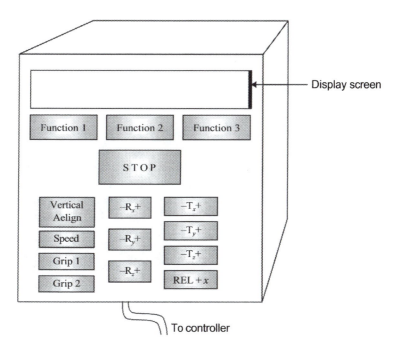

FIGURE 14.16 Components of teach pendant

mechanical stops. These devices determine the sequence in which motion of the robot cycle is completed. Hence this is more of a manual setup rather than a programming method.

Lead-through programming method: This method is used for computer-controlled robots. In this method, the robot is taught the task by moving the manipulator through the desired motion cycle thereby entering the points through which the manipulator has to pass, in the controller memory.

For playback robots with PTP control, the powered lead-through method is employed. This method uses a handheld control box known as "teach pendant" to move the end effector through the desired positions during the teach procedure. Figure 14.16 illustrates various features of a teach pendant. During the playback, the robot moves through the same positions under its own power.

For a playback robot with continuous path control, the manual lead-through method is more suitable. In this method during the teach procedure, the robot operator has to physically grasp the end effector or tool attached to the wrist and move it manually through the motion sequence thereby recording the path into the computer memory.

Robot programming languages: A number of robot programming languages have been developed which make use of computer and appropriate software for control functions of the robot. The programming may be accomplished on-line or off-line. The following are the types of robot programming languages available:

a. Point-to-point motion languages,
b. Motion languages at assembler level,
c. High-level programming languages,
d. Numerical control type programming languages,
e. Object-oriented languages,
f. Task-oriented languages.

Task-oriented languages are very intelligent and have commands which represent real world language e.g., TIGHTEN THE SCREW. The following is a list of some of the most popular programming languages for robots:

VAL – Versatile algorithmic language (Unimation),
AL – Algorithmic language (Stanford University, AI lab),
AML – A manufacturing language (IBM),
MCL – Manufacturing control language (McDonnel Douglas),
RAIL – (Automatrix),
HELP – (General Electric),
ROBEX – ROBOTER EXAPT.

VAL is one of the most popular languages. It was developed by Unimation Inc. for PUMA robots in 1979. In 1984 it was upgraded to VAL II version with interlocking facilities. Most of the robot programming languages including VAL use a combination of textual statements and lead-through techniques. While the textual statements are used to describe the motion, the load-through techniques (that make use of a teach pendant) are used to define the position and orientation of the manipulator or end effector at the end of the motion.

> **Example 14.1:** *Write a program in VAL to pick a part from point A(X_1 = 600, Y_1 = 550, Z_1 = 600) and place it at point B(X_2 = 100, Y_2 = 150, Z_2 = 50).*
>   *Solution:* Using the teach pendant move the gripper to point (600, 550, 600) and record it into memory as point using the following command.

    HERE   A,
    POINT   ARECV = A

Now move the gripper to point (100, 150, 50) and record it into memory as point bussing the following command:

    HERE   AB
    POINT   ADROP = B

Now the program can be written as:

    APPROACH   ARECV, 70
    MOVE   ARECV
    CLOSE
    DEPART   A70
    APPROACH   ADROP, 70
    MOVE   ADROP
    OPEN
    DEPART   A150

14.10   ARTIFICIAL INTELLIGENCE (AI) FOR INTELLIGENT MANUFACTURING

Artificial intelligence is the science concerned with systems that show some characteristics similar to intelligence in human behaviour, such as learning, reasoning and problem solving, etc. AI tries to simulate such human behaviour on a computer. It can also be utilised for design and manufacturing operations. AI is the study of how to make computers do things which at the moment people do better. It focusses on creating machines that can engage in behaviours that humans consider intelligent. It is a scientific analysis of mechanisms' underlying thought and intelligent behaviour and their embodiment in machines such as robots.

LO 8. To understand Artificial intelligence for intelligent manufacturing

   AI has the following elements:

   Knowledge based expert systems,
   Machine vision system,

Neural networks,
Fuzzy logic,
Voice recognition system,
Natural language understanding.

An expert system is an intelligent computer program that can solve complex design or manufacturing problems by making use of an engineering and manufacturing data base also called knowledge base. The knowledge and logic of engineers is incorporated into so called "knowledge base." By making use of a knowledge base and inference engine, an expert system can solve complicated problems starting from scratch.

14.10.1 Machine Vision System

Machine vision (also sometimes called computer vision or intelligent vision) can be defined as means of simulating the image recognition and analysis capabilities of human eye/brain system with electronic and electromechanical techniques. In a human vision system, the eyes sense the image and the brain analyses the information and takes action on the basis of the analysis. Similarly, in a machine vision system, visual sensing of information is done after forming an image of the object and information is analysed to make a useful decision about its content. A machine vision system thus needs both visual sensing and interpretive capabilities.

A schematic diagram of a machine vision system is shown in Figure 14.17.

14.10.2 Neural Networks

Computers are much faster than human brains in performing sequential tasks but humans are still much better in parallel processing. For example, humans can recognise features like voice, face, etc., assess situations quickly and adjust to new and dynamic conditions.

The logic of artificial neural networks is designed on the same principle as neurons of a human brain. A human brain has approximately 100 billion linked neurons. Each neuron performs a simple task. It receives signals from a fixed set of neurons and combines these in a specific way to generate an electrochemical output signal which goes to a fixed set of neurons.

The logic of neural networks is being used in a number of applications such as speech recognition systems, process control in manufacturing, etc.

In the quest to create intelligent machines, the field of AI has divided into several different approaches. The two basic approaches are **bottom-up** and **top-down** approaches. Bottom-up researchers believe that the best way to achieve AI is to make electronic replicas of the human brain's complex network of neurons. It aims at constructing electronic circuits that act as neurons do in the human brain. The complex network of neurons is what gives humans intelligent characteristics. By itself, a neuron is not intelligent but when grouped together neurons are able to pass

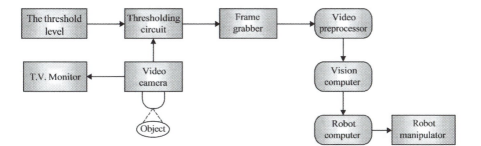

FIGURE 14.17   Block diagram of a robot vision system

electrical signals through networks. The top-down approach attempts to copy a brain's behaviour with computer programs.

14.10.3   Fuzzy Logic

It consists of four principal components:

a. A fuzzification module,
b. A knowledge base,
c. A decision-making logic,
d. A defuzzification module.

The fuzzification interface performs a mapping that converts values of input variables into fuzzy subspaces. The input values may be taken from an existing database or received by the user inter-actively (Figure 14.18).

The knowledge base of the hybrid expert system consists of two components, i.e., a database and a rule base. The database contains the fuzzified values of the input variables into various fuzzy spaces. The values stored in the database are used for finding similarities with the fuzzy subspaces in the rule base and inferencing. The rule base consists of a set of fuzzy if–then rules in the form: "If a set of conditions are satisfied, THEN a set of consequences can be inferred."

The decision-making logic is the module that actually makes the inference from the given infor-mation using the rules stored in the knowledge base.

A defuzzification module converts the fuzzy results into crisp values.

14.10.4   Voice Recognition

In the 1990s, computer speech recognition reached a practical level for limited purposes.

It is possible to instruct some computers using speech.

14.10.5   Understanding Natural Language

Just getting a sequence of words into a computer is not enough. The computer has to be provided with an understanding of the domain the text is about. This is presently possible for very limited domains.

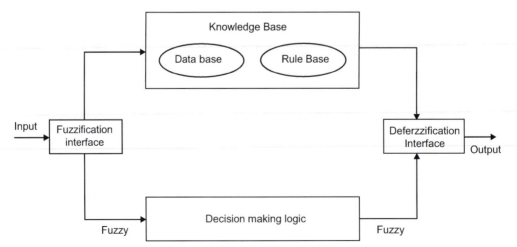

FIGURE 14.18   Structure of fuzzy expert system

Some of the applications of AI are game playing (chess), computer vision, expert systems, etc.

14.11   SUMMARY

1. A robot is a reprogrammable, multifunctional manipulator, designed to move materials, parts, tools or special devices through variable programmed motions for the performance of a variety of tasks.
2. Asimov gave three laws of robotics.
3. A robot can replace humans to operate in hazardous and hostile environments.
4. The basic building blocks of robots are manipulator, controller, sensors and power supply unit.
5. A manipulator makes use of prismatic or revolute joints between links.
6. An end effector may be a gripper or a tool.
7. A gripper may be vacuum cup type, magnetic type, mechanical type or adhesive type.
8. Modern robots make use of computer control.
9. Depending upon the need, a robot may be incorporated with various types of sensors such as touch sensor, force sensor, proximity sensor, range sensor, vision sensor.
10. Sensors are classified into two categories: Contact type and noncontact type sensors.
11. Modern robots usually make use are hydraulic drive or electric drive.
12. Based on manipular, a robot is classified as: Cartesian, cylindrical, polar, jointed-arm robot and SCARA.
13. Robots are also classified as point-to-point or continuous path robots.
14. Robots are used for welding, spray painting, material handling, assembly, medical treatment, firefighting, defence applications, etc.
15. Programming methods used for robots are manual method, lead-through programming and robot programming languages.
16. Artificial intelligence (AI) and expert systems are in rapid advancement phase and have numerous potential applications.

14.12   EXERCISE

1. What is a robot? What are laws of robotics (*BT level 1*)?
2. Explain the working of robot manipulator (*BT level 2*).
3. What is the type of controller used in modern robots? What are the functions of a controller (*BT level 1*)?
4. Describe various types of sensors used in robots (*BT level 1*).
5. Discuss various types of drives used in robots (*BT level 2*).
6. Briefly discuss various classifications of robots (*BT level 2*).
7. Discuss various types of cost associated with robots (*BT level 2*).
8. Discuss the applications of robots in industry (*BT level 2*).
9. What are various robot programming methods (*BT level 1*)?
10. What is artificial intelligence? Discuss various elements of artificial intelligence (*BT level 2*).
11. Under what manufacturing conditions is it suitable to use robots in industry (*BT level 1*)?
12. State the potential advantages and disadvantages of using robots (*BT level 1*).
13. What is an end effect? What are its types (*BT level 1*)?
14. Discuss the control system used in robots (*BT level 2*).
15. Differentiate between point-to-point and continuous path robots (*BT level 4*).
16. Distinguish between open-loop and closed-loop robot control systems (*BT level 4*).
17. Compare between NC machines vs robots. Also briefly write types and generations of robots with applications (*BT level 4*).

14.13   MULTIPLE-CHOICE QUESTIONS

1. What is a robot?
   a.   A computer program.
   b.   A machine that mimics human actions.
   c.   A device used for communication.
   d.   An instrument for measuring temperature.
2. Which of the following is NOT a type of robot?
   a.   Industrial robot.
   b.   Medical robot.
   c.   Service robot.
   d.   Communication robot.
3. What is the purpose of an end-effector in a robot?
   a.   To provide power to the robot.
   b.   To protect the robot from damage.
   c.   To control the robot's movements.
   d.   To perform tasks such as gripping, cutting or welding.
4. Which of the following is an example of a sensor commonly used in robotics?
   a.   GPS sensor.
   b.   Camera sensor.
   c.   Sound sensor.
   d.   All of the above.
5. What is the purpose of a robot controller?
   a.   To provide power to the robot.
   b.   To program the robot.
   c.   To monitor the robot's performance.
   d.   All of the above.

Answers

1. Answer: b. A machine that mimics human actions.
2. Answer: d. Communication robot.
3. Answer: d. To perform tasks such as gripping, cutting or welding
4. Answer: b. Camera sensor.
5. Answer: d. All of the above.

15 Application and Implementation of CAD

Learning Outcomes: After studying this chapter, the reader should be able

LO 1: To understand application of CAD in virtual engineering (BT level 2).
LO 2: To understand application of CAD in virtual prototyping (BT level 2).
LO 3: To understand application of CAD in rapid prototyping (BT level 2).
LO 4: To understand CAD implementation steps (BT level 2).

15.1 INTRODUCTION

In earlier chapters, we have examined the numerous design and manufacturing uses of computer systems. The significance of combining the design and manufacturing operations using CAD/CAM has been underlined throughout the discussions. The purpose of this chapter is to examine the application of CAD in Virtual Engineering, Virtual Prototyping and Rapid Prototyping. We also strive to comprehend CAD/CAM system implementation.

15.2 APPLICATION OF CAD IN VIRTUAL ENGINEERING

The term "virtual engineering" refers to the practice of using computer-generated environments to foster multidisciplinary collaborative product development through the integration of geometric models and related engineering tools such as analysis, simulation, optimisation, decision-making tools, etc. From the design phase onward, virtual engineering allows for the simulation of a wide range of processes, including those involved in the creation of components, their assembly, quality assurance and the provision of after-sales service. Time savings in product development, improved engineering decision-making, more creative design solutions and interfaces for virtual 3-D model manipulation are only few of the ways in which virtual engineering contributes to engineering design.

LO 1. To understand application of CAD in virtual engineering.

The conventional design process, which consists of design works, prototype creation, prototype testing, design analysis and simulation, and redesign, is time-consuming and results in high manufacturing costs. Virtual engineering-based design is commonly regarded as a solution to the aforementioned problems of conventional product design and prototype processes. During the early phases of product development, virtual design simulation and prototyping are vital tools for testing, among other things, the functioning of mechanical motions and features.

Virtual engineering requires multi-disciplinary expertise, and the development of the technology is driven by developments in hardware and software-related technologies, such as CAD/CAM. CAD software is utilised to boost the designer's efficiency, enhance the quality, improve communication through documentation and develop a database for production. It refers to the capacity to represent a dimension using geometric operations that closely resemble actual industrial machining processes. The CAD module is designed to facilitate the production of geometric shapes. Even if CAD provides a precise virtual shape of the products or components, the manufacture of these might vary

DOI: 10.1201/9781003350842-15

significantly, as the prior technology only dealt with faultless mathematical operations. Engineers utilise a production module, which represents a tool that machines the components, in order to take into consideration the successive manufacturing activities in a more realistic manner and to ensure that the final product will be near to the virtual model.

LO 2. To understand application of CAD in virtual prototyping.

15.3 APPLICATION OF CAD IN VIRTUAL PROTOTYPING

In virtual prototyping, designers utilise virtual models instead of physical prototypes and examine them using a variety of simulations that attempt to simulate the real-world operating circumstances under which the product will be required to function. This procedure is facilitated by sophisticated computer software designed to aid contemporary engineers in their work. Typically, a virtual model is built that replicates the real, or as close to real as feasible, image of the future structure or component. The fundamental objective of virtual prototyping is to decrease or eliminate the creation of physical prototypes, hence reducing the time required for product development.

Considering the fact that the creation of virtual prototypes is a multi-step process, and that in most cases each step is performed using a different type of software, there is the issue of purchasing separate licences for each commercially used software and training the individuals who will be operating the software. The use of the CAD system with extra, integrated calculation modules appears to be a viable solution for organisations with reduced budgets.

As a development of CAD, virtual prototype bridges the gap between existing design tools and automated production systems. It enables engineers and designers to use CAD data and methodologies to create interactive simulations that simulate the physical behaviour of a product in the "digital" stage of development. This enables product testing at the earliest feasible stage,

LO 3. To understand application of CAD in rapid prototyping.

which has positive effects on the cost of bringing the concept to market. In light of its maturity, the modular structure of many CAD systems now includes virtual prototype features. Therefore, the technology has reached the mainstream market.

15.4 APPLICATION OF CAD IN RAPID PROTOTYPING

Rapid prototyping (RP) technology was created in 1988. RP permits the creation of a geometrical reproduction of a component in a matter of hours, as opposed to days or weeks using conventional model shop processes. RP of physical components is sometimes referred to as solid-free fabrication, desktop manufacturing and layer manufacturing technology. RP is an important contemporary industrial development. RP is the method of creating a physical model of a component straight from a three-dimensional CAD drawing. The term rapid prototyping also refers to a group of technologies that may generate physical models automatically using CAD data.

Even though there are many ways to do RP, they all follow the same basic five-step process. The procedure is as detailed below.

1) Develop a CAD model of the proposed design.
2) Transform the CAD model into STL format.
3) Cut the STL file into layers with narrow cross-sections.
4) Construct the model in successive layers.
5) Cleanse and complete the model.

Initially, the thing to be constructed is modelled using CAD software. Solid modellers, such as Pro/Engineer, SolidWorks, Inventor and Catiatend to represent three-dimensional items more precisely than wire-frame modellers, such as AutoCAD, and hence will provide superior results.

The CAD file will need to be converted to STL format during the second stage. A collection of planar triangles is used to represent a three-dimensional surface in this presentation format. The file specifies the position and orientation of the three vertices of each triangle, as well as the outward normal.

In the third step, the STL file is pre-processed by an application in preparation for the construction stage. The vast majority of applications that are accessible give the user the ability to change the model's dimensions, location and angle.

The fourth phase involves the fabrication of the component. Using one of the procedures given previously. RP machines construct polymers, paper or powdered metal one layer at a time. The majority of machines are autonomous and require minimal human involvement.

Post-processing is the last phase. This requires disconnecting any supports and removing the prototype from the machine. Before using some photosensitive materials, they must be thoroughly cured.

LO 4. To understand CAD implementation steps

15.5   CAD IMPLEMENTATION STEPS

A CAD/CAM system is comprised of interactive graphics and accompanying design software, manufacturing software packages and a CAD/CAM database. Planned adoption of CAD/CAM systems is fundamental to their effectiveness.

The implementation of CAD/CAM systems is carried out in phases.

The first phase is to form a team of specialists who understand the design, analysis, production and automatic data processing processes. The team will design and comprehend various CAD system implementation criteria, as well as tour various industries employing CAD/CAM systems.

After completing the study, the team should investigate the availability of various systems on the global market. Comparing the proposals obtained from various suppliers, the team decides on the best system.

In the final phase, an existing system is integrated with the selected CAD/CAM system.

15.6   SUMMARY

1. Virtual engineering offers simulation of numerous operations in the design and manufacturing of components, assembly process, quality control and service, beginning with the design phase.
2. Virtual engineering requires multi-disciplinary expertise, and the development of the technology is driven by developments in hardware and software-related technologies, such as CAD.
3. The use of the CAD system with extra, integrated calculation modules appears to be a viable solution for organisations with reduced budgets in virtual prototyping.
4. Rapid prototyping refers to a group of technologies that may generate physical models automatically using CAD data.

15.7   EXERCISE

1. Explain the application of CAD in virtual engineering *(BT level 2)*.
2. Explain the application of CAD in virtual prototyping *(BT level 2)*.
3. Explain the application of CAD in rapid prototyping *(BT level 2)*.
4. Explain CAD implementation steps *(BT Level 2)*.

15.8   MULTIPLE-CHOICE QUESTIONS

1. What is CAD?
   a. Computer-Aided Drawing.

    b.   Computer-Aided Design.

    c.   Computer-Aided Development.

    d.   Computer-Aided Debugging.

2. Which of the following is not an advantage of CAD?

    a.   Faster design iterations.

    b.   Improved accuracy.

    c.   Reduced cost.

    d.   Decreased design complexity.

3. Which of the following is not a software used for CAD?

    a.   AutoCAD.

    b.   SolidWorks.

    c.   Adobe Photoshop.

    d.   CATIA.

4. Which type of CAD allows designers to create 3-D models and simulate real-world conditions?

    a.   2-D CAD.

    b.   3-D CAD.

    c.   CAM.

    d.   CAE.

5. Which of the following is not a common file format used in CAD?

    a.   .dwg

    b.   .pdf

    c.   .dxf

    d.   .stl

6. Which of the following is not a hardware component used in CAD?

    a.   Graphics card.

    b.   CPU.

    c.   Printer.

    d.   Mouse.

7. Which of the following is not a type of CAM?

    a.   2-D CAM.

    b.   3-D CAM.

    c.   Adaptive CAM.

    d.   Computer-aided testing.

8. Which of the following is NOT a type of rapid prototyping technology?

    a.   Fused deposition modelling.

    b.   Stereolithography.

    c.   Computer numerical control.

    d.   Selective laser sintering.

9. Which rapid prototyping technology uses a laser to solidify a liquid resin?

    a.   Fused deposition modelling.

    b.   Stereolithography.

    c.   Selective laser sintering.

    d.   Inkjet printing.

10. Which of the following is a benefit of using rapid prototyping in product development?

    a.   Increased time to market.

    b.   Reduced costs.

    c.   Improved product quality.

    d.   All of the above.

11. Which of the following is NOT a limitation of rapid prototyping?

    a.   Limited range of materials.

     b. Limited accuracy.

     c. Limited size of parts.

     d. Limited speed.

12. Which of the following is NOT an example of a software used for CAD?

     a. AutoCAD.

     b. SolidWorks.

     c. Blender.

     d. Adobe Photoshop.

13. Which of the following is a potential application of rapid prototyping?

     a. Medical implants.

     b. Architectural models.

     c. Custom jewellery.

     d. All of the above.

Answers

1. Answer: b. Computer-Aided Design.
2. Answer: d. Decreased design complexity
3. Answer: c. Adobe Photoshop.
4. Answer: b. 3-D CAD.
5. Answer: b. .pdf
6. Answer: c. Printer.
7. Answer: d. Computer-aided testing.
8. Answer: c. Computer Numerical Control.
9. Answer: B. Stereolithography.
10. Answer: d. All of the above.
11. Answer: d. Limited speed.
12. Answer: d. Photoshop
13. Answer: d. All of the above.

Bibliography

Amirouche, F.M.L. *Computer Aided Design and Manufacturing*, Prentice Hall, New York City, 1993.

Asfahl, C. Ray, *Robots and Manufacturing Automation*, 2nd ed., John Wiley, Hoboken, New Jersey, 1992.

Deb, S. R. *Robotics Technology and Flexible Automation*, Tata McGraw-Hill, New Delhi, 1994.

Gibbs, D., and Crandell, T. M. *An Introduction to CNC Machining and Programming*, Industrial Press, New York, 1991.

Groover, M. P. *Automation, Production Systems, and Computer-Aided Manufacturing*, Prentice Hall, Englewood Cliffs, NJ, 1980.

Groover, M. P., and Zimmers, E. W. *CAD/CAM Computer-Aided Design and Manufacturing*, Pearson Inc., Chennai, 2012.

Groover, M. P. Industrial Control Systems. In *Maynard's Industrial Engineering Handbook*, 5th ed., K. Zandin (ed.), McGraw-Hill Book Company, New York, 2001.

Hannam, R. *Computer Integrated Manufacturing from Concepts to Realisation*, Addison Wesley, England, 1997.

Koren Y. *Computer Control of Manufacturing Systems*, Tata McGraw-Hill, New York, 2012.

Koren, Y., and Tzafestas, S. Robotics for Engineers. In *IEEE Transactions on Systems, Man, and Cybernetics* (Vol. 16, Issue 4, pp. 619–619). Institute of Electrical and Electronics Engineers (IEEE), 1986. https://doi.org/10.1109/tsmc.1986.289270

Kulwiec, R. A. Editor, *Materials Handling Handbook*, 2nd ed., John Wiley & Sons, New York, 1985.

Opitz, H. *A Classification System to Describe Work-Pieces*, Translated by Acton Taylor, Pergamon Press, New York, 1970.

Rao, P. N., Tewari, N. K., and Kundra, T. K. *Computer Aided Manufacturing*, Tata McGraw-Hill, New Delhi, 1993.

Seames, W.S. *Computer Numerical Control: Concepts and Programming*, 2nd ed., Delmar, New York, 1990.

Stenerson, J., and Curran, K. *Computer Numerical Control: Operation and Programming*, 3rd ed., Pearson/Prentice Hall, Upper Saddle River, NJ, 2007.

www.abb.com/robotics

www.wikipedia.org/wiki/Automated_guided_vehicle

www.wikipedia.org/wiki/Automated_storage_and_retrieval_system

www.wikipedia.org/wiki/Automation

www.wikipedia.org/wiki/Barcode

www.wikipedia.org/wiki/Industrial_robot

www.wikipedia.org/wiki/Numerical_control

www.wikipedia.org/wiki/Radio_frequency_identification

Index